# Copyright Law in Photographic Works

This book presents an original theory of copyright authorship tailored for photographic works, grounded in the concepts of categorical intention, channelled selection, and causation. By addressing the unique dual nature of photography, where mechanical processes intersect with creative choices, it offers a fresh perspective on a longstanding legal challenge.

Through a critical examination of select case law with a focus on Anglo-American law, the book highlights the complexities and inconsistencies in the current copyright protection for photographs due to their dual nature, which exhibits both mechanical and creative characteristics. It argues for moving beyond the conventional one-size-fits-all approach for copyright concepts in favour of adopting a tailored, contextual approach that acknowledges the nature and characteristics of the category of work in question. The book also alludes to emerging technologies such as artificial intelligence and machine learning models, considering their implications for copyright and creative expression. It also discusses how the history of copyright protection of photographic works may illuminate the path towards dealing with conflicts between copyright and perceived mechanical mediums of creative expression.

This book will be of interest to researchers in copyright law and intellectual property law, especially those engaged with the legal treatment of mechanically produced creative works. It offers valuable insights into the evolving relationship between law, technology, and authorship in the digital age.

**Faisal Alamri** is an Assistant Professor of Law, specialising in Intellectual Property Law. He holds a PhD in Intellectual Property Law from the University of Leeds and has a strong academic and research background in copyright and trademark law. His work bridges the gap between theory and practice, offering fresh insights into the evolving landscape of intellectual property rights. Recently appointed as the Director of Scientific Publishing and Scientific Societies at Taibah University, he remains actively engaged with researchers across many fields. His expertise reflects a passion for intellectual property rights, legal education, and research.

## Routledge Research in Intellectual Property

**Copyright Law and Translation**
Access to Knowledge in Developing Economies
*Chamila S. Talagala*

**Patent Law, Green Technology and Innovation**
*Ankit Singh and Yogendra Kumar Srivastava*

**Intellectual Property and Development**
Geographical Indications in Practice
*Barbara Pick*

**Collective Management of Music Copyright**
A Comparative Analysis of China, the United States and Australia
*Qinqing Xu*

**Intellectual Property Rights and Competition Law in India**
*Edited by Rajni Malhotra Dhingra and Nisha Dhanraj Dewani*

**Digitization, Copyright and the Law**
Copyleft and the Future of Intellectual Property
*Ettore M. Lombardi*

**Intellectual Property and Emerging Technologies**
Generated Global IP Issues and Challenges
*Tshimanga Kongolo*

**Innovation and Development of Knowledge Societies**
Artificial Intelligence and Knowledge-Based Socioeconomic Growth
*Nadia Naim, Alhanoof AlDebasi and David Price*

**Copyright Law in Photographic Works**
Authorship, Originality, and Protection
*Faisal Alamri*

For more information about this series, please visit https://www.routledge.com/Routledge-Research-in-Intellectual-Property/book-series/INTELLPROP

# Copyright Law in Photographic Works

## Authorship, Originality, and Protection

**Faisal Alamri**

Routledge
Taylor & Francis Group
LONDON AND NEW YORK

First published 2026
by Routledge
4 Park Square, Milton Park, Abingdon, Oxon OX14 4RN

and by Routledge
605 Third Avenue, New York, NY 10158

*Routledge is an imprint of the Taylor & Francis Group, an informa business*



*British Library Cataloguing-in-Publication Data*
A catalogue record for this book is available from the British Library

ISBN: 978-1-032-95263-5 (hbk)
ISBN: 978-1-032-95784-5 (pbk)
ISBN: 978-1-003-58655-5 (ebk)

DOI: 10.4324/9781003586555

Typeset in Times New Roman
by Deanta Global Publishing Services, Chennai, India

# Contents

# Preface

Photographs represent a category of copyright-protected works that are associated with automatism and serendipity. Due to their dual nature, which exhibits both mechanical and creative characteristics, photographs struggled to fit within the traditional paradigm of copyright law. The dual nature of photography has long been the subject of continuous debate about whether photographs should be considered works of art worthy of copyright protection. The courts avoided engaging with the nature of photographs directly, preferring to utilise the proxy of analogy or narrative to address various copyright issues in the context of photographs. This has created a legacy that sits at the heart of the compatibility issues plaguing photographs' copyright protection.

The origins of this book came from a successful doctoral thesis that emerged from the idea that one art should not be judged in terms of its copyrightability according to the paradigms of another art. The importance of this book is illustrated in its systematic analysis of the Anglo-American approach to copyright in photographic works, from the invention of photography through the various stages of its protection, while reflecting on a wide variety of sources. Photographic works represent a significant subject of analysis since they, perhaps, represent one of the first encounters between copyright and perceived mechanical mediums of expression. The lessons learned from this analysis of photographic works may be of value in approaching other emerging mediums of expression, such as ones that incorporate artificial intelligence and complex algorithms to produce highly creative works.

The book examines the concept of authorship and originality in the context of photographs and proceeds to recommend adopting a tailored and contextual approach to photographic works' copyright that considers the nature of the category of work in question. It presents a two-tier system for copyright protection for photographic works anchored to a tailored approach to copyright authorship. In so doing, the book provides an original theory of copyright authorship tailored for photographic works based on the elements of categorical intention, channelled selection, and causation.

# Acknowledgements

This book would not have been possible without the support of many people. To all of you who inspired, encouraged, and guided my journey throughout this work and my academic career, I am deeply thankful for your kind and generous support.

I, Faisal Alamri, dedicate this book to my dear family, who have always blessed me with their unwavering support. I am forever grateful to my beloved parents, Bati and Maha, and my dear siblings, Yousef, Mai, Abdelaziz, and Fai, for their love and support.

# Table of Cases

*16 Casa Duse, LLC v Merkin*, No 13-3865 (2d Cir 2015)
*Aalmuhammed v Lee*, 202 F3d 1227 (2000)
*Alfred Bell & Co v Catalda Fine Arts*, 191 F2d 99 (1951)
*Altman v New Haven Union Co*, 254 F 113 (1918)
*American Mutoscope & Biograph Co v Edison Mfg Co*, 137 F 262 (1905)
*Andrien v Southern Ocean County Chamber of Commerce*, 927 F2d 132 (1991)
*Andy Warhol Foundation Visual Arts v Goldsmith* (2022) 598 US 508 (Supreme Court)
*Antiquesportfolio.com Plc v Rodney Fitch & Co Ltd* [2001] FSR 23
*Apple Corps Ltd v Cooper* [1992] 12 WLUK 29
*Authors Guild v Google, Inc*, 804 F3d 202 (2d Cir 2015)
*Avedon v Exstein*, 141 FSupp 278 (1956)
*Baigent v Random House Group Ltd* [2008] EMLR 7
*Barbera v Grande, No 119-cv-04349* (SDNY May 13, 2019)
*Bauman v Fussell* [1978] RPC 485
*Beckingham v Hodgens* [2003] EWCA Civ 143
*Belair v MGA Entertainment, Inc*, 831 FSupp2d 687 (2011)
*Blanch v Koons*, 467 F3d 244 (2006)
*Bleistein v Donaldson Lithographing Co*, 188 US 239 (1903) 4
*Bolles v Outing Co*, 46 LRA 712 (1897)
*Bolton v Aldin* (1895) 65 LJQB 120
*Boucas v Cooke* [1903] 2 KB 227
*Brammer v Violent Hues Productions, LLC, 922 F3d 255 (2019) (4th Circuit) 13*
*Brattleboro Pub Co v Winmill Pub Corp*, 369 F2d 565 (1966)
*Bridgeman Art Library, Ltd v Corel Corp*, 25 FSupp2d 421 (1998)
*Brighton v Jones* [2004] EMLR 26
*Brod v General Pub Group, Inc*, 32 FedAppx 231 (2002)
*Bryant v Gordon*, 483 FSupp2d 605 (2007)
*Burrow-Giles Lithographic Co v Sarony*, 111 US 53 (1884)
*(C-5/08) Infopaq International A/S v Danske Dagblades Forening* [2009] ECR I-6569
*(C-145/10) Painer v Standard Verlags GmbH* [2012] ECDR 6
*(C-277/10) Martin Luksan v Petrus van der Let*, [2012] EU:C:2012:65
*(C-310/17) Levola Hengelo BV v Smilde Foods BV* [2019] ECDR 2

*Football Association Premier League Ltd and Others v QC Leisure and Others (C-403/08) and Karen Murphy v Media Protection Services Ltd* (C-429/08) [2012] FSR 1
*Football Association Premier League Ltd v Panini UK Ltd* [2003] EWCA Civ 995
*Football Association Premier League Ltd v QC Leisure* (No2) [2008] FSR 32
*Foster v Lee*, 93 FSupp3d 223 (2015)
*Franklin Mint Corp v National Wildlife Art Exchange, Inc*, 575 F2d 62 (1978)
*Fraser-Woodward Ltd v BBC* [2005] EWHC 472 (Ch)
*Fylde Microsystems Ltd v Key Radio Systems Ltd* [1998] FSR 449
*Gambart v Ball* (1863) 14 C B(N S) 305
*Garcia v Google, Inc*, 786 F3d 733 (2015)
*Gentieu v Tony Stone Images/Chicago, Inc*, 255 FSupp2d 838 (2003)
*Gillespie v AST Sportswear, Inc*, Not Reported in FSupp2d (2001)
*Godfrey v Lees* [1995] 3 WLUK 278
*Goldstein v California*, 412 US 546 (1973)
*Google LLC v Oracle America, Inc*, 141 SCt 1183 (2021)
*Gracen v Bradford Exchange*, 698 F2d 300 (1983)
*Graham v Prince*, 265 FSupp3d 366 (2017)
*Graves' Case* (1868-69) LR4 QB 715
*Griner v King* (2021) 568 F Supp 3d 978 (Dist Court)
*Griner v King* (2024) 104 F 4th 1 (Court of Appeals, 8th Circuit)
*Gross v Seligman*, 212 F 930 (1914)
*Hadley v Kemp* [1999] EMLR 589
*Harney v Sony Pictures Television, Inc*, 704 F3d 173 (2013)
*Harper & Row Publishers, Inc v Nation Enterprises*, 471 US 539 (1985)
*Home Legend, LLC v Mannington Mills, Inc*, 784 F3d 1404 (2015)
*Hubbard v Vosper*, [1972] 2 QB 84
*Hyde Park Residence Ltd v Yelland* [2000] EMLR 363
*In re Trade-Mark Cases*, 100 US 82 (1879)
*Infection Control Enterprises Ltd v Virrage Industries Ltd* [2009] EWHC 2602 (QB)
*Interlego AG Appellant v Tyco Industries Inc* [1988] 3 WLR 678 (1988) 105 343
*Jarvis v K2 Inc*, 486 F3d 526 (2007)
*Jewelers' Circular Pub Co v Keystone Pub Co*, 274 F 932 (1921)
*Kaplan v Stock Market Photo Agency, Inc*, 133 FSupp2d 317 (2001)
*Katz v Google Inc*, 802 F3d 1178 (2015) (11th Circuit)
*Kelley v Chicago Park Dist*, 635 F3d 290 (2011)
*Kienitz v Sconnie Nation LLC*, 766 F3d 756 (2014) 4
*Kisch v Ammirati & Puris Inc*, 657 FSupp 380 (1987)
*Kogan v Martin* [2020] EMLR 4
*L Batlin & Son, Inc v Snyder*, 536 F2d 486 (1976)
*Ladbroke (Football) Ltd v William Hill (Football) Ltd* [1964] 1 WLR 273 17
*Leibovitz v Paramount Pictures Corp*, 137 F3d 109 (1998)
*Leigh v Warner Bros, Inc*, 212 F3d 1210 (2000)
*Levy v Rutley* (1870-71) LR 6 CP 523

# Legislations and Treaties

**Legislation**

Copyright Act 1909 (US)
Copyright Act 1911 (UK)
Copyright Act 1956 (UK)
Copyright Act 1976 (US)
Copyright, Designs and Patents Act 1988 (UK)
Directive 93/98/EEC of 29 October 1993 harmonizing the term of protection of copyright and certain related rights [1993] OJ L290/9
Directive 96/9/EC of 11 March 1996 on the legal protection of databases [1996] OJ L77/20
Directive 2001/29/EC of 22 May 2001 on the harmonisation of certain aspects of copyright and related rights in the information society [2001] OJ L167/10
Directive 2006/116/EC of 12 December 2006 on the term of protection of copyright and certain related rights [2006] OJ L372/12
Directive 2009/24/EC of 23 April 2009 on the legal protection of computer programs [2009] OJ L111/16
Directive 2012/28/EU of 25 October 2012 on certain permitted uses of orphan works [2012] OJ L299/5 2012
Directive 2019/790/EC of 17 April 2019 on copyright and related rights in the Digital Single Market and amending Directives 96/9/EC and 2001/29/EC [2019] OJ L130/92
Fine Arts Copyright Act 1862 (25 & 26 Vict.) C. 68
Gesetz über Urheberrecht und verwandte Schutzrechte (Urheberrechtsgesetz, geändert durch das Gesetz vom 01. September 2017) (Germany)
Law No. 57-298 of March 11, 1957 on Literary and Artistic Property
Law No. 92-597 of July 1st, 1992 Relating to The Code of The Intellectual Property (Part Legislative)
Legge 22 aprile 1941, n. 633 sulla protezione del diritto d'autore e di altri diritti connessi al suo esercizio (aggiornata con le modifiche introdotte dal decreto-legge 30 aprile 2010, n. 64 (Italy)
Orrin G. Hatch-Bob Goodlatte Music Modernization Act, Pub. L. No. 115-264 2018

Texto refundido de la Ley de Propiedad Intelectual, regularizando, aclarando y armonizando las disposiciones legales vigentes (aprobado por el Real Decreto Legislativo No 1/1996 de 12 de abril de 1996, y modificado hasta el Real Decreto-Ley No 26/2020 de 7 de julio de 2020) (Spain)
The Civil Procedure Rules 1998 (UK)
The Copyright and Rights in Performances (Licensing of Orphan Works) Regulations 2014
Title 17 of the United States Code
United States Constitution

## Treaties

Agreement on Trade-Related Aspects of Intellectual Property Rights (TRIPS) (as amended on 23 January 2017).
Berne Convention for the Protection of Literary and Artistic Works 1886.
WIPO Copyright Treaty 1996.

# 1 Introduction

## 1.1 Introduction

Photographic works have long occupied a precarious position in the field of copyright law. Since their inclusion, the tensions between their mechanical and creative aspects have been at the centre of the discourse concerning their copyright protection. The tried and tested copyright concepts such as authorship and originality have shown clear foundational weaknesses when it comes to the protection of photographs within the paradigm of copyright law.

This book focuses on the issue of copyright in photographic works by critically and methodologically tracing the story of its inclusion as a protected work within the Anglo-American copyright law. The book pinpoints the core issues plaguing copyright in photographic works along with its struggle to fit within the traditional copyright paradigm. It presents a theory that posits that the concept of originality is ill-equipped to determine the copyrightability of a photograph due to its incompatibility with the characteristics of the medium of photography. Hence, it advances that the concept of authorship, instead, is more suitable for determining the copyrightability of a photograph. However, the concept of authorship must be tailored to fit the medium of photography in order to avoid the issues plaguing copyright in photographic works. Therefore, a two-tier system of protection anchored on the concept of authorship that categorises works into high and low authorship is an effective solution to address copyright in photographic works. For this system to function efficiently, it has to operate within a specific conception of authorship suitable for photographic works. This book then proceeds to provide an original theory of photographs' copyright authorship that states that *copyrightable authorship is a product of a human agent's categorical intention and prior mental conception that influenced a channelled source with channelled selection, expression, to cause a work of authorship to materialise for the purposes of copyright law.*

The book provides an in-depth critical analysis of copyright in photographic works in Anglo-American copyright law. The United Kingdom and the United States were selected as the primary jurisdictions analysed in this book because both adopt a common law legal system and have a rich legal literature and case law that deals with copyright in photographic works. The United Kingdom was chosen because it was a pioneering country with regard to photography (alongside

DOI: 10.4324/9781003586555-1

France). It was the first jurisdiction to expressly grant copyright protection to photographs as fine art.[1] Since that time, the United Kingdom has wrestled with the issue of copyright in photographic works from its earliest inception without the luxury of having any prior examples or precedent from which to draw much-needed guidance. In relation to UK copyright law, the book also examines the influence of European Union (EU) law on the United Kingdom concerning photographic works' copyright.

The United States was chosen because it was where the use of photography expanded and entered many fields. The Eastman Kodak Company is credited for popularising photography by making it widely accessible to most classes of society. Furthermore, the United States is the birthplace of many photo-sharing and social media platforms. Most of these social platforms on cyberspace designate the United States as the legal forum of choice for disputes concerning any issue within their ecosystem.

In addition to the United Kingdom and United States, examples from other jurisdictions are included where appropriate to stress certain points or highlight further issues. Particularly, France is an important jurisdiction to examine regarding copyright in photographic works due to its influence on the Berne Convention 1886,[2] which expressly included photographic works among the list of copyright-protected works following the 1948 Brussels conference. Furthermore, Germany and Italy will be examined briefly as examples of countries implementing a two-tier system of protection for photographic works.

This chapter serves as an introduction to the main parts of this book and presents an overview that outlines how it unfolds. Firstly, the book demonstrates the importance of studying copyright in photographic works since it represents the first encounter between copyright and a perceived mechanical medium of expression. Secondly, the book's core questions and arguments are presented. Finally, an overview of the book's chapters is presented to illustrate how the arguments will unfold across the chapters.

## 1.2 Why Study Copyright in Photographs?

The term "photography" comes from the Greek words "Phos" which means "light," and "Graphos" which means "draw," thus photography means "draw with light."[3] The term is believed to have been popularised in 1839 by Sir John Herschel, an

1 Fine Arts Copyright Act 1862 (25 & 26 Vict.) C. 68.

2 Berne Convention for the Protection of Literary and Artistic Works 1886.

3 Naomi Rosenblum, *World History of Photography* (4 edition, Abbeville Press Inc, US 2008) 195; Beaumont Newhall, *The History of Photography: From 1839 to the Present* (5 edition, The Museum of Modern Art, New York 1984) 35; Mark Osterman, "The Technical Evolution of Photography in the 19th Century" in Michael R. Peres (ed), *The Focal Encyclopedia of Photography: Digital Imaging, Theory and Applications History and Science* (4 edition, Elsevier 2007) 27.

English scientist who himself created his own photographic process.[4] The first ever photographic image made from a camera and fixed permanently is "The View from the Window at Le Gras," which was captured by a French inventor named Joseph-Nicephore Niépce between 1816 and 1829.[5] In 1837, Louis Jacques Mandé Daguerre, building on Niépce's Heliography and his own experiments, managed to produce high-quality detailed images and fix them permanently using a process he invented called the Daguerreotype.[6] Two years later, the details of the Daguerreotype process were published as "a gift to the world" from France, marking the birth of photography. The Daguerreotype process was the first practical photographic process made available to the public without restrictions, and this catapulted its popularity. In the years that followed, numerous photographic processes and innovations emerged to lift photography to prominence as a medium representing one of the most prevalent works of copyright. The advancement of the digital era through the aid of complex computational algorithms has considerably reduced the requisite level of skill needed to take photographs. Furthermore, social media has drastically changed how photographs are utilised, perceived, valued, and disseminated.

"Copyright," or "authors' rights" in civil law countries, is a legal term that refers to an area of intellectual property law that covers a wide range of creative and cultural works such as books, letters, music, songs, paintings, drawings, sculptures, photographs, films, and other types of original works of authorship regardless of their artistic merits. Copyright does not impose any formalities or specific conditions regarding the work's aesthetics or artistic quality to be subject to protection.[7] It subsists automatically, provided that the subject matter was the author's own creative creation that satisfies the originality requirement of the respective jurisdiction, which is generally a low threshold.[8] Once the work's originality is established, copyright confers a set of exclusive rights for a limited duration on the intangible subject matter of the protection, distinct from its physical medium, to the copyright owner.[9] For example, a book's physical form is a tangible representation that contains the expression of the author's thoughts; copyright attaches to the intangible expression itself that was fixed in the book and not the book's physical form. Subsequently, it allows the book copyright owner to prevent unauthorised

4 Sir John Herschel invented the Cyanotype photographic process, which produced permanent blue images. Rosenblum (n 3) 27.

5 ibid 17, 194; Newhall (n 3) 13, 14; Osterman (n 3) 28.

6 Newhall (n 3) 17 18; Osterman (n 3) 28; Rosenblum (n 3) 18.

7 Lionel Bently and others, *Intellectual Property Law* (5 edition, OUP Oxford 2018) 35–37; *Dutfield and Suthersanen on Global Intellectual Property Law: Second Edition* (2 revised edition, Edward Elgar Publishing 2020) 98.

8 *Dutfield and Suthersanen on Global Intellectual Property Law: Second Edition* (n 7) 100; *(C-5/08) Infopaq International A/S v Danske Dagblades Forening [2009] ECR I-6569*; (EU) *Feist Publications, Inc v Rural Telephone Service Co, Inc, 499 US 340 (1991)* (US).

9 Nicholas Caddick, Gwilym Harbottle and Uma Suthersanen, *Copinger and Skone James on Copyright* (18 edition, Sweet & Maxwell Ltd 2020) paras 1–01, 1–04, 1–05; Howard B Abrams and Tyler T Ochoa, *Law of Copyright* (Clark Boardman Callaghan 2020) s 1.1.

reproduction regardless of the form of that reproduction, whether it was an unauthorised direct copy of the book or an unauthorised film adaptation of it. Thus, copyright gives the author and/or owner a bundle of exclusive rights attached to the work that enables them to exert control over the subject matter of the copyright for a limited duration and prevent others from utilising the work without authorisation.

Photographs represent a category of copyright-protected works that are often associated with automatism and serendipity. Consequently, photographs struggled to fit within the traditional paradigm of copyright law. Despite this, photographic depictions saturate the digital landscape at an unprecedented rate. All kinds of photographs are continuously being shared to the farthest reaches of the internet as well as being used and remixed on a scale that renders most attempts to control their spread, for considerations such as copyright protection, often near impossible to implement effectively. The digital revolution and the advent of the internet provided a decentralised platform populated with tools that allow amateurs and hobbyists, with the aid of smart digital cameras, to capture technically challenging photographs that rival those captured by veteran photographers without requiring the same rigour to create. This is attributed to various advancements in photo technologies that automated most of the demanding aspects of photography to the point where a newbie photographer is capable of capturing high-quality technical photographs with minimal effort.[10] In the past, such photographs required the technical knowledge, skill, and expertise of a professional photographer with years of experience. These relatively recent developments in photo technologies may give credence to the old notion that argues against the artistic merits of photography, conceptualising it as merely a mechanical process that demands minimal creative input from the human operator and, consequently, unworthy of copyright protection on the same level as other artistic works. This old argument was kept at a distance by the notion that the true value of a photograph lies in the photographer's artistic judgement, which was independent of the mechanical nature of the camera. It posits that the photographer's creative judgement, regardless of its nature and quantity, elevates a photograph as a work of authorship worthy of copyright protection.[11]

Some critics argue that digital photography negatively impacts the value of photographs as an artistic medium since the physical materials involved in a

10 Tom de Castella, "Five Ways the Digital Camera Changed Us" *BBC News* (28 February 2012) <http://www.bbc.co.uk/news/magazine-16483509> accessed 11 October 2024; Isabella Foreman, "How Digital Technology Has Changed Photography" (*YourStory.com*, 3 August 2017) <https://yourstory.com/mystory/8d00fa40c1-how-digital-technology> accessed 30 September 2021; Olivier Laurent, "How Snapchat, Instagram & Apple Are Reinventing Photography" (*Time*, 24 February 2017) <http://time.com/4659058/snapchat-instagram-apple-photography/> accessed 19 October 2024.

11 John Tagg, *The Burden of Representation: Essays on Photographies and Histories* (Palgrave Macmillan 2002) 113; Christine Haight Farley, "The Lingering Effects of Copyright's Response to the Invention of Photography" (2004) 65 University of Pittsburgh Law Review 385, 428; *Burrow-Giles Lithographic Co v Sarony, 111 US 53 (1884).*

photograph's creation often imbue it with an additional aesthetic value. Indeed, Edwards and Hart argue that the artistic value of photographs is not only represented by the two-dimensional image in isolation, as it is often reduced into as a side-effect of the digital impact on photographs, but it encompasses its material form as a three-dimensional object.[12] The powerful expressive capability of a visual medium such as photography coupled with the internet and social media platforms (such as X – formerly Twitter – Snapchat, Instagram, and Facebook) illuminate its overwhelming impact as an expressive medium that invites pressing commercial, social, political, and legal concerns. The use or distribution of photographs could have legal complications related to copyright, privacy, and media-related laws. In fact, the digital revolution has amplified the reach of copyright issues such as enforcement, fair use/fair dealing, as well as the issue of orphan works, which refer to works without an identifiable rightsholder.[13]

It is difficult to underestimate the impact of photography, with its many forms, on many aspects of our lives. Photographs are utilised for a variety of purposes, and their artistic potential is well established and respected today. Hence, it cannot be denied that photographs, as a class of works, are worthy of copyright protection. However, copyright law must address photographic works in their own capacity as photographs, not through the proxy of analogies or comparisons, in order to be properly equipped to deal with the increasing challenges associated with photographic works in a way that adapts to the changes and demands of society. The legacy approach that dates back to the initial inclusion of photographs within the sphere of copyright protection in Anglo-American copyright law remains impactful to the point that it represents a considerable source of the incompatibility issues that have plagued photographic works' copyright protection. Moreover, photographic works represent one of the first encounters between copyright and a perceived mechanical medium of expression. The lessons learned from analysing copyright in photographic works are valuable in approaching emerging mediums of expression, such as ones that incorporate artificial intelligence and complex algorithms to produce highly creative works.

## 1.3 The Book Core Questions and Argument

The book is built around three core questions formulated to initiate an in-depth critical analysis of the Anglo-American approach to copyright in photographic works. It aims to investigate the legacy of that protection and its links to the incompatibility issues that have plagued photographic works. These three core questions are as follows:

12 See: Elizabeth Edwards and Janice Hart (eds), *Photographs Objects Histories: On the Materiality of Images* (Routledge 2005).

13 US Copyright Office and The Register of Copyrights, "Orphan Works and Mass Digitization" (2015) 2, 7, 9 <https://www.copyright.gov/orphan/reports/orphan-works2015.pdf> accessed 19 October 2024; Intellectual Property Office, "Copyright: Orphan Works" (*GOV.UK*, 12 May 2015) <https://www.gov.uk/guidance/copyright-orphan-works> accessed 19 October 2024; see Chapter 8.

- How did copyright law extend its reach to photographic works, and what are the challenges, justifications, and legacy of their inclusion?
- Why do photographic works represent a contentious and precarious area in copyright law at both the conceptual and practical levels?
- Is the current copyright regime appropriate for photographic works? Can it be modified? Or do we need a sui generis approach to photographic works that take into account their distinct nature? And if so, what should it look like?

The book argues that most of the issues associated with photographic works, and amplified with digital imaging, can be regarded as legacy issues traced back to the earliest debates concerning photographic works' capacity for artistic expression. That is because copyright protection for photographic works was reasoned by drawing parallels to the process of writing or painting to justify its copyright protection. This created an aura of uncertainty since it has become increasingly challenging to regard photographs as having anything remotely in common with the process of writing or painting. Yet, it was on this very notion, which entails that photography is somewhat analogous to writing or painting, where copyright protection for photographic works was deemed appropriate and justifiable. The book argues that this created a legacy issue that intensified the compatibility issues associated with copyright in photographic works. The book posits that these issues can only be appropriately resolved when photographic works are specifically addressed directly. To achieve this, the unique characteristics of photographs must be considered on their merits rather than by virtue of their similarity, whether perceived or otherwise, with other categories of copyright-protected works.

## 1.4 The Book Overview

The book is divided into three main parts that consist of multiple chapters. Each part represents one of the three core questions. These three parts are organised into three themes representing the past, the present, and the possible future. The first part focuses on the formative years of copyright in photographic works and tracks the development of the law in the relevant jurisdictions up to the present. The second part examines the copyright concepts of authorship and originality in the context of photographic works. The third part focuses on the future of copyright in photographic works.

Part 1 examines the inclusion of photographic works within the sphere of copyright law. It focuses on the past, and it endeavours to examine how copyright protection extended to photographic works in Anglo-American copyright law and the Berne Convention 1886. This part is constructed to focus on the development of copyright in photographic works from a socio-legal point of view through chronological historical research. It aims to provide a clear narrative of its history, examining the events, attitudes, and challenges that shaped the development of copyright in photographic works to reach its current state. In addition to examining the selected jurisdictions, this part examines the inclusion of photographic works in the Berne Convention's list of protected works since it represented a big step towards the acceptance of photographs as a class of works worthy of copyright protection. This part aims to show that most of the issues surrounding the nature of the medium of photography were present from the earliest debates regarding its eligibility for copyright protection and posit that the legacy of these issues lingers in the present. Hence, instead of becoming outdated, these arguments resonated more potently in recent times, exposing the extent to which photographic works suffer from legacy issues.

Part 1 is composed of three chapters. The first chapter (Chapter 2) examines the extension of copyright protection to photographs in the Berne Convention. The second chapter (Chapter 3) examines the extension of copyright protection to photographs in the United Kingdom. The third chapter (Chapter 4) examines the extension of copyright protection to photographs in the United States.

Part 2 focuses on the present, and it critically analyses how copyright concepts and rules, particularly the concepts of authorship and originality, were applied in the context of photographic works. It shows how the Anglo-American courts were often forced to distort these concepts and employ analogies to other protected works to find copyright in particular photographs, doing so to reconcile the tried and tested copyright rules and concepts with the medium of photography. This exacerbated the legacy that intensified the incompatibility issues associated with photographic works. This part also highlights the issues emerging from the tendency of copyright law to adopt a one-size-fits-all approach when implementing its concepts in the context of photographic works.

Part 2 is composed of three chapters. The first chapter (Chapter 5) examines the concept of authorship in copyright law and the difficulties associated with locating copyright authorship in the context of photographic works. It argues that the crux of the issue is manifested in the law's tendency to draw parallels to authorship in painting and other categories of works to justify copyright authorship in photographs. The second chapter (Chapter 6) examines the concept of originality in copyright law and the manner in which it was applied to photographic works, revealing its incompatibility with photographic works. The third chapter (Chapter 7) explores the inconsistencies exhibited with originality in photographic works and copyright protection in Anglo-American copyright law. These inconsistencies were manifested in how the courts located originality differently in different types of photographs. The sources of originality in photographs from timing, selection, and rendition are often arbitrarily utilised by the courts to justify contrasting results regarding the originality of a given photograph. Henceforth, it argues that originality, as a concept, is ill-equipped to deal with photographic works.

Part 3 focuses on the future of copyright in photographic works. It presents its own original recommendation by building on the preceding parts to examine the impact of the digital revolution on the medium of photography and on photographic works' copyright protection. It highlights that copyright law remains anchored on an analogue view of photographic works that lay bare the legacy issues carried from the time photographic works were first protected by copyright. Firstly, this part examines copyright-related issues in the context of photographic works that were amplified by the advent of the digital age, such as copyright infringement and enforcement, the scope of fair use/fair dealing, and orphan works, among other related issues. Secondly, this part builds on the earlier chapters to recommend adopting a tailored contextual approach to copyright concepts that considers the categories of works in question. It provides a proposal for a two-tier system for copyright protection tailored to photographic works and anchored on an original conception of copyright authorship. It then presents the proposed model for the recommended two-tier system for photographic work's copyright protection.

Part 3 is composed of three chapters. The first chapter (Chapter 8) examines the impact of the digital age on photography and how it amplifies various copyright-related issues in the context of photographic works. It highlights that copyright law remains anchored on an analogue view of photographic works that lays bare the legacy issues originating from the time photographic works were first protected by copyright. The second chapter (Chapter 9) builds on the analysis and advances that the concept of authorship, instead of the concept of originality, should be the determinative factor concerning the copyrightability of a photograph. It then lays the groundwork to remedy the legacy issues of copyright in photographic works at its core by advocating for a tailored approach to copyright key concepts that actively considers the unique characteristics of the category of works in question. This chapter recalibrates key copyright concepts to better accommodate photographic works under a proposed two-tier system of copyright protection based on Professor Ginsburg's framework of high and low authorship,[14] and Calabresi and Melamed's framework[15] of the types of protection for legal entitlements. It then proceeds to dissect selected theories of copyright authorship to serve as building blocks to construct an original theory for copyright authorship in photographic works. The third chapter (Chapter 10) builds on the previous chapter and consolidates the discussion to present its own original theory of copyright authorship in conjunction with a detailed two-tier system for the copyright protection of photographic works. The theory posits that photographs' copyrightable authorship "is a product of a human agent's categorical intention and prior mental conception that influenced a channelled source with channelled selection, expression, to cause a work of authorship to materialise for the purposes of copyright law." Following this, the chapter explores the merits of the proposed theory and the two tiers system on selected case law.

## 1.5 Conclusion

The book provides a critical and systematic analysis of photographic works' copyright protection in Anglo-American copyright law. It tracks the history of photography from its invention and builds a coherent narrative that illustrates the general

14 Jane C Ginsburg, "Creation and Commercial Value: Copyright Protection of Works of Information" (1990) 90 Columbia Law Review 1865.

15 Guido Calabresi and A Douglas Melamed, "Property Rules, Liability Rules, and Inalienability: One View of the Cathedral" (1971) 85 Harvard Law Review 1089.

attitudes towards photography across the different stages of its development, highlighting the elements and issues that had a lasting impact on the development of copyright protection for photographic works. The book demonstrates the extent to which copyright in photographs suffers from legacy issues pertaining to the time copyright protection first extended to cover photographic works. The book utilises Rodolfo Sacco's theory of legal formants[16] to examine specific interest groups from which the book builds its narrative regarding the development of photographs' copyright protection. These groups include legal practitioners, lawmakers, academics, artists, and photographers. By examining the views of these groups on photography, the book develops a historical account of the development of photographs' copyright protection in the United Kingdom and the United States. This, in turn, illustrates the underlying reasons for the tension between copyright law concepts, such as authorship and originality, and the protection of photographic works.

There is limited research that systematically investigates copyright in photographic works in Anglo-American copyright law through comparative law and even less that attempts to systematically investigate whether current copyright laws regarding photographic works are sufficient to deal with the increasing challenges brought by new photographic technologies and the internet. One focal feature of this book is that it builds on its analysis to examine whether a sui generis approach is more suitable to address the various challenges of copyright in photographic works and what form the new approach should take. The book then provides its own original proposal for a two-tier system of copyright protection for photographic works centred on an original conception of copyright authorship tailored for photographic works. This theory of photographs' copyright authorship provides that "copyrightable authorship is a product of a human agent's categorical intention and prior mental conception that influenced a channelled source with channelled selection, expression, to cause a work of authorship to materialise for the purposes of copyright law." The book argues that the merits of the proposed system would reduce the incompatibility issues that trouble copyright in photographic works and provide a stable ground for the copyright protection of photographs.

16 Rodolfo Sacco, "Legal Formants: A Dynamic Approach to Comparative Law (Installment I of II)" (1991) 39 The American Journal of Comparative Law 1, 22 ("that living law contains many different elements such as statutory rules, the formulations of scholars, and the decisions of judges – elements that he keeps separate in his own thinking…we will call them, borrowing from phonetics, the 'legal formants'").

# 2 The Berne Convention for the Protection of Literary and Artistic Works and Photographic Works

## 2.1 Introduction

The Berne Convention is the oldest and still the supreme international copyright treaty. Its importance rests on its wide and continued success in introducing uniform minimum standards of copyright protection to an expanding range of protected works. This process has been enabled by the principle of national treatment in order that its provisions on the rights of authors can be enjoyed equally by all authors in all member states, as well as by the abolition of specific formalities attached to copyright protection.[1] The Berne Convention demonstrated resilience across the years, showing a remarkable degree of adaptability to technological changes across its revisions, additional acts, and several follow-on treaties ("special agreements") as provided in its Article 20, as well as its incorporation by reference into the World Trade Organization's Agreement on Trade-Related Aspects of Intellectual Property Rights to remain the primary foundational force behind the international copyright regime to this day.[2] Nearly all the countries in the world are legally bound to the Berne Convention's standards in one way or another, or at least their copyright laws have been significantly influenced by it.[3]

The inclusion of photographic works in the list of protected works under the Berne Convention was far from an easy process. This is due to photography occupying a precarious position where traditional views on art, originality, and authorship are often hard to align with the nature of photographic works. The process of capturing a photograph was often regarded as mechanical in that it amounts,

1 Berne Convention for the Protection of Literary and Artistic Works 1886; Peter Burger, "The Berne Convention: Its History and Its Key Role in the Future" (1988) 3 Journal of Law and Technology 1, 16, 50, 51; Jane C Ginsburg, "Berne-Forbidden Formalities and Mass Digitization Symposium: Notice and Notice Failure in Intellectual Property Law: Panel II" (2016) 96 Boston University Law Review 745, 750; Paul Goldstein, *International Copyright: Principles, Law, and Practice* (OUP Oxford 2001) 20; Graham Dutfield and Uma Suthersanen, *Dutfield and Suthersanen on Global Intellectual Property Law* (2 edition, Edward Elgar Publishing 2020) 55; Sam Ricketson and Jane C Ginsburg, *International Copyright and Neighbouring Rights: The Berne Convention and Beyond* (2 edition, OUP Oxford 2006) 53.

2 Burger (n 1) 50.

3 "Berne Convention for the Protection of Literary and Artistic Works" (*WIPO*) <http://www.wipo.int/treaties/en/ip/berne/index.html> accessed 11 October 2024.

DOI: 10.4324/9781003586555-2

in many instances, to nothing more than the pressing of a button.[4] At the same time, it could not be denied that some photographic works exhibit a distinct artistic expression that evidences the intellectual creation of the photographer, challenging the view that sees photographic works as a lesser form of art, or not even art at all. These two views about photography – that it is art, and that it is barely art at all – collided numerous times during the development of the Berne Convention and across its revision conferences.

France was the country at the forefront in advocating the inclusion of photographic works in the list of protected works across the development of the Berne Convention. France's copyright philosophy was built on the notion of the author's right (droit d'auteur), which sits at the core of the Berne Convention. The French Second Republic passed a decree in 1852 that incriminated any piracy of literary or dramatic works regardless of their place of origin.[5] It was French authors who started the movement towards uniting the authors of the world to accord universal copyright protection for their literary works based on the notion of natural rights.[6] Eventually, their efforts accumulated to lead to the creation of the Berne Convention itself.[7]

This chapter is divided into two parts. The first part examines France's early reception to photography, since it was the birthplace of photography, and its legal treatment of photographic works, being the country that strongly advocated for the inclusion of photographic works in the Berne Convention. The second part tracks the history of the Berne Convention and its treatment of photographic works as one of the protected works of expression. This recognition by the Berne Convention represented a significant milestone for the international recognition of copyright in photographic works.

## 2.2 France and Photographic Works

### *2.2.1 France: The Birthplace of Photography and the Site of Its First Struggle for Recognition*

On 19 August 1839, France unveiled the Daguerreotype process, invented by Louis Jacques Daguerre (Figure 2.1), and announced the details as a gift to the world; this marked the birth of photography to the world.[8] While everyone was eager to embrace this process that allows nature to reproduce itself,[9] the traditional art establishment and jurists looked at photography with worried eyes. The famous painter Paul Delaroche, upon hearing about the Daguerreotype, was reported

4 Ricketson and Ginsburg (n 1) 10, 448, 449; The International Bureau of Intellectual Property, "Berne Convention Centenary 1886–1986" [1986] WIPO 243, 112.

5 Ricketson and Ginsburg (n 1) 22; Burger (n 1) 10.

6 Ricketson and Ginsburg (n 1) 22, 44, 45, 49, 50; Burger (n 1) 10.

7 Ricketson and Ginsburg (n 1) 22, 44, 45, 49, 50; Burger (n 1) 10.

8 Beaumont Newhall, *The History of Photography: From 1839 to the Present* (5 edition, The Museum of Modern Art, New York 1984) 17.

9 ibid.

*Figure 2.1* Louis Jacques Daguerre (1787–1851), the inventor of the Daguerreotype.

Photograph by Jean-Baptiste Sabatier-Blot, "Louis Jacques Mandé Daguerre" (Eastman Museum, 1844) https://collections.eastman.org/objects/27621/louis-jacques-mande-daguerre, accessed 11 October 2024.

to have proclaimed, rather dramatically, that "From today, painting is dead."[10] Delaroche had students who ended up being famous as photographers, the most prominent among them being the British photographer Roger Fenton.[11]

One of the first legal responses to photography outside patent law was censorship. To protect public sensibilities, indecent and pornographic photographs were censored, and laws were passed in the 1850s to prevent the selling and making of pornographic photographs; such offences were punishable with prison sentences.[12]

10 Tim J Barringer, "Rethinking Delaroche/Recovering Leighton" (2001) 44 Victorian Studies 9, 11; Naomi Rosenblum, *World History of Photography* (4 edition, Abbeville Press Inc, US 2008) 209.

11 Rosenblum (n 10) 100.

12 John Tagg, *The Burden of Representation: Essays on Photographies and Histories* (Palgrave Macmillan 2002) 104,105; Donald E English, "Anxiety and the Official Censorship of the Photographic Image, 1850–1900" [2012] Yale French Studies 104, 108.

This is not too surprising since the origin of copyright in its infancy, both in France and England, can be traced to the government's desire to control the spread of ideas to maintain a tighter grip on the populace by giving printing privileges only to certain establishments with printing rights.[13]

Photographic works struggled to be recognised as deserving of legal protection on the level of the fine arts. French jurists were met with a difficult challenge regarding the nature of the art of photography since French civil law assigns more emphasis on the author's right (droit d'auteur) compared to the focus on reproduction rights ("copyright") as was the case in English common law.[14] The French jurists dealt with the nature of the mechanical reproduction of photographs and whether or not such a mechanical process gives rise to the author's rights.[15] After all, for intellectual creations to be protected according to the French author's right system, the work must exhibit the author's unique personality, a manifestation of his labour which imbued his soul into the work to become akin to an extension of his soul, his intellectual work.[16] It was from this very notion that the focus was shifted onto appreciating the author's work more than being concerned with pragmatic matters relating to distribution and economic rights, which are characteristic of Anglo-American copyright law.[17] Art was held in high regard by the French elites since it was considered the representation of man's soul. Hence, many were reluctant to allow this "Soulless machine," whose production was close to industrial rather than artistic, to be put on the same pedestal as traditional works of art with the same level of protection.[18]

The prejudicial position adopted by the conservative art establishment towards photography felt like a bitter pill for photographers since there was evidence to suggest that some of these artists used photographs as reference materials in some of their paintings. In contrast, the works of photographers who inspired such paintings were not met with the same respect and legal protection.[19] From that point, it was clear that the notion of whether photography is an art or an industrial process would only be settled when the law had taken the task of determining whether photography is accorded author's rights protection on the same level as paintings and other works of art. This matter was pursued in a series of cases that heightened

13 Simon Newman, "The Development of Copyright and Moral Rights in the European Legal Systems" (2011) 33 European Intellectual Property Review 677, 680, 681.

14 Goldstein (n 1) 10; Catherine Colston and Jonathan Galloway, *Modern Intellectual Property Law* (Taylor & Francis 2010) 281; Newman (n 13) 677.

15 Christine Haight Farley, "The Lingering Effects of Copyright's Response to the Invention of Photography" (2004) 65 University of Pittsburgh Law Review 385, 395; Tagg (n 12) 104, 105, 108.

16 Newman (n 13) 682; Anne Mccauley, "'Merely Mechanical': On the Origins of Photographic Copyright in France and Great Britain" (2008) 31 Art History 57, 67, 76; Bernard Edelman, *Ownership of the Image: Elements for a Marxist Theory of Law* (Elizabeth Kingdom tr, Routledge & Kegan Paul Books 1979) 51; Tagg (n 12) 110.

17 Newman (n 13) 677; Jane C Ginsburg, "Tale of Two Copyrights: Literary Property in Revolutionary France and America" (1989) 64 Tulane Law Review 991, 993.

18 Tagg (n 12) 109; Rosenblum (n 10) 209.

19 Rosenblum (n 10) 209.

the existing tensions regarding photography in the 1860s.[20] This issue persisted due to the fact that the law had established, since 17 February 1852, that photographs, along with other visual media, were subject to registration.[21] However, this requirement was geared towards censorship rather than protection.

### *2.2.2 The Author's Rights and Photographic Works*

The French courts met with a technology that tested the underlining philosophy of the author's rights protection; it was challenging to find precisely where the personality of the creator lies in a photograph because photography was held by the firm belief that it was a mechanical process that reproduces reality, a product of a machine devoid of the personality of the creator.[22] The French courts' decisions in this period were often contradictory, demonstrating the difficulties associated with inducting photography into the existing legal realm of the author's rights protection.[23]

In 1861, Mayer & Pierson, a company that specialised in the Carte de visite[24] and portraiture business, sued Siraudin for their unauthorised use of Mayer & Pierson celebrities' photographs on the cover of their products.[25] The court did not entertain questions about the photographs' eligibility for author's rights but held in favour of the claimant, ordering an injunction and damages on the defendant's use of the claimant's photographs.[26] In the following year, Mayer & Pierson took another legal action in "the Tribunal correctionnel de la Seine" against several companies for their unauthorised use and modification of Mayer & Pierson's Carte de visite photographs. The defendants argued that recycling celebrities' Carte de visite is a common practice among photographers and that Mayer & Pierson must have the rights to the celebrity's image in those disputed images in order to have a legitimate claim. The court held in favour of the defendants, the judge stating that:

> in effect photography does not invent and create…that its works, produced with the aid of mechanical means, can in no way be assimilated to works of intelligence.[27]

20 Mccauley (n 16) 64.

21 ibid 77; English (n 12) 107.

22 Edelman (n 16) 46, 48, 51; Tagg (n 12) 110; Mccauley (n 16) 76.

23 Tagg (n 12) 107; Mccauley (n 16) 59, 64.

24 The Carte de visite process uses a special camera that utilises several lenses and a moving plate holder in order to make several exposures and fix them to a single negative. See: Newhall (n 8) 60–62; Rosenblum (n 10) 62.

25 Kimberly Rhodes, "Mayer and Pierson Company" in John Hannavy (ed), *Encyclopedia of Nineteenth-Century Photography*, vol 1 (Routledge 2008) 909; Mccauley (n 16) 64.

26 Mccauley (n 16) 64.

27 "Art. 775 – Propriété artistique – Portraits photographiques – Trib. corr. de la Seine – 9 janvier 1862 – Mayer et Pierson c. Thiebault et autres," Annales de la propriété, 1862, 75. As quoted and cited in ibid 65.

Consequently, Mayer & Pierson appealed the decision. The Paris Court of Appeal (Cour d'Appel de Paris) overruled the lower court's judgement in favour of Mayer & Pierson, stating that certain photographs are considered artistic works because of the prior setup and work done to prepare the scenes to be photographed, which showed an artistic quality and an "imprint of [the creator's] personality."[28] The case eventually reached the Court of Cassation in November 1862, and the defence argued that based on the 1793 law, a work of art had to be an original work of the mind and "genius" of the author, and had to originate from the artist in order to be eligible for protection as a work of art. They proceeded to say that photography was not a medium of art but a mere mechanical process lacking the capacity to exhibit the author's imprint of personality.[29] The defence also showed a declaration signed by several renowned French artists declaring that photography is not an art.[30]

The claimant's side attempted to build its argument on the premise that art takes many forms and, drawing from the influential French philosopher Victor Cousin, the products of the mind are composed of three categories: "truth, beauty and utility."[31] The claimant argued that while machines denote "uniformity," a photograph of the same person across different portraiture studios are varied in style, the way they depict the subject proves the considerable influence of the photographer's intellectual judgement and creative choices.[32] In other words, it is precisely the human operator who, by imbuing his personality into the photographs, renders null the uniformity that emanates from the products of mechanical processes. In this manner, the photographer's camera is analogous to the painter's brush, directed by the artist's genius to imprint his personality upon the work.[33] The Court of Cassation upheld the ruling made by the appeal court and acknowledged, albeit not conclusively, that certain photographs could be considered art for the purposes of the law and qualify for protection as original works of the mind.[34]

From a legal standpoint, everything depends on the judge's assessment. The photographer could be an artist who imprinted his personality into the photograph to elevate it into a work of art or be relegated to nothing more than an important gear that allows the mechanical process to work as intended. Perhaps it is appropriate to refer to Bernard Edelman's view on this particular notion, where he said that the law "disintegrate [the photographer] into the 'mechanical'" to be nothing more than the machine itself in order to adhere strictly to its legal biases. Thus, it was

28 "Art. 787 – Propriété artistique – Portraits photographiques – C. de Paris – 10 avril 1862 – Mayer et Pierson c. Thiebault et autresl" Annales de la propriété, 1862, 116–117. As cited in ibid; Justin Hughes, "The Photographer's Copyright-Photograph as Art, Photograph as Database" (2011) 25 Harv. JL & Tech. 339, 365.

29 "Photographies – Portraits – Contrefaçon – C. de cass.–28 novembre 1862 – Mayer et Pierson c. Betbéder et Schwalbél," Annales de la propriété, 1862, 423–428. As cited in Mccauley (n 16) 65.

30 ibid.

31 ibid 66.

32 ibid.

33 ibid 67.

34 Hughes (n 28) 364.

not the machine that was at the service of man, but man that was at the service of the machine.[35] However, it is important to stress that there is no doctrine of precedence under the French legal system. Thus, court decisions do not become law as in common law legal systems, but they do exhibit a degree of persuasive power, especially if the decision comes from the upper courts.[36] In 1878, efforts were made to push for special laws that address photography in particular, but without fruition. The uncertain standards for which photography was required to satisfy to gain an author's rights protection was still a matter left to the judge's discretion.[37]

Even though France is considered the birthplace of photography and the country that advocated protecting photographs in the Berne Convention, the law did not address photographs directly until the 1957 law on literary and artistic works,[38] more than a hundred years after the invention of photography. This inclusion was far from being clear, for the law was cautious about photography and expressly designated two categories of photographs in Article 3 by stating that "Photographic works of artistic or documentary character and those of the same character obtained by a process analogous to photography"[39] are considered works of the mind for the purposes of the law. This provision was ambiguous in the sense that it does not specify what was meant by "artistic or documentary character," so it was up to the judges to evaluate the artistic merits of a photograph on an ad hoc basis with inevitably diverging results.[40] This particular issue with the 1957 law regarding photographic works was rightfully addressed in July 1985, removing the mention of "artistic or documentary character" to settle for the simpler provision that states, "Photographic works and those made using techniques similar to photography" are considered works of the mind and are protected as such if they were deemed original without, ideally, a special treatment with regard to the standard of protection granted.[41] This provision remains in force in the 1992 law in the Intellectual Property Code.[42]

35 Edelman (n 16) 45.
36 Newman (n 13) 678.
37 Mccauley (n 16) 67; Hughes (n 28) 364.
38 Law No. 57-298 of March 11, 1957 on Literary and Artistic Property.
39 Article 3, ibid.
40 Hughes (n 28) 395.
41 Law No. 57-298 of March 11, 1957 on Literary and Artistic Property Modified by Law No. 85-660 of July 3, 1985 – art. 1 JORF 4 July 1985 in force on 1 January 1986; Hughes (n 28) 396.
42 Art. L.112-2, 9 in Law No. 92-597 of July 1st, 1992 Relating to The Code of The Intellectual Property (Part Legislative).

## 2.3 The History of the Berne Convention and Its Treatment of Photographic Works

### *2.3.1 The Origin of the Berne Convention*

The origin of the Berne Convention can be traced back to 1858 when the first International Congress of Authors was held in Brussels.[43] The 1858 Brussels conference saw the attendance of diverse interest groups from across the world and advocated for the establishment of universal copyright protection for authors of literary works worldwide.[44] In 1861, an international congress for artists was organised in support of the aforementioned efforts towards universal copyright protection for the benefit of authors and artists.[45] In 1878, an international literary association led by Victor Hugo was established to represent the interests of authors worldwide and continue the campaign towards universal copyright protection.[46] The International Association, which later included artists and was renamed the International Literary and Artistic Association (ALAI),[47] adopted a number of resolutions that served as the bedrock for the Berne Convention 1886.[48] In 1882, the Swiss government took the initiative to organise state-level international conferences from 1883 to 1886 to discuss the matters raised by the ALAI, which culminated in the Berne Convention in 1886.[49]

### *2.3.2 The Berne Convention 1886*

The Berne Convention came into effect in 1887; it recognised certain rights by setting a minimum standard of protection for authors and artists.[50] The original Berne Convention did not set a mandatory minimum duration of protection, due to the lack of uniformity and agreement among union members. The stark differences of views became apparent on the subject of photographic works. Some countries, such as France and the United Kingdom, protected some photographs as artistic works, while other countries, such as Germany, did not regard photographs as artistic works and gave them a lesser form of protection.[51]

On the one hand, those who regarded photography as a medium capable of artistic expression, particularly when combined with sufficient skill and judgement to arrange the scene coupled with choosing the right time, angle, and lighting to capture the image, considered photographs worthy of being protected as original

43 Ricketson and Ginsburg (n 1) 44, 45; Goldstein (n 1) 19; Burger (n 1) 11.

44 Ginsburg (n 1) 749.

45 Ricketson and Ginsburg (n 1) 48, 51; Dutfield and Suthersanen (n 1) 55.

46 Ricketson and Ginsburg (n 1) 49; The International Bureau of Intellectual Property (n 4) 19; Goldstein (n 1) 19; Burger (n 1) 11.

47 Association Litteraire et Artistique Internationale (ALAI)

48 Ricketson and Ginsburg (n 1) 49–51, 54; Burger (n 1) 11; The International Bureau of Intellectual Property (n 4) 19; Dutfield and Suthersanen (n 1) 55.

49 Ricketson and Ginsburg (n 1) 52; The International Bureau of Intellectual Property (n 4) 19.

50 Burger (n 1) 16.

51 Ricketson and Ginsburg (n 1) 443.

artistic works reflecting the author's personality.[52] On the other hand, those who regarded photography as a mechanical process, that renders the human actor as nothing more than a manual operator who merely pushes the button, refused to accord photographs the status of artistic works.[53] These different views clashed and could not be quelled without a compromise.

The original Berne Convention did not include photographic works in the list of protected works; it was left to the national legislator of each union state to decide the standard of protection, if any, conferred upon photographic works.[54] In other words, the countries that did not protect photographic works as artistic works would be under no obligation to protect them as such and were free to determine the level of protection accorded to photographs according to their national laws.[55] However, an exception was given to authorised photographs reproducing protected works of art, in which case the convention applies to these photographs to the extent it applies to the principal work of art.[56] It was worth noting that photographs that reproduced works other than artistic works, such as textual content, are not similarly protected.[57] Nevertheless, the original Berne Convention expressly pointed out that the convention was an ongoing project and mentioned that revision conferences were planned to be held in order to "introduce improvements to perfect the system of the Union."[58]

### *2.3.3 The Berne Convention Revision Conferences and Photographic Works*

#### *2.3.3.1 The 1896 Paris Conference*

The 1896 Paris Conference amendments were limited to minor changes to refine and clarify the Berne Convention.[59] The French delegates, with the support of the Belgian delegation, reiterated their proposal to include photographic works in the list of protected works in Article 4 of the 1886 Convention.[60] This proposal was, again, rejected since several countries still did not protect photographic works as artistic works.[61] However, the German delegation proposed a compromise regarding the formalities requirements that would improve the protection of photographic

52 ibid.

53 ibid.

54 Final Protocol paragraph 1, Berne Convention 1886 (original text), The International Bureau of Intellectual Property (n 4) 230; Burger (n 1) 18.

55 Ricketson and Ginsburg (n 1) 443; Burger (n 1) 18.

56 The International Bureau of Intellectual Property (n 4) 230; Burger (n 1) 18.

57 Sam Ricketson, "International Conventions" in Ysolde Gendreau, Axel Nordemann and Rainer Oesch (eds), *Copyright and Photographs, An International Survey* (Kluwer Law International 1999) 19.

58 The International Bureau of Intellectual Property (n 4) 35; Article 17 of the Berne Convention Act of 1886 (original text) ibid 230.

59 Ricketson and Ginsburg (n 1) 86; Burger (n 1) 22.

60 The International Bureau of Intellectual Property (n 4) 138, 139.

61 ibid.

works under the convention without necessarily including them in Article 4.[62] This compromise entails that the formalities requirement was waived in the countries where protection was sought, provided that the photographic work in question satisfied the formalities of the country of origin. In normal circumstances, the union country where the work was first published was generally considered "the country of origin of the work."[63] This was a convenient improvement since it was easier and less cumbersome to afford national treatment to photographs under the Berne Convention in union states.[64] This was because countries that did not protect photographic works were not obliged to protect them, but their citizens benefitted from the convention when they sought protection in countries that did protect photographic works.

#### *2.3.3.2 The 1908 Berlin Conference*

The 1908 Berlin Conference represented a major revision and introduced significant advancements towards the codification of international copyright law.[65] It consolidated the convention into a single document and introduced several important changes, such as the removal of formalities that hindered the enjoyment of copyright protection, expanded the list of protected works, and introduced the standard minimum duration of copyright protection that extends the term of protection to the life of the author and 50 years after his death as a recommendation along with other important amendments.[66]

On photographic works, it was acknowledged by the countries that some form of protection was required for photographs in all union countries.[67] The delegates agreed that there was an obligation to protect photographic works but decided that the nature and manner of that protection should be left for the national legislator to decide.[68] This stance on photographic works represented a departure from the 1896 Paris Conference, which did not oblige countries to accord protection to photographic works but only recommended that they should be protected.[69] However, the countries could not agree on a uniform standard of protection for photographic works.[70] The protection for photographic works was to remain subject to the national legislator's decision. The duration of protection depended on the country

62 ibid 139; Ricketson and Ginsburg (n 1) 444, 445.

63 Article 2, paragraph 3, the Berne Convention of September 9, 1886 (original text) The International Bureau of Intellectual Property (n 4) 228.

64 ibid 139.

65 Burger (n 1) 23; Ricketson and Ginsburg (n 1) 92, 95, 101.

66 Ricketson and Ginsburg (n 1) 95–97, 101; Ginsburg (n 1) 749; Burger (n 1) 23, 24; Goldstein (n 1) 21.

67 Ricketson and Ginsburg (n 1) 446.

68 ibid.

69 The International Bureau of Intellectual Property (n 4) 147.

70 ibid; Ricketson and Ginsburg (n 1) 447.

where protection was sought, provided that the term of protection claimed does not exceed the period accorded to photographic works in the country of origin.[71]

The Berlin revision conference did not include photographic works alongside other protected works in Article 2 but elected to introduce a special article that expressly addresses photographic works under the convention in the form of Article 3, which stated that "This Convention shall apply to photographic works and to works produced by a process analogous to photography. The contracting countries shall be bound to make provision for their protection."[72] Article 7 stated that:

> For photographic works and works produced by a process analogous to photography…the term of protection shall be governed by the legislation of the country where protection is claimed, provided that the said term shall not exceed the term fixed in the country of origin of the work.[73]

Hence, a uniform standard of protection for photographic works was not yet within reach, owing to the diverging opinions on the nature of photographic works.[74]

The achievement of the Berlin Conference on the subject of photographic works was summarised by the German delegates who stated that:

> Although opinions on the intrinsic nature of photographs still differ a great deal, it matters little whether they are considered to be works of art under the domestic regime or whether they are subject to any particular treatment; the main thing is that, in every country of the Union, they are guaranteed such protection as exists.[75]

#### *2.3.3.3 The 1928 Rome Conference*

The major contribution of the 1928 Rome Conference was the recognition of the moral rights of the authors, such as the right of attribution and the right of integrity to the work, and the expansion of the list of protected works to include oral works.[76] The Rome Conference organised sub-committees to examine particular matters such as photographic works. The Sub-Committee for Cinematography and Photography agreed unanimously that photographic works should remain addressed in Article 3 and not be included alongside other protected works in Article 2.[77] No particular reason was given, but perhaps it was due to the refusal of some countries to regard photographic works as within the meaning of artistic works. The Italian

71 The International Bureau of Intellectual Property (n 4) 147; Ricketson and Ginsburg (n 1) 447.

72 Article 3, Act of Berlin of November 13, 1908. The International Bureau of Intellectual Property (n 4) 229.

73 Article 7 (3), Act of Berlin of November 13, 1908. ibid.

74 ibid 150; Ricketson and Ginsburg (n 1) 447.

75 The International Bureau of Intellectual Property (n 4) 147; Ricketson and Ginsburg (n 1) 447.

76 Ricketson and Ginsburg (n 1) 107, 108; Burger (n 1) 27, 28.

77 The International Bureau of Intellectual Property (n 4) 166.

government proposed an addition to Article 3 that provides that "these works shall, regardless of their merit or purpose, enjoy protection in all the countries of the Union."[78] The Italian proposal would have had the potential to protect all types of photographic works, regardless of whether the work was a banal photograph or an artistic photograph, but the proposal failed to gain approval.[79] Another proposal regarding photographic works was raised by Hungary; however, it was prejudicial to photographers since it proposed the free reproduction of photographs attached to "news of the day and miscellaneous items of information."[80] This proposal was firmly rejected on the grounds that such photographs could have artistic merits.[81]

Perhaps the discussion regarding the protection of cinematographic works in the Rome Conference laid bare the approach that viewed photography as a lesser form of art, a view embodied by the attitude towards photographic works in the Berne Convention. It was stated, in the general report of the Rome Conference, that:

> A film which reproduces street scenes without any staging does not deserve any protection other than that which is afforded by the law to photographs. The protection enjoyed by other works of art should be reserved for cinematographic productions which meet the requirements of originality laid down in paragraph (2).[82]

It is quite apparent that there was an assumption that photographs did not exhibit originality, at least equal to other works of art, despite the fact that even photographic works can involve staging an entirely constructed scene to be photographed. Article 14 of the Rome Revision Act of 1928 stated that "Cinematographic productions shall be protected as literary or artistic works if the author has given the work an original character. If this character is absent, the cinematographic production shall enjoy protection as a photographic work."[83] The wording of this article is prejudicial to photographic works as it stresses the view that photographic works are, by default, a lesser form of art regardless of the artistic merits a photographic work may exhibit.

A few years after the Rome Conference, an international congress for photographers was held in Brussels in June 1935 to discuss copyright protection for artistic photographs.[84] The International Congress on Photographic Rights demanded that the protection for photographic works be in the same league as other artistic works. However, it was observed that the photographic congress stressed their campaign in distinguishing between the artistic photographer, whose work was worthy of protection as an artistic work, and the ordinary photographer, whose work may

78 ibid; Ricketson and Ginsburg (n 1) 448.
79 Ricketson and Ginsburg (n 1) 448.
80 The International Bureau of Intellectual Property (n 4) 166.
81 ibid.
82 ibid 174.
83 Article 14, Act of Rome of June 2, 1928. ibid 230; ibid 174.
84 Ricketson and Ginsburg (n 1) 450.

not be on the same elevated class of work, in a way that exhibits a sense of elitism from those who drafted the photographic congress' resolutions. Perhaps this attitude reflected the need of certain groups of the photographic community to distinguish their works from the massive bulk of mundane and banal photographs that populated the photographic landscape. The French delegation expressed their intention to take the photographic congress' proposal to the next Berne revision conference in Brussels.[85]

### *2.3.3.4 The 1948 Brussels Conference*

The 1948 Brussels Conference continued the movement towards a uniform international copyright law while maintaining the stability of the Union, which had grown to comprise a large membership.[86] The Brussels Conference's significant achievements range from expanding the list of protected works, imposing a mandatory minimum term of protection of the life of the author and 50 years after his death, and requiring the protection of moral rights, among other several amendments.[87]

Remaining steadfast on its campaign, France once again requested that photographic works be placed alongside other protected works in Article 2 and consequently enjoy the same level of protection.[88] The original proposed French amendment, which was inspired by the demands of the International Congress of Photographic Rights, stated that "all photographic works or works realised by an analogous process to photography … constitute intellectual creations, with the exception of ordinary photographic productions."[89] This time, their proposal gained favourable traction and would eventually pass, but not without certain modifications and limitations. A sub-committee that was organised to report on the matter of photographic works favoured the decision to include photographic works alongside other protected works in Article 2, but wondered if additional specific conditions should accompany its inclusion.[90] In particular, the sub-committee questioned whether it should be specified in the text that only photographic works that exhibit "the character of personal creations" were protected under Article 2.[91] This suggestion failed to generate agreement due to the fact that the requirement of originality and personality on a creation applies to all protected works under the convention, and many questioned the need to emphasise these requirements again in relation to a specific class of work.[92] Thus, no specific mention that differentiates artistic and non-artistic ordinary photographic works was adopted. Furthermore, no agreement

85 ibid.
86 ibid 115.
87 ibid 114–116; Burger (n 1) 37; Goldstein (n 1) 22.
88 The International Bureau of Intellectual Property (n 4) 178; Ricketson and Ginsburg (n 1) 450, 549.
89 As quoted in Ricketson (n 57) 24.
90 The International Bureau of Intellectual Property (n 4) 184.
91 ibid.
92 ibid.

could be reached regarding the minimum duration of protection for photographic works.[93]

Following the meeting of the minds on the inclusion of photographic works in Article 2, a question arose about whether it was appropriate to add a general provision that defines what was meant by a "literary or artistic work" in clear terms in order to clarify which class of photographs, among other classes of works, were protected as an artistic work.[94] This proposal, however, did not pass due to a strong objection from the UK delegates, who expressed that such a proposal could lead to works being discriminated against based on their literary or artistic merits, which would run contrary to "the spirit of the convention."[95]

The Brussels Revision Act 1948 omitted Article 3, which addressed photographic works separately from other protected works and included photographic works in Article 2 alongside other protected works.[96] The Brussels Act Article 2 stated that:

> The expression "Literary and artistic works" shall include every production in the literary, scientific and artistic domain, whatever may be the mode or form of its expression, such as... photographic works and works produced by a process analogous to photography...(4) The works mentioned in this Article shall enjoy protection in all countries of the Union.[97]

However, no minimum term of protection for photographic works was specified, and Article 7(3) stated that:

> in case of cinematographic and photographic works, as well as works produced by a process analogous to cinematography or photography...the term of protection shall be governed by the legislation of the country where protection is claimed, but shall not exceed the term fixed in the country of origin of the work.[98]

A definition of what constitutes a photographic work was not adopted despite indications that the term "Photographic works" encompasses technological development in the field of photographic processes. Sam Ricketson explained the phrase "works produced by a process analogous to photography" was meant to be wide enough to include future advancement in photographic processes and also restrictive enough so as not to include other visual works.[99] Ricketson indicated that this was part of the reason why the phrase "analogous effects" was rejected during the succeeding Stockholm revision.

93 Ricketson and Ginsburg (n 1) 548.
94 The International Bureau of Intellectual Property (n 4) 184.
95 ibid.
96 Article 2, 3, Act of Brussels of June 26, 1948. ibid 231.
97 Article 2, Act of Brussels of June 26, 1948. ibid.
98 Article 7(3), Act of Brussels of June 26, 1948. ibid.
99 Ricketson (n 57) 25–26.

### *2.3.3.5 The 1967 Stockholm Conference and the 1971 Paris Conference*

The Stockholm Conference took place in June 1967, and it saw the establishment of the World Intellectual Property Organization (WIPO), which continued the work started by the Berne Convention on the road to a universal international copyright regime.[100] The Stockholm revision aimed to refine and perfect the convention, but maintaining the Union with its broad membership proved to be its greatest challenge since the disagreement between developing and developed countries threatened to rupture the Berne Union itself.[101] The Stockholm revision was not able to receive the minimum number of ratifications and subsequently, the 1971 Paris Conference was held to mitigate the differences and maintain the Union so the Stockholm text could receive the minimum number of ratifications.[102] WIPO, having been established following the Stockholm Conference, played an essential role in conciliating the two opposing sides, which led to the success of the 1971 Paris Conference.[103] The 1971 conference revision text was identical to the Stockholm revision except for the provisions pertaining to developing countries.[104]

On the subject of photographic works, it was recommended that they should be protected for at least 25 years, as a minimum term of protection, from the time the work is made. Consequently, Article 7(4) of the Stockholm 1967 Act provides that:

> It shall be a matter for legislation in the countries of the Union to determine the term of protection of photographic works...in so far as they are protected as artistic works; however, this term shall last at least until the end of a period of twenty-five years from the making of such a work.[105]

Thus, member states are free to determine which category of photographic works falls within the meaning of artistic works according to their national legislation and subsequently satisfy their national originality standard to be eligible for protection, provided that the protection was no less than 25 years from the making of the photographic work.[106]

### *2.3.3.6 The Berne Convention and Beyond*

The Berne Convention in its current iteration, as amended in September 1979, provides in Article 2 that:

100 Ricketson and Ginsburg (n 1) 121, 122, 124; The International Bureau of Intellectual Property (n 4) 22, 61; Burger (n 1) 39.
101 The International Bureau of Intellectual Property (n 4) 22, 23; Ricketson and Ginsburg (n 1) 123–124, 129–131; Burger (n 1) 39–40.
102 The International Bureau of Intellectual Property (n 4) 22, 23; Ricketson and Ginsburg (n 1) 132; Burger (n 1) 39–40.
103 The International Bureau of Intellectual Property (n 4) 23; Ricketson and Ginsburg (n 1) 131–132; Burger (n 1) 41.
104 The International Bureau of Intellectual Property (n 4) 23.
105 Article 7(4) Act of Stockholm of July 14, 1967; ibid 232.
106 Ricketson and Ginsburg (n 1) 405; Burger (n 1) 42.

> The expression "literary and artistic works" shall include every production in the literary, scientific and artistic domain, whatever may be the mode or form of its expression, such as...photographic works to which are assimilated works expressed by a process analogous to photography.[107]

The terms of protection for artistic photographic works are left for national legislation to determine, provided that the protection is no less than the minimum term of 25 years from the making of the photograph and does not exceed the term of protection given to the work in the country of origin.[108]

Moreover, the Berne Convention does not specify what is meant by a "process analogous to photography," but the WIPO Guide to the Berne Convention posited that the wording is construed to encompass all photographic works regardless of the subject depicted and the purpose for which the photograph was made.[109] The provision's construction was meant to cover all processes, either chemical or technical, that are in use or yet to be discovered to produce photographic works, regardless of the specific photographic methods used.[110] Hence, digital photography and computational photography are within the Berne Convention criteria of photographic works.

However, the WIPO Guide pointed out that the Berne Convention does not require protection for all categories of photographic works.[111] The Berne Convention permits union members to deny protection to any particular category of photographs they deem not worthy of protection as artistic works.[112]

Since there are no uniform interpretations in the Berne Convention regarding authorship, originality, or the author's personality reflected in the intellectual work, disparity regarding what constitutes a photographic work of art was bound to exist. Outside the Berne Convention, there were attempts by the European Union (EU) to harmonise the standard of originality in the Berne Convention between EU member states, particularly for photographic works, in the form of recital 16 of EU Directive 2006/116/EC. The recital provides that:

> A photographic work within the meaning of the Berne Convention is to be considered original if it is the author's own intellectual creation reflecting his personality, no other criteria such as merit or purpose being taken into account. The protection of other photographs should be left to national law.[113]

107 Article 2, Berne Convention for the Protection of Literary and Artistic Works.

108 Article 7(4) ibid.

109 World Intellectual Property Organization (ed), *Guide to the Berne Convention for the Protection of Literary and Artistic Works (Paris Act, 1971)* (World Intellectual Property Organization 1978) 16.

110 ibid.

111 ibid 113.

112 ibid.

113 Recital 16, Article 6 Directive 2006/116/EC of 12 December 2006 on the term of protection of copyright and certain related rights [2006] OJ L372/12.

Therefore, photographs that are "original in the sense that they are the author's own intellectual creation" are deemed artistic works under Article 2 of the Berne Convention and protected for the life of the author and 70 years after his death in EU member states, regardless of the date of the making of the photograph, according to Article 1 and 6 of the EU Directive 2006/116/EC.[114]

Nonetheless, outside of the EU's attempt at harmonising the treatment of photographs across its jurisdiction, at least for the photographs that are deemed artistic, photographic works remain a challenging area in the international copyright landscape. The 1996 WIPO Copyright Treaty, which recognised the impact of emerging information technologies on literary and artistic works, addressed the term of protection for photographic works in Article 9 of the treaty by specifically stating that "In respect of photographic works, the Contracting Parties shall not apply the provisions of Article 7(4) of the Berne Convention."[115] Thus, under the WIPO copyright treaty, photographs are treated equally to other works of art in all aspects of copyright protection.

## 2.4 Conclusion

The journey photographic works undertook to be admitted into the scope of literary and artistic work, and consequently becoming one of the protected works, was not one without perils. Photography's mechanical aspects were summoned time and time again to discredit its position as an artistic work worthy of protection. The traditional art establishment acted as gatekeepers that stood in the way of photographs being recognised and protected as an art form. Yet, protecting photographs with copyright was not meant to lessen the status of art. Perhaps it is appropriate to refer to Eugène Pouillet's remarks about what it means to accord photographs the status of art in that "it is not art which is lowered, but industry which is raised and ennobled."[116]

Despite being the birthplace of photography, France wrestled with the dual nature of photography that exhibits both mechanical skill and artistic judgement. Photography's greatest defining characteristic, in that it can capture a reality fixed in time, was also its greatest challenging aspect to be recognised as an artistic medium capable of reflecting the author's personality. On one hand, some described photographs as the labour of soulless machines that cannot carry the essence of the author's personality. On the other hand, some judges found photographs to contain the essence of the author in a manner that reflects his personality. This contradiction serves as a testament to the dual nature of photography in that it contains the characteristics of both the mechanical and artistic processes.

114 ibid; see also: *(C-145/10) Painer v Standard Verlags GmbH [2012] ECDR 6.*

115 Article 9, WIPO Copyright Treaty 1996.

116 Eugène Pouillet, *Propriete Litteraire et Artistique* (William Alexandre tr, 1879) as quoted in *Sarony v Burrow-Giles Lithographic Co, 17 F 591 (1883)* 599.

Nevertheless, France was the leading force behind the recognition of photographic works as a class of works worthy of being included within the Berne Convention's list of protected works. However, this was initially met with strenuous resistance across the Berne revision Acts until the Brussels Revision Act 1948 paved the way for the Paris 1971 Revision Act to include photographic works formally into the list of protected works covered by the Berne Convention. With this, photographs were finally accorded minimal standards of protection on the international level. Nonetheless, even with the inclusion of photographic works into the Berne Convention, the tension between photographic works and copyright law, with concepts such as authorship and originality, remains ever persistent for virtually the same reasons it ever was.

# 3 The United Kingdom and Photographs

## 3.1 Introduction

This chapter explores the path photographic works undertook in the United Kingdom to eventually come under the scope of copyright subject matters. The United Kingdom was the first country to enact a statute that expressly offered legal protection to photographic works as intellectual property. However, this did not come about easily since countless debates ensued – between academics, artists, photographers, and jurists – concerning whether photographs were worth protecting by copyright as artistic works.

The first part of this chapter covers the development of photography within the United Kingdom, the effect of the patent monopoly on the then-infant art of photography, and how it shaped the movement towards photographs' copyright protection. The second part examines the development and impact of the Fine Art Act 1862 on photographic works since it was the first statute in the world to expressly classify photographs as fine art. The third part examines the UK statutory development of copyright law in relation to photographic works, culminating in the Copyright, Design and Patents Act 1988 (CDPA 1988).

## 3.2 Photography: An Art? Or Science?

Britain is credited with being the place where another photographic process, developed in isolation from France's Daguerreotype around the same time, was established as well as being the place that pioneered one of photography's first technological advancements. Henry Fox Talbot (Figure 3.1) (1800–1877), an English scientist, invented the Calotype, also known as Talbotype, a photographic process that pioneered the negative-positive image system. The Calotype was unique compared to the Daguerreotype, which did not lend itself well to reproductions, in that it was naturally compatible with duplication since a single negative image can be used to print multiple positive images.[1]

1 Beaumont Newhall, *The History of Photography: From 1839 to the Present* (5 edition, The Museum of Modern Art, New York 1984) 22, 36; Naomi Rosenblum, *World History of Photography* (4 edition, Abbeville Press Inc, US 2008) 24; Marcy J Dinius, "Daguerreotype" in John Hannavy (ed), *Encyclopedia of Nineteenth-Century Photography*, vol 1 (Routledge 2008) 370.

DOI: 10.4324/9781003586555-3

*Figure 3.1* Henry Fox Talbot (1800–1877).

Photograph by John Moffat, "William Henry Fox Talbot" (1864) https://collections.eastman.org/objects/26706/william-henry-fox-talbot accessed 11 October 2024.

The first book illustrated with photographic images, *The Pencil of Nature* by Talbot, was released in parts between 1844 and 1846. Within it, Talbot accurately predicted potential uses of photography,[2] such as its importance as evidence in court, and also entertained the notion that it was a medium capable of producing art.[3]

The British art community's response to the Daguerreotype announcement was that of a fearful reservation, comparable to the French art community's response, albeit with less intensity. Photography was met with anxiety by the art community to the point that engravers and painters feared for their livelihood.[4] Engravers saw themselves as translators, not copyists, of a painting's original design, a

2 Larry J Schaaf, "Third Census of H. Fox Talbot's The Pencil of Nature" (2012) 36 History of Photography 99, 99.

3 William Henry Fox Talbot, *The Pencil of Nature* (Longman, Brown, Green and Longmans) 19, 20, 25 <https://www.gutenberg.org/files/33447/33447-pdf.pdf> accessed 11 October 2024.

4 Roger Taylor, "The Graphic Society and Photography, 1839: Priority and Precedence" (1999) 23 History of Photography 59, 61–63.

higher grade of reproduction that requires intellectual labour, unlike the perceived mechanical and servile nature of photography.[5] At first, this reassured the opponents of photography since popular sentiments dictated that photographs were products of a mechanical process limited to reproducing reality without colours; hence, the medium was initially perceived to be limited and most closely connected with the realm of science rather than art.[6] This conclusion seems to conveniently neglect the fact that art and science often intertwined, as was evidenced in the Renaissance, a period praised profoundly for its artistic and scientific productions.[7] Instead of being antithetical to each other, art, science, and industry influence one another to rise to new heights. Some of the leading British artists and art critics shared sentiments similar to those of their French counterparts towards photography, albeit with relatively less hostility. In their view, the mechanical and servile nature of photography prevented it from being fine art, and as a result, it should not be held in the same place or offered comparable legal protection.[8]

By contrast, the scientific community welcomed photography with gleaming excitement about the prospects this invention might bring to the development of scientific documentation and science in general.[9] This was unsurprising since the Daguerreotype was an optical and chemical process. The Daguerreotype's first public disclosure in 1839 by François Arago was delivered to a joint audience composed of the Academy of Science and the Academy of Fine Art. It was also apparent that this invention had applications as a new medium for artistic expression, which is equally unsurprising since Daguerre was an accomplished painter.[10]

One could say that photography occupies both the domain of science and art. This fact was a source of tension between the proponents of art photography, on the one hand, and the proponents of scientific photography, on the other hand.[11] Indeed, photography was closely embedded with the scientific community due to its perceived mechanical and objective nature to depict what the camera lay witness to in an authentic and reliable manner. As a result, it lent itself well to the scientific objectivity that the scientific community generally aspired to achieve.[12] In fact,

5 Elena Cooper, *Art and Modern Copyright: The Contested Image* (Kindle edition, CUP Cambridge 2018) 16, 54.

6 See: Jens Jäger, "Discourses on Photography in Mid-Victorian Britain" (1995) 19 History of Photography 316, 317, 319; Kelley E Wilder, "Photography and the Art of Science" (2009) 24 Visual Studies 163, 164.

7 See: Jerry Brotton, *The Renaissance: A Very Short Introduction* (1 edition, OUP Oxford 2006).

8 See: Michael Harvey, "Ruskin and Photography" (1984) 7 Oxford Art Journal 25; Jäger (n 6) 316; Wilder (n 6) 164; Anne Mccauley, "'Merely Mechanical': On the Origins of Photographic Copyright in France and Great Britain" (2008) 31 Art History 57, 70; John Tagg, *The Burden of Representation: Essays on Photographies and Histories* (Palgrave Macmillan 2002) 66, 105.

9 Wilder (n 6) 163, 164; Jäger (n 6) 318.

10 See: Newhall (n 1) 17; Wilder (n 6) 164; Jäger (n 6) 317; Rosenblum (n 1) 17.

11 Jäger (n 6) 317; Wilder (n 6) 164.

12 Wilder (n 6) 164; Jäger (n 6) 318; see: Lorraine Daston and Peter Galison, "The Image of Objectivity" [1992] Representations 81, 120.

the initial primary objective of the Royal Photographic Society (RPS), founded in 1853 as one of the oldest and still active photographic societies that received royal patronage from Queen Victoria and Prince Albert in 1854, proposed at first by Antoine Claudet, was for "The advancement of the science of photography." However, with Roger Fenton's insistence, the society's objective expanded to "promoting the art and science of photography."[13] This close relationship between photography and science reinforced the perceived characteristics of photography as a passive, mechanical, and servile process that merely reproduces reality.[14] These sentiments were the primary reasons behind the reluctance to acknowledge photographs as fine art.

Nonetheless, the RPS was populated with members who were more interested in the science of photography than its potential as fine art.[15] This prompted stern advocates of photography such as Henry Peach Robinson to feel that the medium as a fine art was shackled by the attitudes of the RPS and formed a breakaway group called the Brotherhood of the Linked Ring in 1892 with the primary objective of "bringing together those who are interested in the development of the highest form of Art of which Photography is capable."[16] The Linked Ring was more interested in cementing the artistic status of photographs as fine art, and by extension, photographers' social status as artists, than the law's acknowledgement of photographs as fine art worthy of the same level of copyright protection as other fine arts.[17] Robinson was very vocal about his disdain for the notion that photography was incapable of being fine art due to its primary characteristic of reproducing candid reality, and equally expressed his dislike for the scientific photographers who thought of photography as a machine that tells no lies to the point of considering it a valuable instrument for scientific documentation.[18]

The root of this tension ran deep and was a point of discussion in the Great Exhibition of 1851 and the London International Exhibition of 1862.[19] The Great Exhibition of 1851, also known as the Great Exhibition of the Works of Industry of All Nations, was a marvellous Victorian-era exhibition that was met with an outstanding reception. The exhibition was conceptualised by members of the Royal Society of Arts (RSA), who embraced photography since its introduction and

13 John Hannavy, "Royal Photographic Society" in John Hannavy (ed), *Encyclopedia of Nineteenth-Century Photography*, vol 1 (Routledge 2008) 1218, 1219; Michael Pritchard, "The Royal Photographic Society | History" (*The Royal Photographic Society (RPS)*) <https://rps.org/about/history/> accessed 11 October 2024.

14 Wilder (n 6) 164; Jäger (n 6) 317.

15 Hannavy, "Royal Photographic Society" (n 13) 1220; Pritchard (n 13).

16 Hannavy, "Royal Photographic Society" (n 13) 1220; Rosenblum (n 1) 309.

17 Cooper (n 5) 106.

18 See: Henry Peach Robinson, "Paradoxes of Art, Science, and Photography" (1892), Wilson's Photographic Magazine, Vol. 29 242–245. Reprinted in Nathan Lyons (ed), *Photographers on Photography* (1 edition, Prentice Hall 1966) 82–88.

19 Jeffrey A Auerbach, *The Great Exhibition of 1851: A Nation on Display* (Yale University Press 1999) 93; John Hannavy (ed), *Encyclopedia of Nineteenth-Century Photography*, vol 1 (Routledge 2008) 462, 615, 1305.

played an important role in urging Talbot to ease the restrictions on the Calotype patent for the benefit of the British photographic community.[20]

## 3.3 Photography and the Patent's Leash

Prior to the Fine Art Copyright Act 1862, photographic processes were protected by patent law since it was the means to gain monopoly rights on photography in specified territories.[21] In fact, England, Wales, and the town of Berwick-upon-Tweed were the only places in the world where the Daguerreotype was restricted due to the existence of a valid Daguerreotype patent. An English patent for the Daguerreotype was granted to Miles Berry, Daguerre's agent, a few days before the announcement of the Daguerreotype as free to the world to utilise.[22] The patent granted monopoly rights on the Daguerreotype process within the patent's territorial scope. In 1841, the patent was sold to Richard Beard, an entrepreneur who effectively controlled the Daguerreotype patent in England, Wales, the town of Berwick-upon-Tweed and "the colonies and plantation abroad."[23] Beard had developed a reputation for not being hesitant at all about taking legal action against anyone who infringed upon the patent in his targeted markets.[24]

It is important to mention that the other photographic process, the Calotype, was also subject to a patent owned by Talbot, who enforced his patent rigorously against anyone who infringed upon it while asking for high licence fees for using it.[25] John Dillwyn Llewelyn, a botanist and a photographer, wrote in a letter:

> I heartily grieve to hear of all his present litigation, his first step to secure himself an exclusive monopoly was a most inadvised one.... It seems however to be with him a kind of monomania, he must be a little insane on that point.[26]

To emphasise, this meant that the only known photographic processes at the time were controlled by two individuals who enforced their patents rigorously to the

20 Auerbach (n 19) 9, 10; Renate Wickens-Feldman, "Eastlake, Sir Charles Lock (1793–1865)" in John Hannavy (ed), *Encyclopedia of Nineteenth-Century Photography*, vol 1 (Routledge 2008) 462; Hannavy, "Royal Photographic Society" (n 13) 1219.

21 Michael Pritchard, "Patents: Britain and Europe" in John Hannavy (ed), *Encyclopedia of Nineteenth-Century Photography*, vol 1 (Routledge 2008) 1054; Steve Edwards, "'Beard Patentee': Daguerreotype Property and Authorship" (2013) 36 Oxford Art Journal 369, 370, 393.

22 John Hannavy, "Beard, Richard (1801–1885)" in John Hannavy (ed), *Encyclopedia of Nineteenth-Century Photography*, vol 1 (Routledge 2008) 126; Pritchard (n 21) 1054; Edwards, "'Beard Patentee'" (n 21) 371.

23 Hannavy, "Beard, Richard (1801–1885)" (n 22) 126; Steve Edwards, "Great Britain" in John Hannavy (ed), *Encyclopedia of Nineteenth-Century Photography*, vol 1 (Routledge 2008) 607; Edwards, "'Beard Patentee'" (n 21) 377.

24 Edwards, "'Beard Patentee'" (n 21) 386; Hannavy, "Beard, Richard (1801–1885)" (n 22) 127.

25 Newhall (n 1) 43.

26 Richard Morris, "Llewelyn, John Dillwyn (1810–1882)" in John Hannavy (ed), *Encyclopedia of Nineteenth-Century Photography*, vol 1 (Routledge 2008) 866.

detriment of the photographic industry in England.[27] Aside from England, the rest of the world was able to utilise the Daguerreotype without any restrictions. It is worth noting that Talbot did not enforce his patent in Scotland, which allowed Scotland to utilise the Calotype and advance the use of photography. This was apparent through the work of David Octavius Hill and Robert Adamson and the establishment of one of the first photographic societies in the world, the Edinburgh Calotype Society.[28] Equally, evidence suggests that Richard Beard, like Talbot, did not enforce his patent in Scotland or Ireland despite the fact that he had registered the patent in the designated territories.[29]

In England, Richard Beard fully utilised the Daguerreotype's patent commercially and solidified his position in the portraiture business to great success.[30] The only person who was legally allowed to use the Daguerreotype process without the need to seek Beard's permission was Antoine Claudet, since he retained a licence to use the Daguerreotype from Daguerre himself before Beard purchased the Daguerreotype patent.[31] This was held after Richard Beard lost an injunction claim brought against Claudet, in which the court reaffirmed that Claudet was entitled to use the Daguerreotype process but only within the limit of his licence.[32] In other words, other than Claudet, anyone wishing to use the Daguerreotype process in England and Wales had to be authorised by Beard to avoid infringement claims.

Many photographers disgruntledly claimed that Beard hardly ever handled a camera, yet he was effectively, under the law, the author of every Daguerreotype in England and Wales by virtue of being the owner of the Daguerreotype's patent in the relevant territories.[33] This exposed an enormous flaw since industrial creations are characterised by uniformity, and photographs, at least the Daguerreotype, are in no way uniform. The value of a Daguerreotype radiates from the image fixed and not from the process, materials, or the physical form of the Daguerreotype itself.[34]

Therefore, it was argued that the circumstances surrounding photography during this period had hindered its development in Britain.[35] Effectively, photography was protected as a mechanical industrial process by patent law, and photographs were treated strictly as commodities. Steve Edwards argues that during this period,

27 Hannavy, "Beard, Richard (1801–1885)" (n 22) 127; John Hannavy, "History: 4. 1850s" in John Hannavy (ed), *Encyclopedia of Nineteenth-Century Photography*, vol 1 (Routledge 2008) 682.

28 Roddy Simpson, "Edinburgh Calotype Club" in John Hannavy (ed), *Encyclopedia of Nineteenth-Century Photography*, vol 1 (Routledge 2008) 470.

29 John Hannavy, "Introduction" in John Hannavy (ed), *Encyclopedia of Nineteenth-Century Photography*, vol 1 (Routledge 2008) xxxix.

30 Hannavy, "Beard, Richard (1801–1885)" (n 22) 126; Edwards, "Great Britain" (n 23) 607; John Ward, "History: 3. Photography in the 1840s" in John Hannavy (ed), *Encyclopedia of Nineteenth-Century Photography*, vol 1 (Routledge 2008) 678; Edwards, "'Beard Patentee'" (n 21) 386.

31 Laura Claudet, "Claudet, Antoine Francois Jean (1797–1867)" in John Hannavy (ed), *Encyclopedia of Nineteenth-Century Photography*, vol 1 (Routledge 2008) 303.

32 ibid; Edwards, "'Beard Patentee'" (n 21) 379.

33 Edwards, "'Beard Patentee'" (n 21) 381, 387, 393.

34 See: ibid 393.

35 Hannavy, "Beard, Richard (1801–1885)" (n 22) 127; Hannavy, "History: 4. 1850s" (n 27) 682.

every Daguerreotype produced in England was virtually considered by the law as being authored by Beard since he held the Daguerreotype patent in England.[36] The photographer and the contents of the photographs were virtually immaterial; as long as the images were fixed using the Daguerreotype process without authorisation, it infringed on Beard's patent.[37]

### *3.3.1 Liberation! A New Photographic Process to Break the Shackles*

In the 1850s, photography in England was given a new life. Fredrick Scot Archer, an English inventor and photographer, invented the Wet Collodion photographic process in 1848 and published the details in 1851 without any restrictions on its use; hence, it was given free to the world.[38] After being subject to restrictions, photography in England was finally liberated with a new photographic process available to everyone to use and further develop without any restrictions. Not only that, the Wet Collodion process was superior to both the Daguerreotype and the Calotype. It was faster and capable of making images with the fine details of the Daguerreotype while also being relatively suitable for reproduction like the Calotype since multiple positives can be reproduced from a single negative.[39]

During this time, Talbot had already resigned most of his patent rights over the Calotype process in 1852 after pleas from the RSA and RPS.[40] As a result, amateur photographers and scientists were allowed to use the Calotype process freely, but professional commercial photographers still had to respect the Calotype patent.[41] Given the apparent similarity of the Wet Collodion process to the Calotype, since the Collodion process was based on the negative-positive system, some commercial photographers were still paying licence fees to Talbot to avoid potential infringement claims despite the fact that Archer gave the process for free.[42] The situation regarding the Wet Collodion process was cleared after a court judgement in the 1854 case initiated by Talbot against Martin Laroche,[43] who ran a portrai-

36 Edwards, "'Beard Patentee'" (n 21) 387, 393.

37 ibid 375, 382, 387.

38 Graham Saxby and Kelley E. Wilder, "Archer, Frederick Scott," *The Oxford Companion to the Photograph* (OUP Oxford 2005) <https://www.oxfordreference.com/view/10.1093/acref/9780198662716.001.0001/acref-9780198662716-e-79> accessed 11 October 2024.

39 Newhall (n 1) 43; Martin Barnes, "Archer, Frederick Scott (1813–1857)" in John Hannavy (ed), *Encyclopedia of Nineteenth-Century Photography*, vol 1 (Routledge 2008) 55, 56; Gary D Sampson, "History: 5. 1860s" in John Hannavy (ed), *Encyclopedia of Nineteenth-Century Photography*, vol 1 (Routledge 2008) 688.

40 Newhall (n 1) 43; Roger Watson, "Talbot, William Henry Fox (1800–1877)" in John Hannavy (ed), *Encyclopedia of Nineteenth-Century Photography*, vol 1 (Routledge 2008) 1378.

41 Newhall (n 1) 43; Watson (n 40) 1378.

42 Barnes (n 39) 56; John Hannavy, "Laroche, Martin (William Henry Silvester (1814–1886)" in John Hannavy (ed), *Encyclopedia of Nineteenth-Century Photography*, vol 1 (Routledge 2008) 827.

43 His name is reported differently on different sources, some sources give his name as Silvester Laroche, while others name him William Henry Sylvester. Other sources also report his name as Martin Silvester Laroche. See: Rosenblum (n 1) 632; Newhall (n 1) 43–45; Hannavy, "Laroche, Martin (William Henry Silvester (1814–1886)" (n 42) 827; Watson (n 40) 1378.

ture studio using the Wet Collodion process. The court held that Talbot was the inventor of the Calotype process and the negative-positive system, but the Wet Collodion process was sufficiently different to the point that it did not fall within the scope of his patent.[44] With this decision, the spread of the Wet Collodion process in England was assured.[45]

The success of the Wet Collodion process, which eventually eclipsed both the Daguerreotype and Calotype in popularity around the early 1860s, liberated the English photographic industry and accelerated its growth to constitute a considerable economic value following the popularity of the Carte de visite format, which was based on the Wet Collodion process.[46] The sheer economic value of the photographic industry meant that piracy became a pressing issue, which consequently led to pressure from art societies and commercial establishments demanding some form of legal protection to be given to photographs.[47] In fact, some photographers cleverly placed their initials or signatures in the photographs they owned so they could spot pirated copies and sue under trademark infringements.[48] This was because such inscriptions could be considered protected trademarks.

## 3.4 The Road to the Fine Art Act 1862

In 1862, England enacted the Fine Art Copyright Act 1862, the first legislation in the world that expressly included photographs with other works of art. The Act gave photographs copyright protection on the same level as other works of art without special provisions that considered photography's unique nature, which later served as a point of debate in subsequent parliamentary Bills and reports.[49] There was evidence to suggest that the Bill was rushed in preparation for the International Exhibition of 1862, which may be one of the reasons why the Act and photographs as a subject matter of copyright were later the target of several reports and amendments.[50]

44 Newhall (n 1) 43–45; Barnes (n 39) 56; Edwards, "Great Britain" (n 23) 608.

45 Newhall (n 1) 43; Barnes (n 39) 56.

46 John Plunkett, "Carte-De-Visite" in John Hannavy (ed), *Encyclopedia of Nineteenth-Century Photography*, vol 1 (Routledge 2008) 276, 277; Newhall (n 1) 43, 62; Rosenblum (n 1) 62.

47 Tim Padfield, "Copyright" in John Hannavy (ed), *Encyclopedia of Nineteenth-Century Photography*, vol 1 (Routledge 2008) 337; Ronan Deazley, "Struggling with Authority: The Photograph in British Legal History" (2003) 27 History of Photography 236, 236, 237; Mccauley (n 8) 70.

48 John Plunkett, "Mayall, John Jabez Edwin (1813–1901)" in John Hannavy (ed), *Encyclopedia of Nineteenth-Century Photography*, vol 1 (Routledge 2008) 908.

49 Deazley, "Struggling with Authority" (n 47) 236, 237.

50 The Solicitor General said, "It was of considerable importance in the present year that such a Bill, if the principle was approved by the House, should be passed with despatch," HC, *Copyright (Work of Art) Bill Deb 27 February 1862*, vol 165 (Hansard 1862) col 845; HC, *Copyright (Work of Art) Bill Deb 31 March 1862*, vol 166 (Hansard 1862) col 324; see: Deazley, "Struggling with Authority" (n 47); see also Ronan Deazley, "Breaking the Mould? The Radical Nature of the Fine Arts Copyright Bill 1862" in Martin Kretschmer, Lionel Bently and Ronan Deazley, *Privilege and Property: Essays on the History of Copyright* (Open Book Publishers 2010) 300, 301.

Just as the Great Exhibition of 1851 was instrumental in reforming patent laws, the International London Exhibition of 1862 was equally important for accelerating the enactment of the Fine Art Act 1862, which expressly protected photographs alongside other traditional works of art such as paintings and drawings.[51] It is important to note that even paintings were not protected by copyright law before the Fine Art Act, but ironically, an engraving of a painting was protected by copyright under the Engraving Act.[52] However, this was not to say that painters had no protection whatsoever. In fact, they enjoyed "residual protection" through the engravings of their paintings since the Engraving Act placed a condition that dictated that the express consent of the proprietor of the "main design" had to be acquired before making an engraving from it.[53] That, in a way, created a symbiotic relationship between painters and engravers since painters relied on engravers to reproduce their work and, as a result, increased their reputation and revenue, and engravers relied on painters to generate new engravings.[54] The RSA, along with other societies representing artists, petitioned for copyright protection for works of fine art and noted that the approaching International Exhibition made the matter all the more pressing.[55]

The 1862 International Exhibition organisers, in their preparation for the exhibition, classified photography among industrial machinery, which caused photographers to rally against such an insult to their art. The photographers were outraged by such a proposal to the point of threatening to boycott the exhibition if their demands for the images to be exhibited in the fine art section, and classified as such, were not satisfied.[56] The photographic community RPS pressed on this issue and campaigned for the reclassification of photography in the exhibition.[57] One journalist wrote that the photographers lamented that the organisers: "have thought fit to pass an insult upon Photographic Art, by classing its productions with railway plant and garden tools, small arms and ship's tackle, big guns, and new omnibuses,

51 Section 1, Fine Arts Copyright Act 1862 (25 & 26 Vict.) C. 68; Deazley, "Breaking the Mould? The Radical Nature of the Fine Arts Copyright Bill 1862" (n 50) 300.

52 Lionel Bently and Martin Kretschmer (eds), "Report of the Artistic Copyright Committee, London (1858)," *Primary Sources on Copyright (1450–1900)* 4, 11 <https://www.copyrighthistory.org/cam/tools/request/showRecord.php?id=record_uk_1858> accessed 11 October 2024; For more on the Engraving Copyright Acts, see: Mark Rose, "Technology and Copyright in 1735: The Engraver's Act" (2005) 21 The Information Society 63; David Hunter, "Copyright Protection for Engravings and Maps in Eighteenth-Century Britain" (1987) s6-IX The Library 128.

53 Cooper (n 5) 115; Lionel Bently and Martin Kretschmer (eds), "Engravers' Copyright Act, London (1777)," *Primary Sources on Copyright (1450–1900)* <https://www.copyrighthistory.org/cam/tools/request/showRecord.php?id=record_uk_1777a> accessed 11 October 2024.

54 Cooper (n 5) 115–116.

55 Deazley, "Breaking the Mould? The Radical Nature of the Fine Arts Copyright Bill 1862" (n 50) 301.

56 Edwards, "Great Britain" (n 23) 610; Steve Edwards, "Societies, Groups, Institutions, and Exhibitions in the United Kingdom" in John Hannavy (ed), *Encyclopedia of Nineteenth-Century Photography*, vol 1 (Routledge 2008) 1305.

57 Edwards, "Societies, Groups, Institutions, and Exhibitions in the United Kingdom" (n 56) 1305.

donkey carts and corn extractors."[58] Eventually, photographers had to swallow their pride and accept the organisers' offer for photographs to be exhibited in a separate room alongside cameras and educational devices instead of the fine art section.[59] This situation with the International Exhibition was of great importance to photography in England since it instigated photographers to present their case regarding photography as fine art in a more pronounced fervour.[60] This undoubtedly must have had an impact during the passing of the Fine Art Copyright Act 1862, which was accelerated by the International Exhibition, to include photographs alongside other traditional fine arts.[61]

The history of the 1862 Fine Art Copyright Act can be traced back to December 1857 following the work exerted by the Royal Society of Arts, known as the Society for the Encouragement of Arts, Manufacture and Commerce, to review copyright law on works of fine art and the scope of protection offered to the artists of such works.[62] The committee, tasked to look at this subject, issued a report in January 1858 and provided that the existing copyright laws did not provide sufficient protection to works of art.[63] The report also stated that aside from the right to the first publication of a work of art, there was no further protection for authors or owners of works of art existing in English common law after the publication of the work.[64]

The report revealed that the existing statutory laws did not protect "the new art of photography," regardless of the expenses endured by the photographer, nor give artists any copyright in pictures since the existing laws regarded pictures as only a predesign for an engraving, which was covered by copyright, but ironically, the principal picture used for the engraving was not protected.[65] As a result, the report laid down recommendations that aimed to provide adequate protection to the authors of works of fine art.[66] Lord Lyndhurst, presenting the petitions from various societies calling for the protection of fine arts, described to the House of Lords that artists suffered from illicit copying of their works and argued that the damage it may inflict on the artists' reputation and livelihood might be severe if nothing was done to protect them.[67]

The Copyright Bill of Works of Art was presented to the House of Commons in 1861.[68] The Bill provided that the author of new and original work in "every

58 "Fair Play for Photography" *Punch* (London, England, 6 January 1861) 221 221.

59 Edwards, "Societies, Groups, Institutions, and Exhibitions in the United Kingdom" (n 56) 1305.

60 ibid.

61 Deazley, "Breaking the Mould? The Radical Nature of the Fine Arts Copyright Bill 1862" (n 50) 301.

62 Deazley, "Struggling with Authority" (n 47) 236.

63 Bently and Kretschmer, "Report of the Artistic Copyright Committee, London (1858)" (n 52).

64 ibid 4, 5.

65 ibid 10–13.

66 ibid 31, 32; Deazley, "Struggling with Authority" (n 47) 236.

67 HL, *Law of Copyright. Deb 26 July 1858*, vol 151 (Hansard 1858) col 2090.

68 Deazley, "Struggling with Authority" (n 47) 236, 237; "Sitting of 15 April 1861 Series 3 Vol. 162 (Hansard)" <http://hansard.millbanksystems.com/sittings/1861/apr/15> accessed 30 September 2021.

Picture, Work of Sculpture, and Engraving…shall have the sole and exclusive Right of copying, reproducing, and multiplying such work…by any means… for the Term of natural Life of such Author, and Thirty Years after his Death."[69] Photographs were included within the meaning of "Picture" since the interpretation of the term includes "every Drawing, Painting, Photograph."[70] The Bill failed to pass and was referred for amendments.[71] Later, the Solicitor General brought a new Bill to "amend the law relating to copyright in works of fine art" and stated that it "differed considerably from that of last year. It was simplified, and some of the more questionable provisions of the measure of last year were omitted."[72] This Bill stated in Section 1 that "The Author of every Painting, Drawing, and Photograph" shall enjoy Copyright protection for the duration of the author's life and seven years after his death.[73] Ronan Deazley explained that this duration of protection was modelled after the 1842 Copyright Act.[74]

In the House of Commons' session dated 20 March 1862, the addition of a registration clause was requested to ascertain the copyright of pictures as it was considered an essential element for securing the property in the work.[75] At first, artists objected to the registration requirement, but the measure had gone through regardless.[76] Moreover, the Bill's parliamentary debates focused on issues relating to the status of copyright when the work was purchased and how the Bill affects the owners of such works if the work was duplicated from the original.[77] This was due to the fact that art collectors, who had considerable influence on the debates regarding artistic copyright and paintings in particular, tried to regulate artists in a way that prevented them from reducing the value of their collection through repetitions.[78] Thus, collectors were concerned about the possible adverse effects on the value of the material property, represented by the canvas, containing the immaterial property, represented by the painting's design, if the author of the painting was allowed to reproduce the immaterial property without restrictions.

69 Section 3, Fine Art Copyright Bill (1861) in Lionel Bently and Martin Kretschmer (eds), "Fine Art Copyright Bill, London (1861)," *Primary Sources on Copyright (1450–1900)* <https://www.copyrighthistory.org/cam/tools/request/showRecord.php?id=record_uk_1861> accessed 11 October 2024.

70 Section 2, Subsection 3 ibid.

71 HC, *Copyright (Work of Art) Bill Deb 6 May 1861*, vol 162 (Hansard 1861) col 1634; Deazley, "Struggling with Authority" (n 47) 236, 237.

72 HC, *Copyright (Work of Art) Bill Deb 27 February 1862* (n 50) col 844.

73 Section 1, Fine Art Copyright Bill (1862) in Lionel Bently and Martin Kretschmer (eds), "Fine Art Copyright Bill (27 Feb.), London (1862)," *Primary Sources on Copyright (1450–1900)* <https://www.copyrighthistory.org/cam/tools/request/showRecord.php?id=record_uk_1862i> accessed 11 October 2024.

74 Ronan Deazley, "Commentary on Fine Arts Copyright Act 1862" in Lionel Bently and Martin Kretschmer (eds), *Primary Sources on Copyright (1450–1900)*, (2008) <https://www.copyrighthistory.org/cam/tools/request/showRecord.php?id=commentary_uk_1862> accessed 11 October 2024.

75 HC, *Copyright (Work of Art) Bill Deb 20 March 1862*, vol 165 (Hansard 1862) cols 1889–1890.

76 The Solicitor General in HC, *Copyright (Work of Art) Bill Deb 31 March 1862* (n 50) col 324.

77 HC, *Copyright (Work of Art) Bill Deb 20 March 1862* (n 75) cols 1890–1891.

78 Cooper (n 5) 7, 160.

Another particularly relevant concern was raised by Mr Harvey Lewis about the inclusion of photography, where he argued that "it would be dangerous at present to include photographs in a Bill of the kind. Photography was not a fine art, but a mechanical process."[79] The Solicitor General conceded that photography, strictly speaking, may not be a work of fine art, but argued that photographers endure significant expenses to acquire good photographs and to allow the products of their "large expenditure of time, labour, and money" to be copied by other persons to "enrich themselves at their expense?" was something he could not stand for and should not be allowed to continue.[80] Another concern was raised regarding portrait photographs where Mr Hennessy suggested that they should be excluded from the Bill entirely since it would be difficult to "prevent the public from obtaining a copy of his likeness."[81]

Perhaps one notion that could be deduced from what was raised in these parliamentary debates was the view that photographs ought to be treated differently as intellectual property, not only because of their mechanical nature but also according to the nature of the images captured. Henceforth, it was hinted that different considerations, with regard to copyright and other relevant matters, may be required depending on the type of images depicted.

In May 1862, the Bill was presented to the House of Lords. Lord Overstone noted that the Bill was only concerned with the interests of artists, neglecting the interests of other stakeholders, and proposed that the statement of "new and original" should be included next to the addressed works of art since these concepts are considered essential conditions for the special privileges granted by copyright.[82] He argued that "The Bill was drawn for the sole purpose of giving extraordinary and comprehensive powers, which were not only unnecessary, but dangerous."[83] Lord Overstone's comments were met with clear disagreement by Earl Stanhope, who said that the Bill balanced the interests of purchasers with that of artists and stated that giving protection to artists does not present any more issues than that of authors of literary works.[84] He argued that "there was no difference in principle between a poem and a picture," but he admitted that photographs present a particularly difficult issue.[85] He illustrated this through a hypothetical situation where more than one photographer took photographs of the same scene under the same conditions to produce similar results, and these results might be the subject of disputes and litigation that may prove difficult to

79 HC, *Copyright (Work of Art) Bill Deb 20 March 1862* (n 75) col 1890.

80 ibid 1891.

81 ibid.

82 *Copyright (Work of Art) Bill Deb 22 May 1862*, vol 166 (Hansard 1862) cols 2017, 2019; Lord Overstone in HL, *Copyright (Work of Art) Bill Deb 23 May 1862*, vol 166 (Hansard 1862) col 2094.

83 *Copyright (Work of Art) Bill Deb 22 May 1862* (n 82) col 2015.

84 ibid 2015–2017.

85 "Copyright (Work of Art) Bill, Second Reading. Lords Sitting of 22 May 1862 Series 3 Vol. 166 (Hansard, 22 May 1862)" para 2016 <http://hansard.millbanksystems.com/lords/1862/may/22/second-reading> accessed 30 September 2021.

dismantle. After all, "A person, for instance, might make a photograph copy of a photograph—say of the Coliseum—originally taken by another; who could say that the copy was not an original photograph?"[86]

Photography proved very challenging to equate to literary works as a product of authorship since it demands, by its perceived mechanical nature, little intellectual involvement from the photographer. Thus, the pronounced rationale for protecting photographs was to reward the photographer for his labour and expenses and prevent others from benefitting from his labour without due remuneration. Elena Cooper observed that the debates concerning photographic copyright, and artistic copyright in general, centred around a "taxonomy of authorship: a division between mental and mechanical labour."[87] Indeed, this appears pronounced in the debates surrounding photographic copyright, as the concept of authorship was often invoked to argue against the copyright protection of photographs.

## 3.5 The Fine Art Copyright Act 1862 and Authorship in Photographs

The Fine Art Copyright Act received royal assent on 29 July 1862. The Act provided that the author of every original painting, drawing, and photograph, and the negative of a photograph, shall have the exclusive right of reproduction of any copies for the life of the author and seven years after his death.[88] For commissioned photographs made for a "good or valuable consideration," then the owner of the photograph retains the copyright unless there was an agreement to the contrary.[89] Furthermore, the Act stated that registration to the Stationers Company was a mandatory requirement to bring a copyright action under the 1862 Act.[90] The Fine Art Act rejuvenated the photographic industry and influenced the behaviour of photographers in England to register their works and seek to profit from them.[91] For the first time, photographs were legally protected as fine art and illicit copying, which plagued the photographic industry, could finally be met with legal repercussions.[92] This was not the only high mark of the Fine Art Act; the Act also introduced the concept of "originality" to British copyright law as one of the important standards that made a work eligible for copyright protection.[93] However, the inclusion of the requirement that the work must be "original" was not included for considerations regarding authorship or originality; instead, it was meant to prevent the emergence of new copyrights for repeat works by the same artists, as this would have created multiple conflicting copyrights on the same work if that copyright was already

86 ibid 2017.
87 Cooper (n 5) 13.
88 Section 1, Fine Arts Copyright Act 1862 (25 & 26 Vict.) C. 68.
89 Section 1, ibid.
90 Section 4 ibid.
91 Mccauley (n 8) 70.
92 Padfield (n 47) 337; Edwards, "Great Britain" (n 23) 610.
93 Deazley, "Breaking the Mould? The Radical Nature of the Fine Arts Copyright Bill 1862" (n 50) 319.

purchased. Henceforth, Ronan Dezealy explained that "the originality requirement would prevent the artist from relying upon a copyright-protected repetition of that work to interfere with the purchaser's commercial exploitation of the original picture."[94]

One of the first cases that came after the 1862 Act involving photographs was *Gambart v Ball 1863*.[95] The case set out to tackle whether photographs of an engraving, which resemble the said engraving, were considered copying within the Engraving Act's meaning and if the Fine Art Act was applicable in this situation. The defence argued that duplicates by the process of photography did not fall under the Engraving Act since it was unknown by the time the legislation was enacted. The court held that reproducing an engraving with the process of photography was an act of copying that falls under the Engraving Act; therefore, the defendant was liable for copyright infringement.[96]

Another notable case was the *Graves Case 1868–1869*[97] that involved photographs of engravings of a picture. An argument was raised that the photographs assigned to Graves, which were of his engravings from a picture, did not have copyright since the photographs were based on another work of art. Thus, "they are mere copies of the engraving, and not original in the sense intended by the first section [of the 1862 copyright act]."[98] Blackburn J responded by stating that

> All photographs are copies of some object, such as a painting or a statue. And it seems to me that a photograph taken from a picture is an original photograph, in so far that to copy it is an infringement of this statute...although it is unlawful to copy a photograph or the negative, it is permitted to copy the subject matter of the photograph by taking another photograph.[99]

On these grounds, it was held that, in a photograph of a copyrighted subject matter, the fact that the object depicted has copyright does not prevent the photograph itself from having its own copyright. Furthermore, an infringement claim regarding the photograph was valid if the photograph itself was copied and not necessarily the subject matter depicted.

The judgement in the *Graves case* served to stop a practice adopted by engravers in which they employed photographers to take photographs of their engravings in order to bring legal action against individuals infringing upon their engraving's copyright under the Fine Art Act.[100] Hence, by using the copyright in the photographs to bring a claim under the Fine Art Act 1862, instead of bringing the action under the Engraving Act, they benefitted from the Fine Art Act's favourable

94 ibid 320.
95 *Gambart v Ball (1863) 14 C B(N S) 305.*
96 See: applied in *Ex Parte Beal (1867–68) LR 3 QB 387.*
97 *Graves' Case (1868–69) LR4 QB 715.*
98 ibid 720.
99 ibid 723.
100 Deazley, "Struggling with Authority" (n 47) 239; Elena Cooper, "We Are Experienced! Jimi Hendrix in Historical Perspective" (2016) 38 European Intellectual Property Review 196, 199.

provisions.[101] This practice also artificially prolonged the copyright in engravings, which was 28 years according to the Engraving Act, since photographs under the Fine Art Act were protected for the life of the author and seven years after his death.[102] Judges may have been aware of this practice since Blackburn J clearly stated that an infringement claim could be brought only for an unauthorised copy of the copyrighted photograph itself and not for the subject matter depicted in the photograph by another original photograph.[103]

The cases involving photographs under the Fine Art Act 1862 raised questions about the copyright owner in portraiture photographs made for a good consideration by the sitter or on his behalf. The courts conclusively ruled that, according to Section 1 of the Fine Art Act 1862, the sitter, or for whom on his behalf the photograph was made, owns the copyright in the portraiture photograph made for a "good and valuable consideration" unless there was an agreement to the contrary.[104] The property in the negative of that photograph, not the copyright, may still be owned by the photographer in the absence of an agreement to the contrary.[105] Even though the photographer may own the negative, the copyright owner may still prevent him from producing positives from it under the Fine Art Act 1862.[106] This was because it was routine practice to leave the negative as the property of the photographer in case the photograph's copyright owner wanted more copies to be produced.[107]

In *Boucas v Cooke*,[108] Collins MR quoted an excerpt from Scrutton on Copyright that laid down the appropriate test for locating the copyright owner in a photograph.[109] The test provides that if the photograph was made on behalf of the photographer and at his request, then the photographer owns the copyright, but if the photograph was made on behalf of the sitter for good and valuable consideration, then the copyright is held by the sitter; if it was not clear on whose behalf the photograph was made or if the sitter paid for select copies then the decision regarding copyright ownership depends on the facts of each individual case.[110] In the present case, it was held that, based on the facts of the case, the sitter owns the copyright according to the Fine Art Act 1862.

101 Deazley, "Struggling with Authority" (n 47) 239; Cooper (n 100) 199.
102 *Graves' Case (1868–69) LR4 QB 715* (n 97) 723; Deazley, "Struggling with Authority" (n 47) 239; Cooper (n 100) 199.
103 *Graves' Case (1868–69) LR4 QB 715* (n 97) 723; Deazley, "Struggling with Authority" (n 47) 239; Cooper (n 100) 199.
104 *Boucas v Cooke [1903] 2 KB 227* 227, 236, 238–239; *Stackemann v Paton [1906] 1 Ch 774* 774; *Pollard v Photographic Company [1888] L.R. 40Ch 345* 353.
105 See: *Boucas v Cooke [1903] 2 KB 227* (n 104); *Stackemann v Paton [1906] 1 Ch 774* (n 104); *Pollard v Photographic Company [1888] L.R. 40Ch 345* (n 104).
106 See: *Boucas v Cooke [1903] 2 KB 227* (n 104); *Stackemann v Paton [1906] 1 Ch 774* (n 104); *Pollard v Photographic Company [1888] L.R. 40Ch 345* (n 104).
107 *Boucas v Cooke [1903] 2 KB 227* (n 104) 231.
108 *Boucas v Cooke [1903] 2 KB 227* (n 104).
109 ibid 235.
110 ibid 235, 236.

*Figure 3.2* Australian Cricket Team (1882).

"Australian Cricket Team, 1882" (State Library New South Wales, 1882) https://archival.sl.nsw.gov.au/Details/archive/110328367 accessed 11 October 2024.

Under the Fine Art Act 1862, most copyright cases involving photographs were pursued to find out who was the copyright owner of a photograph and not so much about the author of the said photograph.[111] However, some early cases tackled the issue of authorship in photographs, and one notable case was *Nottage v Jackson (1883)*.[112] In *Nottage*, the plaintiffs were two photographers who co-owned a company in the photography business that employed several photographers and managers across different studios. One of their managers arranged for photographs of the 1882 Australian cricket team (Figure 3.2) and sent photographers to take these photographs accordingly. The photographers prepared the scene, made the necessary arrangements, took photos of the team as tasked, and sent the negatives to the company. The plaintiffs registered the photographs in the Stationers Company, as required by Section 4 of the Fine Art Act 1862, and put themselves as the owners, as it was fit, and also as the authors despite not being actively and physically

111 Deazley, "Struggling with Authority" (n 47) 237.
112 *Nottage v Jackson (1883) 11 QBD 627.*

involved in capturing these photographs. The plaintiffs brought legal action against the defendants for copyright infringement since the defendants were selling pirated copies of the photographs in question. The defendants argued that the photographers who took the negative were the authors and not the plaintiffs, who were only the owners of the negative, and since the registration was false, the copyright was, accordingly, void.

The appeal court upheld the lower court's judgement that the plaintiffs were not the authors of the photograph in question. Before reaching this conclusion, the appeal judges struggled with authorship in photographs since the Fine Art Act 1862 did not specify who was the author of a photograph. For the purposes of the Act, photographs were considered fine art on the same level as paintings and drawings. However, can locating the authorship of different works of art be achieved in the same manner regardless?[113] Brett MR struggled to find any guidance in the legislation about what was meant by the author of a photograph and expressed accordingly that:

> I should like to know whether the person who drew this Act of Parliament was clear in his mind as to who can be the author of a photograph.... I confess I cannot be very clear about it, all I can do is to see who is the nearest person—the nearest like the author of a painting or the author of a drawing. Certainly it is not the man who simply gives the idea of a picture.[114]

Brett MR concluded that the one nearest to becoming the author of a photograph is the "person who has superintended the arrangement, who has actually formed the picture by putting the people into position and arranging the place in which the people are to be—the man who is the effective cause of that."[115] Thus, it was held that neither the plaintiffs nor the managers were the authors. Instead, the individuals who took the negatives were deemed as the photographs' authors. This attempt at locating the authors of the photographs echoed strongly and remained a sound way to find authorship in photographs for the purposes of copyright. The other appeal judges shared the same opinion; Cotton LJ further stated that the "'author' Involves originating, making, producing, as the inventive or Mastermind, the thing which is to be protected, whether it be a drawing, or a painting, or a photograph."[116] The *Nottage case* showcased the difficulties of forcing photography, a unique medium, into the existing copyright paradigm without special rules that take into account its unique nature.

*Melville v Mirror of Life Co [1895]*[117] was another case that examined authorship in photographs under the Fine Art Act. The case concerned an infringement claim involving a celebrity photograph brought against a publisher for the unau-

113 *Nottage v Jackson (1883) 11 QBD 627* (n 112) 637 (Bowen LJ).
114 ibid 631, 632 (Brett MR).
115 ibid 632 (Brett MR); see: *Wooderson v Raphael Tuck & Sons (1887) 4 TLR 57.*
116 *Nottage v Jackson (1883) 11 QBD 627* (n 112) 635 at 635 (Cotton LJ).
117 *Melville v Mirror of Life Co [1895] 2 Ch 531.*

thorised duplications of the photograph owned by the plaintiff. The plaintiff was a photographer who took the photograph on his behalf since he thought this photograph of the celebrity would sell well for himself. The plaintiff and his son worked together to take the photograph of the celebrity and gave him copies as a courtesy. The defendant wanted to use the photograph, so they sent a request to Melville but did not receive any reply. As a result, the defendant requested a copy of the photograph from the celebrity himself and subsequently received a copy of the photograph from his friend that was later used in unauthorised prints.

The plaintiff brought a copyright infringement claim against the defendant. An issue was raised regarding the author of the photograph since the son was the one who made the preparations, posed the celebrity, and worked to set out the scene; his father only gestured that everything was set and took the photograph afterwards. The defendant argued that the son was the author and not the father since he was the "effective cause" of the photograph by virtue of the arrangement and preparations to capture the photograph. The defendant proceeded to cite *Nottage* to support the conclusion that even if the plaintiff was to be considered an author, he would not be the sole author. The plaintiff replied that the son was merely an agent acting under the father's direction, who was the photograph's principal author.

The court attempted to apply the *Nottage* test regarding the authorship of photographs in the *Melville* case; Kekewich J examined whether the principal photographer, the father, could be regarded as the author of the photograph. The judge concluded that the son was merely an assistant for the father, who was the principal photographer, and his son's preparations and arrangements amounted to "matters of detail."[118] Therefore, the father was the author of the photograph. Kekewich J explained that this conclusion still falls within *Nottage*'s definition and stated that "an agent is not an author within s.1 of the Fine Arts Copyright Act, 1862, and that the principal cannot be the author unless he is the active principal."[119]

## 3.6 The 1911 Copyright Act, a Setback for Photographic Works?

The early copyright cases involving photographs in the United Kingdom were often pursued against photographers who used photography to reproduce paintings, engravings, and other designs, and commercially exploit the produced illegal copies.[120] In 1875, a royal commission was set up to review and evaluate the laws regarding copyright. The royal commission presented a report in 1878, stating that the existing copyright laws were "bad[ly]" organised and "in many parts so ill-expressed that no one who does not give study to it can expect to understand it."[121] The report examined the Fine Art Copyright Act and suggested that the terms of

118 ibid 535.

119 ibid.

120 Deazley, "Struggling with Authority" (n 47) 237, 238.

121 Lionel Bently and Martin Kretschmer (eds), "Royal Commissioners' Report, London (1878)," *Primary Sources on Copyright (1450–1900)* para 7 <https://www.copyrighthistory.org/cam/tools/request/showRecord.php?id=record_uk_1878> accessed 11 October 2024.

protection for works of fine art should be the same as literary works, which was the life of the author and 30 years after his death.[122] However, photographs were expressly excluded from this recommendation as they represented a problematic matter since they were "essentially different from drawings and paintings" due to their mechanical nature.[123] As a result, the report recommended that the appropriate term of protection for photographs, as an art of reproduction more in common with engravings, should be 30 years from the date of its first publication; if it was published as a part of a book then the term of protection shall be the same term given to books.[124] Another drastic proposal was that the copyright in a photograph should belong to the owner of the negative as opposed to the author of the photograph.[125] One can say that this represented a departure from the principle established since *Pope v Curl (1741)*[126] that emphasised the demarcation between the material (tangible) and immaterial (intangible) property, pointing that copyright attaches to the immaterial expression itself, not to the specific tangible material it was manifested upon.[127]

The following year, a Bill to consolidate and amend the law relating to copyright was presented to the parliament in 1879, and it included the commission's recommendation regarding copyright in photographs. This Bill, along with the Bills introduced in the following years between 1881 and 1886, failed to pass.[128] In all of these Bills, the photograph was presented as distinct from fine arts and was grouped with engravings and other mechanical processes of reproduction.[129] In the 1881 Copyright Bill, the term of protection for photographs was increased; the first owner of the negative of any photograph was entitled to copyright protection for 50 years from the date of registration.[130] In the following year, the Copyright Bill went back to adopting the Fine Art Act 1862 provisions that state that the first owner of the copyright was "the author of every photograph" while still retaining the extended term of protection proposed by the earlier Bill.[131]

In 1883, another Copyright amendment Bill that specifically targeted photographs and authorship proposed that the author of the photograph:

122 ibid 95.
123 ibid 118.
124 ibid 118, 119.
125 ibid 121.
126 *Pope v Curl (1741) 26 ER 608.*
127 Mark Rose, *Authors and Owners: The Invention of Copyright* (Harvard University Press 1993) 64–65.
128 Deazley, "Struggling with Authority" (n 47) 238; Thomas Edward Scrutton, *The Laws of Copyright : An Examination of the Principles Which Should Regulate Literary and Artistic Property in England and Other Countries* (William Clowes and Sons, Limited 1883) Vi <http://hdl.handle.net/2027/hvd.32044077699510> accessed 17 October 2024.
129 Deazley, "Struggling with Authority" (n 47) 238.
130 ibid 239.
131 ibid.

> shall mean the person at whose house or studio, being a house or studio used for the purpose of taking and selling photographs, or by means of whose instruments and materials whereof the negative thereof shall have been made, and who shall have been permitted or employed to make such negative by the person on whose behalf such photograph shall have been taken.[132]

This amendment underlined the notion that photography was nothing more than an industrial and mechanical process. Hence, the author was not the one who actually captured the image, but instead, the one who owned the equipment and materials utilised to capture the image and produce the photographs. In other words, the commercial establishment owner would be regarded as the photographs' author if he was present and aware of its creation.[133] Surely, an author was not synonymous with an owner, but perhaps in the case of photography, this notion was suggested to regulate commercial establishments that employed young and healthy photographers as an attempt to prolong their copyright.[134] Nonetheless, this amendment Bill failed to pass, as did the Bills that came in the following years. These Bills have dropped the concept of authorship for photographs in favour of the one who "made a photograph."[135]

It was not until 1898 that a Bill to consolidate the law related to copyright, based mainly on the 1878 royal commission's report, was brought to the House of Lords. This Bill restated that photographs should remain in the realm of artistic works, not adhering to the 1878 royal commission's report, which deemed photography vastly different to the point that it should not be considered as fine art.[136] Given that photographs fall within the meaning of artistic works, the Bill provided that "the author of an original literary or artistic work" shall have the copyright for the duration of his life and 30 years after his death.[137] The House of Lords struggled immensely with authorship in photographs, with some of the Lords questioning if such a thing was even possible in the context of photographs.[138] Hence, the term of protection as attached to the life of the author was seen as not suitable for photographs. Henry T. Wells, a painter and member of the Royal Society of Art, reasoned that "the use of copyright is to foster the arts of design, and a copyist scarcely deserves it for the full term."[139]

132 As quoted in ibid.
133 Cooper (n 5) 65.
134 Deazley, "Struggling with Authority" (n 47) 239.
135 ibid.
136 ibid 240.
137 ibid.
138 Select Committee of the House of Lords, *Report from the Select Committee of the House of Lords on the Copyright Bill [H.L] and the Copyright (Artistic) Bill [H.L] Together with the Proceedings of the Committee, Minutes of Evidence, and Appendix. Session 1899* (Wyman and Sons 1899) 164 <https://catalog.hathitrust.org/Record/001759237> accessed 11 October 2024.
139 As quoted in Cooper (n 5) 83.

In 1899, a Bill was presented by Lord Monkswell, which was supported by the Royal Academy and those interested in works of art.[140] The Bill proposed that copyright protection for a photograph should last up to 30 years from the date of publication.[141] It was suggested that this term of protection was derived from the normative assumption of the life expectancy of commercial firms.[142] Hence, the term of protection for photographs was not attached to the author's life. In fact, the Kodak cameras were mentioned as justification for granting lesser copyright protection to photographs, a testament to how photography as an art was intricately linked to technology. Thomas Edward Scrutton, a professor of law who helped draft the Bill, explained that

> the author of a painting, an original statue, or an original engraving, should have higher rights and a longer term than the man who merely used a Kodak, and went through the mechanical operation of copying, with the aid of light, some pleasing scenery.[143]

The persons representing the photographic community's interests objected to this term of protection granted to photographs since it denoted that photography was of a lower grade of art than paintings.[144] They instead argued that photographs should receive a term of protection equal to whatever term was granted to paintings.[145] Elena Cooper explained that the insistence of photographers to be treated on equal terms with painters originated from the desire to preserve the social status of photographers as artists, and the status of photographs as artistic works, more than any aspirations to gain higher standards of copyright protection.[146]

Mr Bolton, a member of the Zoological Society that was involved in a successful copyright claim against an artist who traced a photograph of his,[147] was asked by Lord Monkswell why photographs should be seen on equal footing with paintings. Mr Bolton answered that there was no reason why paintings and photographs should be separated since both were considered works of art for years. He quoted Oscar Rejlander's view on art in that art is

> a means of making thought visible in a picture which people can understand and be moved by it to laughter or tears, it is a work of art, whether I produce it by the aid of the camera or of the pencil. It is the mind of the artist, and not the nature of his materials which makes his production a work of art.[148]

140 HL, *Copyright (Artistic) Bill Deb 28 April 1899*, vol 70 (Hansard 1899) cols 805–806.
141 HL, *Copyright (Artistic) Bill Deb 28 April 1899* (n 140).
142 Cooper (n 5) 105.
143 As quoted in ibid 84.
144 Select Committee of the House of Lords (n 138) 132, 162, 165.
145 ibid 162, 165.
146 Cooper (n 5) 86–87, 257.
147 *Bolton v Aldin (1895) 65 LJQB 120.*
148 As quoted in Select Committee of the House of Lords (n 138) 163.

A point was raised about whether a photograph was considered a work of art emerging from the photographer's original design.[149] While acknowledging the difficulty in finding an original design in photographs, those supporting photography as fine art argued that it all depended on the type of photograph created. A compositional work created to capture a particular picture to tell a story certainly evidences an original design as opposed to a photograph of nature.[150] However, both are considered works of art worthy of copyright. They merely follow a different class of photography; one was based on an original design and the other was a work of art not based on an original design. Both classes may have considerable value in warranting copyright protection for "practical reasons."[151] Thus, "value" was invoked to support copyright in photographs, and that value was argued to emerge precisely from photography's perceived mechanical nature that serves as a "certificate" that supports documentary photographs' authenticity as factual records and, consequently, their value as such.[152] Ironically, the illustrated press industry attempted to use the same line of argument to attack the legitimacy of photographic copyright as a way to advance their interests since they often used photographs without authorisation.[153]

Sir Frank Dicksee, a painter and an academic from the Royal Academy, when questioned by Lord Monkswell about photography, stated that a photograph might exhibit an original design, "but it is not a work of fine art, because it is all produced by a mechanical process. You see it is the sun that does the chief part of the work."[154] Dicksee's views regarding photography echoed the early popular views towards photography despite the fact that photography was already considered fine art by the law for several years under the 1862 Fine Art Act. Like those that came before it, this Bill failed to pass.

In 1911, a Bill "To amend and consolidate the Law relating to Copyright" was presented to the House of Commons on 30 March.[155] The Bill proposed that the term of protection for a photograph should be 50 years from the making of the original negative.[156] This did not sit well with the Royal Photographic Society, who protested the "Invidious manner in which photographic copyright was dealt with."[157] Despite that, their disapproval fell on deaf ears.[158] During the parliamentary

149 ibid 140.

150 ibid 140, 141.

151 via Mr. Edward Cutler and Mr. John Little Mitchell in ibid 140, 141, 167.

152 Cooper (n 5) 97–98.

153 ibid 74–75, 77–78.

154 Sir Frank Dicksee in Select Committee of the House of Lords (n 138) 157 at para 2266.

155 HC, *Copyright Bill Deb 30 March 1911*, vol 23 (Hansard 1911).

156 HC, *Clause 5. (Ownership of Copyright, Etc.) Deb 17 August 1911*, vol 29 (Hansard 1911); HC, *Clause 21 (Provisions as to Photographs.) Deb 17 August 1911*, vol 29 (Hansard 1911).

157 Sir W De W Abney (ed), "Council Meeting," *The Photographic Journal*, vol 51 (The Royal Photographic Society (RPS) 1911) 246 <https://archive.rps.org/archive/volume-51/726896-volume-51-page-228> accessed 11 October 2024.

158 Sir W De W Abney (ed), "The Fellowship," *The Photographic Journal*, vol 51 (The Royal Photographic Society (RPS) 1911) 223 <https://archive.rps.org/archive/volume-51/726952> accessed 11 October 2024.

debates concerning the Bill, a specific amendment proposed by Frederick Handel Booth echoed the state of photography in relation to unsolicited photographs of individuals.[159] Booth suggested that if a photographer took a photograph of a person without his consent, then the person whose features were identified should hold the copyright as if he were the photographer; his reasoning was "to protect various distinguished people from being subjected to snapshotters."[160] This proposal was undoubtedly influenced by the popularity of the Kodak Brownie and other detective cameras that made taking a photograph an activity that amounted to little more than pointing the camera and pressing a button.[161] Nonetheless, this proposed amendment failed to gain support.[162]

The Bill eventually received royal assent in December 1911. The Copyright Act 1911 stated that copyright subsists in "every original literary, dramatic, musical and artistic work" and the author of such a work was the first owner of the copyright, and the term of protection shall be the life of the author and 50 years after his death.[163] The 1911 Copyright Act did not specifically mention cinematographic films in the list of copyright subject matter, but the courts confirmed in 1912 that cinematographic films were protected as a collection of photographs.[164] The 1911 Copyright Act removed copyright formalities to the benefit of photographs, considering their production output compared to other works of art made it costly for photographers to register every photograph produced. However, the term of protection for photographs was 50 years "from the making of the original negative from which the photograph was directly or indirectly derived."[165] Moreover, on the difficult question regarding authorship in photographs, the 1911 Act provided that "the person who was the owner of such negative at the time when such negative was made shall be deemed to be the author of the work."[166] Thus, even though photographs were within the meaning of artistic works, photography seems to have been regulated to a lower degree of art as long feared by photographers.[167] Henceforth, Elena Cooper observed that the

> links between copyright and artistic status were severed by 1911. Photographs were protected on a mechanical paradigm alone in 1911, just at the point at which, as art historical literature shows, there was art institutional evidence

159 HC, *Clause 21 (Provisions as to Photographs.) Deb 17 August 1911* (n 156); HC, *Clause 5. (Ownership of Copyright, Etc.) Deb 17 August 1911* (n 156).
160 HC, *Clause 21 (Provisions as to Photographs.) Deb 17 August 1911* (n 156).
161 Deazley, "Struggling with Authority" (n 47) 241.
162 HC, *Clause 21 (Provisions as to Photographs.) Deb 17 August 1911* (n 156).
163 Section 1, Section 5 Copyright Act 1911.
164 Nicholas Caddick, Gwilym Harbottle and Uma Suthersanen, *Copinger and Skone James on Copyright* (18 edition, Sweet & Maxwell Ltd 2020) paras 2–68.
165 Section 21 Copyright Act 1911.
166 Section 21 ibid.
167 Section 35 ibid; Select Committee of the House of Lords (n 138).

> that photography, in the ideal case, was a fine art involving the expression of the ideas of a creator.[168]

The 1911 Copyright Act effectively dictated that the author of a photograph was no longer considered different from the first owner of the negative.[169] Whoever owns the material and equipment used to make the photograph was, for the purposes of the law, the author of the said photograph. Regardless of the skill utilised to produce images of profound beauty or mundane quality, photographs were not regarded by the law as works of artistic authorship. Henceforth, effectively, this means that if one owns the film which another person used to make 100 captures – during this time the Kodak made photography vastly accessible – the author of the photographs was, to the law, the film owner. This goes contrary to common law, which regarded the author of a photograph as "the effective cause" of it.[170] Surely, the effective cause of the photograph was the photographer, at least in the act of fixing the images at the moment he chose to do so, not necessarily him creating the scene, which in itself could also be regarded as the effective cause of the photograph. But one could understand from Section 21 of the 1911 Copyright Act that even if the photographer created the scene as a compositional work to be photographed, without owning the negative in which to fix the image, his actions were not regarded as acts of authorship according to the legislation. This was quite the opposite of the attitudes adopted by the French legal system that focused on the author's personality embedded in the work to find authorship.

## 3.7 The Copyright Law 1956, Photographic Copyright Threatened Again

A committee was set up in 1951 to review the copyright laws and see whether any changes were desirable in reference to recent technological developments.[171] The copyright committee produced a report in 1952, known as the Gregory Report, which recommended changes to copyright law to meet the needs of the times.[172] The Gregory Report regarded photographs as artistic works but recommended that the term of protection should be reduced to only 25 years from the time the original photograph was taken; this recommendation was for no reason other than stating that the current term was "unduly long."[173] On 14 February 1956, during the House of Lords session regarding the Copyright Bill, Lord Mancroft, perhaps expressing the general anxiety towards photographs and their invasive nature, remarked that

168 Cooper (n 5) 6.

169 For more on the impact this approach had had on the ownership of photographs and on Canadian copyright law, see: Ysolde Gendreau, "Copyright Ownership of Photographs in Anglo-American Law" (1993) 15 European Intellectual Property Review 207 (Canadian copyright law provisions discussed in this journal article had been repealed by 2012).

170 *Nottage v Jackson (1883) 11 QBD 627* (n 112) 632 at 632.

171 HC, *Copyright Law (Committee) Deb 10 April 1951*, vol 486 (Hansard 1951) cols 64–5W.

172 Board of Trade, "Report of the Copyright Committee" (1952) Cmd. 8662 1, 2.

173 ibid para 312.

the expiry of the term of protection in 25 years from "the end of the calendar year in which the photograph was taken" was a cause for concern, but not necessarily for its potential effects on photographers' livelihood.[174] He explained that "This reduction…seems to increase the risk that private photographs, particularly of public people, will be published in ways that will be a source of embarrassment to the subjects."[175] Lord Mancroft suggested amending this provision so that photographs shall be protected for 25 years from the date of first publication since this would allow the owner to keep control over his photograph indefinitely because it could only be legally published subject to the owner's consent.[176]

In the House of Commons session in June 1956, Mr Andrew Greenwood voiced his objections on two grounds. The first ground, from the public's point of view, echoed Lord Mancroft's concerns about the reduced term of protection for photographs and its effects on privacy.[177] On the second ground, from the photographers' point of view, he stated that it would be grossly unfair to discriminate against photographers' work and deny them an adequate term of protection. He continued by stating that the protection offered for photographers was already less than other works of art and suggested that reducing it even further was disheartening.[178] Mr Greville Howard, who was a member of the Royal Photographic Society and self-described as an amateur photographer, wholeheartedly expressed his agreement with Mr Greenwood and remarked:

> I do not see why photographers should not be considered to be artists…I maintain that we should be considered to be artists… .The many photographers whom I know feel that it is most unfair that they should have been singled out for only 25 years' protection, especially when films are protected for 50 years.[179]

Mr Walker Smith, while expressing his sympathies with the arguments raised, stated that the report did not suggest the reduced term out of prejudice to photography but instead did so to give "quasi-mechanical or quasi-industrial subjects" a copyright term in between literary and industrial works.[180] He further argued that:

> we are not differentiating against photographs here. A photograph is different in that respect from a film and it is different from a portrait and an engraving, because one is in essence a mechanical process, albeit not without artistic contribution, and the others are done by hand.[181]

174 HL, *Copyright Bill Deb 14 February 1956*, vol 195 (Hansard 1956) col 895.
175 ibid.
176 ibid.
177 HL, *Copyright Bill Deb 4 June 1956*, vol 553 (Hansard 1956) col 727.
178 ibid 727, 728.
179 ibid 742–743.
180 ibid 803.
181 ibid.

Furthermore, this session also discussed the distinction between commissioned portrait photographs, commissioned landscape photographs, and photographs of non-human subjects and whether the provisions concerning the ownership of the copyright in a photograph should be regarded differently for each example.[182]

The Copyright Act was passed on 5 November 1956. Section 3 provided that copyright shall subsist in "every original artistic work" irrespective of the work's artistic quality.[183] The term of protection shall be for the life of the author and 50 years after his death, except for photographs, where the term of protection was 50 years from the date of first publication.[184] Photography avoided the reduced copyright term in part due to the effort exerted by the representatives of photographers' interests to keep the term of protection at 50 years from the date of first publication.[185] The 1956 Copyright Act specifically protected films as subject matter, distinguishing them from photographs.[186]

The Copyright Act 1956 provided that the author of the photograph was "the person who, at the time when the photograph is taken, is the owner of the material on which it is taken."[187] The author of the photograph was still considered by the law to be the owner of the materials; hence, no emphasis was placed on the operator or the "effective cause" that led to the photograph's creation. Moreover, Section 4(3) of the 1956 Copyright Act provided that the copyright owner of a commissioned photograph was the "person who so commissioned the work" and paid for it or agreed to pay for it.[188]

## 3.8 The Copyright Law 1988, What Has Become of Photographic Copyright?

In the years after the Copyright Act 1956, a committee was tasked to consider what "changes are desirable in the law relating to copyright" and produced a report in March 1977.[189] The committee's report to consider the law on copyright and designs 1977, known as the Whitford Report, put forward recommendations concerning copyright in photographs. The report recommended that in the case of "still

182 HL, *Copyright Bill Deb 4 June 1956* (n 177).
183 Section 3 Copyright Act 1956.
184 Section 3(4) ibid.
185 The president of the Royal Photographic Society, Dr A.J.O. Axford, in the society's annual dinner speech in Kenneth R Warr and Pat Jessop (eds), "The Society Annual Dinner and Dance," *The Photographic Journal*, vol 110 (The Royal Photographic Society (RPS) 1970) 34 <https://archive.rps.org/archive/volume-110/743846-volume-110-page-21?q=copyright> accessed 11 October 2024; "The Copyright Bill," *The Photographic Journal*, vol 96 (The Royal Photographic Society (RPS) 1956) 199 <https://archive.rps.org/archive/volume-96/740455?q=copyright> accessed 11 October 2024.
186 Section 13 Copyright Act 1956.
187 Section 47 ibid.
188 Section 4(3) ibid.
189 John Whitford and The Committee to Consider the Law on Copyright and Designs, "Report of the Committee to Consider the Law on Copyright and Designs" (1977) Cmnd 6732 1.

photographs," the author of the photograph shall be the one who was "responsible for the composition of the photograph."[190] This recommendation was supported by the photographers who argued that the author of a photograph was not necessarily the one who owned the equipment or pressed the shutter but was the one who composed the photograph.[191] The report pointed out that photographers were not content with the term of protection offered but nonetheless recommended that it remain unchanged.[192] In 1981, a green paper on the law relating to copyright, designs, and performers' protection was released but did not bring any additional recommendations for photographs.[193]

In light of these endeavours to update the copyright laws, the photographic community demanded equal rights for photographers. The photographic committee, which consisted of representatives from the leading photographic organisations at the time, was established in 1981 to advance the interests of photographers in the forthcoming legislation.[194] In *The Photographic Journal* issue in 1983, an excerpt titled "Photographers Demand Equal Rights, Says Photographic Committee" protested that "no other artistic work is authorship allocated to the owner of the material (canvas, clay, paper etc.,) on which the work is imposed."[195] Hence, the photographic committee demanded equal treatment for photographs with other artistic works and put forth two recommendations. Firstly, "The 'author' of a photograph should be defined as the Photographer."[196] Secondly, "Copyright should be vested in the Photographer, unless agreed otherwise in writing."[197]

In April 1986, the White Paper on Intellectual Property and Innovation was presented, and it stated that the 1956 Act's definition of the author of a photograph was "arbitrary" since it was not fitting to regard the owner of the materials as an author of a photograph based only on this ground.[198] Equally, the White Paper regarded the Whitford Report's recommendation that the author of a photograph was the one who composed it as representing yet another problematic issue. That was because it might prove difficult to discern who had a better claim in the copyright based on their contribution to a photograph's composition. Therefore, the White Paper opted to recommend a simple definition that provides that the photographer was the author of a photograph, a proposal deemed attractive by the government.[199] The term of protection was suggested to be 50 years from the photograph's capture

190 ibid 148.

191 ibid 148, 154, 223.

192 ibid 160–162.

193 Deazley, "Struggling with Authority" (n 47) 242; "Reform of the Law Relating to Copyright, Designs and Performers' Protection A Consultative Document" (1981) Cmnd. 8302.

194 RH Mason (ed), "Photographers Demand Equal Rights, Says Photographic Committee," *The Photographic Journal*, vol 123 (The Royal Photographic Society (RPS) 1983) 402 <https://archive.rps.org/archive/volume-123/747497-volume-123-page-231?q=copyright> accessed 11 October 2024.

195 ibid.

196 ibid.

197 ibid.

198 Department of Trade and Industry, "Intellectual Property & Innovation" (1986) Cmnd 9712 67.

199 ibid.

instead of the date of first publication. This proposal was presented to remove the perpetual copyright in unpublished photographs and "to provide a more readily identifiable commencement date."[200]

In the following two years leading to the enactment of the Copyright, Designs and Patents Act 1988, the parliamentary debates regarding photographs centred around the proper definition of a photograph,[201] the term of protection,[202] the author of a photograph,[203] copyright in commissioned photographs,[204] and privacy.[205] The House of Lords strongly objected to the prejudicial attitude towards photographs and opposed the special term of protection given to photographs, expressing their disapproval for treating photographers differently from the authors of other artistic works.[206] The Lords stated that photographs were works of art on equal footing with other works of art and should be treated as such.[207] However, the Lords struggled to provide a technology-neutral and appropriate definition of photographs given its current development but opted to do so.[208] The compounding result of these efforts from 1977 eventually produced the Copyright, Designs and Patents Act of 1988.

The Copyright, Designs and Patents Act 1988 was enacted on 15 November 1988. The Act implemented the Berne Convention provisions in relation to moral rights and brought photographs back to the position they lost since the Fine Art Act 1862. The Act effectively declared that copyright in photographs was not regarded any differently from other artistic works. The 1988 Act provided that copyright subsists in every "original literary, dramatic, musical or artistic works"[209] until "the end of the period of 50 years from the end of the calendar year in which the author dies."[210] The duration of protection was raised to 70 years after the author's death

200 ibid 64.

201 HL, *Copyright, Designs and Patents Bill Deb 30 November 1987*, vol 490 (Hansard 1987); HL, *Copyright, Designs and Patents Bill Deb 23 February 1988*, vol 493 (Hansard 1988); HL, *Copyright, Designs and Patents Bill Deb 29 March 1988*, vol 495 (Hansard 1988).

202 HL, *Copyright, Designs and Patents Bill Deb 12 November 1987*, vol 489 (Hansard 1987); HL, *Copyright, Designs and Patents Bill Deb 30 November 1987* (n 201); HL, *Copyright, Designs and Patents Bill Deb 3 December 1987*, vol 490 (Hansard 1987); HL, *Copyright, Designs and Patents Bill Deb 23 February 1988* (n 201); HL, *Copyright, Designs and Patents Bill Deb 29 March 1988* (n 201).

203 HL, *Copyright, Designs and Patents Bill Deb 12 November 1987* (n 202).

204 HL, *Copyright, Designs and Patents Bill Deb 23 February 1988* (n 201).

205 HL, *Copyright, Designs and Patents Bill Deb 29 March 1988* (n 201).

206 HL, *Copyright, Designs and Patents Bill Deb 12 November 1987* (n 202); HL, *Copyright, Designs and Patents Bill Deb 3 December 1987* (n 202).

207 HL, *Copyright, Designs and Patents Bill Deb 12 November 1987* (n 202) cols 1496, 1517; HL, *Copyright, Designs and Patents Bill Deb 30 November 1987* (n 201); HL, *Copyright, Designs and Patents Bill Deb 3 December 1987* (n 202); HL, *Copyright, Designs and Patents Bill Deb 25 February 1988*, vol 493 (Hansard 1988).

208 HL, *Copyright, Designs and Patents Bill Deb 30 November 1987* (n 201); HL, *Copyright, Designs and Patents Bill Deb 23 February 1988* (n 201); HL, *Copyright, Designs and Patents Bill Deb 29 March 1988* (n 201) col 613.

209 Section 1(1) Copyright, Designs and Patents Act 1988 (UK).

210 Section 12(2) ibid.

following the transposing of the 1993 EU Term Directive.[211] A photograph was defined as "a recording of light or other radiation on any medium on which an image is produced or from which an image may by any means be produced, and which is not part of a film."[212] Furthermore, the first owner of the copyright was the author of the photograph. For the purposes of copyright, an author was simply defined as "the person who creates [the work]."[213] After the long and arduous journey, photographs were finally respected as intellectual creations deserving of the same level of copyright protection on par with other copyright eligible works. Thus, they were no longer treated as a lower grade of art.

## 3.9 Conclusion

Photographs represent a precarious place for copyright concepts such as authorship and originality due to their dual nature that exhibits both mechanical and creative characteristics. On the one hand, opponents of photographic works' copyright diminished photographs to their mechanical and servile characteristics to argue against copyright protection. On the other hand, supporters of photographic works' copyright analogised photographs with paintings in a bid to gain protection. They demanded that photographic works be treated on par with paintings not only for copyright considerations but also to preserve their social status as artists and their photographs as art. Even though the Fine Art Act 1862 protected photographs as fine art without discrimination, the debates surrounding the legitimacy of photographs' artistic capacity were not quelled.

As art was seen as the domain of authors, authorship in photographic works was a point that skewed the debates back and forth due to the difficult nature of locating authorship in photographs. The difficulties surrounding authorship in photographs led many to question if such a thing as authorship can ever be applied to photographs. In the early cases involving authorship in photographs, the courts' method of locating the author depended on finding the person who was the nearest to the position of the author of the work. It was deemed that a person's directorial actions might be sufficient to have him regarded as the author, even if the camera was operated by someone else, if he was an active principal during the capture of the photographs. Some saw this as a way to give the owner of the commercial establishment that owned the equipment and employed the photographers a better claim for authorship if he was present during the photographs' capture. The 1911 Act reaffirmed this view by refusing to tackle the issue of authorship in photographs altogether and opting to regard the owner of the negative and equipment as the

211 Directive 93/98/EEC of 29 October 1993 harmonizing the term of protection of copyright and certain related rights [1993] OJ L290/9.

212 Section 4(2)(b) Copyright, Designs and Patents Act 1988 (UK).

213 Section 9(10) Copyright, Designs and Patents Act 1988 (UK).

owner of the copyright in photographs. Hence, photographic works were deemed as "machine-made thing[s]"[214] unworthy of a full term of protection.

The position regarding the authorship of photographs did not change until the CDPA 1988 Act, where photographs were protected equally to other copyright subject matters with the same term of protection. Furthermore, the 1988 Act presented a universal approach to copyright authorship that regards the author of the work to be the one who created it. Nonetheless, this universal approach to authorship was not simple to apply to photographic works as it was not always clear which party should be considered as the author and creator of a given photograph. A more tailored approach that takes into account the unique characteristics of photographs may be more effective in determining authorship in photographic works.

214 E. C. Elliott (1909) as quoted in Cooper (n 5) 102.

# 4 The United States of America and Photographs

## 4.1 Introduction

This chapter explores the history of photographic works' copyright in the United States, highlighting its path towards being protected by copyright law. Firstly, it examines the early attitudes of Americans towards photography compared to those in Europe. Secondly, it explores the circumstances surrounding copyright protection for photographs in the United States. Thirdly, it examines the US Supreme Court's case of *Burrow-Giles Lithographic Co v Sarony*,[1] a landmark case that confirmed the constitutionality of copyright protection of photographic works. Finally, it tracks the development of photographic works' copyright to the 1976 Copyright Act.

Compared to the United Kingdom, the United States, by not having a centralised base or established artistic institutions during the forming years of photography, reacted differently to photography. The United States extended copyright protection to photographs without necessarily indulging in the discourse about their artistic capability or even defining what the term "photograph" meant. This was in contrast with the United Kingdom, where the discourse about the definition of photographs and their capacity for original artistic expression featured prominently during the debates surrounding the extension of copyright protection to photographic works.

## 4.2 Photography in the United States

### *4.2.1 The Early Years of Photography in America*

The United States first received news about the Daguerreotype through a private letter from Samuel F.B. Morse, an inventor and artist, sent to his brother in March 1839, describing his experience seeing the Daguerreotype for the first time following his visit to Daguerre.[2] Morse described that the Daguerreotype displayed

1 *Burrow-Giles Lithographic Co v Sarony, 111 US 53 (1884).*

2 William Welling, *Photography in America: The Formative Years, 1839–1900* (Crowell 1978) 7; Reese V Jenkins, *Images and Enterprise: Technology and the American Photographic Industry, 1839 to 1925* (Johns Hopkins University Press 1975) 12; François Brunet, "Societies, Groups, Institutions, and Exhibitions in the United States" in John Hannavy (ed), *Encyclopedia of Nineteenth-Century Photography*, vol 1 (Routledge 2008) 1307.

DOI: 10.4324/9781003586555-4

"exquisite minuteness of the delineation....No painting or engraving ever approached it."[3] The press took this private letter and published it in newspapers throughout America to an eager public curious about this mysterious invention and the prospects it may bring to their way of life.[4] James F. Ryder, also one of the earlier American photographers, wrote about the environment surrounding the Daguerreotype in America that

> In the first few years most practitioners were plodding in the dark, something like the "blind leading the blind". There was no literature bearing upon the subject beyond the mere statement of routine description, no sure road yet opened to successful work.[5]

Indeed, the conditions surrounding the Daguerreotype in America were quite different from those in Europe.

The Daguerreotype came at a time when the United States was dealing with an economic depression, which encouraged the entrepreneurial spirit towards photography in America from the very beginning.[6] After the full disclosure of the details of the Daguerreotype process, many Daguerreotypists started to appear around the United States, making Daguerreotypes in small towns and cities in a decentralised and autonomous manner.[7] In fact, the decentralised beginnings of the American photographic industry created an environment described by Reese V. Jenkins as exhibiting "perfect competition,"[8] which refers to a market environment where all the relevant information is available to all the buyers and sellers to the point that acquiring a monopoly or controlling the prices is not possible.[9]

The decentralised nature allowed the business side of photography to have low entry barriers. The Daguerreotype being free to use along with the public enthusiasm towards it created the perfect environment for the Daguerreotype to flourish in America.[10] There was little to no involvement from trade organisations, formal or academic institutions, or even photographic unions to guide photography in its infancy, allowing the customs to vary and develop independently.[11] Consequently, due to the absence of centralised channels and the lack of many established businesses, craftsmen, and artists, the Daguerreotype was not met with anxiety and

3 Samuel Morse quoted in Welling (n 2) 7.
4 ibid 8, 15; Jenkins (n 2) 12; Brunet (n 2) 1307, 1308.
5 James F. Ryder quoted in Welling (n 2) 63.
6 Jenkins (n 2) 12, 13; Welling (n 2) 17; Brunet (n 2) 1307, 1308.
7 Jenkins (n 2) 12, 13; Welling (n 2) 8, 17; Brunet (n 2) 1307, 1308.
8 Jenkins (n 2) 16.
9 John Black, Nigar Hashimzade and Gareth Myles, "Perfect Competition," *A Dictionary of Economics* (5 edition, OUP Oxford 2017) <https://www.oxfordreference.com/view/10.1093/acref/9780198759430.001.0001/acref-9780198759430-e-2315?rskey=h1xbGq&result=1> accessed 17 October 2024.
10 Jenkins (n 2) 12, 16; Brunet (n 2) 1307, 1308; Welling (n 2) 17.
11 Welling (n 2) 3; Jenkins (n 2) 12, 16, 18, 20, 32; Brunet (n 2) 1307; François Brunet, "United States of America" in John Hannavy (ed), *Encyclopedia of Nineteenth-Century Photography*, vol 1 (Routledge 2008) 1424, 1425.

resistance from these communities as was the case in Europe. Instead, it was embraced.[12]

#### *4.2.2 The Art of Photography and the Forming of a Photographic Community*

While Europe had already established artistic and scientific communities and formal institutions that guided the discourse about the place photography occupies in the landscape of art and science, the United States was comparably a young nation yet to define its culture and identity. Thus, the early discourse regarding photography's status as art or its potential implication on art was not significantly present in American cycles, aside from a few people and journals that entertained the idea by talking about the state of the discourse regarding photography in Europe.[13] In 1840, Thomas Cole, an English-born American painter, wrote that the Daguerreotype might have led people to believe that "the poor craft of painting was knocked in the head by this new machinery for making nature take her own likeness, and we [artists] nothing to do but give up the ghost."[14] However, he reaffirmed that "the art of paintings is creative, as well as an imitative art, and is in no danger of being superseded by any mechanical contrivance."[15]

Photographic journals and societies soon spawned in the 1850s to build a sense of community for the photographers and establish a platform for men interested in the science and art of photography to share their ideas.[16] In March 1859, the American Photographic Society, renamed later as the Photographic Section of the American Institute, was established with the desired aim "to place the art [of photography in America] in a position equally as elevated as in Europe."[17] It was hard to gather amateur photographers into an organised society, not least one specifically established for advancing the science and art of photography. That was because many photographers at the time focused on the business dimension of photography. In other words, the development of photographic processes so far was driven to gain a competitive edge and make the processes more efficient and profitable.[18]

The *American Journal of Photography*, in its 1858 July issue, described that photography in America was mainly utilised:

> almost solely as a means of making money, and though in the pursuit of the cash, we have necessarily brought the mere manipulations to almost

12 Jenkins (n 2) 11, 12; Brunet (n 2) 1307, 1308; Welling (n 2) 3, 17.

13 Jenkins (n 2) 2, 11; Brunet (n 2) 1307; Brunet (n 11) 1424, 1425, 1427; Welling (n 2) 3.

14 Thomas Cole quoted in Welling (n 2) 8.

15 ibid.

16 ibid 135; Brunet (n 2) 1308.

17 Charles A. Seely quoted in Welling (n 2) 135.

18 Jenkins (n 2) 18; Brunet (n 2) 1308; Charles A Seely (ed), *The American Journal of Photography and the Allied Arts & Sciences*, vol I (Seely & Garbanati 1858) 48 <http://archive.org/details/americanjournalo11858newy> accessed 30 September 2021.

> perfection, yet it cannot be denied that we neglect the higher and nobler uses it is now available for. We are too mechanical...photographers...[should] strive to be artists... .Photography can and will rank as one of the "fine arts."[19]

The journal emphasised that photography represents a vast unexplored field and Americans should look to the Europeans who "are far ahead of [America] in endeavours to make the art scientific and really artistical."[20] Despite the effort to divert attention towards the service of the American art of photography, the business side of photography remained a priority for the vast majority of photographers. Many companies had risen to meet the needs of photographers and provide them with the necessary equipment, such as plates, cases, and specific chemicals.[21]

The Daguerreotype charm was left uncontested in America for some time until the late 1850s when the Wet Collodion-based processes became the dominant photographic process in America until the 1880s when the Gelatin-based process prospered until the advent of digital imaging. The Gelatin-based dry process sprung the development of photography towards more centralised production channels, away from the decentralised hands of photographers during the Wet Collodion days.[22] In this period of competition between enterprises, information regarding manufacturing processes had become a closely guarded secret; equally, information related to improvements and modifications became increasingly scarce in journals that were once an avenue for sharing ideas and improvements on photographic processes.[23]

### *4.2.3 The Kodak and the American Photographic Fine Art Movement*

One of the biggest innovations that changed how people viewed photography, not only in America but all over the world, was attributed to the American company Eastman Kodak, founded by George Eastman in the 1880s.[24] Kodak introduced an innovative system with its flexible roll-film emulsion that paved the way for photography to reach unprecedented accessibility and popularity.[25] It expanded

19 Seely (n 18) 48.
20 ibid.
21 Jenkins (n 2) 3.
22 ibid 67, 68.
23 ibid 73.
24 Becky Simmons, "Amateur Photographers, Camera Clubs, and Societies" in John Hannavy (ed), *Encyclopedia of Nineteenth-Century Photography*, vol 1 (Routledge 2008) 33; Elizabeth Brayer, "Eastman, George (1854–1932)" in John Hannavy (ed), *Encyclopedia of Nineteenth-Century Photography*, vol 1 (Routledge 2008) 463; "George Eastman | Kodak" (*Kodak*) <https://www.kodak.com/en/company/page/george-eastman-history> accessed 17 October 2024.
25 Jenkins (n 2) 95, 96; Steve Edwards, "Great Britain" in John Hannavy (ed), *Encyclopedia of Nineteenth-Century Photography*, vol 1 (Routledge 2008) 612; Simmons (n 24) 33; "Photography | Kodak" (*Kodak*) <https://www.kodak.com/en/company/page/photography-history> accessed 17 October 2024.

the photographic industry greatly into new untapped markets and made cameras ubiquitous.[26]

The innovation brought by Eastman Kodak can be summarised by its slogan, "You Press the Button, We Do the Rest."[27] Eastman Kodak separated the act of taking a picture from developing and making the picture, making photography, as a result, hugely accessible to all kinds of photographers.[28] George Eastman aimed to "furnish anybody, man, woman or child, who has sufficient intelligence to point a box straight and press a button...with an instrument which altogether removes from the practice of photography the necessity for...any special knowledge of the art."[29] He achieved his goal with the introduction of the Kodak Brownie in 1900, priced at only $1, with a film that can take up to 100 captures. Then, the consumer can, for a fee, send it to Eastman Kodak to develop the photographs and refill the camera with a new film.[30] This system proved to be highly successful. Eastman noted that ordinary people thought they would not be able to take pictures themselves since the process seemed complicated. However, with Eastman Kodak's advertising campaign that focused on novice photographers with the highly accessible Kodak Brownie product line, the vast majority were the targeted market.[31]

The simplification of photography and the attractive price of the Kodak Brownie opened the doors far and wide for previously untapped markets and radically changed how photography was perceived.[32] By then, anyone could pick up a Kodak camera and take photographs. Photographers no longer had to possess sufficient knowledge about photographic processes and chemicals, nor did they need to learn the skills necessary to develop photographs. This contrasts with the early Daguerreotype days when itinerant photographers were often called "professors" by ordinary people.[33] Eastman Kodak did all the messy and mundane work, and the photographer needed only to point the camera and "press the button."

The immense success of Eastman Kodak revolutionised photography's landscape and influenced people to develop new applications and uses for photography. The spread of cameras to all kinds of people prompted a movement that sought to differentiate artistic photographs from the masses of amateur, professional, and snapshot photographs by pursuing the limit of artistic expression in photography.

26 Welling (n 2) 321.

27 Jenkins (n 2) 112.

28 ibid 112, 236; Colin Harding, "Camera Design: 6 Kodak (1888–1900)" in John Hannavy (ed), *Encyclopedia of Nineteenth-Century Photography*, vol 1 (Routledge 2008) 251; Renate Wickens-Feldman, "Domestic and Family Photography" in John Hannavy (ed), *Encyclopedia of Nineteenth-Century Photography*, vol 1 (Routledge 2008) 433; Brayer (n 24) 463.

29 Colin Harding, "Kodak" in John Hannavy (ed), *Encyclopedia of Nineteenth-Century Photography*, vol 1 (Routledge 2008) 804.

30 Jenkins (n 2) 112, 115; "Photography | Kodak" (n 25); Harding, "Kodak" (n 29) 804; Brayer (n 24) 464; Welling (n 2) 395, 398.

31 Jenkins (n 2) 115–117; Harding, "Kodak" (n 29) 804.

32 Johan Swinnen, "History: 7. 1880s" in John Hannavy (ed), *Encyclopedia of Nineteenth-Century Photography*, vol 1 (Routledge 2008) 700; Harding, "Kodak" (n 29) 804; Jenkins (n 2) 68, 112, 113.

33 Welling (n 2) 63.

At the helm of this movement was Alfred Stieglitz, whose pursuit to distinguish artistic photography from the rest elevated the American visual art scene.[34] In 1902, Stieglitz led the Photo-Secessionist movement, composed of like-minded individuals who sought to elevate photography to the fine arts, and it was the American equivalent to the Brotherhood of the Linked Ring in Britain.[35]

The Photo-Secessionists aimed to advance photography's application as a pictorial art.[36] That was because art was the venue of the few, but the unparalleled ubiquity of photographs compared to all of the visual arts combined lessened its perception as an art form.[37] Stieglitz and other like-minded individuals fought to distinguish and promote artistic photographs and elevate photography's position in America to an equal level alongside other forms of visual art.[38]

The popularisation of photography due to Eastman Kodak's efforts unintentionally sent ripples to proponents of artistic photography in an attempt to establish a class of photographs worthy of being perceived as an art form, that is, a class of photographs distinct from photographs produced by amateurs and professional photographers, which comprised the vast majority of photographs. However, the copyright protection of photographic works in America was not dependent on their status as art. This is in contrast to the United Kingdom, where the very status of photography as a fine art was the catalyst for the debates regarding whether or not it deserved copyright protection.

### *4.2.4 American Photographers and the Battle against Patents*

A significant event during the early American photographic scene concerns the controversy surrounding the Ambrotype patent. The Ambrotype was a photographic process based on the Wet Collodion process with a slight variation. It was made on

34 John Glaves-Smith and Ian Chilvers, "Stieglitz, Alfred," *A Dictionary of Modern and Contemporary Art* (3 edition, OUP Oxford 2015) <https://www.oxfordreference.com/view/10.1093/acref/9780191792229.001.0001/acref-9780191792229-e-2615?rskey=5Ia7oY&result=1> accessed 17 October 2024; Welling (n 2) 293, 295; Simmons (n 24) 34; Johan Swinnen, "History: 8. 1890s" in John Hannavy (ed), *Encyclopedia of Nineteenth-Century Photography*, vol 1 (Routledge 2008) 703, 704; Colin Harding, "Snapshot Photography" in John Hannavy (ed), *Encyclopedia of Nineteenth-Century Photography*, vol 1 (Routledge 2008) 1278; Brunet (n 2) 1310.

35 Brunet (n 2) 1310; Sarah B Wheeler, "Stieglitz, Alfred (1864–1946)" in John Hannavy (ed), *Encyclopedia of Nineteenth-Century Photography*, vol 1 (Routledge 2008) 1341; Welling (n 2) 353, 355; Ann Lee Morgan, "Photo-Secession," *The Oxford Dictionary of American Art and Artists* (1 edition, OUP Oxford 2007) <https://www.oxfordreference.com/view/10.1093/acref/9780195373219.001.0001/acref-9780195373219-e-1048?rskey=L8H0B5&result=1> accessed 17 October 2024; Christian A Peterson, "The Little Magazine of the Photo-Secession" (2010) 34 History of Photography 96, 96, 97; Alfred Stieglitz (ed), "Camera Work" (1903) 13 Camera Work a Photographic Quarterly 15, 16 <https://catalog.hathitrust.org/Record/100835958> accessed 17 October 2024.

36 Morgan (n 35); Stieglitz (n 35) 15, 16.

37 John Taylor, "Pictorialism" in John Hannavy (ed), *Encyclopedia of Nineteenth-Century Photography*, vol 1 (Routledge 2008) 1130; Welling (n 2) 291, 297; Stieglitz (n 35) 15, 16.

38 Stieglitz (n 35) 15, 16; Wheeler (n 35) 1341; Taylor (n 37) 1130; Welling (n 2) 291.

glass as a negative image and fitted into a case with a dark background to show the positive image.[39] Every Ambrotype was a unique positive like the Daguerreotype but cheaper to make since glass plates were used instead of silver plates.[40] In 1854, James A. Cutting patented some elements of the process in America. The most troublesome of the patents issued for him was the one regarding the use of bromide of potassium because it affected all other processes that were based on the Wet Collodion process.[41] The bromide patent itself was questionable since the use of bromide was not novel, and experiments with the bromide of potassium were conducted and published before the patent was issued.[42]

Nonetheless, the patent issuance did not generate wide criticism until years later, perhaps owing to the scattered photographic scene at the time.[43] In order to fight the patent, the photographers organised against Cutting and his agents, who were sort of the villains of the American photographic scene between 1854 and 1868, and many photographers intentionally ignored the patent and used the Ambrotype regardless in spite of threats of litigation from those who bought a licence and Cutting himself.[44] The photographers viewed Cutting as having no right to patent the process in the first place and were generally hostile towards any attempts to patent improvements on photographic processes, regarding such attempts as greedy, unethical, and contrary to the spirit of the profession.[45] After one of Cutting's agents sued the photographer C.D. Fredricks in 1860, the photographers organised a gathering to aid Fredricks in this case and formulate a resistance plan.[46] The resistance team set up funds to continue the fight, and the case dragged on until it proved expensive for Cutting and his agents, who passed the case to Thomas H. Hubbard.[47] Hubbard managed to reach a settlement with Fredricks, for whom the case had devoured the funds raised on top of a large sum of his savings, and consequently, the battle was suspended.[48]

The flames of the battle were reignited again in 1865 when Hubbard took control of the patent management – the patent was due to expire in 1868 and continued

39 William O Griggs, "The Daguerrotype, the Ambrotype, and the Photograph" (1909) 167 Journal of the Franklin Institute 99, 6; Martin Barnes, "Archer, Frederick Scott (1813–1857)" in John Hannavy (ed), *Encyclopedia of Nineteenth-Century Photography*, vol 1 (Routledge 2008) 57; Brunet (n 11) 1426.

40 Welling (n 2) 111.

41 ibid 107, 198; Sarah Templeton, "Court Cases and Photography" in John Hannavy (ed), *Encyclopedia of Nineteenth-Century Photography*, vol 1 (Routledge 2008) 342; Brunet (n 11) 1426.

42 Welling (n 2) 107, 198; John Hannavy (ed), *Encyclopedia of Nineteenth-Century Photography*, vol 1 (Routledge 2008) 1426.

43 Welling (n 2) 107, 196.

44 ibid 107, 109, 118, 134, 145; Templeton (n 41) 342; Lynn Ann Davis, "Wet Collodion Positive Processes" in John Hannavy (ed), *Encyclopedia of Nineteenth-Century Photography*, vol 1 (Routledge 2008) 1486.

45 Jenkins (n 2) 32; Welling (n 2) 145.

46 Welling (n 2) 145.

47 ibid 145, 180.

48 ibid.

to charge licence fees; by this time, Cutting was admitted to an insane asylum.[49] The photographic community could not tolerate this abuse any longer and once again gathered in order to formulate a plan to attack the validity of the patent and end this debacle once and for all.[50] The photographers in these meetings took the matters very seriously and pledged "their lives, their fortunes and their sacred honours" to protect and promote the art of photography.[51] In 1868, the National Photographic Convention was held in New York to gather photographers from across the United States to fight the plans to renew Cutting's patents by the administrator of his estate Cutting had died in 1867 and prepare a resistance campaign.[52] The gathering included the leading American photographers at the time, which gave the movement broad recognition among the photographers.[53] They established a national photographic union and resolved to organise in order to combat the predatory encroachments on the photographic scene that were encouraged by "the state of isolation among photographers" that made them vulnerable.[54] The patent renewal was rejected, and the US Patent Office upheld the opinion found in the examiner's report, issued in June 1868, stating that the bromide patent was invalid from the beginning and was wrongfully granted.[55]

American photographers benefitted from this experience because it was the first time the fragmented photographic community came together and organised a movement for the benefit of their community as a whole.[56] A fraternity was born to represent the American photographers' interests and advance their art. This unity later proved useful for the lobbying effort to extend copyright protection to photographs.[57]

## 4.3 The Push for Copyright Protection for Photographs

During the 1860s, American photographic organisations campaigned for copyright protection, since they considered photographs to exhibit enough authorship to be protected as works of authorship, and to combat the issue of piracy that had plagued the photographic scene.[58] Moreover, photographers were aware of the situation between the British photographic scene and the London International Exhibition 1862 and expressed their solidarity with the British photographers who were protesting the classification of photographs alongside machinery by stating that "the

49 ibid 177, 188, 195.
50 ibid 177, 180, 188.
51 ibid 180.
52 ibid 195.
53 ibid.
54 ibid 196.
55 ibid 197, 198.
56 ibid 199; Brunet (n 2) 1309; François Brunet and others, "Unions, Photographic" in John Hannavy (ed), *Encyclopedia of Nineteenth-Century Photography*, vol 1 (Routledge 2008) 1422.
57 Welling (n 2) 199; Brunet (n 2) 1309; Brunet (n 11) 1429.
58 Brunet (n 11) 1429; Welling (n 2) 209.

[exhibition] committee on Classification should be taught better manners… .This attempt to bring the cloth down to the level of 'greasy mechanics' and 'mud-stills' must be resisted."[59] One could argue that given the developments regarding photography's copyright protection in Europe and the American photographic scene's newly found confidence after their union against Cutting's patents and other predatory practices, photographers set their eyes towards acquiring copyright protection for photographs on par with other protected works.

The American Copyright Act 1831 provided that the author of any

books, map, chart, or musical composition…or who shall invent, design, etch, engrave, work or cause to be engraved, etched, or worked from his own design, any print or engraving, and…legal assigns of such person…shall have the sole right and liberty of printing, reprinting, publishing…[such works] in whole or in part, for the term of twenty-eight years from the time of recording the title thereof

with a chance to renew the protection for an additional 14 years from the expiry date of the first term.[60] Sec. 7 provides that after recording the title for copyright in compliance with the Act, any person who, without the consent of the copyright holder and within the term of copyright, "engrave, etch, or work, sell, or copy… either on the whole, or by varying…with the intent to evade the law; shall print or import for sale any such [protected works]" or causing these activities was offending on the copyright and liable for copyright infringement.[61]

Following the photographers' calls for copyright protection, Congress passed an amendment to the Copyright Act 1831 on 3 March 1865 to include photographs in the list of copyright-protected works under strict formalities.[62] The amendment provided that the provisions of the Copyright Act 1831 and its amendments shall apply to photographs and the negatives in the same manner as applied to other protected works, "and to the same extent, and upon the same conditions as the authors of prints and engravings."[63] The Act further provided that in order for a work to be protected, copies of the work must be sent to the Library of Congress within one month from the date of publication. If the work was not deposited, the Congress librarian was obligated to make a demand in writing for a copy of the work to be

59 "Is Photography a Mechanic Art?," *Humphrey's Journal of the Daguerreotype and Photographic Arts and the Sciences and Arts Pertaining to Heliography*, vol 13 (S D Humphrey 1861) 160 <https://catalog.hathitrust.org/Record/003781653> accessed 17 October 2024.

60 Sec. 1, 2, 3 and 4 of the Copyright Act 1831 (US), Lionel Bently and Martin Kretschmer, "Copyright Act, Washington D.C. (1831)," *Primary Sources on Copyright (1450–1900)* <https://www.copyrighthistory.org/cam/tools/request/showRecord.php?id=record_us_1831> accessed 11 October 2024.

61 Copyright Act 1831 (US), Sec. 7, ibid.

62 Copyright Act 1865 (US) The Library of Congress, "An Act Supplemental to an Act Entitled 'An Act to Amend the Several Acts Respecting Copyright,' Approved February Third, Eighteen Hundred and Thirty-One, and to the Acts in Addition Thereto and Amendment Thereof. 38th Congress, 2nd Session.Ch 126" (*A Century of Lawmaking for a New Nation: U.S. Congressional Documents and Debates, 1774–1875*, 1865) <https://memory.loc.gov/cgi-bin/ampage?collId=llsl&fileName=013/llsl013.db&recNum=569> accessed 30 September 2021.

63 Copyright Act 1865 (US) Sec. 1 ibid.

deposited within one month; failure to do so would mean that the copyright was forfeited.[64]

Around the time of the 1865 Copyright Amendment Act, a copyright case that involved photographs, *Wood v Abbott (1866)*,[65] was undergoing trial. In *Wood v Abbott (1866)*,[66] the claimant brought an infringement claim under the 1831 Act against the defendant regarding a photograph the defendant rephotographed to produce and sell multiple pirated copies of the claimant's original photograph. The claimant's principal argument rested on the notion that photographs were "prints" within the meaning of Sec. 1 of the 1831 Act and thus protected by copyright. In response, Judge Shipman stated that photography was "an entirely original and independent method of producing and multiplying pictures – an art, not of printing or engraving, but of securing the delineation of pictures by light operating on sensitive surfaces" and therefore was not subject to copyright protection within the meaning of "print" under the 1831 Act.[67] Furthermore, while the 1865 amendment extended copyright protection to photographs, the claim was brought under the 1831 Act and before the 1865 amendment Act, and consequently, the case was dismissed.[68]

In *Rossiter v Hall (1866)*,[69] the claimant sought an injunction against the defendant, who photographed and reproduced the claimant's engraving. The defendant argued that the process of photography was not subject to the 1831 Copyright Act and cited *Wood v Abbott* to support his defence. The district judge examined the claim in light of Sec. 7 of the 1831 Copyright Act and said that the 1831 Act intended to "disclose a clear intent to protect a copyrighted work from such a mode of duplication" and "The word 'copy' is a general term,… if it covers anything, should cover the photographic method, which, more nearly than any other, produces a perfect copy."[70] The judge supported this construction by citing the English case of *Gambart v Ball*.[71] He pointed out that Judge Shipman in *Wood v Abbott*[72] did not discuss whether the word "copy" included photographs, but that photography, before the 1865 amendment Act, was not subject to copyright. Judge Benedict stated that the 1865 amendment Act was passed to protect original photographs and remove doubts that the provisions of the 1831 Act extended to photography as far as infringement was concerned. Therefore, it was held in favour of the claimant since the defendant infringed upon the engraving's copyright.

These two cases led photographers to believe that while everyone was protected from photographic copying, photographs themselves were not protected from

64 Copyright Act 1865 (US), Sec. 2, 3 ibid.
65 *Wood v Abbott, 5 Blatchf 325 (1866).*
66 ibid.
67 ibid at 425.
68 *Wood v Abbott, 5 Blatchf. 325 (1866)* (n 65).
69 *Rossiter v Hall, 20 F Cas 1253, 5 Blatchf 362 (1866).*
70 ibid (per Benedict at 1254).
71 *Gambart v Ball (1863) 14 C B(N S) 305.*
72 *Wood v Abbott, 5 Blatchf. 325 (1866)* (n 65).

copying.[73] This was because the courts' application of the 1865 amendment Act could be interpreted to mean that photographic reproduction was within the acts of reproduction covered in the 1831 Act. However, the 1865 amendment Act did not (at least for photographers), beyond doubt, confirm that photographs were subject to copyright protection within the meaning of the 1831 Act before the 1865 amendment Act.[74] Hence, photographs produced after 1831 but before 1865 are left in an uncertain state with regard to their copyright status. Nonetheless, original photographs were believed to be copyright protected as works by virtue of the 1865 Act and Sec. 7 of the 1831 Act. Therefore, it was argued by Judge Benedict in *Rossiter v Hall (1866)*[75] that for the 1865 Act's construction to be beneficial to photographs, it ought to be understood as extending the term "copying" under the 1831 Act Sec. 7 to include photographic copies. Without this construction, even photographs were vulnerable to being copied by rephotographing them. Therefore, the defendant's argument had to fail. However, it ought to be understood that any photograph published before the 1865 Act was not subject to copyright protection; hence, pre-1865 photographs were within the public domain.[76] With this, Judge Benedict cleared the confusion regarding the copyright status of the pre-1865 photographs.

A few years after the 1865 Act, a bill "to revise, consolidate, and amend the statutes relating to Patents and Copyright" was in Congress. The National Photographic Association (NPA), formed in 1869 "To improve the science and art of photography,"[77] set up a committee led by Alexander Gardner, a famous photographer, to lobby for the photographers' interests and put an end to the "piratical stealing of the negative."[78] The work exerted by the NPA committee bore fruit, and the 1870 Copyright Act expressly included photography alongside other copyright-protected works to remove the confusion surrounding its inclusion. The Copyright Act 1870 stated that "the author…or proprietor of any book,…engraving, cut, print, or photograph or negative thereof and his…assigns, shall, upon complying with the provisions of this act, have the sole liberty of printing, reprinting, publishing, completing, copying, executing, finishing, and vending the same" for the term of 28 years, renewable for an additional 14 years, from the date the title was recorded in compliance with the Act's requirements.[79]

73 Talcott Williams, "The Copyright of Photographs" in Edward L Wilson (ed), *The Philadelphia Photographer* (Benerman & Wilson 1884) 184 <http://archive.org/details/philadelphiaphot1884phil> accessed 30 September 2021.

74 ibid.

75 *Rossiter v Hall, 20 F Cas. 1253, 5 Blatchf. 362 (1866)* (n 69).

76 Welling (n 2) 186.

77 Edward Wilson (ed), *The Philadelphia Photographer*, vol VI (Benerman & Wilson 1869) 17, 60 <http://archive.org/details/philadelphiaphot1869phil> accessed 30 September 2021.

78 Edward Wilson (ed), *The Philadelphia Photographer*, vol VII (Benerman & Wilson 1870) 299 <http://archive.org/details/philadelphiaphot1870phil> accessed 30 September 2021; Wilson, *The Philadelphia Photographer* (n 77) 60; Welling (n 2) 206.

79 Sec. 86, 87, 88 of the Copyright Act 1870 (US), Lionel Bently and Martin Kretschmer (eds), "Copyright Act, Washington D.C. (1870)," *Primary Sources on Copyright (1450–1900)* <https://www

In order to acquire copyright protection, a set of strict formalities had to be satisfied; otherwise, the copyright would be forfeited. Two crucial formality requirements were that two copies of the photograph had to be sent to the Library of Congress before or within ten days from the date of publication and that the registration fees were 50 cents for every copy.[80] Moreover, every new edition of the photograph that contains substantial changes had to also be deposited to the Library of Congress to avoid a penalty for non-compliance.[81] For example, if a photograph was hand coloured, this version had to be sent to be copyright protected. Moreover, another formality requirement stated that in order to bring an infringement action for a copyrighted photograph, the photograph in question must have had a copyright notice inscribed on the copies published.[82]

Despite the fact that photographs were formally protected alongside other protected works in the same manner, photographers soon realised that the formality provisions affected them more severely than other works because of the nature of their medium. This is because unlike books or paintings, which generally require a long time to produce, a photographer's output was not comparable to that of the writers' or painters' output since a photographer can take hundreds of photographs each month, and it was not feasible to endure the expenses of satisfying the copyright requirements for each and every photograph they made.[83] For example, if a photographer neglected to copyright his photographs or did not consider a certain photograph, at first, valuable enough to copyright, and then suddenly that photograph grew popular, the aforementioned photograph would be in the public domain for failure to comply with the copyright Act requirements in the designated timeframe. This issue became very clear after the technological developments of photography and the popularity of the Kodak. Understandably, photographers became troubled with the requirements of the copyright law. Expressing this, Benjamin J. Falk wrote that

> copyright law…although, perhaps, sufficient for the needs of the art in its earlier days, are now utterly inadequate; because they entail upon the photographer who would avail himself of their protection an enormous and almost prohibitory amount of trouble and expense.[84]

While British photographers demanded that photographs be treated on equal terms with other artistic works, US photographers complained that copyright protection

.copyrighthistory.org/cam/tools/request/showRecord.php?id=record_us_1870a> accessed 11 October 2024.

80 Copyright Act 1870 (US) Sec. 90–95 ibid.

81 Copyright Act 1870 (US) Sec. 90–95 ibid.

82 Copyright Act 1870 (US) Sec. 97 ibid.

83 Benjamin Falk, "A New Copyright Law" in Edward L Wilson (ed), *The Philadelphia Photographer* (Benerman & Wilson 1888) 691 <http://archive.org/details/philadelphiaphot18882phil> accessed 30 September 2021.

84 ibid.

requirements did not consider the nature of their medium, which led many photographers not to copyright the majority of their photographs.

Archive records about the details of the congressional debates that led to the 1865 amendment Act and the 1870 Copyright Act were not available, since until 1873, Congress only recorded the resolutions and not the verbatim minutes of the debate.[85] Nonetheless, given the Act's structure, which did not seem to impose originality or an artistic classification for copyright, unlike the United Kingdom's Fine Arts Copyright Act,[86] perhaps it was safe to assume that such considerations were not thought to be necessary to justify granting photographs copyright protection similar to other protected works.

## 4.4 A Fierce Attack on the Legitimacy of Copyright Protection for Photographs

Photographs' copyright protection in the United States was soon challenged on the grounds of the constitutionality of such protection for photographs in the first place. That was due to the fact that photography occupies a precarious position between art and science, cementing photographs' dual nature between the creative and mechanical paradigms. It appears mechanical, yet different images lack uniformity, a defining trait of industrial processes. The Supreme Court case of *Burrow-Giles Lithographic Co v Sarony*[87] in 1884 was a landmark case that dealt with questions regarding the eligibility of copyright protection for photographs according to the US Constitution.

In *Burrow-Giles Lithographic Co v Sarony*,[88] Napoleon Sarony was a famous photographer renowned for taking portraiture photographs of celebrities. In 1882, Sarony took several photographs of Oscar Wilde, a famous Irish writer and poet, and registered some of the photographs for copyright protection and put a copyright notice on the photographs showing his initials. Burrow-Giles Lithographic Co, a company specialising in lithography, made a lithographic copy of one photograph titled "Oscar Wilde No.18" (Figure 4.1) without authorisation from Sarony. Subsequently, Sarony filed an infringement claim in the Southern District Court of New York in which the court held in his favour and ordered Burrow-Giles to pay damages. Burrow-Giles appealed the decision and attacked the constitutionality of copyright protection for photographs in the first place, arguing that Congress should not have been able to extend copyright protection to photography by virtue of Section 8 of the US Constitution that provides that "The Congress shall have Power…To promote the Progress of Science and useful Arts, by securing for limited Times to Authors and Inventors the exclusive Right to their respective

85 U.S Senate, "Reporters of Debate and the Congressional Record" (*Senate.gov*) <https://www.senate.gov/about/officers-staff/secretary-of-the-senate/reporters-debate-congressional-record.htm> accessed 17 October 2024.

86 Fine Arts Copyright Act 1862 (25 & 26 Vict.) C. 68.

87 *Burrow-Giles Lithographic Co v Sarony, 111 US 53 (1884)* (n 1).

88 *Sarony v Burrow-Giles Lithographic Co, 17 F 591 (1883).*

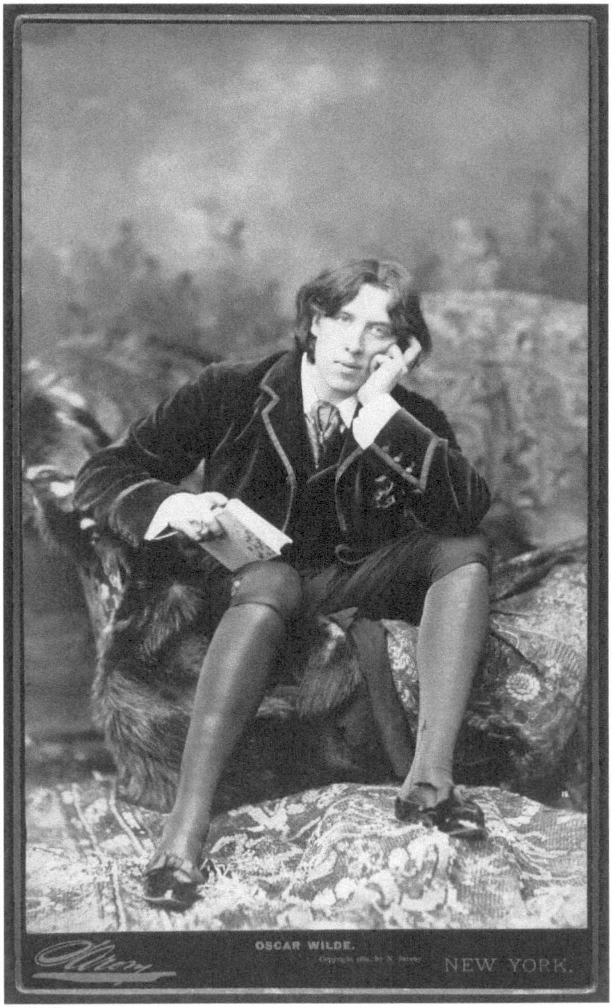


*Figure 4.1* Oscar Wilde (1854–1900), "Oscar Wilde No.18."

Photograph by Napoleon Sarony (The Metropolitan Museum of Art, 1882) https://www.metmuseum.org/art/collection/search/283247 accessed 17 October 2024.

Writings and Discoveries."[89] They further argued that photographers were not authors, nor were photographs synonymous with writings. Henceforth, they argued that photographs should not have been eligible for copyright protection, making the 1865 Copyright Amendment Act unconstitutional.

89 Section 8 U.S. Constitution.

The circuit court affirmed the earlier judgement and stated that the prevailing presumption was that the Acts of Congress were constitutional and valid unless it was clear beyond a reasonable doubt that a particular law was unconstitutional. The case eventually reached the US Supreme Court to rule on the constitutionality of copyright protection for photographs.

The Supreme Court was presented with a fundamental question regarding photographs' copyright protection and whether the Congress decision to extend copyright protection to photographs in the 1865 Act was constitutional. Both parties presented their briefs to the Supreme Court, each arguing their point extensively.

### *4.4.1 Against Photographs' Copyright Protection, the Burrow-Giles Brief*

The Burrow-Giles brief, presented by David Calman, denied the very notion of copyright protection for photographs and argued that the Congress extension of copyright protection to photographs in the 1865 Act was unconstitutional since a photograph showed "No genius and no laborious thought…nothing but mechanical skill."[90] He stressed that only original works were the subject of protection, and photography, by its very nature, cannot produce original works, in the sense of being new, that did not exist before they were captured and reproduced. Therefore, photographs and negatives "are not original works of art, but reproductions of existing objects by the application of physical laws."[91]

From this premise, Calman claimed that the 1865 Act was unconstitutional and void because Congress had gone beyond the Constitution by granting copyright protection for "merely an application of scientific principles."[92] He further stipulated that since the Constitution only permits Congress to secure "to authors and inventors, the sole right…to their respective writings and discoveries,"[93] the photographer had to fall within the meaning of "author," and the photograph had to be considered comparable to "writings" to be eligible for copyright protection, a proposition he quickly dismissed.[94] He laid his arguments against such propositions by stating that an author was an originator and creator in a way that satisfies the idea of originality because something new emerged from the act of authorship, producing a work from the author's original intellectual labour based on his own design.[95] However, photographs were "the work of the chemical forces of light on prepared plates, and that no intellectual labor, or other than the mechanical skill and manual dexterity of the photographer, contributed to the result."[96] Calman

90 Lionel Bently and Martin Kretschmer (eds), "Burrow-Giles' Brief, Washington D.C. (1883)," *Primary Sources on Copyright (1450–1900)* 21 <https://www.copyrighthistory.org/cam/tools/request/showRecord.php?id=record_us_1883b> accessed 11 October 2024.

91 ibid 5, 19.

92 ibid 5, 21.

93 U.S. Constitution Section 8.

94 Bently and Kretschmer, "Burrow-Giles' Brief, Washington D.C. (1883)" (n 90) 7.

95 ibid 9.

96 ibid 10.

argued that *Wood v Abbott*[97] supported the notion that the "true author [of a photograph] is the sun, not the photographer."[98]

To further illustrate his point, Calman cited the English case of *Nottage v Jackson (1883)*[99] to showcase the difficulties of finding authorship in photography in accordance with the legislation. He explained that the only way the judge was able to find the author was to look for the one nearest to being the author in analogy to the author of a painting.[100] Calman argued that the court was forced to do so because the UK legal system considers the parliament as the supreme law-making body. Thus, it cannot pass void laws. He argued that the court in *Nottage* was arbitrarily trying to fix authorship to photographs solely out of the necessity to apply the law as it was. However, in the United States, the courts were not forced to do that since they have the right and the duty to declare an Act of Congress unconstitutional and consequently void if it goes beyond what the Constitution allowed, which was the case in the matter in question.[101]

Calman continued to downplay the photographer's role, denying him the position of the author. He stated that an author was the one who created a new work that did not exist before. He claimed that this does not apply to the photographer whose work in a photograph was "but a copy, the original must be before extant, not only in substance, but in every minute particular."[102] The photographer can only have a claim regarding his personal judgement and skill that might have contributed to the creation of the photograph, which alone, in his view, did not give a photograph value or place the photographer's work in a position comparable to the work of a painter.[103] Calman explained that photographs were fundamentally different from paintings, engravings, and sculptures, since these works embody the ideas in visible form from the creator's own intellectual design, and the value of the work itself stems from the aforementioned design.[104] When compared to photography, "nothing of such a nature is required. The subject once arranged, there remains nothing to do but to allow the forces of nature to act."[105] The photographer cannot change or modify his vision once the creation process of the photograph begins; "he cannot, by any means, change the same from the exact way in which the subject appears to the eye."[106]

Moreover, Calman emphasised that the photograph in question was only valuable because it depicted Oscar Wilde; it did not owe its value to Sarony's work. After all, if one replaced Oscar Wilde with an unknown person in exactly the same

97 *Wood v Abbott, 5 Blatchf. 325 (1866)* (n 65).
98 Bently and Kretschmer, "Burrow-Giles' Brief, Washington D.C. (1883)" (n 90) 8.
99 *Nottage v Jackson (1883) 11 QBD 627.*
100 Bently and Kretschmer, "Burrow-Giles' Brief, Washington D.C. (1883)" (n 90) 7.
101 ibid 7, 10.
102 ibid 19.
103 ibid 9, 12, 14, 17.
104 ibid 14.
105 ibid 15.
106 ibid.

conditions and arrangement, it was highly doubtful that it would have nearly the same value as it has now. He further stated that if we considered the elements of arrangements and prior work to be sufficient to show originality, then a landscape photograph, where the photographer cannot arrange the natural scene, by this notion, should not be eligible for copyright protection.[107] However, the 1865 Act granted the same protection to all photographs and negatives regardless of the subject displayed or how it was depicted.[108] He stated that as "useful as the art may be, it is clearly not one in which originality is an essential element."[109] Therefore, he reasoned that granting photographs copyright protection was unconstitutional.[110]

The Burrow-Giles arguments rested on the notion that photography only appropriated and reproduced what was already there without any power to deviate or express individuality or personality since one, according to them, cannot identify the photographer from his works as opposed to other protected works where the author's personality shines in the work.[111] This same argument against legal protection for photography and its position as fine art had been raised from the dawn of photography in France and the United Kingdom, and it was employed yet again to challenge the legitimacy of photography's copyright protection. While Sarony did not make Oscar Wilde, he did create the photograph depicting him. Sarony fixed the image in the manner it was depicted, which was conveniently ignored in the Burrow-Giles brief. After all, doubting the value of the photograph if it showed an unknown person instead of Oscar Wilde was immaterial since Sarony did, in fact, choose to take a photograph of Oscar Wilde in those arrangements based on his own judgement, which amounts to a great deal in a medium such as photography, and it was unfair to diminish this fact.

Furthermore, Calman did not take into account the practice of retouching and never considered it in his brief. He remained steadfast in diminishing or even removing the human and intellectual elements in photography. Photography was surely not writing in the literal sense but if writing was the way to record the fruits of one's intellectual labour, could this "essence" of "writing" apply to photography? He claimed that this was worthy of consideration only if photographs were the product of intellectual labour from the photographer's own design, but in Calman's view, photography was incapable of satisfying such a requirement.[112] For him, a photograph was "the reproduction by natural means [of] something already existing."[113] He refused to consider that just as the painter can manipulate colours to reach his desired image, the photographer can prepare the scene and adjust the direction of light to achieve the desired results.

107 ibid 16.
108 ibid.
109 ibid 19.
110 ibid 22.
111 ibid 12, 17.
112 ibid 18.
113 ibid 21.

### *4.4.2 The Photographer Is an Author! Sarony's Brief*

Sarony's brief, presented by Augustus T. Gurlitz, stated that Burrow-Giles's arguments were construed to justify infringing with impunity upon this valuable copyrighted photograph.[114] He explained that the Constitution's general terms were deliberately construed in a manner that did not limit or restrict necessary developments.[115] Gurlitz cited Joseph Story's judgement in *Martin v Hunter*[116] which provided that the delegated powers by the Constitution

> are expressed in general terms, leaving to the legislature, from time to time, to adopt its own means to effectuate legitimate objects, and to mould and model the exercise of its powers, as its own wisdom, and the public interests, should require.[117]

The Constitution gives Congress the power "To promote the Progress of Science and useful Arts."[118] Thus, Congress has the power "to make all necessary and proper laws" to secure rights for limited terms to promote useful arts, which photography most certainly was.[119] He continued by saying that only upon the assertion beyond a reasonable doubt that a particular law was manifestly wrong and went beyond the Constitution would such a law be declared void. He reasoned that this did not apply to the law extending copyright protection to photographs since it did not go beyond the powers delegated by the Constitution.[120] Only extending protection to the ideas that remained unexpressed and existed solely in the mind was the place where the lines were crossed.[121] This was because the law, out of necessity, gives protection "indirectly to certain materialization" of the expressed ideas because the law's reach can only cover the manifestation of these ideas. The law aims to protect the expression of ideas fixed in permanent form and not the medium or the form itself that was used to create and fix the ideas.[122]

By the same token, photography was a medium that conveyed ideas and the photograph was the visible vessel in which the ideas were manifested, and subsequently, that law could reach and protect.[123] "The conception, inventions and creations of the mind may be manifested, expressed, or discovered in many ways according to various arts."[124] For the purposes of the law, the particular medium and

114 Lionel Bently and Martin Kretschmer (eds), "Sarony's Brief, Washington D.C. (1883)," *Primary Sources on Copyright (1450–1900)* 19 <https://www.copyrighthistory.org/cam/tools/request/showRecord.php?id=record_us_1883a> accessed 11 October 2024.

115 ibid 17, 18.

116 *Martin v Hunter's Lessee, 14 US 304 (1816).*

117 ibid at 826; Bently and Kretschmer, "Sarony's Brief, Washington D.C. (1883)" (n 114) 2.

118 Section 8 U.S. Constitution.

119 Bently and Kretschmer, "Sarony's Brief, Washington D.C. (1883)" (n 114) 3, 17.

120 ibid 3, 19.

121 ibid 8, 9.

122 ibid 7, 8.

123 ibid 9, 13.

124 ibid 9.

form of manifestation were not of utmost importance for protection compared to the importance of the original expression of the idea that was fixed in a permanent form.[125] Thus, the 1865 Act does not seek to protect all photographs, by virtue of them being photographs, indiscriminately, but it seeks to protect the exact expression depicted in the photograph from direct copying. The courts would decide the copyright validity of any photograph in the same manner as other copyrighted works, and that decision would be based on the merits of each individual case.[126]

Gurlitz further argued that the terms "authors," "inventors," "writings," and "discoveries" are correlative terms constructed to cover every form "In which authorship or invention is capable of being communicated and expressed."[127] So the author was to be understood as the originator and "the efficient cause of a thing"; the inventor was to be understood as the "one who find[s] out something new."[128] Moreover, in essence, "writings" are a way to record ideas and were construed in the Constitution to include other methods of conveying and fixing ideas.[129] This was supported by the fact that copyright protection was extended to cover engravings, prints, and photographs.[130] Therefore, one can see that the art of photography does require elements of authorship, such as the photographer's directory activities and invention, in the sense that the image in the photograph was something new that did not exist in a fixed form before it was made.[131]

Gurlitz argued that since art takes many forms and can be achieved through different mediums, one cannot deny protection for an original expression of an idea solely because of the medium used,[132] because doing so would beat the purpose of the law that did not aim to offer protection to the medium itself but the expression of the ideas instead. Photography is an art with particular rules, limitations, and methods that allow the artist to express and convey his ideas. Just as the painter or sculptor was limited by the rules and requirements of the art of painting or sculpting, the photographer was also limited by the rules of photography. This does not diminish an artist's contribution; it just limits his creative expression within the boundaries of that particular art.[133] One cannot fault a work of one art just because the same rules of another art did not bind it. One cannot fault a sculpture because the steps taken to manifest the ideas were not similar to painting or writing. Equally, the art of photography has its own unique practices to convey the expression of ideas and manifest it in a permanent form, no matter what the limitation was, as long as it was capable of conveying the author's ideas. The limitations of the art were left for the

125 ibid 10.
126 ibid 14.
127 ibid 6.
128 ibid 4.
129 ibid 7.
130 ibid 6.
131 ibid 7, 10.
132 ibid 10, 11.
133 ibid 11.

artist to deal with and should not be used to deny photography copyright protection by virtue of its limitation.[134]

With regard to Burrow-Giles's claims that Sarony was not an author since he only appropriated what already existed through the process of photography, Guriltz responded that the photograph in question was "the original invention and design of Sarony, made by him entirely from his own original mental conception."[135] Through Sarony's judgement, the photograph, which did not exist before, was conveyed and fixed permanently in the form it took. Sarony, as the principal photographer:

> posed Oscar Wilde before the camera, selected and arranged the costume, draperies and other various accessories in said photograph; arranged the subject to present graceful outlines, arranged and disposed the light and shade, suggested and evoked the desired expression…these various acts constitute an author, inventor and designer in the art of photography.[136]

Gurlitz concluded that the court judgement should be affirmed so as not to encourage acts of gross infringement, stressing that Burrow-Giles knew very well that the photograph was copyrighted, and yet, they infringed upon the copyright to illegally profit from the work's exploitation.[137]

One could see that Gurlitz's argument was built on the notion that photography was merely the vessel conveying the expression dictated by the photographer. Photography was a medium of expression. However, the tools which the photographer utilises to achieve his vision in this medium were different from the tools utilised by a painter, but that did not diminish his role as an author to a level that regulated the photographer as subservient to the camera when, in reality, the camera was still subservient to the photographer. Thus, the point of the 1865 Act was to extend protection to photography, giving its established status as a useful art capable of artistic expression. Gurlitz stressed the pre-capture work done by Sarony in order to create the photograph and reasoned that all the steps that Sarony took positioned him as the author within the art of photography. Due to Sarony's activities, the resulting photograph was "invented," in that it did not exist before he prepared and fixed it in the form it took.

### *4.4.3 The Supreme Court Decision, a Victory for Photographic Copyright?*

Justice Miller at the Supreme Court confessed that the question about the constitutionality of photographs' copyright protection was "not free from difficulty."[138] Nevertheless, looking at the history of the US Constitution, US

134 ibid 15.
135 ibid 12.
136 ibid.
137 ibid 19.
138 *Burrow-Giles Lithographic Co v Sarony, 111 US 53 (1884)* (n 1) 56.

copyright law, and the copyright law of England, Miller J stated that the construction intended:

> to include all forms...by which the ideas in the mind of the author are given visible expression. The only reason why photographs were not included in the extended list in the act of 1802 is, probably, that they did not exist, as photography, as an art, was then unknown.[139]

Therefore, there was no doubt that "the constitution is broad enough to cover an Act authorizing copyright of photographs, so far as they are representatives of original intellectual conceptions of the author."[140]

Afterwards, Miller J turned to the question of authorship in photographs and whether a mere mechanical reproduction of whatever the camera represents, in which "the accuracy of this representation being its highest merit" without regard to originality and invention, was eligible for copyright protection.[141] Miller J noted that copyright might not subsist in such servile photographs, but this certainly did not apply to the photograph in question. In the photograph titled "Oscar Wilde No.18," the findings showed that Sarony had prepared the scene and was actively involved in the creation process by posing Oscar Wilde and taking care of all the arrangements necessary to achieve the result manifested in the photograph. Therefore, the photograph appears "to be an original work of art, the product of [Sarony's] intellectual invention, of which [he] is the author."[142] Miller J cited the English case of *Nottage v Jackson*[143] and stated that the judges' views in that case mirrored their own views regarding the nature of authorship and originality in photographs. In that, the author was the one "who has superintended the arrangement...who is the effective cause of [the photograph]."[144] Following this, the Supreme Court affirmed the circuit court's judgement in favour of Sarony.

With the US Supreme Court decision, the copyrightability of photographs in the United States was no longer a matter of dispute.[145] However, the Supreme Court was cautious of drawing the line for what constitutes a copyrightable photograph. Miller J avoided the question altogether.[146] As important as this case was, one can say that it only affirmed that prior arrangement and judgement were indeed evidence of authorship and originality in photographs to the degree that renders it a copyrightable work. Soon the Kodak revolution arrived to render an ordinary photographer's effort, on many occasions nothing more than pointing the camera and pressing the shutter, a snapshot of what was already there independent of the prior arrangement and influence of the photographer.

139 ibid 58.
140 ibid.
141 ibid 59.
142 ibid 60.
143 *Nottage v Jackson (1883) 11 QBD 627* (n 99).
144 *Burrow-Giles Lithographic Co v Sarony, 111 US 53 (1884)* (n 1) 60, 61.
145 *Thornton v Schreiber, 124 US 612 (1888).*
146 *Burrow-Giles Lithographic Co v Sarony, 111 US 53 (1884)* (n 1) 59.

## 4.5 The Aftermath of the Supreme Court Decision on the *Burrow-Giles Case*

The *Burrow-Giles case* settled the matter regarding the copyrightability of photographs in the affirmative. However, it did not conclusively provide the minimum requirements for any specific type of photograph for copyright protection. Consequently, it was left to the courts to decide disputes regarding the copyrightability of a given photograph on a case-by-case basis, drawing guidance regarding authorship, originality, and copyrightability by following the *Burrow-Giles standard* firmly.[147]

Benjamin J. Falk, an artistic photographer and the president of the Photographers' Copyright League of America,[148] brought several successful infringement claims against unauthorised copying of his copyrighted photographs following the *Burrow-Giles case.*[149] In *Falk v Brett Lithographing Co (1891)*,[150] a photograph of a mother and child arranged by the photographer, where the child placed her finger in her mouth, was the subject of a copyright dispute. The defendant, who copied the photograph with minor adjustments, argued that Falk was not the author since he did not direct the child to put her finger in her mouth, an amusing argument which can be foreseen if one understood the *Burrow-Giles standard* as one to be applied extremely rigidly. Thankfully, however, the judge stated that the photographer had taken all the necessary steps and employed his judgement, taking advantage of the proper time, to produce the photograph. This sufficiently rendered him the sole author of the photograph, and the court decided in Falk's favour.

The cases that came after *Burrow-Giles* show that a degree of arrangement and judgement must be sufficiently evident, even if there were elements outside the photographer's directorial control. What constitutes sufficient arrangements to evidence the authorship and originality of a photographic work were left to the courts to decide on an ad hoc basis in the light of the *Burrow-Giles standard.*[151] Furthermore, it was worth noting that in cases regarding the copyright ownership of commissioned photographs, there was a strong presumption that if the work was ordered, paid for, and delivered as per the wishes of one party, then the copyright ownership passed to the commissioning party in the absence of an agreement to the contrary.[152]

147 See: Christine Haight Farley, "The Lingering Effects of Copyright's Response to the Invention of Photography" (2004) 65 University of Pittsburgh Law Review 385.

148 Dixon Tennant and Mrs Edward L Wilson (eds), *Wilson's Photographic Magazine*, vol XLIV (Edward L Wilson 1907) 2 <http://archive.org/details/wilsonsphotogra07unkngoog> accessed 30 September 2021.

149 See: *Falk v TP Howell & Co, 37 F 202 (1888)*; *Falk v Gast Lithograph & Engraving Co, 48 F 262 (1891)*; *Falk v Brett Lithographing Co, 48 F 678 (1891)*; *Falk v Donaldson, 57 F 32 (1893).*

150 *Falk v Brett Lithographing Co, 48 F 678 (1891)* (n 149).

151 *Bolles v Outing Co, 46 LRA 712 (1897)* "Whether a photograph is a mere manual reproduction of subject matter, or an original work of art, is a question of fact" (per Judge Wallace, at 970); see: *Cleland v Thayer, 121 F 71 (1903).*

152 *Dielman v White, 102 F 892 (1900)*; *Press Pub Co v Falk, 59 F 324 (1894).*

In 1903, an important Supreme Court decision on *Bleistein v Donaldson Lithographing Co (1903)*,[153] which cited *Burrow-Giles*, had the effect of lowering the authorship and originality threshold required for photographic works' copyright protection. The case involved a circus advertisement illustration that was copied without authorisation. The Supreme Court reversed the lower court's judgement and held that advertisement illustrations were subject to copyright. Justice Holmes declared that:

> Personality always contains something unique. It expresses its singularity even in handwriting, and a very modest grade of art has in it something irreducible, which is one man's alone. That something he may copyright unless there is a restriction in the words of the act.[154]

Thus, it was to be understood that the threshold requirements for a photograph to be copyright protected were not subject to strict, predetermined standards; as long as it contains elements of the author's personality, then it may well be subject to copyright protection.

It is worth mentioning that during these years, a new art, closely connected to photography, was plagued by piracy and sought to be protected by copyright under the category of photographs. The art of motion pictures was beginning to form its identity as an art, and to combat pirated copies of its films, the Edison company brought an infringement lawsuit under photographic copyright since films, they argued, were essentially an extension of photographs.[155] This led to the Third Circuit Court of Appeals case of *Edison v Lubin (1903)*[156] where the court held, after considering the *Burrow-Giles* and *Bleistein* standards, that motion picture films were protected under the category of photographs since "the reproduction is a light-written, and therefore a photographic picture or photograph."[157]

Moreover, it was held in *American Mutoscope & Biograph Co v Edison Mfg Co (1905)*,[158] that even if the film depicted scenes from different camera locations that were later joined as one continuous shot, it was still protected as if it was a single photograph since it tells a single story despite the different scenes depicted. Motion picture films would continue to be protected as photographs until the 1912 amendment Act reintroduced them as a separate copyright-protected class of works.[159]

153 *Bleistein v Donaldson Lithographing Co, 188 US 239 (1903).*

154 ibid at 250.

155 See: Peter Decherney, "Copyright Dupes: Piracy and New Media in Edison v Lubin (1903)" (2007) 19 Film History: An International Journal 109; *Edison v Lubin, 119 F 993 (1903)*; *Edison v Lubin, 122 F 240 (1903).*

156 *Edison v Lubin, 122 F 240 (1903)* (n 155).

157 per Buffington, at 242 ibid.

158 *American Mutoscope & Biograph Co v Edison Mfg Co, 137 F 262 (1905).*

159 See *Townsend Copyright Amendment : Complete File of Arguments before the Committee on Patents, House of Representatives, on H.R. 15263 and H.R. 20596, Commencing January 24, 1912.*

## 4.6 The 1909 Copyright Law Revision and the New Foe, the American Newspaper Publishers' Association

In an address to Congress in December 1905, President Theodore Roosevelt echoed the general sentiments regarding the state of copyright law by stating that:

> Our copyright laws urgently need revision. They are imperfect in definition, confused and inconsistent in expression…; they are difficult for the courts to interpret and impossible for the Copyright Office to administer with satisfaction to the public.[160]

During this revision period, the Photographers' Copyright League of America, led by Benjamin Falk, was tasked with lobbying for the interests of photographers as per the resolution of the 26th annual convention of the Photographers' Association of America, held in August 1906.[161] The Photographers' Copyright League was established "to secure and protect Photographic Copyrights, to suppress piracies, and generally to promote the interests of the profession."[162] As the representative of the photographic community, they voiced their support for the Copyright Bill (1906) H.R. 19853[163] proposed in 1906, which did not introduce any significant changes to the protection of photographs without any additional amendments.[164]

The American Newspaper Publishers' Association,[165] hereafter referred to as the Newspaper Association, was surely not amused with copyright law in relation to photographs remaining unchanged and voiced a loud protest.[166] The Newspaper Association copyright committee declared that:

(Government Printing Office 1912) 107, 108 <http://hdl.handle.net/2027/chi.73606950> accessed 17 October 2024; see also: Decherney (n 155).

160 As quoted in *Arguments before the Committees on Patents of the Senate and House of Representatives, Conjointly, on the Bills S. 6330 and H.R. 19853, to Amend and Consolidate the Acts Respecting Copyright. June 6–9, 1906.* (Government Printing Office 1906) 3 <http://hdl.handle.net/2027/hvd.hx7dvf> accessed 17 October 2024.

161 LW Wilson (ed), *Wilson's Photographic Magazine*, vol XLIII (Edward L Wilson 1906) 385, 435 <http://archive.org/details/wilsonsphotogra01unkngoog> accessed 30 September 2021.

162 ibid 397.

163 E Fulton Brylawski and Abe Goldman (eds), "The Copyright Bill S.6330; H.R. 19853 Fifty-Ninth Congress, First Session Compared With Copyright Statutes Now in Force and Earlier United States Copyright Enactments 1906," *Legislative History of the 1909 Copyright Act*, vol 1 (Fred B Rothman 1976) <https://heinonline.org/HOL/P?h=hein.leghis/lhcav0001&i=31> accessed 30 September 2021.

164 Wilson, *Wilson's Photographic Magazine* (n 161) 435; *Arguments before the Committees on Patents of the Senate and House of Representatives, Conjointly, on the Bills S. 6330 and H.R. 19853, to Amend and Consolidate the Acts Respecting Copyright. June 6–9, 1906.* (n 160) 147.

165 Known now as News Media Alliance, "About News Media Alliance" (*News Media Alliance*) <https://www.newsmediaalliance.org/about-us/> accessed 17 October 2024.

166 *Arguments before the Committees on Patents of the Senate and House of Representatives, Conjointly,on the Bills S.6330 and H.R.19853. To Amend and Consolidate the Acts Respecting Copyright. December 7–11, 1906.* (Government Printing Office 1906) 169 <http://hdl.handle.net/2027/njp.32101068559879> accessed 17 October 2024.

> injustice is done (1) by giving to the mechanical maker of a Kodak snap shot the same protection that is given to the author of a literary, artistic, or musical composition; (2) by treating the imperfect reproduction or imitation in a newspaper of a copyrighted photograph as causing every copy of the offending issue to become in the eyes of the law an infringing, damage-producing copy of such photograph, subject to penalty of not less than $1 for every such copy and to other punishment; and (3) by failing to recognize that newspaper reprints of photographs are not such reproduction as can be substituted in sales for originals, and that instead of inflicting injury by reducing sales they often tend to advertise and to increase the sales of the original photographs.[167]

The Newspaper Association copyright committee followed their outcry with proposing the following amendment to be included which provided that "the reproduction of a photograph in any newspaper by the process known as stereotyping shall not be construed as an infringement of the copyright of such photograph."[168]

It does not seem far-fetched that the Newspaper Association wanted to reproduce photographs with impunity without regard to established copyright principles that consider a copy as a copy regardless of whether it was reproduced using a different medium. A prompt response came to the aid of photographers from the president of the Print Publishers' Association, W.A. Livingstone, who responded to this protest by saying that

> it will not do to say that because some unimportant kodak picture is not seriously injured by reproduction that all other photographic pictures must submit to infringement with impunity. As a matter of fact, not 1 per cent of the photographs taken are copyrighted at all, and nobody copyrights a photograph unless he believes there is certain value to him in its exclusiveness.[169]

Livingstone expressed that it would be an injustice to single out photographs' copyright with limited protection or reservations just because many photographs were not considered valuable.[170] That was because the same could be said across all other protected works just as well, and just as it was not a ground for restricting copyright for other protected works, by the same principle, it should not be used as a ground to restrict copyright protection for photographs.[171] Livingstone further pointed out that some photographs were copyrighted for the sole purpose of preserving privacy and avoiding potential damages that the publication may cause.[172] Moreover, he noted that the newspaper appropriation of copyrighted pictures, in fact, can cause the sales of the said photograph to decline as people

167 ibid.
168 ibid.
169 ibid 112.
170 ibid 111.
171 ibid.
172 ibid 112, 113.

already acquired a copy of it, no matter how imperfect a copy it was, and if one assumed that publishing in newspapers attracts sales then the photographer out of his own volition would be happy to provide a photograph to the newspaper to reproduce.[173]

The Photographers' Copyright League, represented by Benjamin Falk and Pirie MacDonald, as soon as they became aware of the Newspaper Association protest, sent their response while scorning the apparent purposeful delay of the Newspaper Association objections up until close to the adjourning of the hearings in order to put themselves at an advantage.[174] They pointed out that the newspaper industry always adopted questionable practices in relation to photographs. Moreover, they stressed that the Newspaper Association's claim that their reproduction benefitted the photographers was flawed and diverted the attention away from the important fact that many people copyright their photographs to preserve their privacy by controlling the photographs' publication. They emphasised that "either a copyright belongs to its owner or it is not a copyright at all."[175]

The Photographers' Copyright League did not stop only at a response. Benjamin Falk immediately published an appeal in leading photographic journals, urging all photographers to send letters to their Senators and Congressmen expressing their utmost refusal of the Newspaper Association's proposed amendments. He urged the photographers to stand together against "the newspaper people" who demanded "that our country shall legislate our rights out of existence as far as newspapers are concerned."[176]

In 1908, in the hearings regarding the Bills "To Amend and Consolidate the Acts Respecting Copyright,"[177] the Newspaper Association once again tried to reduce, or rather they wished to remove, the risk of infringement for newspapers by proposing a couple of amendments that essentially advocated for a special treatment for newspapers with regard to photographs' copyright.[178] The Newspaper Association proposed a requirement that a "conspicuous notice of copyright" should be placed on the face of the photographs to protect newspapers from "unintentional" infringement due to the sheer volume of photographs that they encounter.[179] Additionally, they claimed, rather shamelessly, that this was also for the benefit of the photographer since he would receive his due credit and the copyright notice would serve as an advisement for him, which was "part of this reasonable and just compensation for the newspaper use of his work."[180] They persisted, quite heavily, on the

173 ibid.
174 ibid 388.
175 ibid.
176 Tennant and Wilson (n 148) 2.
177 E Fulton Brylawski and Abe Goldman (eds), "Legislative History of the 1909 Copyright Act. Hearings before the (Joint) Committees on Patents, March 26–28, 1908 Part K" (1976) 5 Legislative History of the 1909 Copyright Act [i].
178 ibid 152–156.
179 ibid 151, 152.
180 ibid 152.

flawed argument that newspapers' reproduction or imitation of a photograph was not a substitute for the original photograph, arguing that "Newspaper reproduction means advertising of and benefit to sale of photographs as photographs."[181] Hence, in their view, it should not be regarded as an infringement.[182]

The revised Copyright Law Bill was enacted in July 1909. The Copyright Act of 1909 simplified the law and eased the formalities required while maintaining that no action regarding copyright infringement shall be accepted until compliance with the Act's registration requirement.[183] Sec. 4 provided that "the works for which copyright may be secured under this Act shall include all the writings of an author"[184] and the copyright duration shall be for the term of 28 years, renewable for another 28 years, from the date of first publication, as opposed to the date of registration.[185] The Act did not specify any definition for the terms "writings" or "author" other than clarifying that in work for hire, the employer was to be regarded as the author for the purposes of the Act.[186] Moreover, in the case of commissioned photographs such as portrait photographs, the prevailing presumption remains that the one who solicited the photograph was the copyright owner in the absence of an agreement to the contrary.[187]

Despite the fact that there were no definitions for the terms mentioned in the Act, it was evidenced that the terms "author" and "writings" were to be understood along the lines suggested in the *Burrow-Giles case*. That means that an "author" was to be understood as the "originator" of the work, and any medium that can record and convey ideas, such as photographs, were within the meaning of "writings" for the purposes of the copyright law.[188] It is worth noting that even though photographs were expressly classified in the non-exhaustive list of copyrightable work for the purposes of copyright registration, no attempt at defining what constituted a photograph was entertained.[189] This was, in a way, beneficial for motion picture films since they were regarded by the courts as an extension of photographic works and were protected as such until the 1912 amendment Act.[190] The US copyright law lacked a definition concerning what was meant by photographic works,

181 ibid 155.
182 ibid 154, 155.
183 Sec. 10–13 Copyright Act 1909 (US).
184 Sec. 4 ibid.
185 Sec. 4, Sec. 23 ibid.
186 Sec. 62 ibid.
187 *Avedon v Exstein, 141 FSupp 278 (1956)*; *Brattleboro Pub Co v Winmill Pub Corp, 369 F2d 565 (1966)*; *Lumiere v Pathe Exch, 275 F 428 (1921)*; *Lumiere v Robertson-Cole Distributing Corporation, 280 F 550 (1922)*.
188 *Burrow-Giles Lithographic Co v Sarony, 111 US 53 (1884)* (n 1); see: *Goldstein v California, 412 US 546 (1973)* at 561 "although the word 'writings' might be limited to script or printed material, it may be interpreted to include any physical rendering of the fruits of creative intellectual or aesthetic labor" per Chief Justice Burger.
189 Sec. 5 Copyright Act 1909 (US); Farley (n 147) 404.
190 See: Decherney (n 155); *Edison v Lubin, 122 F 240 (1903)* (n 155).

in contrast to UK copyright law, where a definition regarding what constituted a photographic work was provided.[191]

In the end, it appears that the legislators attempted to reach a middle ground between the photographers and the interests of the newspaper industry. In an attempt to please the Newspaper Association, the Copyright Act 1909 Sec. 25, which addressed infringements, provided a special provision for cases involving newspapers' reproductions of copyrighted photographs by limiting the damages awarded when the courts exercised their discretion in assessing the damages to $200 as a maximum and $50 as a minimum,[192] a stark difference from the damages available at the courts' discretion in other cases, which were set to a maximum of $5000 and a minimum of $250.[193] At the same time, the legislators also took heed of the complaints raised by photographers regarding the increase of the registration fees to $1 and provided an exception to photographs by keeping the registration fees at 50 cents.[194]

It appears that the photographic community lost the battle against their powerful adversary, the Newspaper Association.[195] The Photographers' Copyright League fought valiantly for four years but lost to the "underhand methods" of the Newspaper Association.[196] The photographers expressed their bitterness over this amendment, which effectively robbed them of protection against the biggest offender of their copyright because the litigation costs would be higher than the amount of damages that could be recovered.[197] The *Wilson's Journal* lamented that when newspapers reproduce the photographer's work, "the law does not recognise his work as being of any value, not over $200 in any event."[198] Perhaps the Newspaper Association statement about the injustice of punishing the newspaper for "the crude newspaper reproduction of a crude newspaper imitation of a kodak snapshot photograph"[199] persuaded the legislators to grant them an exception. Kodak, after all, changed how people perceived and valued photographs by making them ubiquitous. Aside from this setback, the photographers were satisfied with the Copyright Act 1909.[200]

The court cases under the Copyright Act 1909 gradually extended the criteria of elements that confer originality to allow for more types of photographs to be copyrightable, often citing the reasoning of *Burrow-Giles* and *Bleistein*[201] and expand-

191 See Chapter 3, Section 3.8.

192 Sec. 25 Copyright Act 1909 (US).

193 ibid.

194 Sec. 61 ibid; *Arguments before the Committees on Patents of the Senate and House of Representatives, Conjointly, on the Bills S. 6330 and H.R. 19853, to Amend and Consolidate the Acts Respecting Copyright. June 6–9, 1906.* (n 160) 149; Falk (n 83) 691.

195 Dixon Tennant (ed), *Wilson's Photographic Magazine*, vol XLVI (Edward L Wilson 1909) 145 <http://archive.org/details/wilsonsphotogra04unkngoog> accessed 30 September 2021.

196 ibid 145, 146.

197 ibid 145; see: *Altman v New Haven Union Co, 254 F 113 (1918).*

198 Tennant (n 195) 145; *Altman v New Haven Union Co, 254 F 113 (1918)* (n 197).

199 Brylawski and Goldman (n 177) 155.

200 Tennant (n 195) 146.

201 *Bleistein v Donaldson Lithographing Co, 188 US 239 (1903)* (n 153).

ing on them to justify protecting the photographs in question. In *Pagano v Chas. Beseler Co (1916)*,[202] where it was held that a photograph of a public building was copyrightable, Judge Mayer stated that:

> Any one may take a photograph of a public building and of the surrounding scene. It undoubtedly requires originality to determine just when to take the photograph, so as to bring out the proper setting for both animate and inanimate objects, with the adjunctive features of light, shade, position, etc.[203]

Similarly, in *Jewelers' Circular Pub Co v Keystone Pub Co (1921)*,[204] Judge Learned Hand stated that:

> no photograph, however simple, can be unaffected by the personal influence of the author, and no two will be absolutely alike…under section 5 (j) photographs are protected, without regard to the degree of 'personality' which enters into them…. The suggestion that the Constitution might not include all photographs seems to me overstrained.[205]

Thus, effectively, any photograph, even the seemingly mindless "Kodak snapshot," may be copyrightable.

The General Counsel of the Photographers' Copyright League of America, Benno Lewinson, expressed his disillusion with leaving photographs' copyrightability as a matter subject to the judges' subjective views regarding what constitutes copyrightable photographs. He explained that the risk of having conflicting results concerning the copyrightability of different photographs had created a sense of unease, because even if one successfully registered a photograph for copyright, the courts may find that the photograph was not copyrightable.

## 4.7 The Fourth Copyright Law Revision, the Copyright Act 1976

In 1947, the copyright law was codified in the US Code as Title 17.[206] By the 1950s, a new general revision to meet the needs of the time was underway.[207] The Copyright Office stated in its 1961 report that the copyright law was "uncertain, inconsistent, or inadequate in its application to present-day conditions." [208] Hence, a general revision was deemed to be long overdue.

202 *Pagano v Chas Beseler Co, 234 F 963 (1916).*

203 ibid at 964.

204 *Jewelers' Circular Pub Co v Keystone Pub Co, 274 F 932 (1921).*

205 ibid at 934, 935.

206 U.S. Copyright Office, "Timeline 1900–1950" (*Copyright.gov*) <https://www.copyright.gov/timeline/timeline_1900-1950.html> accessed 18 October 2024.

207 The Committee on the Judiciary, "Copyright Law Revision Report of the Register of Copyrights on the General Revision of the U.S. Copyright Law" (*Copyright.gov | U.S. Copyright Office*, 1961) IX, X <https://www.copyright.gov/history/1961_registers_report.pdf> accessed 18 October 2024.

208 The Committee on the Judiciary, "Copyright Law Revision Report of the Register of Copyrights on the General Revision of the U.S. Copyright Law" (n 207).

The 1961 report recommended that the registration requirement for photographs be eased. The 1909 copyright law required a separate registration for every individually published photograph, which placed an undue economic burden on photographers.[209] Thus, the report recommended remedying this in a manner that made it possible for photographers to register multiple photographs under a single application, even if they plan to publish each one separately.[210] Photographers had long complained about this issue, and it seemed it was finally being addressed.[211] It further recommended that unregistered photographs that contain a copyright notice should be protected but with limited remedies until formally registered.[212] The report also drew attention to an issue faced by photographers who published their photographs in periodicals since many publishers preferred to include one general copyright notice for the periodical and not for each individual photograph. This placed a lot of pressure on photographers to assign their copyrights to the publisher or risk losing the copyright in the photograph due to the absence of a copyright notice on it.[213] For this, the report suggested that a publisher's general notice of copyright should be sufficient to cover the photographs' copyright notice requirement in periodicals.[214]

In the years leading to the 1976 Copyright Act, the discussion about photographs centred around the copyright registration requirements, the special provisions addressed to newspapers' use of copyright photographs, and the work made for hire in relation to portrait photographs. A recommendation was presented regarding the exceptions addressed to certain infringements and the limited statutory damages available for them, such as the one related to newspapers' use of copyrighted photographs.[215] That recommendation proposed eliminating the special provisions to introduce one general provision that dealt with situations involving innocent infringements by placing the burden of proof of innocence on the infringer, leaving the court to decide upon the appropriate statutory damage in such cases within a defined limit.[216] Of course, this would remove the special treatment newspapers enjoyed with regard to their use of copyright photographs since they

209 ibid 78, 133.
210 ibid.
211 Falk (n 83) 691.
212 The Committee on the Judiciary, "Copyright Law Revision Report of the Register of Copyrights on the General Revision of the U.S. Copyright Law" (n 207) 80, 133.
213 ibid 133.
214 ibid.
215 ibid 104; The Committee on the Judiciary, *Copyright Law Revision Part 2. Discussion and Comments on Report of the Register of Copyrights on the General Revision of the U.S. Copyright Law* (Washington, 1963) 172–175 <http://hdl.handle.net/2027/mdp.35112100697905> accessed 18 October 2024.
216 The Committee on the Judiciary, "Copyright Law Revision Report of the Register of Copyrights on the General Revision of the U.S. Copyright Law" (n 207) 104; The Committee on the Judiciary, *Copyright Law Revision Part 2. Discussion and Comments on Report of the Register of Copyrights on the General Revision of the U.S. Copyright Law* (n 215) 172–175.

would have to prove that their infringement was innocent, aligning them with any other case that involves an innocent infringement defence.

Predictably, the Newspaper Association was not too fond of this recommendation and again employed the same arguments from 50 years ago to argue in favour of keeping the special provision as "it would be in the public interest to retain" it.[217] By this time, the Photographers' Copyright League of America ceased to exist, and the photographers did not have the vigour or enough interest to resume the old fight, so it was up to the legislators to see if the newspapers' argument still held as well as it did 50 years ago.[218] This recommendation advocating a general provision in all situations involving innocent infringement to streamline the law, despite the Newspaper Association protest, persisted so it would "not allow a defendant to escape simply because the plaintiff failed to disprove his claim of innocence."[219] Thus, after a long 50 years, the photographers finally gained a victory against their old enemy.

Moreover, it was recommended that commissioned portrait photographs should be expressly mentioned within the categories of "work made for hire" in the absence of an agreement to the contrary.[220] It seems that this might have been specifically suggested to cement the prevailing presumption of common law about the copyright ownership of portrait photographs, which was regarded as generally vesting on the party that commissioned it and not the photographer who made it.[221] This was thought of as a way to preserve the privacy of the people who ordered the portrait to be taken.[222] This recommendation, however, was strongly contested by the Copyright Office; it voiced its objection by saying that:

> The addition of portraits to the list of commissioned works that can be made into "works made for hire" by agreement of the parties is difficult to justify.

217 The House Committee on the Judiciary, *Supplementary Register's Report on the General Revision of the U.S. Copyright Law* (House Committee Print (89th Congress, 1st Session) 1965) 78 <https://ipmall.law.unh.edu/sites/default/files/hosted_resources/lipa/copyrights/Supplementary%20Register%27s%20Report%20on%20the%20General%20Revision%20of.pdf> accessed 18 October 2024; The Committee on the Judiciary, *Copyright Law Revision Part 5. 1964 Revision Bill with Discussions and Comments* (US Government Printing Office 1965) 230–232 <http://hdl.handle.net/2027/mdp.35112203450541> accessed 18 October 2024.

218 The Committee on the Judiciary, *Copyright Law Revision Part 2. Discussion and Comments on Report of the Register of Copyrights on the General Revision of the U.S. Copyright Law* (n 215) 140.

219 The Committee on the Judiciary, *Copyright Law Revision Report Additional Views (Senate Report 94-473) | U.S. Copyright Office* (1975) 145 <https://www.copyright.gov/history/law/clrev_94-473.pdf> accessed 18 October 2024.

220 ibid 105.

221 The Committee on the Judiciary, "Copyright Law Revision, Sept. 3, 1976 (House Report 94-1476)" (*Copyright.gov | U.S. Copyright Office*, 1976) 121 <https://www.copyright.gov/history/law/clrev_94-1476.pdf> accessed 18 October 2024.

222 The Committee on the Judiciary, *Copyright Law Revision Part 2. Discussion and Comments on Report of the Register of Copyrights on the General Revision of the U.S. Copyright Law* (n 215) 374.

> Artists and photographers are among the most vulnerable and poorly protected of all the beneficiaries of the copyright law, and it seems clear that, like serious composers and choreographers, they were not intended to be treated as "employees" under the carefully negotiated definition in section 101. The Copyright Office recommends deleting this reference or, at the very least, calling it to the attention of the various groups now concerned with artists' rights.[223]

Congress followed the Copyright Office recommendation and abandoned this special address to portrait photographs altogether.[224] The photographer was to be presumed as the copyright owner in portrait photographs unless there was an agreement to the contrary. In other words, the prevailing presumption was now reversed to favour the photographer's position.[225]

The Copyright Act 1976 came into effect in January 1978, amending Title 17 of the United States Code. It provides that copyright subsists "in original works of authorship fixed in any tangible medium of expression, now known or later developed, from which they can be perceived, reproduced, or otherwise communicated, either directly or with the aid of a machine or device."[226] It further explains that works of authorship include "pictorial, graphic, and sculptural works," which is a category that includes photographs.[227] The language used was more inclusive by eliminating the term "writing" to reflect the broad mediums of expression existing or coming to exist in the future. Strikingly, the 1976 Copyright Act did not attempt to define what constitutes a photograph; it seems that the legislators were content with simply regarding photographs as one of the protected classes of works without defining what a photograph was. Under the 1976 Act, photographs no longer needed to be considered "writings" to be granted protection. For works created on or after January 1978, the general term of copyright protection subsists from its creation and lasts until the author's life and 50 years after his death.[228] The general duration of copyright was later raised to the life of the author and 70 years after his death.

Furthermore, the formality requirements were relaxed considerably as registration was no longer a condition for copyright protection, albeit still necessary to bring an infringement lawsuit and to be eligible for statutory damages and certain

223 The Register of Copyrights, *Second Supplementary Register's Report on the General Revision of the U.S. Copyright Law (1975)* (The Register of Copyrights 1975) 100 <https://ipmall.law.unh.edu/sites/default/files/hosted_resources/lipa/copyrights/Second%20Supplementary%20Register%27s%20Report%20on%20the%20General%20Revision.pdf> accessed 18 October 2024.

224 The Committee on the Judiciary, "Copyright Law Revision, Sept. 3, 1976 (House Report 94-1476)" (n 221).

225 R Scott Miller Jr, "Photography and the Work-for-Hire Doctrine" (1994) 1 Texas Wesleyan Law Review 81, 100.

226 Sec. 102 Copyright Act 1976 (US).

227 Sec. 101, 102, ibid.

228 Sec. 302(a) ibid.

remedies.[229] The Act allowed the registration of a group of photographs under a single registry for a single fee within 12 months if the photographs were from the same author.[230] This removed much of the economic burden on photographers that previously prevented them from registering their works. Furthermore, the absence of copyright notice and the default of registration does not forfeit the copyright, albeit copyright notices were still required on published works to limit cases of innocent infringements.[231] Regarding innocent infringers, the general provisions applied equally to all such cases that involve an innocent infringer defence; the newspaper industry was no longer afforded special treatment when it came to their use of copyright photographs.[232] The work-for-hire provisions were streamlined and no longer prejudiced portrait photographs. The photographers were the initial owners of the copyright in portrait photographs in the absence of an agreement to the contrary.[233]

The Copyright Act of 1976 was highly beneficial to photographs' copyright since the old grievances voiced by photographers were addressed, and their work was protected in the same manner as other protected works without any special provisions that limited the protection.

The US accession to the Berne Convention in 1989 led to the creation of the Visual Artists Rights Act 1990, which introduced a particular class of photographs that enjoyed greater moral rights protection.[234] It provided that a still photograph was considered to be within the meaning of a "work of visual art" if the "image [is] produced for exhibition purposes only, existing in a single copy that is signed by the author, or in a limited edition of 200 copies or fewer that are signed and consecutively numbered by the author."[235] The author's moral rights, such as the right of attribution, among other moral rights, in the visual work of art, cannot be assigned and are distinct from the copyright.[236]

## 4.8 Conclusion

The decentralised nature of photography since its introduction to the United States created a fertile ground for innovation and expanded the use of the medium. The artistic capacity of photographs was not a matter that took centre stage as the new medium was enthusiastically embraced by American society. Photographs gained copyright protection equal to other copyrighted works via the 1865 Copyright Amendment Act without intense debate regarding their artistic capacity. However,

229 Sec. 408, 411, 412 ibid.
230 Sec. 408(c)(2) ibid.
231 Sec. 405–408 ibid.
232 Sec. 504(c)(2) ibid.
233 Sec. 201(b) ibid.
234 U.S. Copyright Office, "Timeline 1950–1997" (*Copyright.gov*) <https://www.copyright.gov/timeline/timeline_1950-1997.html> accessed 18 October 2024.
235 Sec. 101 Title 17 of the United States Code (US).
236 Sec. 106a ibid.

the constitutionality of that protection was affirmed following the 1884 US Supreme Court's decision in *Burrow-Giles v Sarony*.

Nonetheless, the journey of photographs in the US copyright law was not free from challenges since the law's strict formalities did not synchronise well with the nature of the medium. By the 1909 Copyright Act, photographs were treated similarly to other protected works, but there was a special provision that, in a way, sanctioned the use of photographs without permission by newspapers. The legislators were quick to allow newspapers to use photographs due to the nature of both works, yet they were reluctant to offer special rules for copyright registration of photographs. By the 1976 Copyright Act, the law treated photographs like other classes of protected works without exceptions or special rules that single photographs out or seek to address certain types of photographs in particular.

Copyright in photographs still presents a complex matter. Copyright law increasingly struggles to reconcile concepts such as authorship, originality, and the boundaries between ideas and expressions with photographic works. The US Copyright Code did not attempt to define what constitutes a photograph since it considered it a class of copyright-protected works without the need for a definition. This was in stark contrast with the UK copyright law, where the extension of copyright protection to photographs followed attempts to define what constitutes a photograph side by side with intense debates regarding the artistic capability of photography and whether or not it was worthy of copyright protection.

# 5 Authorship and Photographs

## 5.1 Introduction

This chapter is divided into two parts. The first part examines the concept of authorship in copyright law with reference to photographs. The second part will critically examine and compare authorship in the context of photographic works in Anglo-American copyright law.

This chapter unfolds in the following structure: First, it begins with a discussion of the literature surrounding authorship for the purposes of copyright law. The first part aims to illuminate the fact that even though authorship was a key concept that justified copyright protection, it eluded a firm consensus regarding its meaning in copyright law. This plays an essential part in forming the discussion in the later chapters pertaining to the proposed sui generis approach for photographic works' copyright protection.[1]

In the second part, this chapter examines the definition of photographs in Anglo-American copyright law before analysing their approach to authorship in photographs. Afterwards, this chapter delves deeper into the concept of authorship in order to identify the Anglo-American courts' approach to photographs' copyright authorship.

This chapter focuses only on authorship and avoids examining originality. The courts often use originality and authorship interchangeably. However, even though they are closely linked, the two concepts are distinct. Originality in the context of photographs is examined in a subsequent dedicated chapter.[2] Therefore, to highlight the subtle difference between these two concepts, this chapter only focuses on the concept of authorship in the context of photographic works. It conceptualises authorship as the road that may lead to originality.

## 5.2 The Concept of Authorship

Authors are considered as one of the core building blocks of copyright law from which the basic tenets of the scope of protection were drawn. Copyright scholars affirmed the importance of authorship as an integral part of copyright law, being a

1 See Chapter 9.
2 See Chapter 6.

DOI: 10.4324/9781003586555-5

necessary element for the establishment of copyright in any protected work as well as one of the rationales employed for the legitimacy of the bundle of rights granted by copyright.[3] Despite that, the copyright laws of various countries shied away from providing a clear and concrete definition of authorship for the purposes of copyright.[4] Even the premier convention on copyright law, the Berne Convention, does not address the figure of the author beyond superficial treatment despite its utmost importance to copyright protection.[5]

The reluctance to provide a clear definition of authors in the Berne Convention, whose primary purpose was to provide a universal standard of protection to authors, was perplexing. This is because even the expression of "literary and artistic works" was explained in a way that defines its boundaries, yet the term "authors" was not, in any meaningful way, addressed sufficiently.[6] Legal scholars argued that the definition of "authors" was intentionally left out in order to accommodate different views regarding authorship within the Berne Convention by leaving the matter for each member state to define within their jurisdiction.[7] Still, this justification does not lessen the fact that the Berne Convention's central subject was not defined in any shape or form and was simply referred to as "authors" without setting out what was meant by the term for the purposes of the convention.

Whenever there is a valid copyright, there must be an author behind it. Such a fundamental figure in copyright regimes was strikingly difficult to define with

3 See: Jane C Ginsburg, "The Concept of Authorship in Comparative Copyright Law" (2003) 52 DePaul Law Review 1063, 1064; Lionel Bently, "Copyright and the Death of the Author in Literature and Law" (1994) 57 The Modern Law Review 973, 980; Peter Jaszi, "Toward a Theory of Copyright: The Metamorphoses of 'Authorship'" (1991) 1991 Duke Law Journal 455, 466, 467; Mark Rose, *Authors and Owners: The Invention of Copyright* (Harvard University Press 1993) 2; Mireille van Eechoud, "Voices near and Far" in Mireille van Eechoud (ed), *The Work of Authorship* (Amsterdam University Press 2014) 7; Lionel Bently and Laura Biron, "Discontinuities between Legal Conceptions of Authorship and Social Practices. What, If Anything, Is to Be Done?" in Mireille van Eechoud (ed), *The Work of Authorship* (Amsterdam University Press 2014) 237; Niva Elkin-Koren, "Does Discursive Authorship Justify User Rights?" (2018) 9 Jurisprudence 174, 177; Shyamkrishna Balganesh, "The Folklore and Symbolism of Authorship in American Copyright Law" (2016) 54 Houston Law Review 403, 404, 430.

4 Ginsburg, "The Concept of Authorship in Comparative Copyright Law" (n 3) 1066, 1069; Balganesh (n 3) 430.

5 Berne Convention for the Protection of Literary and Artistic Works 1886; Jane C Ginsburg, "People Not Machines: Authorship and What It Means in the Berne Convention" (2018) 49 IIC – International Review of Intellectual Property and Competition Law 131, 131; Alina Ng Boyte, "The Conceits of Our Legal Imagination: Legal Fictions and the Concept of Deemed Authorship" (2013) 17 New York University Journal of Legislation and Public Policy 707, 743; Ginsburg, "The Concept of Authorship in Comparative Copyright Law" (n 3) 1069; Sam Ricketson and Jane C Ginsburg, *International Copyright and Neighbouring Rights: The Berne Convention and Beyond* (2 edition, OUP Oxford 2006) 358, 369.

6 Article 2, Berne Convention for the Protection of Literary and Artistic Works; Ginsburg, "People Not Machines" (n 5) 131.

7 Ginsburg, "The Concept of Authorship in Comparative Copyright Law" (n 3) 1069; Ginsburg, "People Not Machines" (n 5) 131; Ricketson and Ginsburg (n 5) 358, 369.

certainty amidst different theories and different kinds of works of authorship.[8] Scholars who have examined the concept of authorship and its development across human history have found three prominent views of authorship that identify the author's position in the act of authorship.[9] The first view regards the author's activities as imitative, guided by the desire to create replicated forms of reality.[10] The second view, often referred to as the idea of the romantic author, posits that the author is individually inspired to create original works that embody his personality.[11] The third view, which recently gained traction, regards authorship as a collaborative and collective endeavour in contrast to the individual romantic author notion of authorship.[12] Collective or collaborative authorship reflects the modern creative environment popularised by the advent of the internet in that authors engage with other authors to produce works that only came about due to the collaborative nature of the internet (e.g. Remixes, memes).[13]

All of these views about authorship left their traces on copyright law, but none more so than the romantic notion of authorship, which featured predominantly within copyright law's rendition of authorship.[14] Scholars such as Peter Jaszi, Martha Woodmansee, and James Boyle traced the development of the romantic author idea and argued that the romantic author notion was highly prevalent in

8 See: Oren Bracha, "The Ideology of Authorship Revisited: Authors, Markets, and Liberal Values in Early American Copyright" (2008) 118 The Yale Law Journal 186, 188, 189; Jessica Reyman, "The Rhetoric of Intellectual Property" 188, 8, 11–13, 19; Ginsburg, "The Concept of Authorship in Comparative Copyright Law" (n 3) 1066; Erlend Lavik, "Romantic Authorship in Copyright Law and the Uses of Aesthetics" in Mireille van Eechoud (ed), *The Work of Authorship* (Amsterdam University Press 2014) 57.

9 See: Bracha (n 8) 188, 189; Reyman (n 8) 11–13; Ginsburg, "The Concept of Authorship in Comparative Copyright Law" (n 3) 1066; Lavik (n 8) 57; see also: Sean Burke (ed), *Authorship: From Plato to the Postmodern* (Edinburgh University Press 1995); Shyamkrishna Balganesh, "Causing Copyright" (2017) 117 Columbia Law Review 1, 9; Jisuk Woo, "Genius with Minimal Originality: The Continuity and Transformation of the Authorship Construct in Copyright Case Law Regarding Computer Software" (2004) 15 Albany Law Journal of Science & Technology 109, 111,112; Boyte (n 5) 758.

10 Reyman (n 8) 11. See also: Burke (n 9).

11 Reyman (n 8) 11. See also: Burke (n 9); Jaszi (n 3) 455,463; Lavik (n 8) 45, 46; Martha Woodmansee, "The Genius and the Copyright: Economic and Legal Conditions of the Emergence of the 'Author'" (1984) 17 Eighteenth-Century Studies 425, 426, 427.

12 Bently (n 3) 985; Margaret Chon, "The Romantic Collective Author Copyright and Creativity: Perspectives on Originality, Authorship, and Expression January 27, 2012" (2011) 14 Vanderbilt Journal of Entertainment and Technology Law 829, 831; Anne Jamison, "Collaboration v. Imitation: Authorship and the Law" (2006) 18 Law and Literature 199, 203, 216; see also Jack Stillinger, *Multiple Authorship and the Myth of Solitary Genius* (OUP Oxford 1991).

13 Chon (n 12) 838; Alina Ng, "When Users Are Authors: Authorship in the Age of Digital Media" (2009) 12 Vanderbilt Journal of Entertainment and Technology Law 853, 860, 861, 864; Elena Cooper, "Reassessing the Challenge of the Digital An Empirical Perspective on Authorship and Copyright" in Mireille van Eechoud (ed), *The Work of Authorship* (Amsterdam University Press 2014) 175; see also: Daniela Simone, *Copyright and Collective Authorship: Locating the Authors of Collaborative Work* (Kindle edition, CUP Cambridge 2019).

14 Jaszi (n 3) 471; Ginsburg, "The Concept of Authorship in Comparative Copyright Law" (n 3) 1065; Bracha (n 8) 189; Lavik (n 8) 45, 46, 47.

our conception of authorship.[15] They argued that the notion of the romantic author highly influenced the development of copyright law and was the culprit behind many of the issues associated with copyright.[16] The romantic author's idea was also one of the driving philosophies behind the Berne Convention construction.[17]

On the other hand, Professor Lionel Bently opposed the view that the notion of the romantic author had the lion's share in influencing the development of copyright law and argued that the romantic author certainly played a role in the development of copyright law, but this was only alongside other economic, cultural, social, and legal factors. He further stated that the influence of the romantic author's notion on copyright law development was marginal compared to the other factors.[18] Moreover, Bently emphasised that authorship for the purposes of copyright law was not necessarily dependent on the meaning of authorship in literary theories.[19] While these different fields may influence each other, they are nevertheless designed to occupy different functions.[20] Considering the history of copyright law, one could argue that the scales tilt in favour of the view held by Professor Bently, in that the notion of the romantic author was only used as a vehicle to further different interests influenced by various other factors that played a bigger role in the course of copyright law development. Perhaps the push towards emphasising the position of authors was taken in order to decentralise the copyright marketplace instead of having it subject to the centralised control of publishers, as was the case in the early days of copyright.[21]

Furthermore, legal scholars argued that if the romantic author notion was the core ideal behind copyright, at least in Anglo-American law, then the provisions that designate an employer as an author could not be compatible with copyright law since the employer was by no means an author according to the romantic author's conception of authorship.[22] Moreover, the moral right of attribution, which was an author's right, was not available in the US copyright law except on certain conditions laid out in the Visual Artists Rights Act 1990.[23] Henceforth, copyright law

15 See: Jaszi (n 3); Woodmansee (n 11); James DA Boyle, "The Search for an Author: Shakespeare and the Framers In Re Shakespeare: The Authorship of Shakespeare on Trial" (1987) 37 American University Law Review 625.

16 See: Jaszi (n 3); Woodmansee (n 11); Boyle (n 15) 629.

17 Ricketson and Ginsburg (n 5) 20, 21, 44; Ginsburg, "People Not Machines" (n 5) 134.

18 Bently (n 3) 974, 979–981, 985; Lionel Bently, "R. v. the Author: From Death Penalty to Community Service – 20th Annual Horace S. Manges Lecture, Tuesday, April 10, 2007" (2008) 32 Columbia Journal of Law and the Arts 1, 21, 77–78.

19 Bently (n 3) 979, 982.

20 ibid.

21 Lyman Ray Patterson, *Copyright in Historical Perspective* (Vanderbilt University Press 1968) 43; Rose (n 3) 4, 49, 58, 135; Tim Wut, "On Copyright's Authorship Policy" [2008] The University of Chicago Legal Forum 335, 342.

22 Boyte (n 5) 710; Balganesh (n 3) 482; Ginsburg, "The Concept of Authorship in Comparative Copyright Law" (n 3) 1088; Lavik (n 8) 53; Jaszi (n 3) 485, 486.

23 Section 106A (a); Section 106A (b) provides that "Only the author of a work of visual art has the rights conferred by subsection (a) in that work" Title 17 of the United States Code (US); see: Jane

used the concept of authorship to facilitate the operation of the law and legitimise the level of protection afforded; looking at it from this angle may serve to justify the provisions that designate an employer as an author, even though such provisions are contrary to the romantic author notion of authorship that was arguably at the core of copyright.[24]

Due to the diverging views regarding authorship, Anglo-American copyright law opted to avoid providing a clear definition or theory of authorship for copyright law purposes.[25] Instead, the courts are left to develop copyright authorship slowly on a case-by-case basis. The courts struggled to remain consistent in their rendition of the element of authorship when faced with certain types of protected works that represent a real challenge to finding authorship.[26] The difficulties of locating copyright's authorship in a work vary in intensity depending on the kind of work produced. Photographic works are one specific category of protected works that proved very challenging, with its various applications, to the element of authorship in copyright law. The unique characteristics of photography, in that it reflects reality by simply fixing it with the aid of a mechanical process, represented a tremendous challenge to the element of authorship as it was understood in other literary and artistic works.

Photographic works illustrated the difficulties associated with locating authorship; these difficulties are often amplified depending on the type of photograph in question. While locating authorship for photographs that evidenced prior arrangement and setup may be relatively consistent, photographs that follow the "decisive moment"[27] style, which demands no prior arrangement or setup, may prove to be a pressing challenge to the consistency of locating authorship in photographs for the purposes of copyright. This was because when copyright protection extended to photographs, as we explored in the previous chapters about the history of Anglo-American photographic copyright,[28] the technology was vastly different and demanded a sufficient level of skill and prior arrangement to create high-quality photographs. In other words, at the time when copyright protection was extended to photographs, photographic technologies required long exposure times and were not capable of depicting motion or scenes without prior arrangements. Photographers had to adjust the camera, prepare the shoot, and make prior arrangements to assemble the subjects where they had to remain still for the duration needed to complete the necessary exposure to fix the desired image. The extension of copyright

C Ginsburg, "The Right to Claim Authorship in U.S. Copyright and Trademarks Law" (2004) 41 Houston Law Review 263.

24 Boyte (n 5) 710–711; Bently (n 3) 979, 982; Woo (n 9) 125.

25 Ginsburg, "The Concept of Authorship in Comparative Copyright Law" (n 3) 1066.

26 ibid.

27 The French photographer Henri Cartier-Bresson's coined the term "the decisive moment" to refer to a style of photography that depicts balanced scenes without the photographer's involvement. See Nadya Bair, "The Decisive Network: Producing Henri Cartier-Bresson at Mid-Century" (2016) 40 History of Photography 146, 148.

28 See Chapters 2–4.

protection to photographs was rationalised by analogising these activities associated with picture making with the process of writing and painting to justify protecting photographs; this was along with a desire to remunerate the cost and reward the skill and labour that went into creating high-quality photographs.[29]

However, the current state of photographic technologies vastly differs from what it once was during the 19th century. Modern digital photography is hardly limited by resources, a feature that lessened the need to employ judgement on each individual photograph and popularised the continuous shooting technique. Continuous shooting, employed mainly by photojournalists and sports photographers, refers to photographers' tendency to take a large number of photographs and then later go through the pile of photographs captured to select the most pleasing one.[30] It often relegates the photographer's judgement while capturing these individual photographs to a minimum; each individual photograph is most often captured without requiring much thought. At a later stage, the photographs would be examined in order to select the most desired photographs out of the collection, a task that might even be taken without the original photographer's involvement.[31] Furthermore, digital cameras come equipped with a variety of software that takes care of many tasks that had once required the expertise of a skilled photographer.[32] The authorial process of writing or painting to produce a work has not, in essence, changed at all from the time when the products of writings and paintings became copyright-protected works. The same was certainly not true with the process of photography, where copyright protection was extended during a time when photography required sufficient skill and prior arrangement, along with other tasks, to evidence copyright's authorship. In contrast, modern digital photography regulated most of the tasks that had once required a skilled photographer to be nothing more than mechanical tasks that do not require prior conceptualising for a photograph to be "authored."

29 See Part 1 regarding the history of photographs' copyright. See also: HC, *Copyright (Work of Art) Bill Deb 20 March 1862*, vol 165 (Hansard 1862) col 1891.

30 Sean Gentry, "Tip: Generally Only Share About 5 Photos From Any Set of Pictures" (*PetaPixel*, 3 May 2013) <https://petapixel.com/2013/05/03/why-you-should-generally-only-show-5-photos-from-any-set/> accessed 18 October 2024; "What Is Continuous Shooting?" (*Canon Australia*) <https://www.canon.com.au/explore/glossary/continuous-shooting> accessed 18 October 2024.

31 Scott Kelby, "So, How Many 'Keepers' Do You Get From a Shoot? – Scott Kelby's Photoshop Insider" (*ScottKelby*, 15 October 2013) <https://scottkelby.com/so-how-many-keepers-do-you-get-from-a-shoot/> accessed 18 October 2024.

32 The photographer Bob Martin said "along came the technology that has engulfed this marketplace. You've got autofocus, auto-exposure, auto-flash and god knows what other toys…That has levelled the playing field to a degree – I could now teach a monkey to photograph Linford Christie with both feet off the ground." In Matt Higgs, "Top of the Game – An Interview with Sports Photographer Bob Martin" (*Wex Photo Video*, 22 September 2017) <https://www.wexphotovideo.com/blog/interviews/top-of-the-game--an-interview-with-sports-photographer-bob-martin/> accessed 18 October 2024.

The element of authorship in photographs is often challenging to find when employing the same authorship tests of other literary or artistic works.[33] That is because photographs are viewed as something that reflects reality in nature, and nature is not "authored"; the photographer was not "individually inspired" to originate the scene depicted in nature.[34] The photographer's role can be argued to be, for the vast majority of photographs, no more than the individual who fixed reality as reflected by the camera.[35] Thus, the romantic author notion may prove challenging to contend with in a manner that supports the extension of copyright protection to engulf the vast majority of photographs. A new understanding of authorship that takes into account the different characteristics of different types of works may lend itself well to untraditional works of authorship, such as photographs.

## 5.3 Photographs in Anglo-American Copyright Law

### *5.3.1 What Is a Photograph?*

What we refer to as photographs may be quite obvious in this day and age; however, defining what is meant by photographs to differentiate them from other visual works, such as paintings, may prove helpful for the purposes of copyright law. This is because if one opted to develop a sui generis approach to photographic works, defining what constitutes photographic works would be essential for its sound application. After all, when photographs were first introduced, some intellectuals defined them as paintings made by artists collaborating with the sun or as the product of an operator facilitating the sun to do its magic on chemicals in order to fix images.[36]

The UK Copyright, Designs and Patents Act 1988 (hereafter referred to as CDPA 1988) classified photographs as artistic works and defined photographs within the category of graphic works in Section 4(2)(b) as "a recording of light or other radiation on any medium on which an image is produced or from which an image may by any means be produced, and which is not part of a film."[37] The CDPA 1988 provided a direct definition of photographs that was quite inclusive of various types and applications of photography that range from the standard digital or analogue photographs to holograms and more specialised applications

33 See Part 1 regarding the history of photographs' copyright. See also: *Burrow-Giles Lithographic Co v Sarony, 111 US 53 (1884)*; *Nottage v Jackson (1883) 11 QBD 627.*

34 Ginsburg, "The Concept of Authorship in Comparative Copyright Law" (n 3) 1075; Christine Haight Farley, "The Lingering Effects of Copyright's Response to the Invention of Photography" (2004) 65 University of Pittsburgh Law Review 385, 393, 395, 396.

35 Farley (n 34) 395, 396.

36 Beaumont Newhall, *The History of Photography: From 1839 to the Present* (5 edition, The Museum of Modern Art, New York 1984) 75. See also: William Henry Fox Talbot, *The Pencil of Nature*, vol 1 (Library of Alexandria 1969) 12.

37 Section 4(2)(b) Copyright, Designs and Patents Act 1988 (UK).

such as medical imaging, X-rays, and scientific photographs.[38] However, it does not seem that modified photographs fit this definition because they include elements not recorded by light; hence, such altered images may be considered to fall under graphical works instead.[39] Furthermore, Section 4 clearly distinguishes photographs from films. Therefore, even a one-frame capture from a film would be considered infringing on the film itself and not regarded as a separate photograph as established in Section 17(3).[40]

In comparison, US copyright law does not define photographs specifically but considers them works of authorship under the general criteria of "pictorial, graphic, and sculptural works."[41] This vague treatment of photographs may raise issues regarding the classification of modified photographs, as it is unclear whether such works still fall under the criteria of photographs or are generally regarded as pictorial works. The courts do regard digitally modified images, those adding new elements and alterations to photographs, as graphical works.[42] However, it is not clear whether digitally enhanced photographs, without adding new elements, such as enhancing only the existing features of a photograph, are still considered photographs.[43] This lack of definition may seem inclusive at first; however, some types of photographs, such as X-rays and similar works produced by mechanical processes or photographs taken for utilitarian purposes, are denied copyright protection.[44] This is contrary to UK copyright law, which protects such photographs if it is evidenced that sufficient skill and labour were expended to produce them.[45]

One of the earliest attempts in the US copyright law to define what is meant by photographs was to be found in the case of *Edison v Lubin*,[46] regarding a copyright dispute involving motion picture films, where Buffington J stated that the process of "reproduction is a light-written, and therefore a photographic picture or

38 Nicholas Caddick, Gwilym Harbottle and Uma Suthersanen, *Copinger and Skone James on Copyright* (18 edition, Sweet & Maxwell Ltd 2020) paras 3–142. See also: *Nottinghamshire Healthcare NHS Trust v News Group Newspapers Ltd [2002] EWHC 409 (Ch).*

39 Caddick, Harbottle and Suthersanen (n 38) paras 3–142. See also: *Temple Island Collections Ltd v New English Teas Ltd [2012] EWPCC 1.*

40 Section 17(3) state that "Copying in relation to a film includes making a photograph of the whole or any substantial part of any image forming part of the film." Copyright, Designs and Patents Act 1988 (UK); Caddick, Harbottle and Suthersanen (n 38) paras 3–142. See also: *Football Association Premier League Ltd v QC Leisure (No2) [2008] FSR 32* 800.

41 Sec. 101 Title 17 of the United States Code (US).

42 *Reinsdorf v Skechers USA, 922 FSupp2d 866 (2013)* 871, 872 (Involving modified photographs); *Tiffany Design, Inc v Reno-Tahoe Specialty, Inc, 55 FSupp2d 1113 (1999)* (Involving digitally enhanced photographs); *Cariou v Prince, 714 F3d 694 (2013)* (Additions to photographs by appropriation artist transformed the photographs into painting).

43 *Tiffany Design, Inc v Reno-Tahoe Specialty, Inc, 55 FSupp2d 1113 (1999)* (n 42).

44 Sec. 313.2 *Compendium of U.S. Copyright Office Practices, Third Edition (US)* (US Copyright Office 2014); *Pohl v MH SUB I, LLC, 314 FSupp3d 1225 (2018)* (US). cf. *Nottinghamshire Healthcare NHS Trust v News Group Newspapers Ltd [2002] EWHC 409 (Ch)* (n 38) (UK).

45 *Nottinghamshire Healthcare NHS Trust v News Group Newspapers Ltd [2002] EWHC 409 (Ch)* (n 38); *Walter v Lane [1900] AC 539*; Caddick, Harbottle and Suthersanen (n 38) paras 3–233, 3–234.

46 *Edison v Lubin, 122 F 240 (1903).*

photograph."[47] Motion picture films were protected first as a collection of photographs in the pre-1912 US copyright law before being formally protected under its own category in 1912.[48] This is in stark contrast to the United Kingdom's approach which specifically excluded still images that are part of a film from being classified as photographs for the purposes of copyright law.[49] Perhaps the definition of photographs from *Edison v Lubin*[50] was not given any importance since it was provided in order to justify extending copyright protection to motion picture films at the time when the case was decided. An express distinction between stills from films and photographs is absent from the US copyright law, perhaps because the US legislators did not bother to define photographs, let alone distinguish them from other related works. However, the US Copyright Code did distinguish between motion pictures and other audio-visual works in that images in works classified as motion pictures must "impart an impression of motion."[51]

One could see that the approach taken by the two jurisdictions differed in addressing photographs. The United Kingdom provides a clear definition of photographs under the CDPA 1988, differentiating photographs from still images taken from films, while the United States only classified photographs under a specific umbrella without delving into a direct objective definition of what was meant by photographs. Perhaps defining photographs was not particularly important for their copyright protection since, within the two jurisdictions, the level of copyright protection offered to photographs was, once established, nothing less than other protected works of authorship produced using different mediums of expression.[52] In fact, it could be argued that acknowledging that photographs were works of authorship was all that was needed because the current UK and US copyright law does not differentiate between photographs and other works of authorship when assessing their copyrightability.

Nonetheless, a clear definition of what a photograph means in the context of copyright law may prove beneficial in the face of new technologies. This is because, based on the definition, a work would be classified under a certain group, where copyright concepts such as authorship and originality could be shaped specifically for the characteristics of that class of works. This would strengthen the consistency of these concepts instead of straining them by stretching their interpretation to all mediums of expression in a one-size-fits-all approach. Hence, one can argue that the direction the CDPA 1988 took regarding the definition of photographs was the better approach. Based on the work's definition, the same concepts

47 ibid at 242.

48 *Compendium of U.S. Copyright Office Practices, Third Edition (US)* (n 44) 18.

49 Section 4(2)(b) Copyright, Designs and Patents Act 1988 (UK).

50 *Edison v Lubin, 122 F. 240 (1903)* (n 46).

51 Sec. 101 Title 17 of the United States Code (US); Section 808.2(A) *Compendium of U.S. Copyright Office Practices, Third Edition (US)* (n 44).

52 Sec. 102 Title 17 of the United States Code (US); Section 1 Copyright, Designs and Patents Act 1988 (UK).

of copyright could be applied, with different standards, depending on the class of work presented.

Nevertheless, the issues associated with defining what constitutes a work of copyright in the context of photographic works may not be entirely due to the nature of photographs as much as to the nature of the overarching concept of work as the subject matter of copyright law. What constitutes a work of copyright is increasingly showing strain in the face of claims involving different kinds of creative endeavours that range from the taste of foods,[53] design of gardens,[54] face makeup,[55] football matches,[56] a designed scene,[57] stormtrooper helmet,[58] fragrance,[59] clothing,[60] to an actress's performance in a film[61] with more challenges expected to arise as creative practices evolve. Yan Han Lee argues that part of this strain, at least in the UK copyright law, was due to the persistence of the formalist conception of copyright works, particularly the influence of a text-centred model on what constitutes a work.[62] She argues that the co-existence of the dematerialised model for copyright works alongside the formalist text-centred model rendered copyright law unstable. On the other hand, Jonathan Griffiths argued that the strict adoption of a fully dematerialised conception of work, beyond its material perceptible boundaries, might risk depriving the courts of the tools used to limit and resist the undue expansion of copyright law to all immaterial properties.[63] Hence, the persistence of the formalist approach to copyright work alongside a dematerialised conception of copyright work may have served as a vital balancing tool that prevents the overexpansion of copyright law.

Scholars stressed that the parameters of the concept of work in copyright law are far from a settled matter beyond its emphasis on the intangible aspect of copyright works.[64] Jani McCutcheon argued that it may be nearly impossible to define

53 *(C-310/17) Levola Hengelo BV v Smilde Foods BV [2019] ECDR 2* (CJEU).

54 *Kelley v Chicago Park Dist, 635 F3d 290 (2011)* (US).

55 *Merchandising Corp of America Inc v Harpbond, [1983] FSR 32 (1981)* 11 (UK).

56 *Football Association Premier League Ltd and Others v QC Leisure and Others (C-403/08)* and *Karen Murphy v Media Protection Services Ltd (C-429/08) [2012] FSR 1* (UK).

57 *Creation Records Ltd v News Group Newspapers Ltd [1997] EMLR 444* (UK).

58 *Lucasfilm Ltd v Ainsworth, [2011] FSR 41* (UK).

59 Kamiel Koelman, "Copyright in the Courts: Perfume as Artistic Expression?" (*WIPO*, September 2006) <https://www.wipo.int/wipo_magazine/en/2006/05/article_0001.html> accessed 18 October 2024.

60 *(C-683/17) Cofemel v G-Star Raw CV [2020] ECDR 9* (CJEU); see also: *Response Clothing Ltd v Edinburgh Woollen Mill Ltd [2020] FSR 25* (UK).

61 *Garcia v Google, Inc, 786 F3d 733 (2015)* (US).

62 Yin Harn Lee, "The Persistence of the Text: The Concept of the Work in Copyright Law – Part I" (2018) 1 Intellectual Property Quarterly 22; Yin Harn Lee, "The Persistence of the Text: The Concept of the Work in Copyright Law – Part 2" 2 Intellectual Property Quarterly 107.

63 Jonathan Griffiths, "Dematerialization, Pragmatism and the European Copyright Revolution" (2013) 33 Oxford Journal of Legal Studies 767.

64 See e.g. Justine Pila, "An Intentional View of the Copyright Work" (2008) 71 The Modern Law Review 535; Griffiths (n 63); Michael Madison, "IP Things as Boundary Objects: The Case of the Copyright Work" (2017) 6 Laws 13; Justine Pila, "Pluralism, Principles and Proportionality in Intel-

the boundaries of a work of copyright independently from copyright subsistence requirements. She argues that a work of copyright "may only be possible to define it as the intellectual conception of an author that emerges from copyright's exclusionary filtration process."[65] Hence, authorship, originality, idea/expression dichotomy, and fixation act as refineries that elevate subject matters into being classified as works for copyright law purposes.

Indeed, the Court of Justice of the European Union (CJEU) cases of *Levola Hangelo*[66] and *Cofemel*[67] arguably lend credence to McCutcheon's observation. The CJEU held that the concept of work, even though it was not defined, was to be regarded as an EU autonomous concept with uniform interpretation across EU member states. It declared that for a subject matter to be classified as a work, two cumulative conditions must be satisfied. The first condition dictates that the subject matter must be original in that it is the author's own intellectual creation.[68] The second condition states that only the expression of the author's own intellectual creation classifies a subject matter as a work for copyright purposes.[69] For these two conditions to be assessed on the subject matter under question, the subject matter need not be expressed in a permanent form, but it must be expressed in a sufficiently precise and objective manner that makes the subject matter firmly identifiable without any room for subjectivity.[70] Thus, instead of conceptualising copyright works separately from copyright requirements, a work is classified effectively as such for copyright purposes through the proxy of originality and the idea/expression dichotomy. This is despite the fact that the CJEU stressed that the concepts of work and originality are distinct concepts that should remain separate.[71]

It seems that the CJEU does not perceive work as separate from the copyrightability requirements. It merely sees it as a subject matter that only constitutes a work by satisfying the aforementioned conditions that could make up part of the work but do not necessarily constitute the whole expression. This may lead to potential complications down the line where a work may be dissected to what constitutes elements of the work and what does not, instead of identifying the copyright eligibility of the work and then locating the original elements of expression that constitute the protectable elements of the author's own intellectual creation. It seems paradoxical that a subject matter is only classified as work if it is the original expression of the author's own intellectual creation and must simultaneously be identified as

lectual Property" (2014) 34 Oxford Journal of Legal Studies 181; Jani McCutcheon, "Shape Shifters: Searching for the Copyright Work in Kinetic Living Art" (2017) 64 Journal of the Copyright Society of the USA 63; Pamela Samuelson, "Evolving Conceptions of Copyright Subject Matter" (2016) 78 University of Pittsburgh Law Review 17.

65 McCutcheon (n 64).

66 *(C-310/17) Levola Hengelo BV v Smilde Foods BV [2019] ECDR 2* (n 53).

67 *(C-683/17) Cofemel v G-Star Raw CV [2020] ECDR 9* (n 60).

68 *(C-310/17) Levola Hengelo BV v Smilde Foods BV [2019] ECDR 2* (n 53) para 36.

69 ibid 37.

70 ibid 40–41.

71 ibid H9, AG46.

work prior to the originality assessment. This is because a work can be uncopyrightable or copyrightable based on satisfying the conditions of copyrightability, but it remains a work that warrants copyright assessment. For example, if a photograph is not original, it should not cease to be a work altogether. It might be an uncopyrightable work but should not be degraded to a non-work. This is also true for entrepreneurial works such as sound recordings, broadcasts, and other related rights since they do not require originality to be covered by copyright. Hence, the CJEU's conception of work is problematic.

## 5.4 Authorship in Photographs

Photographs, owing to their unique nature, represent an ideal point of discussion to strip down the concept of authorship to its core. This part examines authorship in Anglo-American copyright law within the context of photographs in order to identify the essence of a photograph's copyright authorship. It is generally accepted in copyright law that the author's status, although a question of law, is a matter closely related to facts and cannot be assigned to a person purely by virtue of an agreement.[72] The facts determining the authorship of copyright might be approached differently depending on the jurisdiction.

EU copyright law has not addressed authorship directly, but it alluded that an author must be a human author involved in the intellectual creation of the work.[73] In the United Kingdom, the CDPA 1988 addressed authorship directly, placing a clear distinction between it and copyright ownership. CDPA 1988 Section 9 points out that the term "author" refers to "the person who creates [the work]" of authorship.[74] This simple definition of the term "author" is useful as a starting point since it clearly differentiates between the first owner of a copyright, who in normal circumstances would also be the author,[75] and the person designated as the author of the copyrighted work. However, in cases involving joint authorship, Daniela Simone observed that the courts tend to conflate joint ownership with joint authorship out of fear that too many joint owners could prevent the work from being exploited, effectively rendering joint authorship with a higher threshold than single authorship.[76] Despite this, the courts' fear is warranted and has support from the field of economics in what is known as the Gridlock economy, described by Professor Michael A. Heller as "a free market paradox. When too many people own pieces

72 Caddick, Harbottle and Suthersanen (n 38) paras 4–16.

73 Article 4, Directive 96/9/EC of 11 March 1996 on the legal protection of databases [1996] OJ L77/20; Recital 16, Directive 2006/116/EC of 12 December 2006 on the term of protection of copyright and certain related rights [2006] OJ L372/12; *(C-277/10) Martin Luksan v Petrus van der Let, [2012] EU:C:2012:65* [67–72]; see: Johannes Fritz, "The Notion of 'Authorship' Under EU Law—Who Can Be an Author and What Makes One an Author? An Analysis of the Legislative Framework and Case Law" (2024) 19 Journal of Intellectual Property Law & Practice 552.

74 Section 9(1) Copyright, Designs and Patents Act 1988 (UK).

75 Section 11(1), (2) ibid.

76 Simone (n 13) 9, 15, 249–250.

of one thing, cooperation breaks down, wealth disappears, and everybody loses."[77] In situations involving a work made as a work for hire,[78] the employer is only designated as the first owner of the copyright in the work and not as the author of the work under the CDPA 1988.[79] Such distinction is not clearly present in the US Copyright Code, which does not differentiate between first copyright ownership and copyright authorship.[80]

The US Copyright Code Sec. 201 only affirms that the author is the initial copyright owner in a work but does not define what was meant by an "author."[81] For works made for hire,[82] Sec. 201(b) regards the author, for the purposes of copyright law, to be the employer.[83] Therefore, the employer was not only the initial owner of a work made for hire but also the author of that work. Perhaps what led to this construction was the fact that the question regarding what constitutes an author of copyright was shunned entirely in the US Copyright Code. Hence, Sec. 201(b) confers the title of "author" to, quite often, a non-author party.[84] In contrast, the United Kingdom clearly separates the two in the sense that, in a work made for hire, only the first ownership of copyright was given to the employer, and the author designation remains with the person who actually created the work.[85] In other words, it could be argued that authorship in the US copyright law was used merely as a legal fiction to facilitate the operation of copyright law to advance the purposes of Section 8 of the US Constitution, "To promote the Progress of Science and useful Arts."[86]

The UK CDPA 1988 expanded further on authorship by clarifying who is to be regarded as an author according to the specific classification of the work in

77 Michael Heller, *The Gridlock Economy: How Too Much Ownership Wrecks Markets, Stops Innovation, and Costs Lives* (1 edition, Basic Books 2008) xiv.

78 Section 11(2) provides that a work made for hire is a work made in the course of employment by an employee, the first copyright ownership in such works vest in the employer. For commissioned works, an agreement should specify whether the work is made for hire, in the absence of such agreement the copyright ownership vest in the author. Copyright, Designs and Patents Act 1988 (UK). See: *Infection Control Enterprises Ltd v Virrage Industries Ltd [2009] EWHC 2602 (QB).*

79 Section 11(2) Copyright, Designs and Patents Act 1988 (UK).

80 Section 201(a), (b) Title 17 of the United States Code (US); for more on the development of copyright ownership of photographs, see: Ysolde Gendreau, "Copyright Ownership of Photographs in Anglo-American Law" (1993) 15 European Intellectual Property Review 207.

81 Sec. 201(a) Title 17 of the United States Code (US).

82 Sec. 101 defines work made for hire as "(1) a work prepared by an employee within the scope of his or her employment; or (2) a work specially ordered or commissioned for use…if the parties expressly agree in a written instrument signed by them that the work shall be considered a work made for hire." ibid.

83 Sec. 201(b) ibid. See: *Community for Creative Non-Violence v Reid, 490 US 730 (1989)*; *Marco v Accent Pub Co, Inc, 969 F2d 1547 (1992)*; *Schiller & Schmidt, Inc v Nordisco Corp, 969 F2d 410 (1992).*

84 *Marvel Characters, Inc v Kirby, 726 F3d 119 (2013)* (Held that, for the purposes of copyright law, the statutory author is presumed to be the employer in a work made for hire).

85 Section 11(2) Copyright, Designs and Patents Act 1988 (UK).

86 Article 1 Section 8, US Constitution. See also: Boyte (n 5).

question.[87] It provides that for computer-generated works, and it could be argued by analogy that it covers works produced by mechanical means such as medical imaging, the author "shall be taken to be the person by whom arrangements necessary for the creation of the work are undertaken."[88] One could see that the incline towards causality was firmly evident from the CDPA's treatment of authorship, yet Section 9 does not elaborate further on the characteristics that make one specific causal element the principal cause as to designate a certain person as an author over other causal elements attributed to other individuals.[89] Photographic works are an ideal example of this issue since, oftentimes, the subjects depicted might have contributed an undeniable causal element to how the photograph was depicted.

Moreover, the person who directed the photographer to create the work can be argued to be a necessary element that led to the creation of the work; equally, the one who fixed the work may also claim that his act was the necessary causal element for the work's creation. In fact, one of the earliest cases involving photographic works that had directly dealt with this issue predates the CDPA 1988 by more than a century. In *Nottage v Jackson (1883)*,[90] the court concluded that the "person nearest" to be the author is the one who "has superintended the arrangement, who has actually formed the picture by putting the people into position and arranging the place in which the people are to be – the man who is the effective cause of that."[91] The "effective cause," however, must be an active principal to be regarded as an author.[92] Thus, merely pressing the shutter does not necessarily make a person an author nor make him the "effective cause" of a photograph in UK copyright law since other factors linked closely to the level of control, skill, and independent artistic judgement are also given adequate consideration.[93]

The UK case *Creation Records Ltd v News Group Newspapers Ltd [1997]*[94] involved a dispute regarding the authorship of unauthorised photographs, taken by the defendants, that depict a subject matter created by the plaintiffs. The photograph is the album cover of *Be Here Now* (1997) by Oasis, which features a surreal outdoor scene with a white Rolls-Royce submerged in a swimming pool, with the lead singer leaning on a vintage scooter, and various scattered objects like a clock, a globe, and a gramophone. The plaintiffs claimed that they owned the copyright in the photographs, which were taken independently by the defendants, by virtue of being the ones who created the scene that was the subject matter of the photograph.

87 Section 9 Copyright, Designs and Patents Act 1988 (UK).
88 Section 9(3) ibid.
89 On copyright causality, see: Balganesh (n 9).
90 *Nottage v Jackson (1883) 11 Q.B.D. 627* (n 33).
91 ibid 632 (Brett MR). See: *Wooderson v Raphael Tuck & Sons (1887) 4 TLR 57.*
92 *Melville v Mirror of Life Co [1895] 2 Ch 531*; *Nottage v Jackson (1883) 11 Q.B.D. 627* (n 33); see Chapter 3.
93 *Ray v Classic FM Plc [1998] ECC 488* ("penmanship did not have to be exercised," actual physical involvement is not needed to establish joint authorship as long as the contribution was significant enough); see also: *Slater v Wimmer [2012] 2 WLUK 475.*
94 *Creation Records Ltd v News Group Newspapers Ltd [1997] EMLR 444* (n 57).

The plaintiffs created the scene by arranging specific objects to make an album cover for the rock band Oasis. The plaintiffs claimed that the scene attracted copyright as an artistic work, and because they created the unique subject matter, they owned all photographs that depict the subject they created. The court held that the scene was not a copyrightable subject matter since it was ephemeral and did not fit into the categories of works protected by copyright under the CDPA. The judge stated that in normal circumstances involving photographs, "the creator of a photograph is the person who takes it."[95] He elaborated on the photographs' authorship by stating that:

> where one person sets up the scene to be photographed (the position and angle of the camera and all the necessary settings) and directs a second person to press the shutter release button at a moment chosen by the first,...it would be the first, not the second, who creates the photograph. There may also be cases of collaboration between the person behind the camera and one or more others in which the actual photographer has greater input, although no complete control of the creation of the photograph, in which case it may be a work of joint creation and joint authorship.[96]

Lloyd J further clarified that if the subject matter was not, itself, a copyright, then anyone could take a photograph of the same subject matter without risking infringement on other photographs, even if the photographs virtually depicted the subject matter in a similar manner provided that there was no direct copying involved.[97]

Similarly, on the US side, the Eleventh Circuit Court of Appeals came to the same conclusion in *Leigh v Warner Bros., Inc (2000)*,[98] where it was held that copyright protection does not extend to cover the photographer's choice of the subject matter, it only extends to cover his expression reflected by his creative choices regarding elements such as "lighting, shading, timing, angle."[99]

In both jurisdictions, it was clear that the subject matter of photographs was not seen as part of the authored elements in photographs. However, the authorial process associated with preparing the subject, and other pre-shutter activities, that amount to the author's expression was firmly considered for locating authorship in photographs.[100] One does not dispute that the law had to take this approach since, otherwise, there would be a detrimental monopoly on subject matters for photographs based on the priority of appropriation. Furthermore, to reconcile the

95 at 450 (per Lloyd J.) ibid.

96 at 450, 451 (per Lloyd J.) ibid.

97 at 450 ibid; see also: *Shelley Films Ltd v Rex Features Ltd [1994] EMLR 134* (it was argued that copyright could exists in a film set provided it evidenced clear artistic craftsmanship).

98 *Leigh v Warner Bros, Inc, 212 F3d 1210 (2000)*.

99 at 1215 ibid.

100 *Burrow-Giles Lithographic Co. v Sarony, 111 US 53 (1884)* (n 33) (US); *Nottage v Jackson (1883) 11 Q.B.D. 627* (n 33) (UK).

mechanical aspects of the medium of photography with copyright law, the courts emphasised the pre-shutter stage to stress the human reliant side of photography when copyright protection was extended to photographs.[101]

The US Copyright Code addressed authorship only in the context of joint authorship and work-for-hire situations, but it did not address authorship directly.[102] The US Copyright Code Sec. 102(a) provides that:

> Copyright protection subsists…in original works of authorship fixed in any tangible medium of expression, now known or later developed, from which they can be perceived, reproduced, or otherwise communicated, either directly or with the aid of a machine or device.[103]

The term "works of authorship" was also not defined in the Copyright Code; it was only to be understood as a flexible category that includes any work that evidences authorship and, consequently, is eligible for copyright protection.[104] Photographs are considered one of the works of authorship that are covered by copyright protection despite the fact that what constitutes authorship was not defined in the US Copyright Code.

Professor Russ VerSteeg attempted to define authorship as per US copyright law and managed to boil down copyright authorship to three core criteria that evaluate the authorship of a given work. VerSteeg posits that:

> In order to be a copyright author…one must meet three criteria: (1) the putative author must communicate something that is original; (2) that original something communicated must be expression; and (3) the putative author must communicate that original expression (a) directly himself through the act of fixation or (b) indirectly by authorizing another to fix it.[105]

The point of focus in this chapter is directed towards what constitutes a "putative author" in the context of photographs. The landmark US Supreme Court case of *Burrow-Giles Co v Sarony (1884)*[106] defined the term "author" by stating that "An author…is 'he to whom anything owes its origin; originator; maker; one who completes a work of science or literature.'"[107] The *Burrow-Giles case* affirmed that photographs are works of authorship where the elements of authorship were to be

101 Farley (n 34) 389–391, 427.

102 See: Sec. 101, 201 Title 17 of the United States Code (US).

103 Sec. 102(a) ibid.

104 Melville Nimmer and others, *Cases and Materials on Copyright and Other Aspects of Entertainment Litigation Including Unfair Competition, Defamation, Privacy by The Late Melville B. Nimmer* (LexisNexis 2012) 52.

105 Russ VerSteeg, "Defining 'Author' for Purposes of Copyright" (1996) 45 The American University Law Review 1323, 1342.

106 *Burrow-Giles Lithographic Co. v Sarony, 111 US 53 (1884)* (n 33). See also: Chapter 4, Section 4.4.

107 ibid at 58 per Miller J.

derived from the process undertaken by the putative author to create the work.[108] The Supreme Court expressly stated that their view regarding authorship in photographs aligned with the view of the judges in the UK case *Nottage v Jackson*.[109]

While the *Burrow-Giles case* remains good law, the US Supreme Court's case *Community for Creative Non-Violence v Reid (1989)*[110] provided another important definition of the term "author." In *Reid*, a copyright ownership claim was brought involving a commissioned sculpture; the court defined authorship in a manner identical to the UK CDPA 1988. The US Supreme Court stated that "As a general rule, the author is the party who actually creates the work, that is, the person who translates an idea into a fixed, tangible expression entitled to copyright protection."[111] Thus, US copyright law's general definition of the term "author" is seemingly identical to the one found in the UK CDPA 1988; it emphasised that the person who produced the fixed expression of the work into existence was the author of that work.

The *Burrow-Giles case*[112] remains the primary authority on copyright authorship in the context of photographs. The case continues to be followed rigorously by the courts.[113] The emphasis regarding authorship was always placed on the pre-shutter activities, which was the stage where human authorship was to be located in photographs.[114] The US Supreme Court in *Burrow-Giles* did not elaborate on the level of pre-shutter activities needed, nor whether authorship exists in ordinary photographs; these matters were left to the courts to decide on a case-by-case basis. Nonetheless, the level of pre-shutter activities needed was not high, as even pointing the camera and pressing the shutter to take a spontaneous photograph was found to be subject to copyright.[115]

In *Time Inc v Bernard Geis Associates (1968)*,[116] frames from the film of President Kennedy's assassination, known as the Zapruder film (named after Abraham Zapruder, the one who filmed it), were reproduced by sketches in a book about the incident. The copyright owner in the Zapruder film, the plaintiffs, sued the book author and the publishers for reproducing the frames in the book without authorisation. The defendants questioned the copyrightability of the Zapruder film itself, arguing that it does not have a valid copyright since it was not original as it appropriates the film's subject matter. The court held in favour of the plaintiffs and stated that the Zapruder pictures evidenced authorship since:

108 See Chapter 4.

109 *Burrow-Giles Lithographic Co. v Sarony, 111 US 53 (1884)* (n 33) at 61; *Nottage v Jackson (1883) 11 Q.B.D. 627* (n 33).

110 *Community for Creative Non-Violence v Reid, 490 U.S. 730 (1989)* (n 83).

111 ibid at 731.

112 *Burrow-Giles Lithographic Co. v Sarony, 111 US 53 (1884)* (n 33).

113 See: Farley (n 34).

114 See: ibid 447, 448.

115 *Otto v Hearst Communications, Inc WL 6510801 (2018) 25* (A photograph by a wedding guest of President Trump crashing a wedding was deemed to have a valid copyright regardless of its factual nature).

116 *Time Inc v Bernard Geis Associates, 293 FSupp 130 (1968)*.

> The Zapruder pictures in fact have many elements of creativity. Among other things, Zapruder selected the kind of camera (movies, not snapshots), the kind of film (color), the kind of lens (telephoto), the area in which the pictures were to be taken, the time they were to be taken, and (after testing several sites) the spot on which the camera would be operated.[117]

Hence, the court was forced to look at the activities prior to the film's capture to showcase the human involvement evidenced in the choices taken by Zapruder, even elements involving the camera's specifications, that led to the film's creation in the manner it was depicted. Professor Christine Farley observed that:

> In order to find authorship, the court could not list pre-shutter choices, but had to engage with the technology much more so than had previously been done. The court recognized that the selection of the camera, film and lens were creative choices. However, as if that were not enough, the court went on to assert that Zapruder had selected the location from which to film and the time to film. Thus, the court felt it necessary to describe happenstance as creative direction in order to come within Burrow-Giles. The court describes in detail all of the testing of spots from which to film as if to absurdly suggest that Zapruder had nothing but aesthetic considerations in mind.[118]

The fact that *Burrow-Giles* expressed doubt over the authorship of ordinary candid photographs was not enough to negatively affect the approach of US courts regarding the copyrightability of candid photographs.[119] Even candid photographs could express authorship in elements such as the camera angle, lighting, arrangements, and choice of equipment, among others, to a sufficient degree that renders the photograph in question a work of authorship.[120] Thus, one could argue that the vast majority of photographs would likely be regarded as works of authorship except for those found to exhibit nothing beyond utilitarian features.[121] UK copyright law was even more inclusive when it comes to various types of photographs since even the most candid photographs could evidence authorship if they involved sufficient skill, labour, and judgement.[122]

117 ibid 143.

118 Farley (n 34) 447.

119 See: *SHL Imaging, Inc v Artisan House, Inc, 117 FSupp2d 301 (2000)*; *Time Inc v Bernard Geis Associates, 293 FSupp 130 (1968)* (n 117); *Los Angeles News Service v Tullo, 973 F2d 791 (1992)*.

120 Ibid; see *Fitzgerald v CBS Broadcasting, Inc, 491 FSupp2d 177 (2007)*.

121 *Custom Dynamics, LLC v Radiantz LED Lighting, Inc, 535 FSupp2d 542 (2008)* (Held that photographs taken for "purely utilitarian purposes" are not copyrightable); *Pohl v MH SUB I, LLC, 314 FSupp.3d 1225 (2018)* (n 44) (Held that before-and-after photographs for dental work was not a work of authorship).

122 *Walter v Lane [1900] AC 539* (n 45); *Antiquesportfolio.com Plc v Rodney Fitch & Co Ltd [2001] FSR 23*; *Nottinghamshire Healthcare NHS Trust v News Group Newspapers Ltd [2002] EWHC 409 (Ch)* (n 38).

The famous US case, often referred to as the *monkey selfie case*,[123] may prove helpful in illustrating the difference in approach regarding photographs' authorship between the two jurisdictions. The case involved photographs taken by a monkey after several arrangements made by the photographer, David Slater, who set out the camera parameters and left the camera in a place where the monkeys would be able to interact with it and press the shutter to capture the photographs.[124] People for the Ethical Treatment of Animals claimed that the monkey, Naruto, was the author of the selfie photograph and consequently the copyright owner. The Ninth Circuit Court of Appeal dismissed the case and affirmed that an animal could not be regarded as an author under copyright law.[125] It was long established in both jurisdictions that only works created by humans are subject to copyright; as a result, works created solely by non-humans are not subject to copyright and are considered in the public domain.[126]

The US court did not question Slater's status as an author, so it was not clear whether US courts would consider Slater as the author of the photograph based on the facts surrounding its creation. Many commentators expressed opposing views regarding the photograph's copyrightability, pushing the Copyright Compendium to directly address this case to indicate that the monkey selfie photograph does not contain copyright.[127] Others criticised the US Copyright Compendium Section 313.2, which expressly mentioned an example that provides that "a photograph taken by a monkey" would be found to lack authorship, and they argued that it prioritises fixation over human creative input.[128] However, one could argue that the fear was

123 *Naruto v Slater, 888 F3d 418 (2018)*; *Naruto v Slater No 15-cv-04324-WHO, 2016 WL 362231 unreported (2016)* 4.

124 *Naruto v Slater, 888 F3d 418 (2018)* (n 124); see how Slater described the photographs' creation David J Slater, "Sulawesi Monkey – Photographs by David J Slater" (*DJS Photography*) <http://www.djsphotography.co.uk/original_story.html> accessed 18 October 2024.

125 *Naruto v Slater, 888 F3d 418 (2018)* (n 124).

126 See: *Cummins v Bond [1927] 1 Ch 167* (UK); *Naruto v Slater, 888 F3d 418 (2018)* (n 124) (US); Sec. 313.2 *Compendium of U.S. Copyright Office Practices, Third Edition (US)* (n 44).

127 See: Andrés Guadamuz, "The Monkey Selfie: Copyright Lessons for Originality in Photographs and Internet Jurisdiction" (2016) 5 Internet Policy Review <https://policyreview.info/articles/analysis/monkey-selfie-copyright-lessons-originality-photographs-and-internet-jurisdiction> accessed 18 October 2024; Andres Guadamuz, "Can the Monkey Selfie Case Teach Us Anything about Copyright Law?" (*WIPO Magazine*, February 2018) <http://www.wipo.int/wipo_magazine/en/2018/01/article_0007.html> accessed 18 October 2024; Sophie Duffy and Dori Ann Hanswirth, "Monkey See, Monkey Do…Monkey Own? The Curious Case of Naruto v Slater" (*Lexology*, 20 September 2017) <https://www.lexology.com/library/detail.aspx?g=5deafb41-a767-4319-bf93-cff2bc5d726a> accessed 18 October 2024; "Monkey 'Selfie' Picture Sparks Wikipedia Copyright Row" (*ITV News*, 6 August 2014) <https://www.itvcom/news/2014-08-06/wikipedia-refuses-to-delete-photo-as-monkey-owns-it/> accessed 18 October 2024; Andrew Orlowski, "Cracking Copyright Law: How a Simian Selfie Stunt Could Make a Monkey out of Wikipedia" (*The Register*, 24 August 2014) <https://www.theregister.co.uk/2014/08/24/wikipedia_monkey_selfie_backfire/> accessed 18 October 2024.

128 See: Jennifer L Muse, "Monkeys and Elephants and Koalas, Oh My! Is Originality Still the Touchstone of Authorship in the United States Copyright Law?" (2015) 97 Journal of the Patent and Trademark Office Society 736, 740, 756.

overstated. The US Copyright Compendium does not refer strictly to fixation, as a critical point of authorship, but to creation since, in normal circumstances, the creator of a photograph was usually the one who had taken it.[129] Fixation was indeed an important element in solidifying and expressing the ideas created in a tangible form within reach of the law, but it does not represent the core of copyright. After all, it was clearly stated in *Feist*,[130] that "The sine qua of copyright is originality."[131]

Notwithstanding, it would be more likely that the court would regard Slater as the photograph's author since he superintended the work and made the necessary arrangements for the work to be created, as evidenced by his description of how the photograph was taken.[132] The fact that he did not press the shutter, which usually in normal circumstances would be enough to designate the photographer as an author, did not necessarily pre-empt his claim of authorship as it was established in the US case of *Lindsay v RMS Titanic (1999)*.[133]

In *RMS Titanic*, the plaintiff wrote up the screenplay and directed the creation of undersea footage, but he did not actively occupy the role of the cameraman or the photographer, who was capturing the images following the plaintiff's instructions. Thus, they argued that the plaintiff did not operate the cameras, nor did he control the timing of the capture, and therefore, he was not the author of the photographs. The defendants argued that the photographers were the authors of the undersea footage. The court responded by stating that the fact that the plaintiff did not operate the camera nor was he present at the site to be photographed, in the sense that he did not participate with the photographers, does not automatically invalidate his claim of authorship. The court stated that:

> All else being equal, where a plaintiff alleges that he exercised such a high degree of control over a film operation – including the type and amount of lighting used, the specific camera angles to be employed, and other detail-intensive artistic elements of a film – such that the final product duplicates his conceptions and visions of what the film should look like, the plaintiff may be said to be an "author" within the meaning of the Copyright Act.[134]

Thus, even if the author did not physically perform the actions necessary to fix his expression or, in the case of the monkey selfie photographs, press the shutter to capture the selected subject, that fact alone does not invalidate his authorship claim provided that the claimant showed a sufficient level of control over the creation process.[135] As a result, it seems more likely that Slater would be the author since he

129 See: VerSteeg (n 106) 1339, 1349–1351, 1362.

130 *Feist Publications, Inc v Rural Telephone Service Co, Inc, 499 US 340 (1991).*

131 ibid 345 (per Justice O'Connor).

132 Slater (n 125); *Burrow-Giles Lithographic Co. v Sarony, 111 US 53 (1884)* (n 33).

133 *Lindsay v Wrecked and Abandoned Vessel RMS TITANIC, not reported WL 816163 (1999)* 7.

134 ibid 5.

135 See: *Andrien v Southern Ocean County Chamber of Commerce, 927 F2d 132 (1991)* ("writers are entitled to copyright protection even if they do not perform with their own hands the mechanical tasks of putting the material into the form distributed to the public").

was the creator of the monkey photographs, even though he did not fix the photographs by pressing the shutter himself, regardless of the fact that an animal cannot hold a copyright. In principle, a photographer should not be denied authorship because he employed an unorthodox creative process to produce his photograph. Furthermore, what Slater did was not drastically different from what sports photographers and artists did when they employed assistants to help them create their works.[136] Andy Warhol relied on his assistants to do the actual physical labour to create his artworks per his instructions and approval.[137] Bob Martin, the famous sports photographer, regularly uses assistants to create his photographs of sporting events.[138] Slater set the camera parameters himself and incited the monkeys to play with the camera; hence, his effort resulted in the creation of the monkey selfie photographs.

The fact that there was an indeterminate element, since the monkey was the one who took the photograph at that specific timing and angle and did not act on instruction, was still not enough to render the work uncopyrightable or incapable of authorship.[139] In the US case of *Alfred Bell & Co v Catalda Fine Arts (1951)*,[140] Frank J pointed out that the fact that some elements in a work were stumbled upon does not automatically diminish the work's authorship. He stated that "A copyist's bad eyesight or defective musculature, or a shock caused by a clap of thunder, may yield sufficiently distinguishable variations. Having hit upon such a variation unintentionally, the 'author' may adopt it as his and copyright it."[141] Therefore, the fact that the monkey represented the indeterminate factor that caused the photographs to be created in that manner should not be enough to deprive Slater of authorship because he "adopted" these variations as his own and produced the photographs in question.

Likewise, Slater can almost certainly be regarded as the author of the photographs under UK copyright law due to his involvement as the principal creator in setting the camera's parameters and maintaining control over the creation process despite the fact that one could argue that the monkey had the final say in terms of

136 Henri Neuendorf, "Art Demystified: Why Do Contemporary Artists Use So Many Studio Assistants?" (*artnet News*, 14 July 2016) <https://news.artnet.com/art-world/art-demystified-the-use-of-assistants-549284> accessed 30 September 2021; Sanja Lazic, "Artist Assistants – The World Of Anonymous Helpers" (*Widewalls*, 4 November 2014) <https://www.widewalls.ch/magazine/the-world-of-artist-assistants-feature-november-2014> accessed 18 October 2024.

137 Ian Youngs, "The Artist Making 'New' Warhol Paintings, 30 Years after His Death" (18 October 2017) <https://www.bbc.com/news/entertainment-arts-41634496> accessed 18 October 2024.

138 Frank Walker, "Meet a Pro: Elite Sports Photographer Bob Martin" (*Adorama Learning Center*, 5 August 2016) <https://www.adorama.com/alc/meet-a-pro-elite-sports-photographer-bob-martin> accessed 18 October 2024.

139 For more discussion regarding indeterminacy and authorship see: Alan L Durham, "The Random Muse: Authorship and Indeterminacy" (2002) 44 William and Mary Law Review 569.

140 *Alfred Bell & Co v Catalda Fine Arts, 191 F2d 99 (1951).*

141 ibid 105.

angle and timing.[142] That was because the act of pressing the shutter, while important, was not enough in itself to evidence a photograph's authorship. The relevant contribution to a photograph must be more significant.[143]

On the issue of non-human involvement and copyright authorship, it would be hard to find mechanically produced works, such as surveillance footage, copyrightable following the US copyright law approach to authorship.[144] That is because the operations that produce such works are, more often than not, automatic, hardly requiring human involvement. The US courts would most likely not find surveillance footage as works of authorship because it is produced automatically without human control.[145] It was established that authorial contributions must go beyond simple mechanical tasks, such as setting a camera on a tripod without further involvement, and must include dynamic contributions that evidence authorship, such as camera angles, lighting, and composition.[146]

On the other hand, prior to the CJEU harmonisation of certain copyright concepts, UK courts regarded skill, labour, and judgement alone as legitimate grounds to establish copyright in a work.[147] Therefore, even though authorship in automatically recorded footage, such as surveillance footage, hardly exhibits conscious authorial activities, UK courts would deem such works as worthy of copyright protection provided that sufficient investment of skill, labour and judgement was established to the court's satisfaction.[148] Nonetheless, following the shift brought by the EU Information Society Directive (InfoSoc)[149] and the CJEU case of *Infopaq,*[150]*,* the skill, labour and judgement must be of the kind that evidences the author's own intellectual creation in order for the work to be eligible for copyright protection.[151]

## 5.5 Joint Authorship and Photographs

If authorship was a difficult concept to grasp with uniformity across different jurisdictions and categories of works, even for a sole claim of authorship, one may

142 Slater (n 125); see: *Nottage v Jackson (1883) 11 Q.B.D. 627* (n 33); *Melville v Mirror of Life Co [1895] 2 Ch. 531* (n 92); *Slater v Wimmer [2012] 2 WLUK 475* (n 93); *Cummins v Bond [1927] 1 Ch. 167* (n 127).

143 *Ray v Classic FM Plc [1998] E.C.C. 488* (n 93); *Nottage v Jackson (1883) 11 Q.B.D. 627* (n 33); *Melville v Mirror of Life Co [1895] 2 Ch. 531* (n 92).

144 Section 313.2, 906.6 *Compendium of U.S. Copyright Office Practices, Third Edition (US)* (n 44).

145 Farley (n 34) 388.

146 See: *Easter Seal Society for Crippled Children and Adults of Louisiana, Inc v Playboy Enterprises, et al, 815 F2d 323 (5th Cir 1987)* 337; *Lindsay v Wrecked and Abandoned Vessel R.M.S. TITANIC, not reported WL 816163 (1999)* (n 134).

147 *Walter v Lane [1900] AC 539* (n 45); *Express Newspapers Plc v News (UK) Ltd [1991] FSR 36.*

148 Art 9 (3) does not deny authorship for computer generated works, which are not different in principle than works created through an automatic process. Copyright, Designs and Patents Act 1988 (UK); see: *Walter v Lane [1900] AC 539* (n 45).

149 Directive 2001/29/EC of 22 May 2001 on the harmonisation of certain aspects of copyright and related rights in the information society [2001] OJ L167/10.

150 *(C-5/08) Infopaq International A/S v Danske Dagblades Forening [2009] ECR I-6569.*

151 See Chapter 6.

expect that joint authorship would be even more perplexing to pin down. However, in reality, joint authorship was given its fair share of principles and rules that clarify the elements that must be present in a joint work by the putative authors to substantiate their joint authorship claim. In a way, one could even argue that the rules regarding joint authorship are more nuanced than copyright law treatment of the concept of authorship itself.

### *5.5.1 Joint Authorship and Photographs in the United Kingdom*

Section 10(1) of the UK CDPA 1988 provides that works of joint authorship are "produced by the collaboration of two or more authors in which the contribution of each author is not distinct from that of the other author or authors."[152] All joint authors are considered "tenants in common"[153], they all hold shares in the joint work and have the same rights over the copyright subject to any contractual agreements between the owners.[154] Furthermore, permissions from all joint owners are required for the exploitation of the joint work; one owner cannot license a joint work without the consent of all other joint owners.[155] This is a particularly troublesome rule that affects the distribution of power since if 10 out of 11 joint authors approved a particular use of the joint work, the last joint author would have immense power to deny that use, potentially overriding the wishes of all other joint authors.[156]

A common intention to be regarded as joint authors of a work is not considered a requirement for joint authorship.[157] Hence, there is a level of flexibility regarding what constitutes a joint author depending on the level of skill and labour expended and the facts of the case.[158] This flexibility is due to joint authorship being fact specific even though authorship is ultimately a question of law.[159] For a person to be considered a joint author of a work, his contribution must be significant and non-trivial compared to the other authors in order to be regarded as a joint author

152 Art 10(1) Copyright, Designs and Patents Act 1988 (UK).

153 "In the case of a tenancy in common, the deceased co-owner's share passes with the rest of his estate." DL Marchese, "Joint Ownership of Intellectual Property" [1999] European Intellectual Property Review 364, 364.

154 *Powell v Head (1879) 12 Ch D 686* 690 (per Jessel MR); Marchese (n 154) 364; Caddick, Harbottle and Suthersanen (n 38) paras 4–46, 4–47, 4–48, 4–49, 5–198, 5–199.

155 Art 173(2) Copyright, Designs and Patents Act 1988 (UK); Caddick, Harbottle and Suthersanen (n 38) paras 5–199, 5–202; Marchese (n 154) 367; *Powell v Head (1879) 12 Ch. D. 686* (n 155); *Cescinsky v George Routledge & Sons, Limited [1916] 2 KB 325*; *Ray v Classic FM Plc [1998] E.C.C. 488* (n 93); *Fisher v Brooker [2009] 1 WLR 1764.*

156 Bently and Biron (n 3) 260.

157 *Beckingham v Hodgens [2003] EWCA Civ 143.*

158 Elena Cooper, "Joint Authorship in Comparative Perspective: Levy v Rutley and Divergence between the UK and USA Part I" (2014) 62 Journal of the Copyright Society of the USA 245, 248; Bently and Biron (n 3) 238.

159 Simone (n 13) 42–43.

of the work in question.[160] Daniela Simone points out that the contribution must be more than de minims intellectual contribution of the right kind, the kind relevant to copyright, in order to qualify an individual as a joint author of the work under question.[161] Furthermore, each contribution must not be distinct, in that each separate contribution should not be a separate work, such as a book consisting of separate essays authored by different authors, but the contributions must be integrated, such as films, for example.[162] Therefore, the contributions must form an integral part of the work in the pursuit of a common design for it to be considered a work of joint authorship.[163]

*Martin v Kogan (2020)*[164] concerned a dispute regarding the joint authorship of a screenplay where the plaintiff claimed joint authorship by virtue of her contribution to the screenplay even though she was not involved in writing the final draft that was adapted into a film. On appeal, the Court of Appeal stated that, based on Section 10(1), four main requirements must be satisfied to evidence joint authorship in a work. These requirements were collaboration, authorship, contribution, and non-distinctness of contribution.[165] The Court of Appeal reviewed the law on joint authorship and boiled down the principles to the following tenets. Firstly, the work must be created by collaboration in the pursuit of a common design "where the labour of working out the design was shared."[166] The court highlighted that the intention to create a work of joint authorship was not a requirement for joint authorship.[167] Secondly, a joint author must have expanded a significant amount of skill and labour towards creating the work. Thirdly, only authorial contributions are considered relevant for joint authorship, and what counts as authorial depends on the nature of the work in question.[168] A contribution was considered "authorial" if, taking into consideration the work's nature, it shows "a significant amount of the skill and intellectual creation, in terms of free, expressive and creative choices, which went into the making of the work.."[169] Hence, a mere contribution of ideas is not considered sufficient grounds for joint authorship.[170] Finally, each author's contribution must not be distinct from that of the other authors, and any contribution that did not become an integral part of the work would not be included in

160 Caddick, Harbottle and Suthersanen (n 38) paras 4–49; see: *Cala Homes (South) Ltd v Alfred McAlpine Homes East Ltd (No1) [1995] FSR 818*; *Hadley v Kemp [1999] EMLR 589*; *Godfrey v Lees [1995] 3 WLUK 278*; *Brighton v Jones [2004] EMLR 26*; *Levy v Rutley (1870–71) LR 6 CP 523*; *Fylde Microsystems Ltd v Key Radio Systems Ltd [1998] FSR 449*.

161 *Kogan v Martin [2020] EMLR 4* 8, 13, 254.

162 Caddick, Harbottle and Suthersanen (n 38) paras 4–46, 4–50.

163 ibid 4–46, 4–49, 4–50; *Godfrey v Lees [1995] 3 WLUK 278* (n 161).

164 *Kogan v Martin [2020] EMLR 4* (n 162).

165 ibid 31.

166 ibid 32 quoting Levy v Rutley (1871) L.R. 6 C.P. 523.

167 ibid H7, 48.

168 ibid H9, 42.

169 ibid.

170 ibid 34.

the assessment of a joint authorship claim.[171] Furthermore, the court stressed that penmanship is not on its own a determinative factor for joint authorship, nor the fact that one of the authors had the final say be considered as a piece of conclusive evidence that determines joint authorship.[172] The Court of Appeal held that the first instance judge erred in law and ordered a retrial of the case. Upon retrial, it was held that the screenplay was a work of joint authorship, and consequently, the plaintiff was entitled to the copyright as a joint author.[173]

In the context of photographs, one could argue that the subject of a photograph may have contributed a significant amount to be regarded as a joint author. After all, the subject collaborated with the photographer, and his contribution to the photograph was integral in the pursuit of a common design with the photographer. The subject was a significant contribution that was not distinct or separate from the way the photograph was depicted. However, a close inspection of UK copyright law would reveal that this was not the case, it would be very hard to claim joint authorship in photographs by virtue of being the one depicted.[174] Even if the subject forced his way into the photograph out of the photographer's control, commonly referred to as "photobomb," the photographer was the one who eventually approved and produced the photograph.

In other words, the photographer was the one who chose to appropriate that indeterminate factor to his advantage by virtue of being the author of the photographs in question. Equally, the mere fact that the photographer was the one who pressed the shutter to capture the photograph would not necessarily elevate his status to be a joint author in a photograph directed and controlled by another person acting as the principal photographer and creator.[175] Even if a photo-shot session was considered a team effort and general instructions and suggestions were given to the photographer, the nature surrounding the work's environment was not itself evidence for joint authorship if the contributions were not sufficiently significant as it was illustrated in *Celebrity Pictures Ltd v B Hannah Ltd [2012]*.[176]

Pre-shutter activities are given primary importance in a photograph's authorship. This is because they occur during the creation of a photograph where the objects depicted in a photograph are subject to the photographer's control, such as

171 ibid H10, 47.

172 ibid 37–38, 41, 51.

173 *Martin v Kogan (NO2) [2021] FSR 10.*

174 *Celebrity Pictures Ltd v B Hannah Ltd [2012] EWPCC 32*; *Levy v Rutley (1870–71) L.R. 6 C.P. 523* (n 161).

175 See: *Melville v Mirror of Life Co [1895] 2 Ch. 531* (n 92); *Ray v Classic FM Plc [1998] E.C.C. 488* (n 93) ("penmanship did not have to be exercised"); *Fylde Microsystems Ltd v Key Radio Systems Ltd [1998] FSR 449* (n 161) (Merely mechanical acts such as testing or proofreading was not enough to support joint authorship claim).

176 *Celebrity Pictures Ltd v B Hannah Ltd [2012] EWPCC 32* (n 175) (Held that "Neither the very general instructions [the photographer] was given as to the type of photographs required, nor the very general acceptance that there was a team effort involved in the photo-shoot, was sufficient to make anyone else other than [the photographer] the first owner of the copyright in the photographs as the creator of the photographs…").

his control over the timing, angle, and camera parameters. It was established that for the authorship of joint works, the contribution of each potential joint author was assessed at the time of the work's creation process when that contribution formed an integral part of the work in question. Therefore, post-shutter work, such as alterations using Photoshop or other apps that enhance images as usually performed in fashion photography,[177] does not make a person a joint author of the original photograph since the enhancements as a contribution were made after the photograph was created and not during its creation even if it was in the pursuit of a common design.[178] Such alterations and enhancements might be considered derivative works, which refer to works derived from other existing original works.[179] The CDPA 1988 does not address derivative works from artistic works, it only addresses adaptation of literary, dramatic or musical works in Section 21.[180] However, it is established that a derivative artistic work, such as a photograph of a copyrighted work, may contain separate copyright from the original work's copyright if the differences were deemed significant and exhibit skill, labour and judgement sufficient enough to create separate copyright for the derivative work in question.[181]

### *5.5.2 Joint Authorship and Photographs in the United States*

Unlike the UK copyright law, the US copyright law adopted a different conception of joint authorship built on the element of "intent," in that the putative joint authors must have intended to be joint authors when they merged their copyrightable contributions to form a joint work, that intent had to be manifested at the time the work was created.[182] Sec. 1 of the US Copyright Code defines "joint work" as "a work prepared by two or more authors with the intention that their contributions be merged into inseparable or interdependent parts of a unitary whole.."[183] The general rule was that all joint authors are co-owners and, unlike the United

177 *Body Evolution – Model Before and After Photoshop* (Directed by Timothy David, 2013) <https://www.youtube.com/watch?time_continue=59&v=xKQdwjGiF-s> accessed 18 October 2024; Aaron Horwath, "Photoshop, Models, and the Law: How Far Is Too Far?" (*Pixelz*, 19 April 2016) <https://www.pixelz.com/blog/photoshop-models-laws/> accessed 18 October 2024; Rhiannon Lucy Cosslett, "Thinner, Smoother, Better: In the Era of Retouching, That's What Girls Have to Be" *The Guardian* (8 September 2016) <https://www.theguardian.com/commentisfree/2016/sep/08/thinner-retouching-girls-image-manipulation-women> accessed 18 October 2024.

178 See: *Apple Corps Ltd v Cooper [1992] 12 WLUK 29* 293 ("It is clear that in the case of a photograph, the statutory vesting of copyright takes place at the moment at which the shutter is opened and light strikes the film").

179 Caddick, Harbottle and Suthersanen (n 38) paras 4–24.

180 See Art 21 Copyright, Designs and Patents Act 1988 (UK).

181 Caddick, Harbottle and Suthersanen (n 38) paras 3–197, 4–24, 4–37; *Sawkins v Hyperion Records Ltd [2005] EWCA Civ 565* [31, 82].

182 Section 505.1, 505.2 *Compendium of U.S. Copyright Office Practices, Third Edition (US)* (n 44); Mutual intent by the putative authors is required for joint authorship. See: *Childress v Taylor, 945 F2d 500 (1991)* 507, 509; *Erickson v Trinity Theatre, Inc, 13 F3d 1061 (1994)* 1068, 1069; *Thomson v Larson, 147 F3d 195 (1998)* 201.

183 Sec. 1 Title 17 of the United States Code (US).

Kingdom, each can exploit the copyright without the need to seek the consent of the other joint owners, provided that the obligation to account to the other joint owners regarding any profits made was respected.[184] This rule was subject to exceptions in circumstances where one exploitation may harm the other owners' rights or bind their interest in the work without their consent, such as conferring exclusive licences without the written consent of the other joint owners.[185] The contributions that form a joint work must be parts of a unitary whole.[186] These contributions may be "inseparable," in that they have no meaning alone, or "interdependent," where they can stand alone as works but are much more significant when integrated into other contributions to form a unitary whole.[187] Each contribution that forms the whole should be a copyrightable contribution. Contributions that consist of mere ideas or other uncopyrightable elements are not enough to support joint authorship status under copyright law, but they could be protected under contract law instead.[188]

In *Childress v Taylor (1991)*,[189] a playwright claimed to be the sole author of a play and brought a copyright infringement claim against the defendants. One of the defendants, an actress, disputed the sole authorship claim and asserted that she was a joint author of the play. On appeal, the Second Circuit Court of Appeal examined the law regarding joint authorship and affirmed that the playwright was the sole author of the work in question. The court rejected the notion that joint labour towards a common design was enough to support a joint authorship claim.[190] The court stressed that the "intention" at the time of the work's creation that copyrightable contributions are to be integrated into a unitary whole as a joint work was the "touchstone" of joint authorship.[191] That intent was to be evaluated during the time the contributions were created and whether both putative authors considered themselves joint authors based on the facts of the case. The court proceeded to give an example to illustrate the importance of the intent of the putative authors in establishing joint authorship:

> For example, a writer frequently works with an editor who makes numerous useful revisions to the first draft, some of which will consist of additions of copyrightable expression. Both intend their contributions to be merged into

184 Sec. 201 ibid; *Thomson v Larson, 147 F3d 195 (1998)* (n 183) 199; *Childress v Taylor, 945 F2d 500 (1991)* (n 183) 505; *Maurel v Smith, 271 F 211 (1921)* 214, 215; *Davis v Blige, 505 F3d 90 (2007)* 98, 99; For more on the difference between US and UK approach to joint authorship. See: Cooper (n 159).

185 *Davis v Blige, 505 F3d 90 (2007)* (n 185) 98, 99; *Thomson v Larson, 147 F3d 195 (1998)* (n 183) 205; *McKay v Columbia Broadcasting System, Inc, 324 F2d 762 (1963)* 3.

186 *Childress v Taylor, 945 F2d 500 (1991)* (n 183) 505.

187 ibid.

188 ibid 507; *Erickson v Trinity Theatre, Inc, 13 F3d 1061 (1994)* (n 183).

189 *Childress v Taylor, 945 F2d 500 (1991)* (n 183).

190 ibid 504.

191 ibid 505.

> inseparable parts of a unitary whole, yet very few editors and even fewer writers would expect the editor to be accorded the status of joint author, enjoying an undivided half interest in the copyright in the published work.... What distinguishes the writer-editor relationship... from the true joint author relationship is the lack of intent of both participants in the venture to regard themselves as joint authors.[192]

The court held that the playwright was the sole author of the play. The actress' assistance did not qualify her as a joint author, and the playwright did not share the actress' intention to be regarded as a joint author of the play.

In the context of photographs, it seems that the US approach to joint authorship lends itself well to photographs in a way that prevents depriving a photographer of his sole authorship status just because he depicted a person in a photograph, the "unitary whole." That is because the US copyright law clearly requires the element of intent by the putative authors of joint work to establish joint authorship.[193] A person who was the subject of a photograph would not succeed in a joint authorship claim solely by virtue of his contribution, evidenced by how he was depicted in the photograph. In other words, the subject matter of photographs is not normally entitled to the copyright of the photograph.[194] Only if the photograph's subject itself was a copyrighted work and the photograph was considered a derivative work where it could be found infringing on the copyrighted work depicted.[195] Thus, someone cannot claim to have contributed significantly to a picture because his physical features are depicted in the photograph.[196]

In *Natkin v Winfrey (2000)*,[197] professional photographers sued Oprah Winfrey and her production company for her use of photographs of herself in her book. The plaintiffs claimed they were the authors of the photographs since they were independent contractors, and they took the photographs during a live television show based on their own discretion regarding when and how to take the said photographs. The defendants claimed joint authorship because they hired the photographers and controlled most of the elements depicted in the pictures. Furthermore, they also claimed authorship over Winfrey's looks and expressions. Since all of the

192 ibid 507.

193 Sec. 101 Title 17 of the United States Code (US).

194 *Olan Mills, Inc v Eckerd Drug of Texas, Inc, Not Reported in FSupp WL 90605 (1989)* 3 ("The simple fact that an individual brings his own image to the studio is not enough to give that person a protectable property right in the portrait. The court finds no basis in law, or in facts of the summary judgment record, to conclude that the subject of a portrait is a co-creator of the photograph"); *Leigh v Warner Bros., Inc, 212 F3d 1210 (2000)* (n 99); *Caratzas v Time Life, Inc, Not Reported in FSupp WL 322033 (1992).*

195 *Cooley v Penguin Group (USA) Inc, 31 FSupp3d 599 (2014).*

196 *Toney v L'Oreal USA, Inc, 406 F3d 905 (2005)* at 910 ("A person's likeness – her persona – is not authored and it is not fixed. The fact that an image of the person might be fixed in a copyrightable photograph does not change this").

197 *Natkin v Winfrey, 111 FSupp2d 1003 (2000).*

aforementioned elements were depicted in the photographs, the defendants claimed to be joint authors by virtue of being the ones who supplied the subject matter for the pictures.[198] The court stated that for a claim of joint authorship to be substantiated, the contribution must be a copyrightable contribution. The defendants contributed non-copyrightable elements to the photographs since it was established in copyright law that the subject matter of a photograph was not normally copyrightable.[199] Thus, the court held that the plaintiffs, as the photographers, were the sole authors of the photographs in question.

In *Brod v General Pub Group, Inc (2002)*,[200] the author of a book on vintage televisions was sued by the photographer because it included his photographs. The court found that the author of the book had made significant contributions to the photographs due to the fact that he selected the specific vintage televisions to be photographed, arranged the subjects, suggested camera angles, and was involved in every step during the composition and creation of the photographs to the degree that evidence his intention to render himself as a joint author to the photographs.

In a similar but opposite case, *Clogston v American Academy of Orthopaedic Surgeons (1996)*,[201] a photographer claimed joint authorship to a medical textbook that included photographs he took. He claimed that his contribution and the fact that the book credited him for the photographs supported his joint authorship claim. The court held that the photographer was not a joint author of the book since there was no intention between both parties to regard the work as a joint work, and the fact that there was a collaboration does not, in itself, evidence joint authorship.

Therefore, in the context of photographs, merely selecting the subject matter to be photographed or being the subject matter of a photograph was not enough to support joint authorship claims.[202] In the same token, the sole fact that a person pressed the shutter does not make him automatically an author or even a joint author of the resulting work, provided that he did not exercise sufficient control over the creation process.[203] So even if a person "photobombed" a picture and contributed immensely to the way that photograph was depicted, the photographer would still have the stronger claim since he still controlled other aspects of the photograph's creation, and it was doubtful that there was an intention to be joint authors at the time of the photograph's creation. The fact that this element of the

198 ibid 1007, 1011.

199 ibid 1011.

200 *Brod v General Pub Group, Inc, 32 FedAppx 231 (2002).*

201 *Clogston v American Academy of Orthopaedic Surgeons, 930 FSupp 1156 (1996).*

202 See: *Olan Mills, Inc v Eckerd Drug of Texas, Inc, Not Reported in FSupp WL 90605 (1989)* (n 195); *Tang v Putruss, 521 FSupp2d 600 (2007)*; *Toney v L'Oreal USA, Inc, 406 F3d 905 (2005)* (n 197); *SHL Imaging, Inc v Artisan House, Inc, 117 FSupp2d 301 (2000)* (n 120); *Foster v Lee, 93 FSupp3d 223 (2015).*

203 *Tang v Putruss, 521 FSupp2d 600 (2007)* (n 203); *Robinson v Buy-Rite Costume Jewelry, Inc, Not Reported in FSupp2d (2004)*; *Lindsay v Wrecked and Abandoned Vessel R.M.S. TITANIC, not reported WL 816163 (1999)* (n 134); *Gillespie v AST Sportswear, Inc, Not Reported in FSupp2d (2001)* 6 ("a person need not hold the camera or push a button to be considered the author of a visual work, since one can exercise control over the content of a work without holding the camera").

photograph, which may give it its value, was beyond the intention and control of the photographer at the time of creation does not diminish his sole authorship status because he still appropriated this indeterminate element to his advantage.[204]

Accordingly, control, intention and copyrightable contributions are key elements to establish joint authorship in a photograph. An authorship claim is strengthened if a sufficient level of control over the creation process of a photograph during the pre-shutter activities, such as selecting the subject matter, camera angles, lighting, arrangement, timing, and composition, was evident.[205] These elements represent significant authorial contributions that support authorship claims in photographs. Moreover, the intention to be joint authors is a crucial element in joint authorship since the existence of collaboration does not automatically mean that the collaborators intended to be joint authors.[206] After all, most professional photographers employ assistants or collaborate with a team or with their subjects to create their photographs. This does not, in any way, diminish their sole authorship status since, most often, neither the subject nor the photographer intended to be joint authors.[207]

The pre-shutter activities and contributions are of great importance to joint authorship claims since they ensued at the time the photograph was created. On the opposite side, post-shutter work on photographs, despite being increasingly widespread among photographers,[208] was not considered important in normal circumstances when evaluating the authorship of a photograph.[209] That was because post-shutter work happens after the photograph was created. Even if the enhancements or additions gave the original photograph its value, the courts still look at the pre-shutter stage to determine the photographs' authorship. However, if there was an intention to be joint authors and merge the parties' contributions, the raw photograph and the added alterations, then joint authorship on the resulting image may be substantiated.[210] If there were no intention to be joint authors, the image

204 *Alfred Bell & Co. v Catalda Fine Arts, 191 F2d 99 (1951)* (n 141); see also: Durham (n 140).

205 *Brod v General Pub. Group, Inc, 32 Fed.Appx. 231 (2002)* (n 201); *Foster v Lee, 93 FSupp3d 223 (2015)* (n 203); *Olan Mills, Inc v Eckerd Drug of Texas, Inc, Not Reported in FSupp WL 90605 (1989)* (n 195); *Burrow-Giles Lithographic Co. v Sarony, 111 US 53 (1884)* (n 33); *Lindsay v Wrecked and Abandoned Vessel R.M.S. TITANIC, not reported WL 816163 (1999)* (n 134); *16 Casa Duse, LLC v Merkin, No 13-3865 (2d Cir 2015).*

206 *Reinsdorf v Skechers U.S.A., 922 FSupp2d 866 (2013)* (n 42); *Robinson v Buy-Rite Costume Jewelry, Inc, Not Reported in FSupp2d (2004)* (n 204); *Tang v Putruss, 521 FSupp2d 600 (2007)* (n 203); *Aalmuhammed v Lee, 202 F3d 1227 (2000).*

207 *Burrow-Giles Lithographic Co. v Sarony, 111 US 53 (1884)* (n 33). Sarony employed a cameraman during the creation of his photograph of Oscar Wilde. See Farley (n 34) at 434; *Foster v Lee, 93 FSupp3d 223 (2015)* (n 203).

208 *Body Evolution – Model Before and After Photoshop* (n 178); Horwath (n 178); Cosslett (n 178).

209 *16 Casa Duse, LLC v Merkin, No. 13-3865 (2d Cir. 2015)* (n 206); *Reinsdorf v Skechers U.S.A., 922 FSupp2d 866 (2013)* (n 42); *Tiffany Design, Inc v Reno-Tahoe Specialty, Inc, 55 FSupp2d 1113 (1999)* (n 42).

210 *Reinsdorf v Skechers U.S.A., 922 FSupp2d 866 (2013)* (n 42) 874; *16 Casa Duse, LLC v Merkin, No. 13-3865 (2d Cir. 2015)* (n 206); see also: *Aalmuhammed v Lee, 202 F3d 1227 (2000)* (n 207).

produced from post-shutter modifications would most likely be regarded as a derivative work if the alterations were significant enough.[211]

Derivative work was defined in Sec. 101 as "a work based upon one or more preexisting works…in which a work may be recast, transformed, or adapted…[or] other modifications, which, as a whole, represent an original work of authorship."[212] A derivative work's copyright exists independently from the pre-existing work. Consequently, copyright protection extends only to cover the elements that the derivative work's author contributed, it does not extend to the pre-existing work nor affect its copyright in any way.[213] The copyright protection on the derivative work is only valid if it was made lawfully, in that it does not infringe on the original work's copyright.[214] For example, a photograph of a copyrighted work, such as a sculpture, is a valid derivative work as long as it was lawfully created.[215]

## 5.6 Conclusion

The concept of authorship, despite casting the largest shadow over copyright law, remained difficult to consistently pin down. Such a central figure was ill-defined even in the Berne Convention, the premier international convention that promoted the universal protection of "authors." Many scholars debated that for such a central figure in the construction of copyright law not to have a clear and consistent definition constitutes a challenge to the legitimacy of copyright law. Perhaps owing to its elusiveness, scholars debated the figure of the "author" without managing to reach a unified definition of authorship. The debates regarding authorship were not only discussed within the confines of copyright law; influential literary theorists and philosophers debated the figure of the author and questioned its importance for the resulting work.[216] Some literary and legal scholars examined authorship and posited that the romantic author notion was the dominant conception of authorship in copyright law. Other scholars disagreed and posited that the romantic author notion was only one factor among many that influenced the development of copyright law and by no means the most important one.

Due to the unique nature of photographic works, they represented an ideal point for investigating the core of copyright's authorship in order to find out what constitutes an author. The UK CDPA 1988 conceptualised photographs by clearly defining what was meant by a photograph within the confines of copyright law as a "recording of light…."[217] In contrast, the US Copyright Code was reluctant to define photographs and opted to settle with recognising photographs as works of

211 *Jarvis v K2 Inc, 486 F3d 526 (2007).*
212 Sec. 1 Title 17 of the United States Code (US).
213 Sec. 103(b) ibid.
214 Sec. 103(a) ibid.
215 *Cooley v Penguin Group (USA) Inc, 31 FSupp3d 599 (2014)* (n 196).
216 See e.g. Burke (n 9); Roland Barthes, "The Death of the Author" in Stephen Heath (tr), *Image, Music, Text* (Fontana Press 1987); Michel Foucault, "What Is an Author?" (1979) 20 Screen 13.
217 See: Section 4(2)(b) Copyright, Designs and Patents Act 1988 (UK).

authorship under a general category.[218] Defining what constitutes a photograph may prove helpful for developing a contextual approach to authorship in photographs that take the nature of work into account instead of the one-size-fits-all approach.

This trend regarding definitions between the two jurisdictions continues with regard to the definition of the term "author." The UK CDPA 1988 defined what constitutes an author directly in Section 9 as being the one who created the work of authorship.[219] In comparison, the US Copyright Code did not address what constitutes an author, it only laid down what constitutes an author in joint authorship and work for hire, allocating the status of an author in work for hire to the employer. Moreover, the US Copyright Code combined authorship with first ownership of copyright. In contrast, the UK CDPA 1988 clearly separated the first ownership of copyright from copyright's authorship.

Both jurisdictions allocated a high level of importance to the pre-shutter activities to determine the authorship of a photograph. However, US copyright law allocates considerably more weight to pre-shutter activities such as selection, lighting, arrangements, angle, timing, choice of equipment, and level of control, among other elements, in order to allocate authorship to a specific person. The United Kingdom puts more emphasis on creation as a whole, taking into account pre-shutter activities alongside other elements such as skill, labour, and judgement to allocate photographs' authorship.

In joint authorship, the US emphasises the element of mutual intention by the putative authors, at the time of the work's creation, to be joint authors as the key element to any joint authorship claim. In comparison, the United Kingdom does not give the intention to be joint authors any heightened importance, it examines the joint labour that went towards creating the work in the pursuit of a common design and whether the contributions were significant enough and of the right kind to support a joint authorship claim. Furthermore, post-shutter activities such as modifications to the pictures using photo editing software may not be regarded as a qualifying contribution to deem the photographs as works of joint authorship. Instead, these contributions would be considered to create derivative works since they do not occur at the time of the photograph's creation.

With the advent of the digital age, photographic works continue to strain copyright law concepts, such as authorship and originality. The pillars on which these copyright concepts were built to find photographs' copyright are increasingly eroded as photographic technology advances. Thus, a contextual interpretation of these concepts may be required to better fit with the category of protected work in question. This is in order to preserve the legitimacy of these concepts and stand against straining them beyond their capacity due to applying them to all mediums of expression in a one-size-fits-all approach instead of a nuanced and tailored approach.

218 See: Sec. 101 Title 17 of the United States Code (US).
219 Section 9 Copyright, Designs and Patents Act 1988 (UK).

# 6 The Concept of Originality

## 6.1 Introduction

This chapter is divided into two parts. The first part examines the concept of originality in copyright law and how it was applied to photographs, highlighting its elusiveness by presenting the diverging views surrounding it. The second part will examine originality in Anglo-American copyright law.

The first part of this chapter unfolds in the following manner: firstly, it examines the concept of originality in general with reference to photographic works. It looks at the diverse standards and common elements concerning originality across different jurisdictions. Secondly, it examines originality in photographs and how the courts in various jurisdictions handled it through different originality proxies.

The second part of this chapter examines the concept of originality in Anglo-American copyright law. It aims to familiarise the reader with the standard of originality in the respective jurisdictions in order to support the subsequent chapter, which analyses originality in the context of photographic works.

As mentioned previously in Chapter 5, courts tend to confuse authorship with originality when it comes to a photograph's originality. In the hope of illuminating the difference between the two concepts, this chapter only focuses on the concept of originality, seen as the place (originality) in which the road (authorship) leads.

## 6.2 The Concept of Originality

The concept of originality is a key integral part of copyright law, much on the same level as the concept of authorship, to which it is strongly related.[1] It is an elusive concept that is often addressed and used flexibly to legitimatise and delineate

1 Ryan Littrell, "Toward a Stricter Originality Standard for Copyright Law Note" (2001) 43 Boston College Law Review 193, 222, 225, 226; Lionel Bently and others, *Intellectual Property Law* (5 edition, OUP Oxford 2018) 93; Jane C Ginsburg, "Creation and Commercial Value: Copyright Protection of Works of Information" (1990) 90 Columbia Law Review 1865, 1897; Jane C Ginsburg, "The Concept of Authorship in Comparative Copyright Law" (2003) 52 DePaul Law Review 1063, 1077 ("in most copyright/authors' rights jurisdictions, originality is overarching standard of authorship"); Shyamkrishna Balganesh, "The Folklore and Symbolism of Authorship in American Copyright Law" (2016) 54 Houston Law Review 403, 410; Sam Ricketson, "The Concept of Originality in Anglo-Australian Copyright Law Part I" (1991) 39 Journal of the Copyright Society of the USA 265, 275;

DOI: 10.4324/9781003586555-6

protection as well as to serve as a mechanism to gatekeep copyright protection from works deemed not original, whatever this means, in a manner that satisfies originality's amorphous nature.[2] That is because it is challenging to reach a single definition of originality that fits all manner of intellectual creations, let alone photographs, without unwittingly entering into areas dreaded by lawmakers, such as commercial value as well as aesthetics and artistic merits, not to mention that boldly attempting to define a concept which even artists are not able to agree on may lead to undesirable consequences.[3]

Much like authorship, originality, despite not being mentioned directly, existed in the premier copyright convention, the Berne Convention, without any useful guidance of what was meant by an original work except a hint that it involves an intellectual creation.[4] Originality has a presence in international treaties regarding copyright, but, as with authorship, no clear definition of originality was presented except that it refers to human intellectual creations.[5]

---

see: Oren Bracha, "The Ideology of Authorship Revisited: Authors, Markets, and Liberal Values in Early American Copyright" (2008) 118 The Yale Law Journal 186.

2 Bently and others (n 1) 93, 95; Michael Tappin and others, *Laddie, Prescott and Vitoria: The Modern Law of Copyright* (5 edition, LexisNexis Butterworths 2018) s 1.20, 3.40; Paul J Heald, "The Vices of Originality" (1991) 199 The Supreme Court Review 143, 153, 154; Russ VerSteeg, "Rethinking Originality" (1992) 34 William and Mary Law Review 801, 805, 810, 813, 814; Erlend Lavik and Stef van Gompel, "On the Prospects of Raising the Originality Requirement in Copyright Law: Perspectives from the Humanities" (2012) 60 Journal of the Copyright Society of the USA 387, 434; Roberta Rosenthal Kwall, "Originality in Context Copyright in Context: Institute for Intellectual Property & Informational Law Symposium" (2007) 44 Houston Law Review 871, 872; Robert Brauneis, "The Transformation of Originality in the Progressive-Era Debate over Copyright in News" (2009) 27 Cardozo Arts & Entertainment Law Journal 321, 323, 324; Daniel J Gervais, "Feist Goes Global: A Comparative Analysis of the Notion of Originality in Copyright Law Part I" (2001) 49 Journal of the Copyright Society of the U.S.A. 949, 960, 970; see also: Eva E Subotnik, "Originality Proxies: Toward a Theory of Copyright and Creativity" (2010) 76 Brooklyn Law Review 1487; Bracha (n 1) 200, 201, 209.

3 *Bleistein v Donaldson Lithographing Co, 188 US 239 (1903)*; *University of London Press Ltd v University Tutorial Press Ltd [1916] 2 Ch 601*; Howard B Abrams, "Originality and Creativity in Copyright Law" (1992) 55 Law and Contemporary Problems 3, 4, 5; Nigel P Gravells, "Authorship and Originality: The Persistent Influence of Walter v Lane" [2007] Intellectual Property Quarterly 267, 267; see: Lavik and van Gompel (n 2) 411, 420; Subotnik (n 2) 1512, 1528, 1537; Cameron Hutchison, "Insights from Psychology for Copyright's Originality Doctrine" (2012) 52 IDEA: The Intellectual Property Law Review 101, 121, 129,; Tappin and others (n 2) s 1.20; Bently and others (n 1) 93, 95; Graham Dutfield and Uma Suthersanen, *Dutfield and Suthersanen on Global Intellectual Property Law* (2 edition, Edward Elgar Publishing 2020) 105–106.

4 Article 2(5) Berne Convention for the Protection of Literary and Artistic Works 1886; Elizabeth F Judge and Daniel Gervais, "Of Silos and Constellations: Comparing Notions of Originality in Copyright Law" (2009) 27 Cardozo Arts & Entertainment Law Journal 375, 399–402; Gervais (n 2) 970–972; Nicholas Caddick, Gwilym Harbottle and Uma Suthersanen, *Copinger and Skone James on Copyright* (18 edition, Sweet & Maxwell Ltd 2020) paras 2–02, 2–07.

5 Article 2(5) Berne Convention for the Protection of Literary and Artistic Works; Article 10(2) Agreement on Trade-Related Aspects of Intellectual Property Rights (TRIPS) (as amended on 23 January 2017); Article 5 WIPO Copyright Treaty 1996; Judge and Gervais (n 4) 399–402; Gervais (n 2) 970–972.

Professor Elizabeth Judge and Daniel Gervais examined the concept of originality in copyright law across different jurisdictions and boiled it down to four main standards of originality that appear to influence the global landscape.[6] These four originality standards are as follows: firstly, originality dependent on the author's personality reflected in his intellectual creation, a standard followed in the European Union;[7] secondly, originality that requires a "modicum of creativity," followed in the United States;[8] thirdly, originality as requiring non-trivial and non-mechanical skill, labour, and judgement in producing the work, as followed in Canada;[9] and finally, originality as requiring sufficient skill, labour, and judgement to be exercised in the work, adopted by the United Kingdom, although this is contested in the light of recent development,[10] and Australia.[11]

Judge and Gervais indicated that these standards are broadly viewed as occupying a scale from "the most restrictive to the most generous."[12] However, they acknowledge that these standards often overlap and that the originality assessment of certain works may end up diverging from the hierarchy as described.[13] However, in general, they argued that this originality hierarchy remains valid for the vast majority of works even if not all works fit "neatly and consistently in the hierarchy."[14] While these standards may generally fit the hierarchy described, one can more accurately describe their differences as based on their different conception of originality and not necessarily a difference based on the level of originality required.[15] This is because these four standards interact with different works differently. A work that could easily satisfy the standard based on personality, placed at the higher level of the hierarchy, may not be able to satisfy the standard of skill and labour, which is placed at the bottom of the hierarchy described.[16] In this situation,

6 Judge and Gervais (n 4).

7 ibid 378, 384, 386, 388; Bently and others (n 1) 98, 100; Eleonora Rosati, *Originality in EU Copyright: Full Harmonization through Case Law* (Edward Elgar Publishing 2013) 153, 167.

8 Judge and Gervais (n 4) 389; *Feist Publications, Inc v Rural Telephone Service Co, Inc, 499 US 340 (1991)*.

9 Judge and Gervais (n 4) 389, 390.

10 Bently and others (n 1) 93, 99; Tappin and others (n 2) s 3.40; Rosati (n 7) 207; see: Daniel Gervais and Estelle Derclaye, "The Scope of Computer Program Protection after SAS: Are We Closer to Answers?" (2012) 34 European Intellectual Property Review 565; *(C-5/08) Infopaq International A/S v Danske Dagblades Forening [2009] ECR I-6569*; *SAS Institute Inc v World Programming Ltd [2013] EWHC 69 (Ch)*.

11 Judge and Gervais (n 4) 394, 395.

12 ibid 377.

13 ibid 405, 407.

14 ibid.

15 Bently and others (n 1) 106; Andreas Rahmatian, "Originality in UK Copyright Law: The Old 'Skill and Labour' Doctrine under Pressure" (2013) 44 IIC-International Review of Intellectual Property and Competition Law 4, 12; Paul Goldstein, *International Copyright: Principles, Law, and Practice* (OUP Oxford 2001) 162.

16 Bently and others (n 1) 106–107, 112; Rosati (n 7) 117; *(C-5/08) Infopaq International A/S v Danske Dagblades Forening [2009] ECR I-6569* (n 10); Bracha (n 1) 208, 209, 267; Barton Beebe,

one could argue that the supposedly lower standard paradoxically represented a hurdle for that work more than the other supposedly higher standard.

It is very difficult to delineate originality on any arbitrary standards due to the fact that, in many instances, the concept is close to formless, a changeable variable subject to any desired aim in copyright law.[17] Despite this, there are certain elements that overlap in the different standards of originality across several jurisdictions that may serve as guideposts to draw a rudimentary shape of originality in copyright law. Many legal scholars have highlighted certain common features regarding originality in copyright law in that originality does not refer to novelty and inventiveness, nor does it require "an original form of expression." Furthermore, originality is not concerned with aesthetic qualities or artistic merits nor the value or uniqueness of the work or the idea behind it.[18] However, these principles only reveal what originality is not; they do not reveal what originality actually is.[19]

Professor William Fisher examined the concept of originality across different jurisdictions around the world and boiled it down to six main conceptions that measure the originality of a work for the purposes of copyright law.[20] The first conception that strikes at the heart of originality is independent creation, in that the work was not copied.[21] The second conception is connected to the amount of labour needed for the work's creation.[22] However, this conception is in decline since it is increasingly apparent that originality is more concerned with qualitative rather than quantitative elements.[23] The third conception is related to the measure of skill

---

"'Bleistein', the Problem of Aesthetic Progress, and the Making of American Copyright Law" (2017) 117 Columbia Law Review 319, 367.

17 Bently and others (n 1) 94; Shyamkrishna Balganesh, "Tiered Originality and the Dualism of Copyright Incentives" (2009) 95 Virginia Law Review 67, 67; Gideon Parchomovsky and Alex Stein, "Originality" (2009) 95 Virginia Law Review 1505, 1506, 1550 (Proposing a new theory of originality for copyright law); Subotnik (n 2) 1490, 1494, 1528; Littrell (n 1) 194, 195; Ginsburg, "Creation and Commercial Value" (n 1) 1867, 1870; William W Fisher III, "Recalibrating Originality" (2016) 54 Houston Law Review 437, 438, 455; Bracha (n 1) 200, 201, 209; Ginsburg, "The Concept of Authorship in Comparative Copyright Law" (n 1) 1077.

18 Judge and Gervais (n 4) 404; Bently and others (n 1) 94, 95; Goldstein (n 15) 162, 163; Tappin and others (n 2) s 3.40.

19 Several commentators and scholars attempted to provide a theory of originality in copyright law to advance its coherence and serve particular policy aims. See for example: Samson Vermont, "The Sine Qua Non of Copyright Is Uniqueness, Not Originality" (2011) 20 Texas Intellectual Property Law Journal 327; VerSteeg (n 2); Diane Leenheer Zimmerman, "It's an Original! (?): In Pursuit of Copyright's Elusive Essence" (2004) 28 Columbia Journal of Law & the Arts 187; Dale P Olson, "Copyright Originality" (1983) 48 Missouri Law Review 29; Joseph Scott Miller, "Hoisting Originality" (2009) 31 Cardozo Law Review 451; Fisher III (n 17); Abraham Drassinower, *What's Wrong with Copying?* (Harvard University Press 2015); Parchomovsky and Stein (n 17).

20 Fisher III (n 17).

21 ibid 448.

22 ibid.

23 Bently and others (n 1) 94, 101–103; Rosati (n 7) 78, 113; *Feist Publications, Inc v Rural Telephone Service Co, Inc, 499 U.S. 340 (1991)* (n 8) 362, 363; *Newspaper Licensing Agency Ltd v Meltwater Holding BV [2011] RPC 7* [74, 75]; *(C-5/08) Infopaq International A/S v Danske Dagblades Forening [2009] ECR I-6569* (n 10) para 45.

expended to create the work in question.[24] One could argue that skill and labour should be grouped together since they are nearly inseparable for the purposes of originality in copyright law. The fourth conception, as observed by Fisher, is the degree to which the author's creative choices are reflected in the work in question. The fifth conception is concerned with the author's imprint of personality on the work. One could say that the author's creative freedom and his imprint of personality are closely connected for the purposes of originality.[25] The sixth conception observed by Fisher is only expressed in one country, Switzerland, and it associates novelty with originality.[26] Unsurprisingly, this novelty criterion is solemnly invoked in other jurisdictions except in a very limited sense concerning the work's creation as something, by virtue of being created, new.[27] Fisher explained that these measures of originality are independent of each other yet are not mutually exclusive since a work can satisfy more than one measure of originality.[28]

For the sake of curtailing originality further, Fisher's observation can be narrowed down to three main conceptions instead of six. These three conceptions are independent creation; employing the right kind of skill and labour in the work's creation; and finally, displaying the author's imprint of personality through exercising free and creative choices.

While these conceptions identified may roughly delineate originality in copyright law, it does not define the concept in a way that makes it coherent in practice. Several commentators and scholars highlighted this flaw and pointed out how, due to the elusiveness of the concept of originality, the courts avoided tackling the issue of defining originality by relying on different proxies to evaluate the originality of the work and at the same time, keep the myth of objectivity intact.[29] This tendency is pervasive when it comes to evaluating originality in photographs.[30]

24 Fisher III (n 17) 449.
25 ibid.
26 ibid 449, 450.
27 Bently and others (n 1) 93; Bracha (n 1) 204–205, 208–209.
28 Fisher III (n 17) 450.
29 Justin Hughes, "The Photographer's Copyright-Photograph as Art, Photograph as Database" (2011) 25 Harv JL & Tech. 339, 408; Littrell (n 1) 222, 226; Balganesh, "The Folklore and Symbolism of Authorship in American Copyright Law" (n 1) 405, 411; Hutchison (n 3) 132, 134; VerSteeg (n 2) 854, 879; Ginsburg, "Creation and Commercial Value" (n 1) 1867; Bracha (n 1) 207–209; Lavik and van Gompel (n 2) 432; Subotnik (n 2) 1425.
30 Subotnik (n 2) 1494, 1512, 1529; Hughes (n 29) 410; Christine Haight Farley, "The Lingering Effects of Copyright's Response to the Invention of Photography" (2004) 65 University of Pittsburgh Law Review 385, 456; Teresa M Bruce, "In the Language of Pictures: How Copyright Law Fails to Adequately Account for Photography" (2012) 115 West Virginia Law Review 93, 112.

### *6.2.1 Originality in Photographs, a Place Plagued by Proxies*

Photographs represented a particularly challenging area for the concept of originality in copyright law across its many forms.[31] That is because the art of photography has elements of automation and verisimilitude embedded deep within its DNA.[32] The majority of photographs are often the result of what the camera laid witness to at the time the shutter was pressed. Consequently, copyright law struggled with establishing solid grounds for originality in photographs, given that their very nature makes it hard to reconcile with the traditional notion of works of authorship.[33] Hence, instead of finding originality in the photograph itself, the courts opted to look at other places where they believed that the mechanical nature of photography was the least involved.[34] In other words, the courts neglected the photograph itself in favour of looking at the means and processes that led to the production of the photograph in question to establish its originality.[35] In doing so, the courts distorted the notion of originality in photographs by employing different proxies to evaluate and establish the originality of photographs as something to be located outside the work itself as a photograph.[36]

The courts' tendency to use different proxies of originality when it comes to photographs was examined by Professor Eva E. Subotnik, who examined how US courts used various proxies to tackle originality in photographic works. Subotnik identified three main proxies for originality that US courts routinely employed in the face of a photograph's originality evaluation.[37] The first and simplest proxy is what Subotnik dubbed "the proxy of ontology," which considers a photograph original by virtue of being a photograph captured independently without direct copying.[38] The second is "the proxy of narrative," which finds originality outside the work by looking at certain elements of the process adopted by the author that led to the production of the photographs in question.[39] This proxy considers the pre-shutter choices (such as selection, arrangement, equipment, lighting, and choice of subject) employed by the principal photographer in order to evaluate whether a photograph is original.[40] In other words, originality is found through the "authorial narrative" associated with the photographs and not necessarily the photograph

31 Hughes (n 29) 368, 388; Terry S Kogan, "The Enigma of Photography, Depiction, and Copyright Originality" (2014) 25 Fordham Intellectual Property, Media & Entertainment Law Journal 869, 918.

32 Hughes (n 29) 342, 343; Kogan (n 31) 918–920.

33 Hughes (n 29) 342, 368, 425; Kogan (n 31) 918.

34 Hughes (n 29) 363, 365–367, 408, 417; Kogan (n 31) 931.

35 Hughes (n 29) 410; Kogan (n 31) 910, 931.

36 Hughes (n 29) 387–388, 408, 410, 416; Kogan (n 31) 910, 931.

37 Subotnik (n 2) 1494.

38 ibid 1513.

39 ibid 1517–1518.

40 ibid 1520; *Burrow-Giles Lithographic Co v Sarony, 111 US 53 (1884).*

itself.[41] This proxy of originality was used in the *Burrow-Giles case*[42] and has been applied ever since in cases involving an evaluation of a photograph's originality.[43] The third is "the proxy of comparisons," and it is the only proxy that endeavours to find originality within the confines of the photograph itself by comparing it with other photographs or/and comparing the way the subjects are depicted in it with the potentially infringing photograph.[44]

An additional proxy that associated originality with commercial value was highlighted by Professor Beebe in which he argued that it spawned from the doctrine of aesthetic neutrality, laid down by Judge Holmes in the *Bleistien case*,[45] and may have since served a role in finding whether a work is original.[46] Another possible proxy is the level of investment that went into producing the photographs in question; this was invoked in the earliest debates surrounding the extension of copyright to photographs as a way to reward investment and protect it from unfair competition.[47] Moreover, the Court of Justice of the European Union (CJEU) has used the standard of originality as a substitute for the concept of work.[48]

The courts' reliance on these different originality proxies led to inconsistent results even within the individual proxies themselves, subject to the type of photographs in question.[49] Perhaps this may be due to the fact that different types of photographs are more compatible with one originality proxy over the other.[50] Even though Subotnik's examination focused on US courts, her main points are certainly relevant across different jurisdictions where the courts evaluated a photograph's originality. For instance, the CJEU in the *Painer case*[51] invoked the narrative proxy

41 Subotnik (n 2) 1520; Hughes (n 29) 410; *Burrow-Giles Lithographic Co v Sarony, 111 US 53 (1884)* (n 40); Farley (n 30) 546; Bruce (n 30) 112.

42 *Burrow-Giles Lithographic Co v Sarony, 111 US 53 (1884)* (n 40).

43 See: Farley (n 30).

44 Subotnik (n 2) 1523.

45 *Bleistein v Donaldson Lithographing Co, 188 US 239 (1903)* (n 3).

46 Beebe (n 16) 376, 378.

47 See Chapters 2–4.

48 *(C-310/17) Levola Hengelo BV v Smilde Foods BV [2019] ECDR 2*; *(C-683/17) Cofemel v G-Star Raw CV [2019] ECDR 16.*

49 Subotnik (n 2) 1509, 1529, 1537; Hughes (n 29) 408; Bruce (n 30) 110; Farley (n 30) 456; Hutchison (n 3) 132.

50 Hughes (n 29) 408, 409; Bruce (n 30) 110; Rebecca Tushnet, "Worth a Thousand Words: The Images of Copyright" (2012) 125 Harvard Law Review 683, 713, 715, 732, 740; Patricia L Baade, "Photographer's Rights: Case for Sufficient Originality Test in Copyright Law" (1996) 30 John Marshall Law Review 149, 180; see: Morgan M Stoddard, "Mother Nature as Muse: Copyright Protection for Works of Art and Photographs Inspired by, Based on, or Depicting Nature" (2007) 86 North Carolina Law Review 572; Robert A Gorman, "Copyright Protection for the Collection and Representation of Facts" (1963) 76 Harvard Law Review 1569, 1596–1598; see: *Meshwerks, Inc v Toyota Motor Sales USA, Inc, 528 F3d 1258 (2008)*; *Time Inc v Bernard Geis Associates, 293 FSupp 130 (1968)*.

51 *(C-145/10) Painer v Standard Verlags GmbH [2012] ECDR 6.*

to regard a portrait photograph as an original work protected by copyright and emphasised the creative choices available at the pre-production stage.[52]

The reliance on authorial narrative when it comes to photographs' originality, in particular, brings to the attention another issue pertaining to how the courts, across different jurisdictions, seem, more often than not, to use the concept of originality and authorship interchangeably as if they were synonyms to each other.[53] This further exacerbates the conceptual confusion regarding the two concepts and their function in copyright law. This has been highlighted and criticised by several scholars and commentators since the courts often venture beyond the work boundaries and paradoxically locate originality outside the work itself.[54] This tendency to address authorship and originality interchangeably may be to blame for eroding the difference between the two concepts.

Therefore, the distinction between authorship and originality should be drawn to be more definite. Authorship is and should be confined to the process of creation, the realm outside the work's tangible boundaries. Originality, in contrast, should be confined to the work itself within its tangible boundaries.[55] A person would not be deemed to have created an original work just because he employed a unique and original process to reproduce an existing work. He may be an author, but his work would not be considered original. The opposite is also true; a work may be considered highly original within its boundaries despite the fact that it was not regarded as authored for the purposes of copyright law and thus would not contain copyright.[56] Hence, many scholars have questioned the persistence of this practice by the courts despite the fact that the concept of originality, which only equates with authorship under the "romantic author" notion,[57] long since broke away from authorship to occupy a different function in copyright law.[58]

Professor Balganesh argued that "Even if originality is otherwise a notional stand-in for authorship in modern context, it does so through the 'work of authorship' construct and not as authorship qua act of authoring."[59] Thus, originality is more of an adjective for what constitutes a work of authorship, that is, where its

52 ibid [90–92].

53 Bently and others (n 1) 93, 105; Alan L Durham, "The Random Muse: Authorship and Indeterminacy" (2002) 44 William and Mary Law Review 569, 606, 618; Balganesh, "The Folklore and Symbolism of Authorship in American Copyright Law" (n 1) 405, 411; Ginsburg, "The Concept of Authorship in Comparative Copyright Law" (n 1) 1077; VerSteeg (n 2) 879; Ginsburg, "Creation and Commercial Value" (n 1) 1867; Gravells (n 3) 267; Littrell (n 1) 222, 225.

54 Hughes (n 29) 408, 409; Farley (n 30) 428, 433, 454–456; Bruce (n 30) 112; Hutchison (n 3) 132; VerSteeg (n 2) 855; Kogan (n 31) 935.

55 Balganesh, "The Folklore and Symbolism of Authorship in American Copyright Law" (n 1) 411.

56 ibid.

57 Farley (n 30) 453; Bracha (n 1) 192–193, 200; Peter Jaszi, "Toward a Theory of Copyright: The Metamorphoses of 'Authorship'" (1991) 1991 Duke Law Journal 455, 471, 487, 494, 501; Littrell (n 1) 222.

58 Balganesh, "The Folklore and Symbolism of Authorship in American Copyright Law" (n 1) 403, 405, 410–411; VerSteeg (n 2) 879, 880; Durham (n 53) 617–618; Hughes (n 29) 410.

59 Shyamkrishna Balganesh, "Causing Copyright" (2017) 117 Columbia Law Review 1, 39.

links and origins are located. Originality should not be confused with the authorial process which is concerned with the act of authorship.[60] Therefore, demarcating authorship and originality as one that is akin to a road (authorship), and the other akin to a place (originality), may serve as a starting point to sever the tendencies of the courts in equating the road and the place as if they are one and the same when it comes to a photograph's originality.

## 6.3 The Standard of Originality in Anglo-American Copyright Law

Originality in Anglo-American copyright law did not have a consistent form nor followed a linear path across its development. Rather, originality was used as a policy tool, leveraging its clay-like form to achieve different objectives.[61] The mirage of the originality standard was identifiable, but it still remained a mirage, at least in practice, when different kinds of works were evaluated differently. The requirement of originality was never defined in Anglo-American statutory law; this task was left in the hands of the courts. The courts established that Anglo-American copyright law should adopt a minimalistic standard of originality, requiring little more than origination and a nominal degree of creativity; hence, it hardly served as a limiting factor.[62] Yet, despite the minimalistic approach towards originality, the requirement is still considered the "sine qua of copyright."[63]

This part identifies the main principles of the standard of originality that are currently followed in the United States and United Kingdom. This is done in order to set the stage for the subsequent chapter, which examines how the Anglo-American courts applied the originality standard in the context of photographs.

### *6.3.1 Originality in the United States*

The history of the originality requirement in US copyright law reveals three standards of originality that the US courts applied prior to the US Supreme Court's decision in *Feist Publications, Inc v Rural Telephone Service Co (1991)*.[64] The first of

60 ibid; VerSteeg (n 2) 880.

61 Steven S Boyd, "Deriving Originality in Derivative Works: Considering the Quantum of Originality Needed to Attain Copyright Protection in a Derivative Work" (1999) 40 Santa Clara Law Review 325, 328; Eleonora Rosati, "Originality in US and UK Copyright Experiences as a Springboard for an EU-Wide Reform Debate" [2010] International Review of Intellectual Property and Competition Law 524, 524, 537–538.

62 Jisuk Woo, "Genius with Minimal Originality: The Continuity and Transformation of the Authorship Construct in Copyright Case Law Regarding Computer Software" (2004) 15 Albany Law Journal of Science & Technology 109, 115; Ricketson (n 1) 270–271; Burton Ong, "Originality from Copying: Fitting Recreative Works into the Copyright Universe" (2010) 2 Intellectual Property Quarterly 165, 165, 170–171.

63 *Feist Publications, Inc v Rural Telephone Service Co, Inc, 499 U.S. 340 (1991)* (n 8) 346.

64 Russ VerSteeg, "Sparks in the Tinderbox: Feist, Creativity, and the Legislative History of the 1976 Copyright Act" (1994) 56 University of Pittsburgh Law Review 549, 579; *Feist Publications, Inc v Rural Telephone Service Co, Inc, 499 U.S. 340 (1991)* (n 8).

these originality standards posits that originality requires independent creation in that the work was not the result of copying.[65] The development of this standard can be traced back to early 19th-century cases, and it has been preserved as the most enduring standard of originality in US copyright law.[66] The standard was further elaborated upon in that for the work to be deemed independently created, an exercise of independent skill or labour to create the work was needed and the scope of copyright only covered those portions of the work that were independently created, in other words, not copied.[67] This standard was developed further following the *Trade-Mark cases (1879)*,[68] where the type of labour expended to create the work was considered relevant for the originality assessment of the work. The court stated that, in order for a work to be regarded as an original work of authorship, it should result from an "intellectual labour" or "laborious thought" in a way that confers originality upon the work.[69] This was affirmed in the famous US Supreme Court case *Burrow-Giles v Sarony*,[70] the landmark case that affirmed the extension of copyright protection to photographs, where it stated that originality refers to origination, and a work is original if it was the result of the author's "original intellectual conception."[71]

The second originality standard employed by US courts required independent creation with the addition of distinguishable variation from other similar works.[72] This was affirmed in *Alfred Bell & Co v Catalda Fine Arts*,[73] where the Second Circuit judge stated that originality requires the author to contribute "something more than a 'merely trivial' variation, something recognizably 'his own.'"[74] The aesthetic quality of the contribution itself or whether the variation was produced consciously was irrelevant to this standard as it was only concerned with the variation being more than trivial in order to be regarded as a distinguishable variation that evidences originality.[75] This particular standard of originality enjoyed widespread use in US courts across different circuits.[76] A heightened version of this

65 *Feist Publications, Inc v Rural Telephone Service Co, Inc, 499 U.S. 340 (1991)* (n 8) 345; VerSteeg (n 64) 580–581; Section 308.1 *Compendium of U.S. Copyright Office Practices, Third Edition (US)* (US Copyright Office 2014).

66 Olson (n 19) 36; VerSteeg (n 64) 580; Craig Joyce and Tyler T Ochoa, "Reach Out and Touch Someone: Reflections on the 25th Anniversary of Feist Publications, Inc. v Rural Telephone Service Co. Authorship in America (and beyond): Institute for Intellectual Property & Information Law Symposium: Historical Essay" (2016) 54 Houston Law Review 257, 259; *Emerson v Davies, 13 Hunt Mer Mag 558 (1845)*.

67 Olson (n 19) 36–37; *Emerson v Davies, 13 Hunt Mer. Mag. 558 (1845)* (n 66).

68 *In re Trade-Mark Cases, 100 US 82 (1879)*.

69 ibid 94; Joyce and Ochoa (n 66) 265; VerSteeg (n 64) 584.

70 *Burrow-Giles Lithographic Co v Sarony, 111 US 53 (1884)* (n 40).

71 ibid 58. See Chapter 4.

72 VerSteeg (n 64) 579, 581, 583; *Alfred Bell & Co v Catalda Fine Arts, 191 F2d 99 (1951)*.

73 *Alfred Bell & Co v Catalda Fine Arts, 191 F2d 99 (1951)* (n 72).

74 ibid 103.

75 ibid 103, 105; *Bleistein v Donaldson Lithographing Co, 188 US 239 (1903)* (n 3) (Held aesthetic quality is should not be a part of originality assessment).

76 VerSteeg (n 64) 582–583.

standard was sometimes employed for derivative works, which are works based on pre-existing works.[77] The level of contribution in these types of works was generally required to be higher than the traditional level associated with this standard.[78]

The third standard of originality applied in the US courts requires that the work be the result of independent creation and contain a minimum degree of creativity in order to be an original work of authorship.[79] Professor VerSteeg indicated that this standard was the least applied standard of originality by US courts prior to the US Supreme Court decision in *Feist Publications, Inc v Rural Telephone Service Co.*[80] The reluctance to adopt a creativity-based originality standard prior to *Feist's decision* was not only reflected by the courts but also evidenced in the Congressional reports leading to the 1976 Copyright Act.[81] Professor VerSteeg revealed that there was strong opposition towards including any reference to creativity within the 1976 Copyright Act.[82] Consequently, the 1976 Copyright Act was enacted without any mention of creativity in any of its provisions or even incorporating any definition of originality.

Sec. 102 of the US Copyright Code provides that copyright subsists in "original works of authorship fixed in any tangible medium of expression."[83] The House report leading to the 1976 Copyright Act explained that the term "original works of authorship" was purposely left without a definition in order to "incorporate without change the standard of originality established by the courts."[84] One important point to highlight is that regardless of originality, copyright does not extend to facts or "any idea, procedure, process, system, method of operation, concept, principle, or discovery, regardless of the form in which it is described, explained, illustrated, or embodied in such work."[85] The US Copyright Code does not define the term "original work of authorship," but it does explain how it is to be satisfied in works of compilation.

Works of compilation are defined in Section 101 as "a work formed by the collection and assembling of pre-existing materials or of data that are selected, coordinated, or arranged in such a way that the resulting work as a whole constitutes an original work of authorship."[86] From this provision, one could deduce that originality is, among other things, closely associated with elements related to selection, coordination, and arrangement that result in creating a work of authorship. Examining how originality is found in works of compilation is important since the

77 Boyd (n 61) 353, 362, 377; *L Batlin & Son, Inc v Snyder, 536 F2d 486 (1976).*

78 Boyd (n 61) 353, 362, 377; *L. Batlin & Son, Inc v Snyder, 536 F2d 486 (1976)* (n 77); *Gracen v Bradford Exchange, 698 F2d 300 (1983)* 305.

79 VerSteeg (n 64) 579.

80 ibid 579, 585; *Feist Publications, Inc v Rural Telephone Service Co, Inc, 499 U.S. 340 (1991)* (n 8).

81 VerSteeg (n 64) 551–552, 558–559, 566.

82 ibid 570.

83 Section 102 (a) Title 17 of the United States Code (US).

84 House of Representative, "Copyright Law Revision, 94th Congress, 2d Sess." (1976) No. 94-1476 51 <https://www.copyright.gov/history/law/clrev_94-1476.pdf> accessed 18 October 2024.

85 Section 102 (b) Title 17 of the United States Code (US).

86 Section 101 ibid.

US Supreme Court effectively instated the only originality standard that the US courts are required to follow in *Feist Publications, Inc v Rural Telephone Service Co*,[87] which involved a copyright dispute in a compilation of telephone directories.

In *Feist Publications, Inc v Rural Telephone Service Co*,[88] the original claimant was a telephone service company, Rural, that published annual telephone directories as required by state regulation. The telephone directory was constructed typically. The white pages in the directory contained detailed information about Rural's subscribers, consisting of their names, towns, and telephone numbers arranged alphabetically. The yellow pages in the directory contained information about businesses as well as advertisements. The original defendant, Feist Publications, was a publishing company that published area-wide telephone directories and sought to acquire a licence from Rural to use their white pages directory information in their own telephone directories, which covered a wider geographical range than Rural's directory. Rural did not agree to license their directory to Feist. Subsequently, Feist extracted the data from Rural's directory, without Rural's consent, and followed their own procedure to verify the information in order to incorporate it in their own directory. Rural sued Feist for copyright infringement, and the district court granted summary judgement in favour of Rural, pointing out that "[c]ourts have consistently held that telephone directories are copyrightable."[89] Feist appealed the decision, claiming that the copied information was not under the scope of copyright protection. Subsequently, the Tenth Circuit Court of Appeal affirmed the lower court's decision for the same reasons. The US Supreme Court granted certiorari to determine whether the information contained in Rural's directory was protected by copyright.

The US Supreme Court first firmly stated that the requirement of originality is a constitutional requirement for copyright protection.[90] It further explained that originality is composed of two requirements along the lines that were articulated in the *Trade-Mark cases*[91] and *Burrow-Giles*.[92] The first requirement is independent creation, in that the work was not the result of copying.[93] The second requirement is that the work that was independently created evidence a "modicum of creativity."[94] The Supreme Court further pointed out that "the requisite level of creativity is extremely low; even a slight amount will suffice. The vast majority of works make the grade quite easily, as they possess some creative spark, 'no matter how crude,

87 VerSteeg (n 64) 579; *Feist Publications, Inc v Rural Telephone Service Co, Inc, 499 U.S. 340 (1991)* (n 8).
88 VerSteeg (n 64) 579; *Feist Publications, Inc v Rural Telephone Service Co, Inc, 499 U.S. 340 (1991)* (n 8).
89 *Feist Publications, Inc v Rural Telephone Service Co, Inc, 499 U.S. 340 (1991)* (n 8) 344.
90 ibid 346.
91 *In re Trade-Mark Cases, 100 U.S. 82 (1879)* (n 68).
92 *Burrow-Giles Lithographic Co v Sarony, 111 US 53 (1884)* (n 40).
93 *Feist Publications, Inc v Rural Telephone Service Co, Inc, 499 U.S. 340 (1991)* (n 8) 345–347, 358.
94 ibid 346, 358.

humble or obvious.'"[95] Therefore, originality does not require novelty or consideration of aesthetic value, it only requires "some minimal degree of creativity"; no other criteria is required.[96] The court affirmed that copyright protection only extends to cover the elements in the work's expression that are deemed original and does not extend to cover unoriginal elements, facts, or ideas.[97]

After delineating the originality requirement, the Supreme Court turned to assess originality in works of compilation. It reiterated that originality in a compilation could only be located in the specific way in which the elements of selection, coordination, and arrangement are utilised to satisfy the minimum creativity requirement.[98] One important tenet is that those elements should not be purely dictated for mechanical or technical consideration devoid of creativity.[99] On the Rural's telephone directories, the court ruled that facts are uncopyrightable and that the Rural's directories lack the requisite level of creativity.[100] Thus, there was no copyright infringement.

The *Feist case* has been hailed as a landmark case that has finally put an end to the circuit split regarding the originality requirement and firmly rejected the "sweat of the brow"[101] standard.[102] Despite the history surrounding the notion of creativity and its relation to originality, the US Supreme Court settled the circuit split regarding the different standards of originality by deciding that the only standard of originality that should be applied is the one that requires independent creation plus a minimal degree of creativity.[103] Some commentators and scholars criticised the decision due to the fact that even though it instated creativity as a requirement, it did not define what a "modicum of creativity" means.[104] Nevertheless, as will unfold in the subsequent chapter, this standard of originality did not represent a significant hurdle towards the protection of the vast majority of photographs.

### *6.3.2 Originality in the United Kingdom*

#### *6.3.2.1 The Traditional Originality Standard*

The development of the originality requirement in the UK copyright law could be argued to have followed a slow and linear developmental path while keeping its foundation, based on independent creation plus a degree of skill, labour,

95 ibid 345.
96 ibid 358–361, 363; see: Joyce and Ochoa (n 66).
97 *Feist Publications, Inc v Rural Telephone Service Co, Inc, 499 U.S. 340 (1991)* (n 8) 348, 351, 358, 360.
98 ibid 358–359.
99 ibid 358, 362.
100 ibid 361–362.
101 Sweat of brow is a copyright law doctrine that entails that protection is granted to reward the effort and investment of the author. ibid 352.
102 Joyce and Ochoa (n 66) 311.
103 *Feist Publications, Inc v Rural Telephone Service Co, Inc, 499 U.S. 340 (1991)* (n 8).
104 VerSteeg (n 2) 823.

and judgement, reasonably intact.[105] For a long time, the originality standard in the United Kingdom was believed to largely follow what was referred to as the skill and labour standard, which requires independent creation through expending the authors' own skill and labour to create the work.[106] In statutory law, the word "original" was first implemented in the Sculpture Act 1814 and the Fine Art Copyright Act 1862, the first statute that extended copyright protection to photographs.[107] This inclusion was meant to clarify that copies of existing works are not covered by separate copyright from the original works; it did not invoke any consideration of novelty or original thoughts.[108] At that time, the term "original" was not implemented in other Acts regarding copyright subject matters prior to the 1911 Copyright Act.[109] With the 1911 Copyright Act, originality was solidified as a general statutory requirement necessary for the subsistence of copyright, and for assessing infringements, for all copyright subject matter regardless of the type of work created.[110]

Historically, the standard of originality in the United Kingdom was a low threshold, only requiring the absence of copying and the expense of some degree of skill and labour to create the work.[111] In *Walter v Lane*,[112] the House of Lords established what was later known as the "reporter's copyright,"[113] granting copyright to a reporter who transcribed a public speech verbatim in a written form. The House of Lords examined the report as it relates to authorship and decided that it "involved considerable intellectual skill and brain labour beyond the mere mechanical operation of writing."[114] Hence, the House of Lords found that the reporter exercised a sufficient amount of skill and labour to be regarded as the author of the report in a way that conveyed copyright even though it was written verbatim from the speech. It seems apparent that the basis of this decision was placed on the skill and labour approach towards copyright to prevent one from unfairly reaping the fruits of another. This was evidenced through Lord Davy's declaration that "Copyright has nothing to do with originality or literary merits

105 *Walter v Lane [1900] AC 539*; *Express Newspapers Plc v News (UK) Ltd [1991] FSR 36*; *Sawkins v Hyperion Records Ltd [2005] EWCA Civ 565*.
106 Caddick, Harbottle and Suthersanen (n 4) paras 3–184, 3–186, 3–193; Bently and others (n 1) 97; *Walter v Lane [1900] AC 539* (n 105); *Sawkins v Hyperion Records Ltd [2005] EWCA Civ 565* (n 105).
107 Caddick, Harbottle and Suthersanen (n 4) paras 3–184, 3–186; Fine Arts Copyright Act 1862 (25 & 26 Vict.) C. 68.
108 Caddick, Harbottle and Suthersanen (n 4) paras 3–184, 3–186; Tappin and others (n 2) s 1.21, 3.40.
109 Caddick, Harbottle and Suthersanen (n 4) paras 3–184, 3–186; Bently and others (n 1) 93, 96.
110 Tappin and others (n 2) s 3.41; Bently and others (n 1) 93, 96; Caddick, Harbottle and Suthersanen (n 4) paras 3–184, 3–186.
111 Caddick, Harbottle and Suthersanen (n 4) paras 3–184, 3–186; Tappin and others (n 2) s 1.21; *Sawkins v Hyperion Records Ltd [2005] EWCA Civ 565* (n 105) 696.
112 *Walter v Lane [1900] AC 539* (n 105).
113 Bently and others (n 1) 114; Gravells (n 3) 268; *Express Newspapers Plc v News (UK) Ltd [1991] FSR 36* (n 105) 42.
114 *Walter v Lane [1900] AC 539* (n 105) 556 (per Lord James).

of the author," before proceeding to state that "it is a sound principle that a man shall not avail himself of another's skill, labour, and expense by copying the written product thereof."[115]

Despite the fact that *Walter v Lane* was against evaluating the originality of the composition to confer copyright and was decided before originality became a statutory requirement for the subsistence of copyright in the 1911 Copyright Act, it was paradoxically referenced as a starting point regarding originality, reinstating it as the authority on the low threshold of the originality requirement.[116] In *Express Newspapers Plc v News (UK) Ltd [1991]*,[117] which involved a similar situation to *Walter v Lane*, the court affirmed that the reporter's copyright established in *Walter v Lane* was "undeniably still good law."[118] The reporter's copyright is invoked whenever the reporter exercises a sufficient degree of skill, labour, and judgement in the report's composition.[119] This decision regarding the validity of the reporter's copyright may have been adopted for pragmatic policy reasons regarding copyright in the news instead of being strictly a matter related to the low threshold of originality.[120] Another possible reason was the lack of unfair competition laws that prevent someone from exploiting the efforts of another through copying.[121]

Professor Gravells examined the influence of *Walter v Lane* and argued that "*Walter v Lane* does not provide an appropriate basis for the modern originality requirement."[122] He proceeded to criticise the case by arguing that the "assertions that the case is 'still good law' under the regime of the 1988 Copyright Act are potentially misleading; and that, while the influence of the decision has been persistent, reliance on it is at best inappropriate and at worst misconceived."[123] Indeed, the importance of *Walter v Lane* to the UK originality standard is often misleading since the case, when referenced by the courts, only served as a way to showcase the low threshold of originality, but its standard was seldom applied at its level.[124] In fact, the cases that referred to *Walter v Lane* had applied a standard that required a level of skill, labour, and judgement that was significantly higher than the one deduced from *Walter v Lane*.[125]

115 ibid 552 (per Lord Davey).
116 Gravells (n 3) 268, 278; see: *Sawkins v Hyperion Records Ltd [2005] EWCA Civ 565* (n 105); *Express Newspapers Plc v News (UK) Ltd [1991] FSR 36* (n 105).
117 *Express Newspapers Plc v News (UK) Ltd [1991] FSR 36* (n 105).
118 ibid 43 (per Sir Nicolas Browne-Wilkinson).
119 ibid.
120 ibid 41; Gravells (n 3) 278.
121 Tappin and others (n 2) s 4.15; Rosati (n 7) 143; Gravells (n 3) 278, 291; see: Richard Arnold, "English Unfair Competition Law" (2013) 44 IIC – International Review of Intellectual Property and Competition Law 63.
122 Gravells (n 3) 293.
123 ibid.
124 ibid 292, 293; Bently and others (n 1) 114.
125 See: *Sawkins v Hyperion Records Ltd [2005] EWCA Civ 565* (n 105); *University of London Press Ltd v University Tutorial Press Ltd [1916] 2 Ch. 601* (n 3); *Ladbroke (Football) Ltd v William Hill (Football) Ltd [1964] 1 WLR 273* 17; Gravells (n 3) 292, 293; Bently and others (n 1) 114.

Richard Arnold revisited *Walter v Lane* and pointed out that the case was often misunderstood as relating to the requirement of originality despite the fact that it clearly rejected any consideration for originality.[126] This was because the House of Lords stated unambiguously that the 1842 Copyright Act did not contain any originality requirement. Hence, the House of Lords was occupied with the question of whether the reporter was considered the author of the report transcribed verbatim from a speech in a manner that qualified the report for copyright protection.[127] Arnold revealed that the persistence of *Walter v Lane*, even with the introduction of the originality requirement in the 1911 Copyright Act, was due to the fact that the law did not experience drastic changes prior to the CJEU harmonisation of the originality requirement.[128]

The meaning of originality for the purposes of copyright law was addressed in *University of London Press Ltd v University Tutorial Press Ltd [1916]*,[129] which involved a copyright dispute about university exam papers. In this case, Peterson J defined what was meant by "original" by stating that:

> The word "original" does not in this connection mean that the work must be the expression of original or inventive thought. Copyright Acts are not concerned with the originality of ideas, but with the expression of thought...the work must not be copied from another work...it should originate from the author.[130]

Therefore, in essence, the traditional approach to originality in English copyright law does not require novelty, nor is it concerned with aesthetic merits or the quality of the work; it primarily requires that the work was independently created and involves a sufficient degree of skill, labour, and judgement that elevates it to be a work of expression eligible for copyright protection.[131]

Originality remains an essential statutory requirement for copyright. The UK Copyright, Designs and Patents Act 1988 (CDPA 1988) established in Section 1 that copyright subsists in "original literary, dramatic, musical or artistic works."[132] Despite being a statutory requirement, originality was not defined in the relevant statutes; what was meant by the term "original" was left to the courts to develop.[133] The courts perceived originality, for the purposes of copyright law, as composed

126 Richard Arnold, "Walter v Lane Revisited (Again)" (2021) 2 Intellectual Property Quarterly 67, 74.

127 ibid 74–75.

128 ibid 75, 78.

129 *University of London Press Ltd v University Tutorial Press Ltd [1916] 2 Ch. 601* (n 3).

130 ibid 608, 609.

131 *Sawkins v Hyperion Records Ltd [2005] EWCA Civ 565* (n 105); *University of London Press Ltd v University Tutorial Press Ltd [1916] 2 Ch. 601* (n 3); *Ladbroke (Football) Ltd v William Hill (Football) Ltd [1964] 1 WLR 273* (n 125); Tappin and others (n 2) s 1.21, 3.42–45; Bently and others (n 1) 93.

132 Section 1(1) Copyright, Designs and Patents Act 1988 (UK).

133 Caddick, Harbottle and Suthersanen (n 4) para 3–185; Tappin and others (n 2) s 3.45.

of two principal ingredients: independent creation/origination, in that the work was not the result of slavish copying; and sufficient skill, labour, and judgement should be evident in the creation of the work.[134]

Subsequent cases affirmed the approach towards originality that was adopted in the *University of London Press*[135] *case*, while acknowledging that the originality requirement may be satisfied on an ad hoc basis, depending on the type, degree, and amount of skill, labour, and judgement expended on the creation of the work.[136] The courts acknowledged that certain types of skill and labour, such as mechanical copying, even if it involved considerable skill, would not be enough to satisfy the originality requirement but it did not provide sufficient guidance regarding what constitutes the minimum degree of skill, labour, and judgement required.[137] All that was relatively certain was that the required skill, labour, and judgement must be sufficient and of the relevant kind to confer originality.[138] In other words, the skill, labour, and judgement employed to create a work must "go beyond mere servile copying" in order to be sufficient to satisfy the originality requirement.[139]

In *Sawkins v Hyperion Records*,[140] which involved copyright on new performing editions of public domain musical works, the court held that the new editions contained copyright since Sawkins had expended considerable skill and labour that "go beyond mere servile copying."[141] Mummry LJ explained that the standard of originality does not impose any "objective standards of novelty, usefulness, inventiveness, aesthetic merit, quality or value."[142] He stated that:

> [a] work may be complete rubbish and utterly worthless, but copyright protection may be available for it, just as it is for the great masterpieces of imaginative literature, art and music. A work needs only be "original" in the

134 *University of London Press Ltd v University Tutorial Press Ltd [1916] 2 Ch. 601* (n 3); *Sawkins v Hyperion Records Ltd [2005] EWCA Civ 565* (n 105); Caddick, Harbottle and Suthersanen (n 4) 3–184, 3–186; Tappin and others (n 2) s 1.21, 1.24; Bently and others (n 1) 97.

135 *University of London Press Ltd v University Tutorial Press Ltd [1916] 2 Ch. 601* (n 3).

136 *Sawkins v Hyperion Records Ltd [2005] EWCA Civ 565* (n 105); *Ladbroke (Football) Ltd v William Hill (Football) Ltd [1964] 1 WLR 273* (n 125); *Interlego AG Appellant v Tyco Industries Inc [1988] 3 WLR 678* (1988) 105 343; *Express Newspapers Plc v News (UK) Ltd [1991] FSR 36* (n 105); *Macmillan & Co v K & J Cooper (1923) 93 LJPC 113*; Bently and others (n 1) 93, 97; Tappin and others (n 2) s 3.45, 3.58.

137 *Ladbroke (Football) Ltd v William Hill (Football) Ltd [1964] 1 WLR 273* (n 125) 278, 281; *Sawkins v Hyperion Records Ltd [2005] EWCA Civ 565* (n 105) 698; *Interlego A.G. Appellant v Tyco Industries Inc [1988] 3 WLR 678* (n 136) 268.

138 *Ladbroke (Football) Ltd v William Hill (Football) Ltd [1964] 1 WLR 273* (n 125); *Interlego A.G. Appellant v Tyco Industries Inc [1988] 3 WLR 678* (n 136); *Sawkins v Hyperion Records Ltd [2005] EWCA Civ 565* (n 105) 695, 696; Bently and others (n 1); Caddick, Harbottle and Suthersanen (n 4) paras 3–184, 3–186; Tappin and others (n 2) s 3.58, 3.70.

139 *Sawkins v Hyperion Records Ltd [2005] EWCA Civ 565* (n 105) 707 (per Mummery LJ).

140 *Sawkins v Hyperion Records Ltd [2005] EWCA Civ 565* (n 105).

141 ibid 707.

142 ibid 696.

> limited sense that the author originated it by his efforts rather than slavishly copying it from the work produced by the efforts of another person.[143]

Furthermore, it was established that the assessment of originality examines the work as a whole without fragmentation.[144] This means that when examining whether a work satisfies the originality requirement, it is not dissected into several parts and subsequently, each part is given its own originality evaluation in relation to the amount and kind of skill, labour, and judgement expended upon it.[145] A work must be evaluated first as a whole to determine whether it satisfies the originality requirement; the fragmentation only occurs afterwards to assess whether infringement occurred because the copied part was a protectable original expression.

So, in essence, the traditional originality standard in the United Kingdom was built upon two main tenets. The first is independent creation. The second requires a sufficient degree of skill, labour, and judgement that does not amount to "mere servile copying"[146] to regard a work as original for the purposes of copyright law.[147] However, this traditional view regarding originality in the United Kingdom was met with uncertainty following EU development in the field of copyright law harmonisation that impacted and shifted the United Kingdom's approach to be more aligned with the EU-wide originality standard influenced by the views expressed in continental Europe regarding originality.[148]

#### *6.3.2.2 The Impact of EU Copyright Harmonisation on the UK Traditional Standard of Originality*

The origins of the EU's impact on the UK copyright law standard of originality are attributed to EU efforts to harmonise some aspects of copyright law in order to create legal certainty within the EU.[149] Several directives attempted to standardise the level of protection afforded to specific types of works, such as

143 ibid.

144 *Ladbroke (Football) Ltd v William Hill (Football) Ltd [1964] 1 WLR 273* (n 125) 277; *Sawkins v Hyperion Records Ltd [2005] EWCA Civ 565* (n 105) 701, 707–708.

145 *Ladbroke (Football) Ltd v William Hill (Football) Ltd [1964] 1 WLR 273* (n 125) 277; *Sawkins v Hyperion Records Ltd [2005] EWCA Civ 565* (n 105) 707–708; Bently and others (n 1) 105.

146 *Sawkins v Hyperion Records Ltd [2005] EWCA Civ 565* (n 105) 707.

147 Caddick, Harbottle and Suthersanen (n 4) paras 3–184, 3–186.

148 Tappin and others (n 2) s 3.58; Caddick, Harbottle and Suthersanen (n 4) paras 2–92, 3–04, 3–187, 4–14, 4–15; Bently and others (n 1); Rosati (n 7) 68–69; see: Rahmatian (n 15); see post-Brexit case: *TuneIn Inc v Warner Music UK Ltd, [2021] EMLR 18*.

149 Directive 2001/29/EC of 22 May 2001 on the harmonisation of certain aspects of copyright and related rights in the information society [2001] OJ L167/10; Directive 2006/116/EC of 12 December 2006 on the term of protection of copyright and certain related rights [2006] OJ L372/12; Rosati (n 7) 4; Caddick, Harbottle and Suthersanen (n 4) paras 2–92, 3–04.

databases,[150] computer programs,[151] and photographs,[152] in order to provide them with streamlined rules for the subsistence of copyright across the EU.[153] These directives purported that the standard of originality was satisfied when the work constitutes the "author's own intellectual creation."[154] The databases directive further explained that in the case of works of compilation, the author's own intellectual creation was satisfied through free selection and arrangement.[155] The CDPA 1988 implemented the database directive in Section 3A(2), which provides that "a database is original if, and only if, by reason of the selection or arrangement of the contents of the database the database constitutes the author's own intellectual creation."[156] To examine the extent of the EU's impact on the United Kingdom's traditional standard of originality, one must look at a series of European decisions starting from *Infopaq International A/S v Danske Dagblades Forening (2009)*.[157]

The CJEU laid down the EU-wide standard of originality in a landmark case that involved a copyright dispute regarding newspaper articles.[158] In *Infopaq International A/S v Danske Dagblades Forening (2009)*[159] it was held that even an 11-word extract of a newspaper article may be protected by copyright against reproduction if that extract contained "elements of the work which expressed the author's own intellectual creation."[160] The CJEU clarified that the words themselves do not constitute elements covered by copyright protection; rather, copyright protection extends to words only through "the choice, sequence and combination of those words that the author may express his creativity in an original manner and achieve a result which is regarded as an intellectual creation."[161] *Infopaq* stressed that originality is satisfied when the work constitutes an intellectual creation by the

150 Article 3(1) Directive 96/9/EC of 11 March 1996 on the legal protection of databases [1996] OJ L77/20.

151 Article 1(3) Directive 2009/24/EC of 23 April 2009 on the legal protection of computer programs [2009] OJ L111/16.

152 Article 6 Directive 2006/116/EC of 12 December 2006 on the term of protection of copyright and certain related rights [2006] OJ L372/12.

153 Thomas Margoni, "The Harmonisation of EU Copyright Law: The Originality Standard," *Global Governance of Intellectual Property in the 21st Century* (Draft version, Springer International Publishing 2016) 1, 8; Judge and Gervais (n 4) 384–384; Caddick, Harbottle and Suthersanen (n 4) paras 2–92, 3–04.

154 Article 3(1) Directive 96/9/EC of 11 March 1996 on the legal protection of databases [1996] OJ L77/20; Article 6 Directive 2006/116/EC of 12 December 2006 on the term of protection of copyright and certain related rights [2006] OJ L372/12; Article 1(3) Directive 2009/24/EC of 23 April 2009 on the legal protection of computer programs [2009] OJ L111/16.

155 Article 3 (1) Directive 96/9/EC of 11 March 1996 on the legal protection of databases [1996] OJ L77/20.

156 Section 3(2) Copyright, Designs and Patents Act 1988 (UK).

157 *(C-5/08) Infopaq International A/S v Danske Dagblades Forening [2009] ECR I-6569* (n 10).

158 Bently and others (n 1) 98; Rosati (n 7) 127, 151.

159 *(C-5/08) Infopaq International A/S v Danske Dagblades Forening [2009] ECR I-6569* (n 10).

160 ibid [38].

161 ibid [45]–[46].

author's own creative choices expressed through his composition, arrangement, and other elements that express the intellectual creation that was reflected in the work. *Infopaq*'s conception of originality proved to be very influential in driving the efforts to harmonise the standard of originality within the EU while leaving room for variation on how it operates in practice to national courts.[162] That is because *Infopaq* did not provide a clear definition of what is meant by the "author's own intellectual creation," perhaps due to the fact that it is difficult to have a universal definition regarding what constitutes an intellectual creation.[163] Instead, it only opted to touch on what elements of the creation process evidence the author's intellectual creation for the purposes of copyright, such as the type of selection and arrangement that express an intellectual creation in a newspaper article.[164]

The *Infopaq* decision was applied in *Painer v Standard Verlags GmbH (2011)*,[165] which involved a question regarding the originality of a portrait photograph and whether it is to be afforded weaker copyright protection by virtue of its perceived limitation with regard to its range of expressions. The CJEU held that portrait photographs could satisfy the originality standard and be protected by copyright if it is the author's own intellectual creation in the sense that they reflect the author's personality through his "free and creative choices in the production of that photograph."[166] The CJEU stated that a work might be the author's own intellectual creation if it contained "his personal touch."[167] The exact meaning of what constitutes the author's "personal touch" was not expanded upon, aside from being achieved through the author's "free and creative choices."[168]

The extent of *Infopaq* and *Painer*'s impact on the UK originality standard was questioned in *Newspaper Licensing Agency Ltd v Meltwater Holding BV [2011]*.[169] The *Meltwater case* involved a copyright claim regarding reports from a media monitoring service that reproduced headlines and extracts from news articles. The case presented two questions pertaining to originality: the first question was whether newspaper headlines constitute an independent original work; the second was whether the extracts constitute a substantial part of the article to the extent that it infringes upon the article's copyright. For the former, the court stated that newspaper headlines could be regarded as original literary work independent from the article for the purposes of copyright if they evidence sufficient skill and judgement in their creation to the degree that they constitute the author's own intellectual creation.[170] The court later provided that the question of substantiality regarding the

162 ibid 48; Rosati (n 7) 4, 99, 107; Bently and others (n 1) 98–99.

163 Rahmatian (n 15) 22; Tappin and others (n 2) s 3.55; Bently and others (n 1) 99–101.

164 *(C-5/08) Infopaq International A/S v Danske Dagblades Forening [2009] ECR I-6569* (n 10) para [45] [48] [50]; Tappin and others (n 2) s 3.46, 3.55; Bently and others (n 1) 99–101.

165 *(C-145/10) Painer v Standard Verlags GmbH [2012] ECDR 6* (n 51).

166 ibid [94] [99].

167 ibid [92].

168 Bently and others (n 1) 99–101; Tappin and others (n 2) s 3.46; Rahmatian (n 15) 22.

169 *Newspaper Licensing Agency Ltd v Meltwater Holding BV [2011] RPC 7* (n 23).

170 ibid 212, 228.

reproduced part was related to its quality, not quantity.[171] This is because *Infopaq* confirmed that copyright protected whatever represented the author's intellectual creation regardless of whether it constituted a small or a big part of the work.[172] Thus, the court stated that the effect of *Infopaq* restated the standard of originality to focus on the quality of the process of creation rather than the quantity of the work.[173] That quality assessment is not addressed at the work itself but rather at the quality of the process of creation employed by the author in the sense that it is of the kind that renders the work his own intellectual creation and subsequently eligible for copyright protection.[174] Therefore, the right kind of skill, labour, and judgement that was poured into the expression to the extent that renders the work the author's own intellectual creation satisfies the *Infopaq test*.[175]

In *Football Dataco Ltd v Yahoo! UK Ltd (2012)*,[176] the CJEU attempted to shed more light on what is meant by the author's own intellectual creation. The case concerned the issue of originality in fixture lists of football leagues that were created following certain parameters and rules. The main issue was whether the skill and labour that went into creating the raw database, which was subject to technical considerations, was enough for it to be regarded as original and subsequently eligible for copyright protection under the Database Directive 96/9/EC.[177] Advocate General Mengozzi examined the law regarding databases and explained that copyright is concerned with the structure and external form of the database when embedded with free selection and arrangement that evidence the author's own intellectual creation (his personal touch).[178] He further stated that the copyright in a database does not extend to cover the data creation phase, regardless of the skill and labour that went into creating them, because copyright is only concerned with how the data was represented and not the effort itself.[179] The Advocate General further clarified that in order for a database to be covered by copyright, it must be original beyond mere skill and labour in the sense that it represents the author's own intellectual creation. He stated that this standard of originality "leaves no room for doubt, and echoes a formula which is typical of the continental copyright tradition."[180] Hence, the case confirms the

171 ibid [74].
172 ibid [83].
173 ibid at [81] "the test of quality has been re-stated but for present purposes not significantly altered by infopaq" (per Proudman J).
174 ibid [71] [74] "it is not literary quality which is in issue but the quality of originality which earned the work copyright protection" (per Proudman J at para [74]).
175 ibid [83]; see: Rahmatian (n 15) 30; Tappin and others (n 2) s 3.46, 4.41; Caddick, Harbottle and Suthersanen (n 4) paras 3–28, 3–29, 3–33, 3–180, 3–181, 3–187, 3–188.
176 *(C-604/10) Football Dataco Ltd v Yahoo! UK Ltd [2013] FSR 1.*
177 ibid.
178 ibid 7–9, 10–12, 13.
179 *(C-604/10) Football Dataco Ltd v Yahoo! UK Ltd [2013] FSR 1* (n 176) Opinion of Advocate General Mengozzi, paras [14] [17] [20] [23]–[24] [27] [31]–[34] [45].
180 ibid AG [37].

shift away from the UK traditional originality standard in favour of the EU-wide conception of originality.

One could read the CJEU decision as not necessarily declaring that all types of skill and labour are irrelevant for the originality standard; it only clarified that the type of skill and labour to be expended should be the type that has gone into creating an expression that embeds the work with the author's "personal touch" to constitute the author's intellectual creation.[181] These sentiments regarding the right kind of skill and labour were present in the UK copyright law, albeit not followed strictly, where the type of skill and labour was taken into consideration upon determining a work's originality.[182]

This position was affirmed in another case that further touched on the EU originality standard and its impact on the UK standard of originality. The case of *SAS Institute Inc v World Programming Ltd (2013)*[183] concerned the extent of copyright protection in a computer program that was reverse engineered by a competitor to reproduce its functions in another program. The CJEU provided that only elements that constitute an original expression of the author's own intellectual creation are subject to copyright protection.[184] The functional elements, as well as the ideas and process behind the program, are not subject to copyright protection and are not regarded as original elements regardless of the nature and amount of skill, labour, and judgement that went into creating them.[185]

Upon the case's return to the United Kingdom, the Court of Appeal judges dismissed the copyright claim since the elements in question were regarded as ideas and processes rather than elements related to the expression of the author's intellectual creation.[186] Furthermore, Lewison LJ clarified that the process of intellectual creation itself is not the subject of protection but rather the work itself, the expression, that was spawned from it, that is, if it contained elements of expression that were original in the sense that they were the author's own intellectual creation.[187] Lewison LJ stated that:

> The essence of the term [intellectual creation] is that the person in question has exercised expressive and creative choices in producing the work. The more restricted the choices, the less likely it is that the product will be the

181 Bently and others (n 1) 106; Rahmatian (n 15) 30; Tappin and others (n 2) s 1.21, 4.41.

182 See: *Interlego A.G. Appellant v Tyco Industries Inc [1988] 3 WLR 678* (n 136); *Hadley v Kemp [1999] EMLR 589*; *SAS Institute Inc v World Programming Ltd [2010] EWHC 1829 (Ch)* [205] [207] [255] [260]; see also: *Sawkins v Hyperion Records Ltd [2005] EWCA Civ 565* (n 105); Tappin and others (n 2) s 1.21, 3.40, 3.58, 4.41; Bently and others (n 1) 106; Caddick, Harbottle and Suthersanen (n 4) paras 3–28, 3–29, 3–33, 3–180, 3–181, 3–187, 3–188.

183 *(C-406/10) SAS Institute Inc v World Programming Ltd [2012] RPC 31*; *SAS Institute Inc v World Programming Ltd [2013] EWCA Civ 1482*.

184 *(C-406/10) SAS Institute Inc v World Programming Ltd [2012] RPC 31* (n 183) 950–951, 955–956, 966, 969.

185 ibid.

186 *SAS Institute Inc v World Programming Ltd [2013] EWCA Civ 1482* (n 183) 300–301.

187 ibid [74].

intellectual creation (or the expression of the intellectual creation) of the person who produced it.[188]

Henceforth, the court stressed that no amount of skill and labour is enough to grant copyright protection to elements that fall under ideas, facts, processes, functions, and other elements excluded from copyright protection. The kind of skill and labour required to meet the originality criteria must be the one that went into elements of expression in a way that evidences the author's own intellectual creation.[189] Lewison LJ remarked, regarding the effects of the Information Society Directive (InfoSoc) on the UK traditional originality standard, that "If the Information Society Directive has changed the traditional domestic test, it seems to me that it has raised rather than lowered the hurdle to obtaining copyright protection."[190] This statement is arguably not certain when it comes to other works. This is because the UK traditional standard requires a work to be non-trivial. Hence, one could argue that in instances involving minimal works like short phrases, the EU standard would seem to lower the threshold for such works rather than raising it.[191] Despite Lewison LJ's remark, the general view within the UK courts seems to suggest that the two tests, although different, oftentimes lead to comparable results.[192] Perhaps a piece of evidence supporting this stance was the fact that the French courts, which adopt the author's imprint of personality standard, resolved the *Sawkins case*[193] similarly to the English courts.

Some argue that the *SAS Institute case* did not interpret the CJEU decisions as rejecting the traditional standard of skill, labour, and judgement wholeheartedly but rather elaborated on its relation to the author's own intellectual creation standard.[194] They concur that the CJEU clarified that the only type of skill, labour, and judgement that confers originality is that which expresses the author's personality through his free choices that embedded the work with his "personal touch."[195] One possible view regarding the meaning of the terms "author's own intellectual creation" and "personal touch," as advanced by *Infopaq* and *Painer*, respectively, may

188 ibid [31].

189 ibid 301.

190 ibid [37].

191 Rosati (n 7) 117; Bently and others (n 1) 64, 106–107,111–112; Tappin and others (n 2) s 3.46, 3.48; Caddick, Harbottle and Suthersanen (n 4) paras 3–193, 3–194; *Newspaper Licensing Agency Ltd v Meltwater Holding BV [2011] RPC 7* (n 23) para [78] [81].

192 Caddick, Harbottle and Suthersanen (n 4) paras 3–187, 3–188, 3–189; Tappin and others (n 2) s 4.41; Fisher III (n 17) 443; Judge and Gervais (n 4) 386; Rahmatian (n 15) 15; *Temple Island Collections Ltd v New English Teas Ltd [2012] EWPCC 1.*

193 *Sawkins v Hyperion Records Ltd [2005] EWCA Civ 565* (n 105).

194 *Newspaper Licensing Agency Ltd v Meltwater Holding BV [2011] RPC 7* (n 23) para [81]; Rahmatian (n 15) 8, 11; Tappin and others (n 2) s 3.55, 4.41; Caddick, Harbottle and Suthersanen (n 4) paras 3–187, 3–188, 3–189.

195 *(C-145/10) Painer v Standard Verlags GmbH [2012] ECDR 6* (n 51) para [92].

be related to origination/independent creation in that the work must originate from the author, a product of his "personal touch," and not copied.[196]

A divide existed regarding the real extent of these CJEU decisions' impact on the traditional UK concept of originality. On the one hand, several commentators and scholars considered these series of decisions as evidence for the EU-wide originality standard that applies to all criteria of works and represents a shift in the UK conception of originality to be more aligned with continental Europe.[197] On the other hand, some argued that the impact was marginal, a little more than a semantic change because the traditional UK originality standard was compatible with the author's own intellectual creation standard.[198] Others argued that the full extent of the EU's impact on the UK originality standard remained to be seen with regard to whether it only extended to the specific works addressed by the directives or whether its impact applies universally to all intellectual creations eligible for copyright protection regardless of the type of work in question.[199]

Nonetheless, the cases of the *Duchess of Sussex v Associated Newspapers Ltd [2021]*[200] *and THJ Systems Limited & Anor v Daniel Sheridan & Anor [2023]*[201] confirmed that the EU-wide standard of originality is the originality test followed by UK courts post-Brexit. In the *Duchess of Sussex case*, Meghan Markle successfully claimed for misuse of private information and copyright infringement against Associated Newspapers Ltd for publishing a substantial part of the content of her private letter in their tabloid newspapers. Warby J, now LJ, confirmed that the EU harmonised originality standard moved the United Kingdom away from its traditional originality standard.[202] Hence, Warby LJ confirmed that the originality standard in operation in the United Kingdom is the author's own intellectual creation standard instead of the traditional standard of skill, labour, and judgement. The decision was later affirmed by the Court of Appeal.[203] In *THJ Systems Limited*, which concerned the copyrightability of a graphical user interface, Arnold LJ confirmed that "the correct test" of originality in the United Kingdom is the author's own intellectual creation in that "the author was able to express their creative

196 *Newspaper Licensing Agency Ltd v Meltwater Holding BV, [2012] Bus LR 53 (2011)* 92; Judge and Gervais (n 4) 386; Caddick, Harbottle and Suthersanen (n 4) paras 3–187, 3–188, 3–189; Tappin and others (n 2) s 4.41; Rahmatian (n 15) 15; Fisher III (n 17) 443, 445, 446.

197 See: Rosati (n 7) 207; Deming Liu, "Of Originality: Originality in English Copyright Law: Past and Present" [2014] European Intellectual Property Review 376; Bently and others (n 1) 93, 99, 102.

198 Caddick, Harbottle and Suthersanen (n 4) paras 3–187, 3–188, 3–189; Tappin and others (n 2) s 4.41; see: Rahmatian (n 15) 11, 30; Judge and Gervais (n 4) 386; Bently and others (n 1) 102; Fisher III (n 17) 443.

199 Caddick, Harbottle and Suthersanen (n 4) paras 2–10, 3–187, 3–188, 3–189; Tappin and others (n 2) s 3.55; Bently and others (n 1) 99, 106, 108; Rosati (n 7) 207.

200 *Duchess of Sussex v Associated Newspapers Ltd [2021] ECDR 25.*

201 *THJ Systems Limited & Anor v Daniel Sheridan & Anor [2023] EWCA Civ 1354.*

202 *Duchess of Sussex v Associated Newspapers Ltd [2021] ECDR 25* (n 200) para [142] [143].

203 *Duchess of Sussex v Associated Newspapers Ltd [2021] 12 WLUK 25.*

abilities in the production of the work by making free and creative choices so as to stamp the work created with their personal touch."[204]

Henceforth, the EU standard of originality has refined the traditional UK test by emphasising that the kind of skill, labour, and judgement must be relevant to the expression reflected in the work and must be the type that evidences the author's own intellectual creation. Even with the UK exit from the EU on 31 January 2020, recent case law indicates that the impact of the CJEU harmonisation effort remains persistent and UK courts still apply the EU-wide originality standard, cementing the shift away from the UK traditional originality standard.[205]

## 6.4 Conclusion

Originality is an amorphous concept that has eluded a clear definition since it entered copyright law. Its most basic tenets are closely linked to origination in that the work was independently created and was not the result of copying. However, the originality concept has since developed much further and increased in complexity as well as in the roles it plays in the operation of copyright law. At times, originality was thought of as promoting the production of high-quality works, curtailing the expansion of copyright protection to undeserving works. Another view considered originality as a flexible limiting factor on copyright, protecting only the parts that are deemed original. It is also used to delineate the scope of protection offered to specific elements of a given work by taking the role of a balancing agent that ensures that copyright does not expand to specific realms, such as styles, even if they were original. What is certain about originality is the way the concept has been used flexibly in copyright law to achieve different desired objectives. This is illustrated clearly in the different approaches across the world regarding the concept of originality, which can be boiled down to three predominant conceptions. These three conceptions are first, independent creation; second, the expenditure of the right kind of skill, labour, and judgement in the work's creation; and third, exercising free and creative choices reflected in the work that amount to the author's own intellectual creation representing the author's imprint of personality.

Moreover, the state of originality in photographs showcased originality's amorphous nature as several proxies were used to meet the standard of originality. Professor Subotnik identified several proxies of originality that were more pronounced when dealing with photographs' originality.[206] These proxies were the proxy of ontology, the proxy of narrative, and the proxy of comparison.[207] The proxy of narrative saw ample use when evaluating the originality in photographs in that the courts often look at the authorial narrative of the photograph's creation to

204 *THJ Systems Limited & Anor v Daniel Sheridan & Anor [2023] EWCA Civ 1354* (n 201) para [16], [23].

205 *Duchess of Sussex v Associated Newspapers Ltd [2021] ECDR 25* (n 200); *TuneIn Inc v Warner Music UK Ltd, [2021] EMLR 18* (n 148).

206 See: Subotnik (n 2).

207 ibid 1494–1495.

determine its originality. Thus, the assessment of originality in photographs often extended beyond the confines of the work itself to determine whether a photograph was original, a testament to the elusive nature of originality.

Despite the amorphous nature of the concept of originality, Anglo-American copyright law has adopted a relatively stable delineation of originality as a qualitative assessment with a low threshold that is not concerned with the artistic merits of the work.[208] The US current standard of originality was laid down in *Feist*,[209] and it requires that a work must be independently created and contain a modicum of creativity. In the United Kingdom, the traditional originality standard of sufficient skill, labour, and judgement was replaced by the EU-wide standard of originality laid down in *Infopaq*[210] and *Painer*,[211] which provided that a work was original if it was the author's own intellectual creation reflecting his personal touch. The EU standard of originality refined the traditional UK test by emphasising that the kind of skill, labour, and judgement must be relevant to the expression reflected in the work and must be the type that evidences the author's own intellectual creation.

208 *Feist Publications, Inc v Rural Telephone Service Co, Inc, 499 U.S. 340 (1991)* (n 8) 345; Tappin and others (n 2) s 1.21, 3.40, 3.55, 4.41; Caddick, Harbottle and Suthersanen (n 4) 2–10, 3–184, 3–186; see: *Temple Island Collections Ltd v New English Teas Ltd [2012] EWPCC 1* (n 192) para 27; see also; *Technomed Ltd v Bluecrest Health Screening Ltd [2017] EWHC 2142 (Ch)* [89–90].

209 *Feist Publications, Inc v Rural Telephone Service Co, Inc, 499 U.S. 340 (1991)* (n 8).

210 *(C-5/08) Infopaq International A/S v Danske Dagblades Forening [2009] ECR I-6569* (n 10).

211 *(C-145/10) Painer v Standard Verlags GmbH [2012] ECDR 6* (n 51).

# 7 Originality and Copyright Protection in Photographs in Anglo-American Copyright Law

## 7.1 Introduction

The general standard of originality in Anglo-American copyright law applies to photographic works without major doctrinal adjustments to fit with the unique nature of photographic works.[1] The US standard of originality as laid down in *Feist*[2] requires a photograph to be independently created and contain a modicum of creativity while stressing that the threshold of originality remains extremely low.[3] In the United Kingdom, the European Union (EU) Copyright Term Directive provides that:

> A photographic work within the meaning of the Berne Convention is to be considered original if it is the author's own intellectual creation reflecting his personality, no other criteria such as merit or purpose being taken into account. The protection of other photographs should be left to national law.[4]

Therefore, in the United Kingdom, a photograph is original if it is the author's own intellectual creation reflecting his personal touch.[5] When it comes to photographs, the US and UK standards of originality operate similarly in practice despite the United States having a higher standard of originality in theory.

This chapter focuses on how the courts assessed originality in photographs in Anglo-American copyright law by exploring how they located originality in different types of photographs. Firstly, this chapter identifies the sources of originality in photographs based on Laddie's Treatise on Copyright.[6] Afterwards, this chapter analyses several cases that endeavoured to locate the protectable elements in photographs regarded as evidence of the photographer's original expression.

1 See Chapter 6.

2 *Feist Publications, Inc v Rural Telephone Service Co, Inc, 499 US 340 (1991).*

3 ibid 345.

4 Recital 16 Directive 2006/116/EC of 12 December 2006 on the term of protection of copyright and certain related rights [2006] OJ L372/12.

5 *(C-145/10) Painer v Standard Verlags GmbH [2012] ECDR 6*; *(C-5/08) Infopaq International A/S v Danske Dagblades Forening [2009] ECR I-6569.*

6 Michael Tappin and others, *Laddie, Prescott and Vitoria: The Modern Law of Copyright* (5 edition, LexisNexis Butterworths 2018) s 4.66.

DOI: 10.4324/9781003586555-7

This chapter illustrates the uncertainty surrounding the level of protection offered to photographs as well as the inconsistency associated with the courts' approach concerning what constitutes a photograph's elements of originality that are worthy of protection. It aims to illustrate that originality is not suitable to function as a deciding factor to the copyrightability of a photograph due to its relatively poor compatibility with visual works such as photographs.

## 7.2 The Sources of Originality in Photographs

For a photograph to be copyrightable, it must satisfy the originality standard. What is certain about a photograph's originality in the Anglo-American copyright law is that it could be located in different stages of its creation process and within different aspects of that stage without necessarily referencing a particular feature of the subject matter itself that was depicted in the photograph.[7] In other words, the courts often do not need to locate originality within the confines of the photograph itself, as it can also find it in the realm outside it.[8] The leading copyright treatise in the United Kingdom, Laddie on Copyright,[9] provided an articulate summary regarding the sources of originality in photographs that proved to be influential on the approach taken by the Anglo-American courts when assessing the originality of a photograph. The treatise identified three nonexclusive sources of originality in which photographs may be found to be original.[10] These sources, or categories, of photographs' originality are 1) rendition or composition, 2) creation of the subject matter, and 3) timing.[11]

The first source of originality in photographs may be attributed to its rendition owing to the compositional elements that rendered the photographs' expression.[12] The rendition or composition of a photograph serves as a tangible source of originality that contains the bulk of what the courts regard as elements of expression capable of conferring sufficient originality upon photographs for the purposes of copyright protection.[13] Across case law, courts have recognised a wide range of elements related to composition such as the angle of shot, lighting, shadows, selection of film and camera, background, shading, position, colours, focus, depth of field, motif, posing the subject, evoking a particular expression, colour manipulation,

7 Eva E Subotnik, "Originality Proxies: Toward a Theory of Copyright and Creativity" (2010) 76 Brooklyn Law Review 1487, 1494, 1512; Tappin and others (n 6) s 4.66; William Patry, *Patry on Copyright* (March 2019, Thomson West 2012) s 3.118.

8 Subotnik (n 7) 1494; Justin Hughes, "The Photographer's Copyright-Photograph as Art, Photograph as Database" (2011) 25 Harv. JL & Tech. 339, 408; Terry S Kogan, "The Enigma of Photography, Depiction, and Copyright Originality" (2014) 25 Fordham Intellectual Property, Media & Entertainment Law Journal 869, 935–936.

9 Tappin and others (n 6) s 4.66.

10 ibid.

11 ibid; see: *Mannion v Coors Brewing Co, 377 FSupp2d 444 (2005)* 451, 452; see also: *Temple Island Collections Ltd v New English Teas Ltd [2012] EWPCC 1.*

12 Tappin and others (n 6) s 4.66; Patry (n 7) s 3.118.

13 Patry (n 7) s 3.118; Tappin and others (n 6) s 4.66.

effects due to filters and developing techniques, and framing among many other elements that were deemed to be capable of being protectable original elements of a photograph's expression and evidence its originality.[14] A photograph's rendition could be regarded as the main source of originality in photographs since its elements are inseparable from the other two sources of originality in photographs.

The second source of originality in photographs may be found in aspects related to the creation of the scene itself or the subject of the photograph, which can be located through elements such as preparation, arrangement, and setting up the scene, among other elements related to the creation of the photograph's subject matter that affect the way it was depicted.[15] Professor Terry Kogan touched on this category and explained that if a photograph's subject matter is more akin to a staged tableau, then it should itself be protected as an expression.[16] Nonetheless, it is important to note that this category does not necessarily give the photographer a monopoly in depicting the subject matter or its features.[17] It only posits that creating the subject matter may enhance a photograph's originality in a way that it could be possible to extend protection in so far as to cover the subject matter from being recreated in another photograph along with the way it was depicted.[18] However, this possibility is rarely met, at least in practice, if the expressive elements accompanying the depicted subject matter are different.[19]

The third source of originality in photographs may be attributed to the timing of capture, perhaps the single most identifiable and prevalent aspect in many photographs captured in this era.[20] The level of originality in timing is significantly pronounced when a unique scene is captured "at the right place at the right time."[21] But this does not necessarily mean that a photograph snapped at a whim is excluded from this category of originality in photographs since "the law would be unrealistic

14 See for example: *Burrow-Giles Lithographic Co v Sarony, 111 US 53 (1884)*; *Mannion v Coors Brewing Co, 377 FSupp2d 444 (2005)* (n 11); *Belair v MGA Entertainment, Inc, 831 FSupp2d 687 (2011)*; *Kaplan v Stock Market Photo Agency, Inc, 133 FSupp2d 317 (2001)*; *Harney v Sony Pictures Television, Inc, 704 F3d 173 (2013)*; *Kisch v Ammirati & Puris Inc, 657 FSupp 380 (1987)*; *SHL Imaging, Inc v Artisan House, Inc, 117 FSupp2d 301 (2000)*; *Nottage v Jackson (1883) 11 QBD 627*; *Melville v Mirror of Life Co [1895] 2 Ch 531*; *Temple Island Collections Ltd v New English Teas Ltd [2012] EWPCC 1* (n 11); *(C-145/10) Painer v Standard Verlags GmbH [2012] ECDR 6* (n 5).

15 Tappin and others (n 6) s 4.66; *Burrow-Giles Lithographic Co v Sarony, 111 US 53 (1884)* (n 14); *Temple Island Collections Ltd v New English Teas Ltd [2012] EWPCC 1* (n 11).

16 See: Terry S Kogan, "How Photographs Infringe" (2017) 19 Vanderbilt Journal of Entertainment and Technology Law 354.

17 *Franklin Mint Corp v National Wildlife Art Exchange, Inc, 575 F2d 62 (1978)*; *Bauman v Fussell [1978] RPC 485*.

18 *Creation Records Ltd v News Group Newspapers Ltd [1997] EMLR 444*; *Mannion v Coors Brewing Co, 377 FSupp2d 444 (2005)* (n 11); see: *Harney v Sony Pictures Television, Inc, 704 F3d 173 (2013)* (n 14).

19 See for example: *Gross v Seligman, 212 F 930 (1914)*; *Temple Island Collections Ltd v New English Teas Ltd [2012] EWPCC 1* (n 11).

20 Tappin and others (n 6) s 4.66.

21 ibid.

if it tried to exclude this element of serendipity."[22] The photographer Henri Cartier-Bresson was famous for employing a philosophy of photography referred to as "the decisive moment" that precisely proves that timing is undeniably a considerable aspect of a photograph's composition in a way that serves as a source of its originality.[23] The right timing can imbue a photograph with the dash of originality required to find a photograph copyrightable.[24]

Upon closer inspection of these categories of originality in photographs, they seem to be connected to a higher theme that emphasises the elements associated with free selection and choices that are inherently embedded in each of these three categories. The element of free selection and choice is what gives a photograph its originality, as was illustrated in the Court of Justice of the European Union (CJEU) case *Painer v Standard Verlags GmbH [2012]*.[25] In *Painer* a question was raised regarding whether a portrait photograph satisfies the originality standard laid down in the Copyright Term Directive[26] and *Infopaq*[27] due to the perceived limited "formative freedom" associated with such types of photographs, which may narrow the extent of copyright protection. The CJEU emphasised that the essence of originality is that the author exercises free and creative choices that reflect his personality and imbue the work with his "personal touch" to the degree that it constitutes the author's own intellectual creation.[28] In the context of portrait photographs, the CJEU explained that:

> the photographer can make free and creative choices in several ways and at various points in its production. In the preparation phase, the photographer can choose the background, the subject's pose and the lighting. When taking a portrait photograph, he can choose the framing, the angle of view and the atmosphere created. Finally, when selecting the snapshot, the photographer may choose from a variety of developing techniques the one he wishes to adopt or, where appropriate, use computer software. By making those various choices, the author of a portrait photograph can stamp the work created with his "personal touch."[29]

The CJEU confirmed that the acts that confer originality on a photograph could be found in several ways during the different stages of the photograph's production,

22 ibid.

23 Naomi Rosenblum, *World History of Photography* (4 edition, Abbeville Press Inc, US 2008) 485, 490, 491; Martin W Sandler, *Photography: An Illustrated History* (OUP Oxford 2002) 98.

24 Tappin and others (n 6) s 4.66; *Otto v Hearst Communications, Inc WL 6510801 (2018)* 25 (Held that spontaneous factual photograph has a valid copyright); *Time Inc v Bernard Geis Associates, 293 FSupp 130 (1968)*.

25 *(C-145/10) Painer v Standard Verlags GmbH [2012] ECDR 6* (n 5).

26 Directive 2006/116/EC of 12 December 2006 on the term of protection of copyright and certain related rights [2006] OJ L372/12.

27 *(C-5/08) Infopaq International A/S v Danske Dagblades Forening [2009] ECR I-6569* (n 5).

28 *(C-145/10) Painer v Standard Verlags GmbH [2012] ECDR 6* (n 5) paras 92, 99.

29 ibid 90–92.

similar to how Laddie categorised three sources of originality in photographs. The CJEU stated that the key elements are creative freedom and choice.[30] Whether a photograph satisfies that standard of originality or not is left for national courts to decide on an ad hoc basis, but once it is satisfied, the protection is not inferior to other works subject to the same standard.[31] Nevertheless, in practice, it seems more often than not that photographs are given thin copyright protection in that they are only protected against verbatim copying.

In the United States, the district court in *Mannion v Coors Brewing Co (2005)*[32] examined the nature of originality in photographs by referencing Laddie's three sources of originality in photographs. Judge Kaplan provided an excellent analysis of originality in photographs that showcased how photographs amplified the elusiveness of the concept of originality. He pointed out that "the nature and extent of a photograph's protection differs depending on what makes that photograph original."[33] He continued by stating that the categories of rendition, creation of subject matter, and timing are closely related to each other, and they evidence originality in photographs by affecting how a photograph is depicted in the end product, in other words, expression.[34] The protection of an original photograph subsequently does not extend to the depicted subject matter itself, nor is each compositional element taken in isolation.[35] In other words, the range of selections and choices represented in the photographs in their own isolated capacity are not protected; only the holistic effects that they have left on how the photograph depicted its contents are protected, not the content itself. The court declined to grant summary judgement on the infringement claim since it acknowledged that there are stark similarities and sufficient differences and thus, "a reasonable jury could find substantial similarity either present or absent…images are such that infringement cannot be ruled out – or in – as a matter of law."[36]

This case perfectly illustrates the issue of originality in photographs and its precarious nature. The claimant's image features the basketball player Kevin Garnett posing while wearing multiple jewellery, with a close-up of his jewellery-donned hands and the title "ABOVE THE CLOUDS." Similarly, the defendant's billboard image advertises Coors Light with the phrase "ICED OUT" and features a close-up of a man's jewellery-covered hands in a similar pose to the Garnett image. Through juxtaposing the two images, one could argue that the two photographs in question are identical in terms of rendition and subject matter and the changes amount to mere auxiliary elements that did not have a huge impact on how the photographs depicted their contents. In fact, given the facts of the case, one could firmly take the position that the reshoot photograph copied the original photograph beyond the

30 ibid 90, 99.
31 ibid 94–99.
32 *Mannion v Coors Brewing Co, 377 FSupp2d 444 (2005)* (n 11).
33 ibid 451.
34 ibid 451–454.
35 ibid.
36 ibid 463.

subject matter down to its expressive elements. Yet, the judge was hesitant to rule that infringement took place as a matter of law and, since substantial similarity was a question of fact, deferred the question to a jury trial where they found that the reshoot photographs indeed infringed upon the original photograph.[37] This reluctance to decide whether the original elements of a photograph were copied is quite prevalent in infringement claims regarding photographs.[38]

Originality in photographs, as being derived from several sources that evidence the free selection and choice of the photographer (such as rendition, timing, and subject creation), is the predominant approach followed by the Anglo-American courts in cases involving a photograph's originality, a testament of its utility in tackling the difficult task of locating originality in photographs.[39] A fourth possible source of originality seems to derive from digital manipulation after the capture of the photograph, a stage in the creation process that was traditionally avoided when assessing a photograph's originality.[40] Thus, in order for a photograph to be original, the mentioned categories have to at least accumulate to the degree that satisfies the standard of originality in the United States and United Kingdom since they are not protected in isolation.

## 7.3 Overview of Anglo-American Case Law Regarding Originality in Photographs and the Scope of Its Copyright Protection

This part identifies what elements of photographs' expression were deemed protectable as original parts of a photograph by examining several cases that dealt with the question. In the United States, it seems that these elements are amorphous and their weight changes depending on the subject matter as well as the creation or authorial narrative that accompanies the photographs. In comparison, the United Kingdom seems to readily give the majority of photographs thin copyright protection. Hence, it regards most photographs as satisfying the originality requirement by virtue of being photographs that were independently created.[41] Underneath the surface of each case, legacy issues that date back to the time when copyright protection extended to photographs left a residual imprint upon the various issues associated with copyright in photographic works.

The discussion unfolds through interweaving the analysis of select Anglo-American cases under six sections organised based on different themes that explore the level of protection afforded to photographic works depending on the nature of

37 *Mannion v Coors Brewing Co, 530 FSupp2d 543 (2008).*

38 See: Michael D Murray, "Copyright, Originality, and the End of the Scènes à Faire and Merger Doctrines for Visual Works" (2006) 58 Baylor Law Review 779.

39 Tappin and others (n 6) s 4.66; Patry (n 7) s 3.118.

40 See: *Temple Island Collections Ltd v New English Teas Ltd [2012] EWPCC 1* (n 11) para 28; *Tiffany Design, Inc v Reno-Tahoe Specialty, Inc, 55 FSupp2d 1113 (1999)*; see also: *Apple Corps Ltd v Cooper [1992] 12 WLUK 29.*

41 Nicholas Caddick, Gwilym Harbottle and Uma Suthersanen, *Copinger and Skone James on Copyright* (18 edition, Sweet & Maxwell Ltd 2020) paras 3–233, 3–235, 3–236.

the subject matter and its impact on other compositional elements. A greater number of cases will be from the United States since it has a wealth of cases regarding copyright in photographic works compared to the United Kingdom.

### *7.3.1 The Reluctance to Protect Photographs' Subject Matters*

The originality that comes from the creation of the subject matter can be argued to be only regarded as a source of originality in a photograph when combined with minimal original elements of composition. Therefore, it seems that creating the subject matter of a photograph is only regarded as an element that may help justify the subsistence of copyright in a photograph but does not necessarily represent, in itself, a protectable element of its expression.

The UK case of *Creation Records Ltd v News Group Newspapers Ltd [1997]*[42] perfectly illustrated the notion that the subject matter of a photograph was not a protectable element, or at least extremely hard to protect, even if it was created to the minute detail. In this case, the scene to serve as the subject matter was created from scratch and prearranged in a set to take photographs that served as the cover for an album by the musical band Oasis.[43] The scene created was creative, unusual, and iconic, depicting several scattered objects and a Rolls-Royce partly submerged in a swimming pool. Several photographs were captured so one would be chosen to serve as the album cover. During this process, a photojournalist managed to take a photograph of the scene independently without authorisation from the plaintiffs, which prompted them to bring an infringement claim against the news agency that published the photograph.[44] The plaintiffs claimed that by virtue of creating the subject matter of the photograph, which was an invented reality, they own the copyright in the photographs that captured it.[45] The courts refused to regard the photograph's subject matter as, in itself, an original element of the photograph that prevents others from capturing it. Judge Lloyd clearly stated that:

> If the subject matter is not itself copyright, in principle two different photographers can take separate photographs of the same subject without either copying the other. Of course copyright subsists in the official photograph and if it were the only source of the scene it would be an infringement to copy that, either by a direct copying process or by the scene being recreated and a fresh photograph taken of that recreation. But it is a basic proposition of copyright law that two works created from a common source do not by reason of that fact involve copying one of the other, however similar they are.[46]

42 *Creation Records Ltd v News Group Newspapers Ltd [1997] EMLR 444* (n 18).
43 ibid 444–445.
44 ibid.
45 ibid.
46 ibid 450.

This case serves as a prime example that the subject matters of photographs are themselves not protected, at least outside their particular depiction in the photograph in question. That is because doing so would risk making copyright protection in photographs strictly a matter related to the priority of appropriation, which goes against copyright law's underlying principles. Yet, this case alluded that it is possible to protect the subject matter of a photograph if the photograph is used as a source from which to recreate its subject matter and produce it in another photograph. However, it is not clear whether the said recreation must also reproduce the rendition and depict the subject in a sufficiently similar way to regard the recreated photograph as an infringing work.

In the US case of *Kaplan v Stock Market Photo Agency (2001)*,[47] the district court held that the subject matter of a photograph is considered an unprotectable idea.[48] In this case, the similarity between the two photographs, which both depicted a high vantage point of a businessman's downward point of view from the edge of a tall building, was only attributed to the central idea behind the two photographs, which is "unprotectable in and of itself" as a subject matter.[49] The claimant's photograph shows a pair of polished black dress shoes overlooking a busy street filled with yellow taxis. The defendant's photograph features another pair of dress shoes next to a pigeon, with a vast grid-like pattern of windows in the background. The court held that the similarities in composition were only due to "the necessary sequence of events that follows from the chosen setting" that was attributed to the idea behind the two photographs, not pertaining to the expression of that idea by the photographers.[50] In other words, the court held that the two photographs were not alike with regard to their protectable elements of expression and only similar in their unprotectable features.[51]

Hence, as a principle, courts do not grant a monopoly on the subject matter of photographs since it falls on the ideas side of the idea/expression spectrum.[52] However, the boundaries between expressions and ideas are blurry at best, especially in the context of photographs where copyright concepts manifest their weak compatibility with visual works in a pronounced manner.[53] Professor Terry Kogan raised a central criticism of this case, arguing that the court did not elaborate on the difference between elements that flow from the idea and elements that express the idea, nor did it differentiate from subject matters that are akin to staged tableau and

47 *Kaplan v Stock Market Photo Agency, Inc, 133 FSupp2d 317 (2001)* (n 14).

48 ibid 322.

49 ibid 323.

50 ibid 323–324.

51 ibid 326–327.

52 ibid 323–324; see: *Kisch v Ammirati & Puris Inc, 657 FSupp 380 (1987)* (n 14); *Franklin Mint Corp v National Wildlife Art Exchange, Inc, 575 F2d 62 (1978)* (n 17).

53 See: Murray (n 38); Jennifer L Muse, "Monkeys and Elephants and Koalas, Oh My! Is Originality Still the Touchstone of Authorship in the United States Copyright Law?" (2015) 97 Journal of the Patent and Trademark Office Society 736.

other kinds of subject matters.[54] Kogan lamented that the *Kaplan decision* stripped protection from whole categories of the photograph's expression:

> By equating the photograph's "subject matter" to its unprotected "central idea," the court invokes the idea/expression dichotomy. In so doing, this sleight of hand virtually assures that a court will never recognize a photograph's staged tableau – its "subject matter" – as protected expression.[55]

The shaky grounds for placing a photograph's originality in its subject matter were illustrated in a dispute regarding a recreated photograph brought to the US First Circuit Court of Appeal. In *Harney v Sony Pictures Television, Inc (2013)*,[56] the plaintiff "snapped" a photograph of a little girl riding piggyback on her father's shoulders, which later became famous due to the revelation that the man depicted in the photograph abducted his daughter and was a criminal with multiple identities.[57] Sony Pictures made a documentary about the story and recreated the original photograph to produce a similar photograph with a number of different details.[58] Both photographs depicted a man in formal attire holding a document while carrying a smiling young girl in a pink coat on his shoulders but with different backgrounds. Harney's photograph had a backdrop with a church and leafless tree branches, while Sony's photograph had a darker, leafy background and slight variations in appearance. The plaintiff brought an infringement claim regarding the recreated photograph, claiming that it copied his photograph's expression. Sony responded that the similarity only spawned from the unprotectable elements needed to recreate the photograph's impression.[59] The first instance court found that the two photographs were not substantially similar in their expressive elements as they only shared their factual contents represented by the scene depicted.[60]

On appeal, the First Circuit was set to review the protectable elements of the photographs in question to determine whether infringement took place. The court examined whether the similarities were limited to unoriginal protectable elements or whether there were similarities in the original elements of expression. The court stated that since the scene was not prearranged or created by the photographer, the originality of this photograph is found in its composition and timing. The court stated that "Where the photographer is uninvolved in creating his subject, that subject matter – whether a person, a building, a landscape or something else – is equivalent to an idea that the law insists be freely available to everyone."[61]

Hence, the copyright protection granted to the photograph only covered how its content was depicted and did not extend to the content itself, which is treated as

54 Kogan, "How Photographs Infringe" (n 16) 381–385.
55 ibid 383–384.
56 *Harney v Sony Pictures Television, Inc, 704 F3d 173 (2013)* (n 14).
57 ibid 176–178.
58 ibid.
59 ibid 182–183.
60 ibid 178.
61 ibid 181.

unprotectable facts unattributed to the photographer's creation and does not owe its existence to him. The court emphasised that "The choices made by the photographer to generate a particular image depicting that subject matter, however, ordinarily transform 'the idea' of the subject into a protectible expressive work."[62] The independently existing facts, such as the scene with the father and daughter, are not protectable, but the "holistic" effects of the framing, angle of the shot, and other expressive elements that formed the original composition of the photograph may be considered as the protectable expression of Harney's photograph.[63]

By looking at the two photographs side by side, one can see the difficulties associated with this case. There are clearly strong similarities between the two photographs because one is a recreated version of the other. At the same time, several different details bar it from being identical in its general tone and colours. Whether these similarities are due to elements of facts or expression was a question the court aimed to tackle. Consequently, the court applied *Feist*[64] and regarded the subject matter of photographs as a discovered fact, uncreated by the photographer's expression, and does not owe its existence to him.[65] Therefore, the court distinguished this case from *Mannion v Coors*[66] in that Harney "happened upon" the scene and captured it; "Unlike Mannion, he did not 'create' his subject by 'orchestrat[ing] the scene.'"[67] Thus, the court held that the recreated photograph did not infringe the protectable elements of the original photograph and confidently stated that "no jury could properly conclude that Sony's adaptation of the Photo infringed Harney's copyright in his work."[68]

While this principle of not protecting ideas and facts is sound, the definition of facts as something that is discovered and not created presents problems not just for photographs but also for copyright in general since it seems to ignore the reality of created facts.[69] Professor Justin Hughes defines created facts as those where "the expressive work brings the very facts themselves into existence."[70] One type of created fact is fictional facts, such as the fact that Batman is Bruce Wayne, Superman's alter ego is Clark Kent, Daenerys is a Targaryen, and Voldemort killed Harry Potter's parents. Of course, created facts do not only refer to fictional facts.

62 ibid.

63 ibid 179–181.

64 *Feist Publications, Inc v Rural Telephone Service Co, Inc, 499 U.S. 340 (1991)* (n 2).

65 *Harney v Sony Pictures Television, Inc, 704 F3d 173 (2013)* (n 14) 181, 183–184, 188.

66 *Mannion v Coors Brewing Co, 377 FSupp2d 444 (2005)* (n 11).

67 *Harney v Sony Pictures Television, Inc, 704 F3d 173 (2013)* (n 14) 187–188.

68 ibid 188.

69 See: Justin Hughes, "Created Facts and the Flawed Ontology of Copyright Law" (2007) 83 Notre Dame Law Review 43, 85, 86; Alan L Durham, "Speaking of the World: Fact, Opinion and the Originality Standard of Copyright" (2001) 33 Arizona State Law Journal 791, 795; see also: Matt Kellogg, "The Problem of Fictional Facts: Idea, Expression, and Copyright's Balance between Author Incentive and Public Interest Part I: Articles" (2010) 58 Journal of the Copyright Society of the USA 549.

70 Justin Hughes, "Created Facts and the Flawed Ontology of Copyright Law" (2007) 83 Notre Dame Law Review 43, 45.

Hughes also pointed to another type of "created facts" or "authored facts" that refer to "human facts that result from an act that was the intentional creation of information qua information through the intentional creation of expression qua expression."[71] Hughes indicated that this refers to information created for the sake of information. An example illustrating this is when a person plans to sell his car for a specific amount of money. This situation is a fact that was neither discovered nor fictional; it is a created fact that owed its existence to that person, and it is accompanied by his expression represented by his act of providing that this specific car is offered for this specific price. Hence, this situation could be said to contain "authored facts." Hughes criticised *Feist*'s[72] universal definition of facts as things that are discoverable since they leave out a whole category of facts that are indeed created and were not discovered.[73]

Treating a photograph as a combination of authored facts and expression may illuminate a different understanding regarding the nature of photographs and, subsequently, a different approach to the *Harney v Sony case*. In other words, photographs might be regarded as a side effect of human activities in that the existence of the photograph itself is an authored fact. Harney's photograph may be regarded as a created fact because the photographer did not stumble upon it; he created it, developed it, and published it, and the other photograph was created based on it. Sony's photograph was not created based on the fact that this scene took place but based on the created fact that exists in the original photograph. Depending on how one interprets photographs as being based on a combination of created facts and expression, the situation regarding the subsistence of copyright may clear or complicate the matter surrounding photographs even further. Henceforth, it is understandable that the court did not divulge into this discussion.

In summary, it is safe to say that the creation of a photograph's subject matter alone as a source of originality crumbles quickly as a protectable element, even if it was accompanied by free compositional elements, in infringement claims.[74] At the same time, the courts acknowledge the creation of a photograph's subject matter as a source of originality for the purposes of the subsistence of copyright without necessarily considering it, in itself, a protectable original element of that photograph's expression.[75] This paradoxical treatment is not very shocking since the courts are exceedingly reluctant to grant a monopoly to the subject matter of photographs, even if it was created by the photographer from scratch. So, in a way,

71 Hughes, "Created Facts and the Flawed Ontology of Copyright Law" (n 70) 59.

72 *Feist Publications, Inc v Rural Telephone Service Co, Inc, 499 U.S. 340 (1991)* (n 2).

73 For more on this topic see: Hughes, "Created Facts and the Flawed Ontology of Copyright Law" (n 70) 45.

74 See: *Creation Records Ltd v News Group Newspapers Ltd [1997] EMLR 444* (n 18); *Sahuc v Tucker, 300 FSupp2d 461 (2004)*; *Leigh v Warner Bros, Inc, 212 F3d 1210 (2000)*; *Caratzas v Time Life, Inc, Not Reported in FSupp WL 322033 (1992)*.

75 Tappin and others (n 6) s 4.66; Patry (n 7) s 3.118; *Mannion v Coors Brewing Co, 377 FSupp2d 444 (2005)* (n 11); *Harney v Sony Pictures Television, Inc, 704 F3d 173 (2013)* (n 14); *Creation Records Ltd v News Group Newspapers Ltd [1997] EMLR 444* (n 18).

one could say that the creation of the subject matter of the photograph is a unique source of originality since it could not, in itself, be protected as an original expression of the photograph, but nonetheless, it is capable of evidencing the subsistence of copyright in a photograph. It is an unprotectable original element of sorts that falls under the idea spectrum of the idea/expression dichotomy when invoked in cases involving infringement but is regarded as an expression when strictly used to evidence the subsistence of copyright in a given photograph. Numerous cases in the United States and at least one case in the United Kingdom appear to confirm this hypothesis.[76]

### *7.3.2 The Nature of the Subject Matter, Its Depiction, and the Degree of Originality in Photographs*

On the photograph's subject matter, perhaps what is certain is that the subject matter, whether it was created or not, may only serve to either strengthen or weaken the subsistence of copyright in a photograph in the eyes of the courts but has little impact on the extent of the photograph's protection in case of infringement. This brings to question whether this focus on the subject matter of photographs is needed in the first place since most photographs are considered original if they were independently created, seemingly requiring nothing more than the pointing of the camera and pressing the shutter.[77] In fact, in certain instances, the subject matter of a photograph may have a negative relationship with whether or not a photograph is considered original to the degree protected by copyright.

#### *7.3.2.1 Public Domain Works as a Subject Matter and Accurate Depiction*

In the US case of *Bridgeman Art Library, Ltd v Corel Corp (1998)*,[78] photographs that accurately reproduced public domain paintings were found not to satisfy the originality standard of both the United Kingdom and the United States since the photographs amounted to nothing but slavish copies of public domain paintings.[79] The court stated that a change of medium does not, in itself, confer originality upon the photographs.[80] It seems that, at least in practice, the courts require a higher degree of originality in derivative photographs of public domain works despite the fact that, in theory, derivative works are not subjected to a heightened standard of

76 See: *Creation Records Ltd v News Group Newspapers Ltd [1997] EMLR 444* (n 18); *Mannion v Coors Brewing Co, 377 FSupp2d 444 (2005)* (n 11); *Kaplan v Stock Market Photo Agency, Inc, 133 FSupp2d 317 (2001)* (n 14); *Belair v MGA Entertainment, Inc, 831 FSupp2d 687 (2011)* (n 14); *Gentieu v Tony Stone Images/Chicago, Inc, 255 FSupp2d 838 (2003)*; *Bryant v Gordon, 483 FSupp2d 605 (2007)*; *Kisch v Ammirati & Puris Inc, 657 FSupp 380 (1987)* (n 14).

77 Caddick, Harbottle and Suthersanen (n 41) 3–233, 3–235; Patry (n 7) s 3.118.

78 *Bridgeman Art Library, Ltd v Corel Corp, 25 FSupp2d 421 (1998).*

79 ibid 195–197, 199.

80 ibid 196.

originality.[81] The *Bridgeman decision* and its implication of denying copyright for photographs that accurately depict their subject as mere slavish copies received criticisms from legal scholars and commentators that support protecting recreative works, such as art reproduction, with thin copyright protection.[82]

Professor Kogan criticised the notion that photographic reproduction lacked the requisite level of originality and argued that:

> Simply because a professional photographer follows tried and true techniques to photograph artwork does not reduce his choices to mere skill, lacking originality. He chooses to follow established practices and, in doing so, makes creative choices. This does not demote his art to a mere technical craft.[83]

Thus, Kogan argues that the choice to accurately depict a painting in photography is in itself a creative choice worthy of being granted, at least, thin copyright protection. He points out that it is absurd that "Vacationers' amateur snapshots taken with point-and-shoot cameras are considered original works, while the images of the professional museum photographer are deemed undeserving of copyright protection."[84]

The EU directive on copyright in the Digital Single Market addresses this matter directly in Article 14 by stating that:

> when the term of protection of a work of visual art has expired, any material resulting from an act of reproduction of that work is not subject to copyright or related rights, unless the material resulting from that act of reproduction is original in the sense that it is the author's own intellectual creation.[85]

Henceforth, there is an express acknowledgement that the art of reproduction can express originality to the degree that makes the work eligible for copyright protection if it constitutes the author's own intellectual creation. Article 14 sympathises with artists who accurately reproduce public domain visual works by acknowledging that even the art of reproduction can express the author's imprint of personality

81 See: *Schrock v Learning Curve Intern, Inc, 586 F3d 513 (2009)*; Steven S Boyd, "Deriving Originality in Derivative Works: Considering the Quantum of Originality Needed to Attain Copyright Protection in a Derivative Work" (1999) 40 Santa Clara Law Review 325, 353, 377.

82 See: Robin J Allan, "After 'Bridgeman': Copyright, Museums, and Public Domain Works of Art" (2007) 155 University of Pennsylvania Law Review 961; Terry S Kogan, "Photographic Reproductions, Copyright and the Slavish Copy" (2011) 35 Columbia Journal of Law & the Arts 445; Burton Ong, "Originality from Copying: Fitting Recreative Works into the Copyright Universe" (2010) 2 Intellectual Property Quarterly 165; Ronan Deazley, "Photography, Copyright and the South Kensington Experiment" in Estelle Derclaye, *Copyright and Cultural Heritage* (Edward Elgar Publishing 2010).

83 Kogan, "Photographic Reproductions, Copyright and the Slavish Copy" (n 82) 486.

84 ibid 445.

85 Article 14 Directive 2019/790/EC of 17 April 2019 on copyright and related rights in the Digital Single Market and amending Directives 96/9/EC and 2001/29/EC [2019] OJ L130/92.

through their creative choices reflected upon the reproduced work. This is because a photographer who seeks to accurately reproduce a work of art has to take into consideration many elements such as light, shadows, glare, focus, distance, position, camera, and aperture, as well as effectively utilise various equipment where his creative judgement is consistently channelled to reproduce the artwork.[86] The stream of creative choices even extends to the post-capture stage where the photographs are edited and tweaked to meet the photographer's desired results.

It is understandable that granting thin copyright protection that protects the works of these photographers from direct facsimile copying may be beneficial to support the production of such works. This may ensure that others are not prevented from taking accurate photographs of the subject matter, even if they were virtually identical, since what matters is that the photographs were independently created. In a sense, the protection would not differ from the protection granted to entrepreneurial works such as sound recordings. In the words of Justice Holmes, "Others are free to copy the original. They are not free to copy the copy."[87]

#### *7.3.2.2 Mundane or Generic Subject Matter with Descriptive Depiction and Its Implication on a Photograph's Level of Originality*

Despite the US courts' stance that affirms that originality is a low threshold, it seems that, in rare instances, photographs depicting mundane or generic subject matter combined with descriptive depiction may negatively affect their originality and, consequently, their protectability.[88] One could say that the dividing line regarding whether a generic or descriptive photograph would satisfy the required level of originality depends on the authorial narrative of its creation and the choices that could be deduced from that narrative. A line of cases seems to take the stance that purely utilitarian descriptive photographs may not be enough to satisfy the requisite level of originality in the United States.[89] However, in most situations, descriptive, accurate, or utilitarian photographs are capable of satisfying the originality

86 For examples regarding the range of creative choices that typically involve photographing artworks, see: *Artwork Photography at Klein Imaging* (Directed by Klein Imaging, 2021) <https://www.youtube.com/watch?v=7W2WVcH1K-A> accessed 18 October 2024; *Ask The Expert: Artwork Photography* (Directed by Klein Imaging, 2018) <https://www.youtube.com/watch?v=yNRbwxkHalE> accessed 18 October 2024.

87 *Bleistein v Donaldson Lithographing Co, 188 US 239 (1903)* 249.

88 *Oriental Art Printing, Inc v Goldstar Printing Corp, 175 FSupp2d 542 (2001)*; *Pohl v MH SUB I, LLC, 314 FSupp3d 1225 (2018)*; *Stokes Seeds Ltd v Geo W Park Seed Co, Inc, 783 FSupp 104 (1991)* 5.

89 *Pohl v MH SUB I, LLC, 314 FSupp3d 1225 (2018)* (n 88) 1230–1232; *Oriental Art Printing, Inc v Goldstar Printing Corp, 175 FSupp2d 542 (2001)* (n 88); *Meshwerks, Inc v Toyota Motor Sales USA, Inc, 528 F3d 1258 (2008)*; *Stokes Seeds Ltd v Geo. W. Park Seed Co, Inc, 783 FSupp 104 (1991)* (n 88); *Custom Dynamics, LLC v Radiantz LED Lighting, Inc, 535 FSupp2d 542 (2008)*; *McNeese v Access Midstream Partners, LP, Not Reported in Fed Supp WL 972156 (2017)* 9, 8 ("It is true that purely descriptive photographs are deemed not sufficiently original to be protected by copyright law, in that there is no 'creative spark' in a purely descriptive picture of a product or service").

standard if they contain a minimal degree of creativity, not necessarily evidenced by the photograph itself but through its creation narrative.[90] This was illustrated in the US cases of *Ets-Hokin v Skyy Spirits, Inc (2000)*[91] and *SHL Imaging, Inc v Artisan House, Inc (2000)*.[92]

In *Ets-Hokin v Skyy Spirits, Inc (2000)*,[93] the Ninth Circuit Court of Appeal held that product photographs of Vodka bottles were sufficiently original since "even the slightest artistic touch will meet the originality test for a photograph."[94] What matters is whether the photograph in question contained enough creative choices in its expression, such as the elements associated with its rendition, in a manner that satisfies the originality standard and, therefore, is eligible for copyright protection.[95] The particular purpose behind the photograph's creation, such as being purely for commercial purposes, or the nature of its subject matter, such as being a utilitarian object depicted as the main subject of a photograph, has no bearing on the copyrightability of the photograph in question.[96] The court stated that "The fact that two original photographs of the same object may appear similar does not eviscerate their originality or negate their copyrightability."[97]

*SHL Imaging, Inc v Artisan House, Inc (2000)*[98] concerned a similar dispute regarding product photographs of mirrored picture frames. The district court held that the photographs in question were original due to "the totality of the precise lighting selection, angle of the camera, lens and filter selection."[99] However, the court acknowledged that the photographs, perhaps due to their nature, are only protected from "verbatim copying"; hence, they are covered by "thin copyright," and did not enjoy broad copyright protection.[100]

However, in the US case of *Oriental Art Printing, Inc v Goldstar Printing Corp (2001)*,[101] photographs of Chinese food dishes were deemed too generic and without a creative spark. Therefore, they lacked the requisite level of originality. The court cited the plaintiff's lack of an adequate description regarding how the photographs were taken as further evidence that the photographs were produced for a "purely utilitarian purpose" that lacks originality despite the fact that the photographs were

90 *Pohl v MH Sub I LLC, 770 FedAppx 482 (2019)* 489; *Home Legend, LLC v Mannington Mills, Inc, 784 F3d 1404 (2015)*; *SHL Imaging, Inc v Artisan House, Inc, 117 FSupp2d 301 (2000)* (n 14); *Ets-Hokin v Skyy Spirits, Inc, 225 F3d 1068 (2000)*.

91 *Ets-Hokin v Skyy Spirits, Inc, 225 F3d 1068 (2000)* (n 90).

92 *SHL Imaging, Inc v Artisan House, Inc, 117 FSupp2d 301 (2000)* (n 14).

93 *Ets-Hokin v Skyy Spirits, Inc, 225 F3d 1068 (2000)* (n 90).

94 ibid 1076.

95 ibid 1077.

96 ibid 1075.

97 ibid 1077.

98 *SHL Imaging, Inc v Artisan House, Inc, 117 FSupp2d 301 (2000)* (n 14).

99 ibid 311.

100 ibid.

101 *Oriental Art Printing, Inc v Goldstar Printing Corp, 175 FSupp2d 542 (2001)* (n 88).

prearranged.[102] The court's approach, in this case, fits what Professor Eva Subtonic called "the narrative proxy," where the court looks outside the photographs to the narrative that created them to determine their originality.[103] This case represents a rare situation where photographs were denied copyright protection due to their mundane subject matter.[104] However, this does not mean that all photographs of foods that populate Instagram are without copyright protection. In fact, this is far from it since this genre of images often does not serve purely utilitarian purposes and has enough compositional elements to be regarded as original photographs.

Nevertheless, in the US case of *Pohl v MH SUB I, LLC (2018)*,[105] the district court dismissed a claim regarding before-and-after photographs of dental cosmetics showing patients' teeth because they did not satisfy the originality requirement and did not, according to the judge, merit protection. On appeal, the Eleventh Circuit reversed and amended the lower court judgement since "precedent makes clear that even descriptive photographs of products, like a flooring design, can be sufficiently original to merit copyright protection."[106]

The few cases in the United Kingdom that dealt with similar situations did not question the originality of photographs as long as they originated from the photographer and were not a product of copying. In the UK case of *Antiquesportfolio.com Plc v Rodney Fitch & Co Ltd [2001]*,[107] the court held that photographs of antique objects were subject to copyright despite the seemingly basic skill employed in terms of their depiction.[108] The court stated that a photograph of a static three-dimensional object still has elements such as the angle of the shot, position of the object, lighting, and focus that are capable of conferring originality to the photographs even if they were shown to be rudimentary.[109]

Moreover, in the UK case of *Nottinghamshire Healthcare National Health Service Trust v News Group Newspapers Ltd [2002]*,[110] a patient's portrait photograph taken by the hospital for medical documentation purposes was found to

102 ibid 546, 547; see also: *Custom Dynamics, LLC v Radiantz LED Lighting, Inc, 535 FSupp2d 542 (2008)* (n 89).

103 Subotnik (n 7) 1494–1495, 1517–1518.

104 Patry (n 7) 3:118; see also: *Stokes Seeds Ltd v Geo. W. Park Seed Co, Inc, 783 FSupp 104 (1991)* (n 89); *Custom Dynamics, LLC v Radiantz LED Lighting, Inc, 535 FSupp2d 542 (2008)* (n 89); *Meshwerks, Inc v Toyota Motor Sales U.S.A., Inc, 528 F3d 1258 (2008)* (n 89); *Pohl v MH SUB I, LLC, 314 FSupp3d 1225 (2018)* (n 90).

105 *Pohl v MH SUB I, LLC, 314 FSupp3d 1225 (2018)* (n 90); see also: cf *Stokes Seeds Ltd v Geo. W. Park Seed Co, Inc, 783 FSupp 104 (1991)* (n 89).

106 *Pohl v MH Sub I LLC, 770 Fed.Appx. 482 (2019)* (n 90) 489; see also: *Home Legend, LLC v Mannington Mills, Inc, 784 F3d 1404 (2015)* (n 90).

107 *Antiquesportfolio.com Plc v Rodney Fitch & Co Ltd [2001] FSR 23.*

108 ibid 345.

109 ibid 346–347.

110 *Nottinghamshire Healthcare National Health Service Trust v News Group Newspapers Ltd [2002] RPC 49* (2002) 119 962.

have copyright, even though it was a candid photograph taken as part of a standard procedure.[111]

The United Kingdom is more lenient when it comes to originality in photographs since they are often afforded thin copyright protection.[112] Perhaps this difference in approach between the United States and the United Kingdom might be attributed to the UK copyright law reliance on the categorisation of works to determine whether a work is eligible for copyright protection. On the one hand, the United Kingdom used to regard a photograph that originated from the author as being eligible for copyright protection on the condition that it was original and then by virtue of being a photograph, one of the categories of works eligible for copyright protection.[113] However, after the CJEU decision on the *Levola Hengelo case*,[114] a photograph needs to only be original as the expression of the author's own intellectual creation to be classified as a work of copyright. On the other hand, the United States adopted a different approach in that any work fixed in a medium of expression could be eligible for copyright protection as long as it satisfies the originality standard.[115]

### *7.3.3 The Style or Mood of a Photograph's Subject Matter and Copyright Protection*

The previous sections explored how the source of originality that relies on the photograph's creation of the subject matter crumbles as a protectable element of a photograph in itself. But does the holistic imprint on how the photograph's subject matter was depicted, in the form of the style or mood reflected, serve as a source of originality for photographs? Perhaps a case that sticks out as a controversial example of protecting the subject matter of photographs is a case that dates back to more than one hundred years ago. In the US case of *Gross v Seligman (1914)*,[116] the photographer sold his copyright in a photograph titled "Grace of Youth," depicting a nude woman photographed from a side angle in a particular pose and looking at the camera with a stoic expression. Two years later, the same photographer created a similar photograph titled "Cherry Ripe" of the same model in a similar pose but with several different details, such as the woman smiling while holding a cherry stem between her teeth. The copyright owner of the "Grace of Youth" photograph sued for copyright infringement; the court held in his favour.

This decision was striking since the two photographs (Figure 7.1), while being similar, were in no way identical. The court regarded the fact that the photographs were the product of the same author as evidence to support infringement despite the fact that the similarity could strongly be argued as a product of the artist's style

111 ibid 987.

112 ibid.

113 See: Justine Pila, "Copyright and Its Categories of Original Works" (2010) 30 Oxford Journal of Legal Studies 229; see also: Subotnik (n 7) 1513.

114 *(C-310/17) Levola Hengelo BV v Smilde Foods BV [2019] ECDR 2.*

115 Section 102 (a) Title 17 of the United States Code (US).

116 *Gross v Seligman, 212 F 930 (1914).*

**Grace of Youth Photograph** **Cherry Ripe Photograph**

*Figure 7.1* Left photograph: "Grace of Youth" (1912). Right photograph: "Cherry Ripe" (1914).

Rick Sanders, "Here's a Poser: Can You Protect a Pose?" (Rick Sanders Law, 9 March 2018) https://www.ricksanderslaw.com/heres-a-poser-can-you-protect-a-pose/ accessed 18 October 2024.

or personality being reflected in both photographs. The court regarded the second photograph as merely a recreation and copy of the first photograph despite clear and obvious differences such as the photograph's tone, the invoked expression, shade, and lighting. The court even stated that no infringement would be found if a different artist recreated the photograph.[117] This controversial case remains an anomaly as courts are reluctant to protect the subject matter of photographs.[118]

The US case of *Kisch v Ammirati & Puris Inc (1987)*[119] involved two monochrome photographs with similar compositions and geometric lighting. The claimant's photograph features a woman in formal attire holding an accordion, while the defendant's photograph depicts a man in a suit holding a saxophone, with additional props like a bottle and a filled glass. Other than the model depicted, the two images were strikingly similar. Despite that, it was not granted summary judgement for copyright infringement, even though one could strongly argue that the holistic effects of the compositional elements of the two photographs, which are protectable original elements of the photograph's expression, appear to closely resemble each other besides the model depicted. The court suggested that "the underlying tone or mood" of the photograph may be found similar by a rational trier of facts,

117 *Gross v Seligman, 212 F 930 (1914)* (n 116) 931.

118 *Harney v Sony Pictures Television, Inc, 704 F3d 173 (2013)* (n 14); see: *Franklin Mint Corp v National Wildlife Art Exchange, Inc, 575 F2d 62 (1978)* (n 17); *Sahuc v Tucker, 300 FSupp2d 461 (2004)* (n 74); *Leigh v Warner Bros., Inc, 212 F3d 1210 (2000)* (n 74); *Kisch v Ammirati & Puris Inc, 657 FSupp 380 (1987)* (n 14).

119 *Kisch v Ammirati & Puris Inc, 657 FSupp 380 (1987)* (n 14).

but does the tone of a photograph represent a protectable element of its expression? This question was addressed in *Leigh v Warner Bros (2000)*.[120]

In the US case of *Leigh v Warner Bros (2000)*, it was held that the general tone, theme, "eerie" or "spirit," and mood of a photograph are not protected even if the photographer intentionally produced them with a particular subject matter. The Eleventh Circuit Court of Appeal stated that copyright protection in photographs is concerned with these concrete elements that represent the expressive elements of the photograph and does not extend to cover "relatively amorphous characteristics of the picture as a whole (such as the 'mood' or 'combination of elements')),"[121] since this "creates a danger of unwittingly extending copyright protection to unoriginal aspects of the work."[122]

Similarly, in the UK case of *Norowzian v Arks Ltd (No.2) [2000]*,[123] which involved a dispute regarding a film, it was held that copyright does not subsist in mere styles or techniques. Hence, one could conclude that, as a principle, the mood or general tone of a photograph or its style is not normally protected in isolation and is not considered, in principle, as protectable elements of the photograph. Nevertheless, one could argue that a photograph's tone or style in isolation is not protectable, but it is included in the general combination of all these elements, the holistic effect, that produced the photograph. Thus, in a way, it could be protected indirectly with the other elements, but never in isolation. Furthermore, the UK Copyright, Designs and Patents Act 1988 Section 64 adds another layer of leeway to authors by allowing them to create similar works to their previous work even if they do not own the copyright. Thus, authors of artistic works will not be precluded from producing similar works provided that these works do not constitute a "repeat or [imitation of] the main design of the earlier work."[124]

### *7.3.4 Realistic Depiction and Photographs' Level of Protection*

The photographs that depict objects as they exist in nature, as well as those that provide an accurate and realistic depiction of a given subject matter, are often afforded thin copyright protection that serves only to protect them against verbatim copying.[125]

In the US case of *Satava v Lowry (2003)*,[126] a copyright infringement claim concerning lifelike glass-in-glass sculptures of jellyfish was dismissed. The Ninth Circuit Court of Appeal held that realistic depictions of animals as they appear

120 *Leigh v Warner Bros., Inc, 212 F3d 1210 (2000)* (n 74).

121 ibid 1215.

122 ibid.

123 *Norowzian v Arks Ltd (No2), [2000] EMLR 67 (1999).*

124 Section 64 Copyright, Designs and Patents Act 1988 (UK).

125 Patry (n 7) s 3.117.10; see also: Morgan M Stoddard, "Mother Nature as Muse: Copyright Protection for Works of Art and Photographs Inspired by, Based on, or Depicting Nature" (2007) 86 North Carolina Law Review 572.

126 *Satava v Lowry, 323 F3d 805 (2003).*

in nature are given narrow copyright protection against only identical direct copying.[127] While this case was about sculptural works, the court's reasoning also applies to photographic works.

Furthermore, in the US case of *Psihoyos v National Geographic Society (2005)*,[128] an infringement proceeding was brought before the court regarding a photograph of two dinosaurs in a fossil "locked in mortal combat". The district court stated that "To the extent a photograph captures the characteristics of an object as it occurs in nature, these characteristics are not protectable."[129] The court found that the defendant's works are not substantially similar to the plaintiff's photograph and held that the photograph was not infringed as far as its protectable elements are concerned.[130] The court regarded the background, the overhead angle, and the perspective of the shot, which are normally regarded as protectable elements of a photograph, as not forming the protectable part in the photograph in question since it is a scène à faire and flows naturally from the idea to depict a fossil as a subject matter.[131]

Similarly, in the US case of *Dyer v Napier (2006)*,[132] the plaintiff brought an infringement claim regarding a photograph that depicted a mountain lion standing on a rocky ledge holding her cub with her mouth. The defendant used the photograph, among other references, as a base to create a bronze sculpture that closely mirrors the scene, showing a stylised mountain lion on a geometric pedestal, holding her cub in her mouth, with a similar posture. The district court held in favour of the defendant since "all of the similarities in expression between the two works at issue consist of unprotectable elements or themes that flow predictably from the underlying subject matter."[133]

Moreover, the United Kingdom also follows the same position in that the elements related to the subject matter or that flow naturally from the subject matter, for instance, a natural scene, are not themselves covered by copyright protection.[134] This was illustrated in *Bauman v Fussell*[135] as well as the UK general approach that protects only what was "visually significant" originating from the original elements of expression regarded as the product of the author's skill and labour or intellectual creation.[136]

127 ibid 812.
128 *Psihoyos v National Geographic Society, 409 FSupp2d 268 (2005).*
129 ibid 275.
130 ibid 277.
131 ibid 275–277.
132 *Dyer v Napier, WL 2730747 not reported (2006)* 10.
133 ibid 9.
134 Tappin and others (n 6) s 4.52, 4.61, 4.66; Caddick, Harbottle and Suthersanen (n 41) paras 7–115.
135 *Bauman v Fussell [1978] RPC 485* (n 17).
136 Tappin and others (n 6) s 4.52, 4.61, 4.66; Caddick, Harbottle and Suthersanen (n 41) paras 7–107, 7–111, 7–112, 7–115.

### *7.3.5 Photographs Reproduced in Other Visual Mediums and the Scope of Protection*

There are many instances where artists copy photographs directly into their preferred visual mediums. This practice emerged since the dawn of photography and was one of the main arguments used by photographers to call for copyright protection.[137] Photographs are often used as a reference by many artists as sources of inspiration. Still, some artists take that inspiration a bit too far and reproduce photographs by tracing them or copying them almost line to line. Some artists were accused of plagiarism and attracted heavy criticism for copying outlines of photographs.[138] One example from the world of comics is found in the work of Greg Land, who is infamous for tracing photographs to create some of his comic book panels.[139] The few cases that touch on imitating photographs seem to suggest that, in the absence of direct evidence of copying, as long as the photograph's original elements of expression, such as lighting and shade among others, were not copied, tracing outlines of a photograph's contents or the poses of the subjects do not seem to encroach on the photograph's original elements of expression.[140] Thus, the outline of the contents depicted in a photograph may not be considered an original element of the photograph.

In the UK case of *Bauman v Fussell (1978)*,[141] a photograph of two roosters locked in combat was reproduced in a painting that copied their position and stance but enhanced their features. The plaintiffs brought a copyright infringement claim that rested on the fact that the painting traced the two roosters' position and was not merely a product of inspiration for the painter to depict the idea in his own way. The plaintiffs argued that the position of the subject matter represented the main compositional element of the photograph, and it was a product of his skill illustrated via choosing the right time to capture the scene.[142] On appeal, two judges

137 See Chapters 2–4.

138 See: "A Tradition in Plagiarism" (*ComiPress*, 9 July 2007) <https://www.comipress.com/article/2007/07/09/2267.html> accessed 18 October 2024; Michael Zhang, "Photographer Souvid Datta Appears to Have Plagiarized Mary Ellen Mark" (3 May 2017) <https://petapixel.com/2017/05/03/photographer-souvid-datta-appears-plagiarized-mary-ellen-mark/> accessed 18 October 2024; Shome Basu, "Souvid Datta's Plagiarised Photos Point to an Industry That Needs Higher Standards" (*The Wire*, 7 May 2017) <https://thewire.in/culture/souvid-datta-photography-plagiarism> accessed 18 October 2024; Chris McGreal, "Plagiarism or Remixing? South African Photographer Accuses Artist of Theft" *The Guardian* (13 September 2018) <https://www.theguardian.com/artanddesign/2018/sep/13/graeme-williams-hank-willis-thomas-photograph> accessed 18 October 2024.

139 Jim, "Greg Land: Tracing, Swiping & Recycling" (*JIMSMASH!!! EXTENDED*, 1 July 2008) <http://jimsmashextended.blogspot.com/2008/07/greg-land-tracing-swiping-recycling.html> accessed 18 October 2024.

140 *Antiquesportfolio.com Plc v Rodney Fitch & Co Ltd [2001] FSR 23* (n 107); *Bauman v Fussell [1978] RPC 485* (n 17); *Folkens v Wyland Worldwide, LLC, 882 F3d 768 (2018)* 7; *Reece v Island Treasures Art Gallery, Inc, 468 FSupp2d 1197 (2006).*

141 *Bauman v Fussell [1978] RPC 485* (n 17).

142 ibid 485, 487.

affirmed the lower court's judgement in finding that the painting did not infringe the photograph since the photographer did not arrange the position of the subjects and the painting was only inspired by the photograph and did not copy it.[143] Romer LJ, dissenting, disagreed and remarked that the trial judge's approach to the facts was incorrect since he sought out the differences between the two works to conclude that their "effect" was not similar.[144] Romer LJ explained that the correct test would be to apply the substantial similarities test to seek out the similarities, instead of the differences, between the works and decide whether these similarities are substantial to a degree to prove or disapprove copyright infringement.[145]

One could see that timing demonstrates the photographer's skill and creative choice as well as the originality of the photograph. However, similar to the subject matter creation category, timing does not necessarily represent an original protectable element of the photograph; it just serves as evidence of it. *Bauman v Fussell* showcased the difficulties associated with protecting the original elements of photographs, as even a painting that reproduced a photograph was not found to be an infringing derivative work.[146]

Timing is an element that allows the photographer to express enough skill and intellectual creation when a "decisive moment" reveals itself to be captured by his camera. The issue here is that timing in isolation does not represent a protectable element; only the timing's effects on the overall composition as it was depicted may be protected, and only those elements that were visually significant.[147]

In the United States, a case similar to *Bauman v Fussell* that involved a photograph's subject matter being recreated in another visual medium was concluded with a different result. In *Roger v Koons (1992)*,[148] a photograph titled "Puppies" was recreated in a porcelain sculpture titled "String of Puppies" without authorisation. The claimant's photograph, "Puppies," depicts a couple sitting side by side, smiling and holding a row of puppies, set against a rustic wooden backdrop. The defendant's sculpture, "String of Puppies," reimagines the scene with stylised, brightly coloured figures donned with a couple of flowers holding blue puppies, sitting on a bench. The appellant's photograph was original since he selected the lighting, camera, angle of the shot, and position of the subject and arranged the scene to create the photograph.[149] The court held that the defendant copied the photograph's original elements of expression. In this case, there was clear evidence that the sculpture not only used the photograph as a source but also copied it

143 ibid 485, 487, 490.

144 ibid 491–492.

145 ibid.

146 For more discussion about this case and similar cases within the EU, see: Richard Arnold, "Paintings from Photographs: A Copyright Conundrum" (2019) 50 IIC – International Review of Intellectual Property and Competition Law 860.

147 Tappin and others (n 6) s 4.52, 4.61, 4.66; Caddick, Harbottle and Suthersanen (n 41) paras 7–107, 7–111, 7–112, 7–115.

148 *Rogers v Koons, 960 F2d 301 (1992).*

149 ibid 301, 304, 307.

directly in an attempt to adapt it to a three-dimensional form as a sculpture.[150] The court did not regard the sculpture's additions, such as the colours and flowers, as something significant to distract from the substantial similarity demonstrated to the photograph's protected original elements of expression.[151]

One could say that *Roger v Koons* appears to contrast with *Harney v Sony*,[152] but a closer inspection would reveal that the two cases are not the same. In *Roger v Koons*, the scene was created with direct evidence of actual copying by the defendants. In *Harney v Sony*, what Sony sought to recreate was the original photograph's impression and its factual contents, not the expressive elements of the original photograph, and consequently, the recreated photograph was deemed to be different in terms of the angle, background, position, and posing of the subject, lighting, and shade.[153] In contrast, in *Roger v Koons*, Koons copied the original expression of the photograph, starting from the position of the subjects to their particular facial expression, and reintroduced the expressive elements of the original photograph as a sculptural work.

In the US case of *Reece v Island Treasures Art Gallery, Inc (2006)*,[154] the claimant brought an infringement claim against a stained-glass art of a female hula dancer for the alleged unauthorised copying of his photograph. The claimant's photograph depicts a woman kneeling on the beach, dressed in traditional Polynesian attire with leafy adornments, performing a dance with arms outstretched. The defendant's artwork recreates this scene in a stained-glass style, maintaining the pose and attire but adding a stylised background. The dancer's pose and position showed undeniable similarities, but other elements were different. The court reiterated the protectable original elements of photographs, such as selection, lighting, and shade, before deciding that, although the photograph was original, the stained-glass art was not substantially similar in relation to its original elements of expression, and any similarities are scène à faire that comes from the subject matter.[155]

The position of the hula dancer and her outline in the stained-glass art look strikingly similar to how they were depicted in the photograph to the point that one can argue that the stained-glass art was directly traced from the photograph. The outlines match almost perfectly when the two images are put on top of each other. However, the court decided to dismiss the case, stating that it was unlikely for the two works to be found as substantially similar.

In summary, it seems that the outline of the objects in a photograph is not regarded as a protectable element of the photograph's expression. Hence, if one traced the object or made a silhouette of an object based on a photograph, it would be unlikely that the courts would regard that act alone as copying the expression of the photographs. That is because tracing the outline of an object in a photograph

150 ibid 301, 305, 307.
151 ibid 307, 308.
152 *Harney v Sony Pictures Television, Inc, 704 F3d 173 (2013)* (n 14).
153 ibid 173, 178, 182.
154 *Reece v Island Treasures Art Gallery, Inc, 468 FSupp2d 1197 (2006).*
155 ibid 1206–1208.

often strips the traced part of the expressive elements of the photograph, such as lighting, shade, colours, and angle of the shot. Thus, one may deduce that due to the fact that the outlines of the objects in photographs are not protected, solely tracing a photograph's subject matter would not, in normal circumstances, be considered infringement.

### *7.3.6 Thin or Broad Copyright Protection, a Lose-Lose Situation?*

Perhaps to better illustrate the precarious nature of copyright in photographic works, one can examine the following two cases that had contrasting judgements regarding the issues of copyright in photographic works in their respective jurisdictions. These cases, which generated a sizable reaction for the opposite reasons, are the UK case of *Temple Island Collections Ltd v New English Teas Ltd [2012]*[156] and the US case of *Rentmeester v Nike, Inc (2018)*.[157] These two cases illustrated the difficult nature of originality in photographic works and its scope of protection. What is considered an original element in a photograph may not necessarily constitute a protectable aspect of it, and what is regarded normally as an uncopyrightable element, such as the theme or feel, may influence the photograph's protection negatively or positively on an ad hoc basis. As a result, an aura of uncertainty persisted due to the inconsistent treatment regarding what constitutes a photograph's original elements of expression and the level of protection associated with these elements.

#### *7.3.6.1 UK: Temple Island Collections Ltd v New English Teas Ltd [2012]*

This case involved an infringement dispute regarding a photographic work that depicted a red London bus on Westminster Bridge contrasted with a monochromic background showing the Houses of Parliament and Big Ben. Both photographs were modified through the use of digital software, some features were added or deleted, and showcased the same iconic landmark associated with London in black and white and a red bus moving across Westminster Bridge.[158] The claimant took his photograph and then modified it; the defendants took four separate photographs of the iconic landmarks and combined them to produce the photograph in question.[159] The two photographs contained significant differences in the angle of view, depth of field, and position of the red bus, among several other different details.

On the case at hand, Judge Birss acknowledged that copyright in photographs represents "a tricky area of law" and it would often turn on qualitative judgement.[160] Referencing Laddie's treatise on the sources of originality in photographs, Judge Birss added that digital manipulation could be an additional source of originality and boiled down the source of originality in the images at hand to their

156 *Temple Island Collections Ltd v New English Teas Ltd [2012] EWPCC 1* (n 11).
157 *Rentmeester v Nike, Inc, 883 F3d 1111 (2018)* 19.
158 *Temple Island Collections Ltd v New English Teas Ltd [2012] EWPCC 1* (n 11) 2.
159 ibid.
160 ibid 1.

composition since it was the "aggregate result" of all the other factors combined in different degrees.[161] He continued by pointing out that the end result of that composition is relevant for originality and is protected like other artistic works as long as it was the product of the author's skill and labour or the author's own intellectual creation.[162] Hence, Judge Birss rejected the notion advanced by the defendants that photographs are only protected against facsimile reproduction.[163] Furthermore, he emphasised that what is relevant for originality is the "visual significance" of the elements of the work itself and not "what the artists actually did to create the work."[164] Here, Judge Birss avoided equating authorship with originality by emphasising that originality in photographs is located in the confines of the work itself and not in the narrative of its creation.

After restating the law's stance on originality in photographs at the time, Judge Birss was set to examine the images at hand to decide whether an infringement took place. It is in this part of his analysis that the controversy lies. Judge Birss looked at the different aesthetic features of the photographs and concluded that evidence suggests that the iconic landmarks depicted, the photographic technique used, and the idea behind these photographs are commonplace.[165] However, he pointed out that the claimant's photograph is original since it was:

> the result of [the claimant's] own intellectual creation both in terms of his choices relating to the basic photograph itself: the precise motif, angle of shot, light and shade, illumination, and exposure and also in terms of his work after the photograph was taken to manipulate the image to satisfy his own visual aesthetic sense. The fact that it is a picture combining some iconic symbols of London does not mean the work is not an original work in which copyright subsists. The fact that, to some observers, icons such as Big Ben and a London bus are visual clichés also does not mean no copyright subsists.[166]

This position is sound since even if a work draws from common ideas and expressions, that does not mean that the work is not protected by copyright. However, that also does not mean that the work is given broad copyright protection covering the common features. That is because if two works were drawn from a common source, similarities would inevitably flow naturally from the shared ideas. Judge Birss highlighted that the original expression of the claimant's intellectual creation in the photograph lies in its composition and visual contrast.[167] And since the works are causally related, due to the fact that the defendants had access

161 ibid 5–6.
162 ibid.
163 ibid 6, 12.
164 ibid 6–7.
165 ibid 9.
166 ibid 10.
167 ibid.

to the claimant's work and wanted to create aesthetically similar work, he found that the defendants' work was substantially similar to the claimant's work to the degree that supports the infringement claim.[168] Judge Birss, rather surprisingly, posited that just because there were substantial differences between the two works in their composition does not negate the "causal link" between the works.[169] He did not consider the possibility that the "causal link" led only to adopting the idea behind the work itself and its uncopyrightable elements rather than its protectable expression.

Judge Birss listed the elements of composition and visual contrast and admitted that there were significant differences in the composition where several elements were not reproduced.[170] Yet, he disregarded these differences and stated that "the overall composition" had been reproduced when one could argue that only the feel or tone was reproduced, not the composition itself.[171] Equally, the similarity raised in the visual contrast could be attributed to the idea itself and not necessarily the expression of that idea since the two buses are different as well as the angle of their depiction, with only the monochromatic effect remaining the same. The defendants rightfully argued that they had adopted only the unprotected ideas, but their expression was different in many aspects.[172]

The idea/expression dichotomy is notoriously tricky to apply to visual works to the degree that questions its viability for such works.[173] However, the case here may represent a rare example where the idea/expression dichotomy could have been useful in delineating the scope of protection afforded to the photographs in question. Judge Birss, regarding the framing of the two images, said that "to my eye the essence of the framing effect has been reproduced."[174] He did not elaborate on that "essence"; was it the motif? Or general tone? Or the general aesthetic effect of the image? He did not consider whether that "essence" represented a protectable element of the photograph or merely the general feel, which in itself may come from the idea and, normally, represent an unprotectable element of a visual work. What Judge Birss did was ignore all the tangible elements of a photograph's composition, such as angle of the shot, light, depth of view, and shading, which he acknowledged were different, and instead based his decision on the

168 ibid 10–12.
169 ibid 10, 12.
170 ibid 12.
171 ibid 10, 11.
172 ibid 12.
173 *Mannion v Coors Brewing Co, 377 FSupp2d 444 (2005)* (n 11) 461 ("In the context of photography, the idea/expression distinction is not useful or relevant") (per Judge Kaplan); see: Murray (n 38) 784; Teresa M Bruce, "In the Language of Pictures: How Copyright Law Fails to Adequately Account for Photography" (2012) 115 West Virginia Law Review 93, 97, 118; Stoddard (n 125) 580–581; see also: Rebecca Tushnet, "Worth a Thousand Words: The Images of Copyright" (2012) 125 Harvard Law Review 683; see also: Amy B Cohen, "Copyright Law and the Myth of Objectivity: The Idea-Expression Dichotomy and the Inevitability of Artistic Value Judgments" (1990) 66 Indiana Law Journal 175.
174 *Temple Island Collections Ltd v New English Teas Ltd [2012] EWPCC 1* (n 11) 12.

general aesthetics effect, visual contrast, and the "essence" that he deemed to be reproduced.

Judge Birss elaborated on the factors that helped shape his decision on this case. The first factor was about the nature of the claimant's work, which was not a traditional photograph but more of a photographic work due to the "deliberate choices and also deliberate manipulations by the author."[175] He remarked that there was a discussion regarding whether the two photographs might be closer to photographic collages than traditional photographs, but nevertheless, he considered the two works as photographs since "what has been manipulated is still ultimately a recording of light."[176] The second factor was related to the other similar photographs relied upon by the defendants, which served as evidence against them since it showcased the different independent forms of expression that the same idea could accommodate.[177] Judge Birss further posited that the defendants went to "elaborate lengths" to reproduce the aesthetic effect of the claimant's photograph in a way that was hoped would avoid infringement when the defendants could have simply taken an independent photograph following an independent design without risking infringement even if the photographs had the same aesthetic qualities.[178] In other words, the judge found that a substantial part of the claimant's work was reproduced since the defendants' photograph was created according to the claimant's work design and was not created based on their own independent design. One could counter this by arguing that the defendants did create their own independent design of the same idea to produce a similar aesthetic appeal of the subject matter.

One possible explanation regarding why the judge was more adamant about finding infringement might be due to the existence of a previously settled copyright dispute between the same parties.[179] However, one could argue that their previous attempt infringed on the copyright, but this new attempt was focused on driving inspiration to produce a similar effect without copying the elements of expression found in the original photograph. This is a matter that the defendants admitted and should not be used to regard their image as mere copies producing a substantial part of the claimant's photograph without assessing whether that part was owed to the protectable elements of expression of the claimant's image. It is true that intention was immaterial when it comes to originality, but one could argue that the work in dispute did not copy the claimant's expressive elements, such as the angle of the shot, light, and shadows. Judge Birss, while attempting to focus on the confines of the work to deliver his judgement, almost unknowingly looked outside the confines of the two photographs, summoning the narrative proxy to somehow force a "substantial similarity" upon the two images. This case is controversial

175 ibid 13.
176 ibid 6.
177 ibid 13.
178 ibid.
179 ibid 1–2.

since it effectively protected the subject matter and the idea behind its depiction, the general aesthetic effect, rather than focusing its protection on the tangible elements of expression in photographs, such as the angle of the shot, depth of field, and shading, among other expressive elements.

Many expressed their dismay about the result of this judgement.[180] They feared that this case might have effectively protected the idea behind the photographs. This would risk creating an inclination that could potentially hinder the production of photographs that borrow their ideas from other photographs. After all, it is a common practice in the medium of photography to appropriate ideas and styles and apply them to the same scene but change the angles to showcase a different expression. In this situation, at least, the idea/expression dichotomy would have been useful despite the infamous difficulty regarding its application to visual works such as photographs. This, perhaps, is due to the prevailing view that the purpose of concepts such as originality and idea or facts/expression dichotomy was to curtail the expansion of copyright protection to elements that may hinder the production of new works. Hence, these concepts were not conceptualised as a mechanism to focus protection only on what deserves protection.

#### *7.3.6.2 US: Rentmeester v. Nike, Inc (2018)*

In *Rentmeester v Nike, Inc (2018)*,[181] the claimant sued Nike for infringement in a photograph depicting the basketball player Michael Jordan jumping mid-air in an original pose with legs stretched and the sun low on the horizon as background, as he aims to dunk the ball into the basket. The claimant licensed the photograph to Nike for a period of time until, at a later date, Nike hired a photographer to take their own photograph of Michael Jordan inspired by the claimant's photograph. The defendants' photograph portrayed a similar pose with Michael Jordan in mid-air but features a more stylised urban background with a sunset sky and a

180 See for example: Jane Lambert, "Copyright in Photographs: Temple Island Collections and Creation Records" (*NIPC Law*) <http://nipclaw.blogspot.com/2012/01/copyright-in-photographs-temple-island.html> accessed 18 October 2024; LTC Harms, "Originality and Reproduction in Copyright Law with Special Reference to Photographs" (2013) 16 Potchefstroom Electronic Law Journal 487; Chris Cheesman, "Photographers Face Copyright Threat after Shock Ruling" (*Amateur Photographer*, 1 April 2012) <https://www.amateurphotographer.co.uk/latest/photo-news/photographers-face-copyright-threat-after-shock-ruling-14134> accessed 30 September 2021; Tim Barribeau, "UK Ruling Says Similar Composition Enough Violate Copyright" (*Popular Photography*, 25 January 2012) <https://www.popphoto.com/news/2012/01/uk-ruling-says-similar-composition-enough-violate-copyright/> accessed 18 October 2024; Richard Butler, "Similar, but Not Copied, Image Found to Breach Copyright" (*DPReview*, 25 January 2012) <https://www.dpreview.com/articles/1166562748/imitated-image-copyright-case> accessed 18 October 2024; Cory Doctorow, "Insane English Copyright Ruling Creates Ownership in the Idea of a Photo's Composition" (*Boing Boing*, 25 January 2012) <https://boingboing.net/2012/01/25/insane-english-copyright-rulin.html> accessed 18 October 2024.

181 *Rentmeester v Nike, Inc, 883 F3d 1111 (2018)* (n 157).

Chicago skyline. The district court dismissed the claim with prejudice in favour of the defendants, and the claimant appealed.

The Ninth Circuit Court of Appeal examined the nature of originality in photographs and their protectable elements and stated that, fundamentally, what is protected was "the photographer's selection and arrangement of the photo's otherwise unprotected elements. If sufficiently original, the combination of subject matter, pose, camera angle, etc., receives protection, not any of the individual elements standing alone."[182] Thus, the individual objective elements of a photograph that reflect the author's creative choices, such as angle, pose, choice of subject matter, lighting, and shading, among other elements, are not protected in isolation; rather, what is protected is the effect of the overall combination of these elements in the resulting work.[183] Therefore, the creative pose depicted and the photograph's subject matter are treated similarly to facts and ideas. Hence, what is protected is only the way they were expressed in the photograph as "a product of not just the pose but also the camera angle, timing, and shutter speed," reflecting the author's creative choices.[184] Furthermore, the court explained that whether a photograph is afforded thin copyright protection depends on the level of freedom related to the range of creative choices available for the photograph's creation.[185] Hence, a narrow level of creative choices and freedom invites thin copyright protection, while a broad level of creative choices and freedom invites broad copyright protection in photographs. Despite the fact that the court deemed the claimant's photograph to be highly original and deserving of broad copyright protection, the defendants' photographs did not infringe on it since what was similar was the ideas or concepts behind the photographs and not the expression of it, which was different.[186] The Ninth Circuit affirmed the lower court decision and held that the two photographs were not substantially similar as a matter of law since the details reflected in the expression were not reproduced.[187]

The court regarded the resulting composition, representing the combined effects of various elements, as expression and the components, representing the elements themselves, of the photograph as ideas or facts. This is aligned with Professor Justin Hughes's proposal to treat photographs as compilations of facts and focus the protection on the particular "selection and arrangement" expressed in the photograph.[188] In fact, the court referenced Professor Hughes's article with approval in that the elements of expression in photographs "can be likened to factual compilation" depicted in a visual medium where only its selection and arrangement are protected.[189] The court stated that:

182 ibid 1119.
183 ibid 1119–1120.
184 ibid.
185 ibid 1120.
186 ibid 1120–1121.
187 ibid 1123.
188 See: Hughes, "The Photographer's Copyright-Photograph as Art, Photograph as Database" (n 8).
189 *Rentmeester v Nike, Inc, 883 F3d 1111 (2018)* (n 157) 1119–1120.

> The individual elements that comprise a photograph can be viewed in the same way, as the equivalent of unprotectable "facts" that anyone may use to create new works. A second photographer is free to borrow any of the individual elements featured in a copyrighted photograph, "so long as the competing work does not feature the same selection and arrangement" of those elements. In other words, a photographer's copyright is limited to "the particular selection and arrangement" of the elements as expressed in the copyrighted image.[190]

Strikingly, the result of this case has had completely the opposite reaction from the one received by the *London red bus case*.[191] A petition for a writ of certiorari was filed to the US Supreme Court, raising the following question:

> Is copyright protection for a photograph limited solely to the photographer's "selection and arrangement" of unprotected elements, as the Ninth Circuit held below, or does it also cover elements of the photograph that express original, creative judgments by the photographer, as the First, Second, and Eleventh Circuits have held?[192]

In the petition, Rentmeester's counsel stressed that the photograph was highly creative, being staged and orchestrated down to the minute detail.[193] They argued that Nike pirated the photograph by producing an unauthorised derivative work that copied Rentmeester's original expression.[194] Therefore, in holding that those individual elements of the photograph were uncopyrightable, the Ninth Circuit erred in law and conflicted with the other circuits, creating a circuit split regarding the nature of copyright protection in photographs.[195] The petition complained that the Ninth Circuit embraced a "controversial law review article," referring to Professor Justin Hughes's article, and it "now treats photographs as glorified phonebooks, shielded from piracy only in their selection and arrangement of bare facts."[196]

Several interest groups filed amicus curiae in support of the petition. Among these groups are the American Society of Media Photographers, Inc,[197] the National

190 ibid 1120.

191 *Temple Island Collections Ltd v New English Teas Ltd [2012] EWPCC 1* (n 11).

192 Eric B Fastiff and others, "Petition for a Writ of Certiorari, Jacobus Rentmeester, Petitioner, v. NIKE, INC., Respondent. On Petition for a Writ of Certiorari to the United States Court of Appeals for the Ninth Circuit (No. 18-)" 50.

193 ibid 16, 39.

194 ibid 19, 24.

195 ibid 24, 38; Eric B Fastiff and others, "Reply Brief for Petitioner, Jacobus Rentmeester, Petitioner, v. NIKE, INC., Respondent. On Petition for a Writ of Certiorari to the United States Court of Appeals for the Ninth Circuit (No. 18-728)" 17, 1, 2.

196 Fastiff and others (n 195) 25.

197 Thomas B Maddrey, Mickey H Osterreicher and Alicia W Calzada, "Brief for the American Society of Media Photographers, Inc. and the National Press Photographers Association as Amici Curiae in Support of Petitioner, Jacobus Rentmeester, Petitioner, v. NIKE, INC., Respondent. On Petition for a Writ of Certiorari to the United States Court of Appeals for the Ninth Circuit

Press Photographers Association,[198] and the Digital Justice Foundation.[199] These interest groups urged the grant of certiorari in order to clarify this area of copyright law. They warned that "If the Ninth Circuit ruling is allowed to stand, photographers will be stripped of their ability to protect the creative expression of their work from anything other than wholesale lifting."[200] This, in their view, would be very harmful to photographers since it allows others to pirate their expression by recreating it with impunity as long as they introduce a minimal degree of variations to avoid identical reproduction.[201]

Professor Terry Kogan, having already written an article[202] in response to Professor Justin Hughes's article,[203] filed an amicus brief in support of the petition.[204] He explained that copyright in photographs protects intentionally staged tableau based on the camera-related choices reflected in the photograph.[205] Hence, Kogan argued that Rentmeester's photograph was an intentionally staged tableau, and it is protected as a subject matter representing the photographer's expression.[206] Kogan further pointed out that the Ninth Circuit erred when it regarded camera-related choices (such as angle, depth of field, lights, shade) as similar to facts when viewed in isolation, diverging from the *Burrow-Giles*[207] approach.[208] Thus, Kogan's amicus brief supported the petitioner and advised that the court should grant certiorari.

In opposition, Nike argued that the Ninth Circuit decision was fully consistent with the legal authorities concerning copyright protection to photographs, and there was no fundamental circuit split since one of the fundamental tenets of copyright was that ideas are not copyrightable.[209] The respondent warned that the peti-

(No. 18-728)" (2 January 2019) <https://www.supremecourt.gov/DocketPDF/18/18-728/77988/20190102120945145_18-728%20ASMP-NPPA%20amicus%20brief.pdf> accessed 18 October 2024.

198 ibid.

199 "Brief Amicus Curiae Digital Justice Foundation in Support of Petitioner, Jacobus Rentmeester, Petitioner, v. NIKE, INC., Respondent. On Petition for a Writ of Certiorari to the United States Court of Appeals for the Ninth Circuit (No. 18-728)" 24.

200 Maddrey, Osterreicher and Calzada (n 197) 5.

201 ibid 8.

202 Kogan, "The Enigma of Photography, Depiction, and Copyright Originality" (n 8).

203 Hughes, "The Photographer's Copyright-Photograph as Art, Photograph as Database" (n 8).

204 Terry Kogan, "Brief of Professor Terry S. Kogan as Amicus Curiae In Support of Petitioner, Jacobus Rentmeester, Petitioner, v. NIKE, INC., Respondent. On Petition for a Writ of Certiorari to the United States Court of Appeals for the Ninth Circuit (No. 18-728)" (7 January 2019) <https://www.supremecourt.gov/DocketPDF/18/18-728/78568/20190107162243792_Prof.%20Kogan%20amicus%20brief.pdf> accessed 18 October 2024.

205 ibid 2–3.

206 ibid 7, 10–11.

207 *Burrow-Giles Lithographic Co v Sarony, 111 US 53 (1884)* (n 14).

208 Kogan, "Brief of Professor Terry S. Kogan as Amicus Curiae In Support of Petitioner, Jacobus Rentmeester, Petitioner, v. NIKE, INC., Respondent. On Petition for a Writ of Certiorari to the United States Court of Appeals for the Ninth Circuit (No. 18-728)" (n 204) 2–3, 7, 18–19.

209 "Brief in Opposition, Jacobus Rentmeester, Petitioner, v. NIKE, INC., Respondent. On Petition for a Writ of Certiorari to the United States Court of Appeals for the Ninth Circuit (No. 18-728)" 51, 1–3, 11–12, 24–25.

tioner seeks to copyright ideas by giving photographs special treatment through broadening the protection afforded to photographs beyond all other works.[210] Therefore, they argued that the Ninth Circuit's judgement flowed from established authorities, and thus, the case did not warrant certiorari.

The petition was ultimately denied, perhaps due to the fact that the Ninth Circuit decision was sound and aligned with established authorities. In essence, the effect of the combination of a photograph's original elements is what is protected and not the choices themselves in isolation, similar to how the combination of words in a novel is protected but not the words themselves or how protection extends to the combination of lines and colours in a painting and not to the individual colours themselves. The petitioner attempted to argue that the individual elements themselves are protected in isolation, showing a misunderstanding of the scope of photographs' copyright protection. This was demonstrated when the petitioners cited cases that did not support their main arguments and attempted to manufacture a circuit split to advance the writ of certiorari request.

## 7.4 Conclusion

The sources of originality in photographs often fall within three main categories. These categories are composition or rendition, the creation of the subject matter, and timing. Other sources of originality may be attributed to digital manipulation, but it could still fall under the category of rendition. The essence of these sources of originality is in the elements of creative freedom and selection, represented by the creative choices that influenced the creation of the photograph in the form it took. These sources of originality are not independent of each other, nor are they perceived in equal standing by the courts. It appears that compositional elements triumph over the other two categories as the one that represents the bulk of the protectable elements of a photograph's expression in a manner that evidences its originality. The courts identified an expanding list of tangible elements of a photograph's expression such as "angle of shot, light and shade, exposure, effects achieved by means of filter, developing techniques"[211] as well as focus, depth of field, motif, posing the subject, evoking a particular expression, selection of film, the subject's position, selection of camera, background, positioning, colour manipulation, and framing, among many other elements that were deemed to be capable of being a protectable original element of the photograph's expression. The combined holistic effects of these compositional elements, together with the other two sources of originality, are covered by copyright protection but not the individual elements themselves in isolation.

The weakest category of originality in photographs appears to be the one associated with the creation of the subject matter as it is increasingly apparent that courts do not consider the subject matter of photographs as, in itself, a protectable element

210 ibid 2–3, 11–12, 19.
211 Tappin and others (n 6) s 4.66.

of a photograph even if it was a completely invented unique scene or a staged tableau. It seems that the level of originality in the subject matter only serves to strengthen the subsistence of copyright in photographs without necessarily forming a protectable element of it.

Anglo-American courts have taken the difficult task of delineating where to locate originality in photographs with mixed results in terms of consistency and coherence. The courts stated that original photographs are not to be given inferior copyright protection, yet it seems that more often than not, photographs are granted thin copyright protection that covers only a little more than identical copying.[212] Originality in a photograph and its scope of protection in relation to its sources of originality were examined by the courts on an ad hoc basis with inconsistent results, especially so in the scope of protection granted.

The extent of photographs' copyright protection is, in practice, a difficult matter that continues to produce inconsistent results. One could argue that this difficulty might be more of a product of the courts struggling with the tools rather than being the fault of the tools themselves. Or perhaps the tools are not yet optimised to deal with copyright protection in photographs to the point that they adequately provide consistent protection. What is apparent is that the courts are reluctant to protect features related to the subject matter of photographs and the concepts behind them since that would risk broadening the protection in a way that could hinder the production of new photographs as a result of seemingly making copyright in photographs a matter related to the priority of appropriation. Even if the courts did broaden the scope of protection in photographs to cover a photograph's general concept, as was the case in *Temple Island Collections Ltd case*[213] in the United Kingdom, it would risk harming photographers' ability to produce new works. Photographers call for a clear and broad scope of protection for their works, but they are quick to raise fears that broadening the protection might risk their ability to produce works similar to the ones that inspired them. Yet, if the courts curtailed the umbrella of protection to minimise that risk, photographers would also be quick to complain that the courts give free rein to recreate photographs with impunity, as was illustrated following the reaction to the *Rentmeester case*[214] in the United States. Thus, it is a lose-lose situation for precisely the same reasons.

The inconsistency could also be argued to spawn from the fact that the courts still carry the legacy issues of equating photographs with other works in order to rationalise their analysis and judgement. Photographs were analogised to writing, databases, paintings, photocopies, and a compilation of facts in a way that only served to feed into the inconsistency of its position. Hence, the issue did not only produce inconsistent results as there is also inconsistency within the same use of the proxy of analogy. This use of analogy for photographs also laid bare the flaws regarding traditional tests such as the idea/expression test and the tests related to

212 Caddick, Harbottle and Suthersanen (n 41) ss 7–115.

213 *Temple Island Collections Ltd v New English Teas Ltd [2012] EWPCC 1* (n 11).

214 *Rentmeester v Nike, Inc, 883 F3d 1111 (2018)* (n 157).

substantial similarity in visual works, illuminating its weak compatibility with visual works such as photographs. Perhaps it is time to stop treating photographs other than as photographs and start acknowledging that photographs should be examined in their own capacity as photographs without the proxy of analogy. This is because the art of photography has been developed well enough to stand on its own as an art form.

# 8 The Impact of the Digital Age on Photography and Copyright

## 8.1 Introduction

The digital revolution introduced fundamental changes to many aspects of our lives. It has brought countless advantages and greatly enhanced creative endeavours. The digital revolution, coupled with the internet, brought unprecedented distribution and instant access to creative works. It established a fertile ground for the colossal mass production and reproduction of creative works, cultivating a predominant "remix culture" in cyberspace.[1]

The digital era and the internet created an environment that amplified various issues related to copyright, such as the scale of infringement, the scope of fair use and fair dealing, orphaned works, piracy, and enforcement, among other issues. Copyright law, which remains deeply rooted in its analogue past, struggles to deal with the challenges of the digital era.[2] The Anglo-American copyright law is strongly anchored in its analogue past with its trusted concepts, which tend to be designed as a one-size-fits-all, becoming antiquated under increasing pressure from the realities of the digital era. This is especially the case with photographs and works closely connected with technology.[3]

This chapter examines the impact of the digital age and social media on photography and photographic copyright. The first section discusses the impact of digital technology on the art of photography. This section highlights the fundamental changes to photographic technologies that impacted the level of creative control exerted by the photographer. The second section examines how the anchors of photographic expression that were traditionally relied upon to justify the

1 See: Lawrence Lessig, *Remix: Making Art and Commerce Thrive in the Hybrid Economy* (Penguin Books 2009); Lawrence Lessig, *Free Culture: How Big Media Uses Technology and the Law to Lock Down Culture and Control Creativity* (Penguin 2004); Alina Ng, "When Users Are Authors: Authorship in the Age of Digital Media" (2009) 12 Vanderbilt Journal of Entertainment and Technology Law 853; Guilda Rostama, "Remix Culture and Amateur Creativity: A Copyright Dilemma" (*WIPO*, June 2015) <https://www.wipo.int/wipo_magazine/en/2015/03/article_0006.html> accessed 19 October 2024.

2 Mira Burri, "Global Cultural Law and Policy in the Age of Ubiquitous Internet" (2014) 21 International Journal of Cultural Property 349, 352.

3 See: Thomas B Maddrey, "Photography, Creators, and the Changing Needs of Copyright Law" (2013) 16 SMU Sci. & Tech. L. Rev. 501.

DOI: 10.4324/9781003586555-8

subsistence of copyright in photographs are increasingly being eroded. The third section examines the impact of social media on how photographs are perceived and utilised as a communicative unit and how social media platforms' terms of service propagated this phenomenon. Furthermore, it considers fair use/fair dealing, orphan works, and copyright enforcement in the context of photographs in the United Kingdom and the United States. Finally, this chapter examines the effect of the UK's Intellectual Property Enterprise Court Small Claims Track (IPEC SCT) on copyright enforcement in relation to photographs. Moreover, it also looks at the US Copyright Alternative in Small-Claims Enforcement Act of 2019 (CASE Act), which has seen an extensive lobbying effort by US photographic organisations that led to its adoption into law.

## 8.2 The Impact of the Digital Age and Social Media on Photography

The digital revolution, coupled with the internet, brought fundamental changes to photography on nearly all fronts, to the point of affecting how images are perceived and valued.[4] The abundance of smartphones equipped with digital cameras combined with the internet and social media contributed to the unprecedented ubiquity of photographs.[5] The digital revolution allowed amateurs and hobbyists equipped with smartphones to take technically challenging photographs with ease. This is due to the fact that digital cameras come equipped with multiple image-enhancing processes and are powered by artificial intelligence (AI) technology, which can automatically adjust several parameters such as the focus, depth of field, and angle, along with other elements in a way that enables a newbie photographer to

4 See: Adrian Hadland, David Campbell and Paul Lambert, "The State of News Photography 2015" (*World Press Photo*, September 2015) 10 <https://www.worldpressphoto.org/getmedia/da4e7234-9f18-4036-8320-9397bf70cd89/The-State-of-News-Photography.pdf> accessed 18 October 2024; see: Peter Suciu, "A Photo Used to Be Worth a Thousand Words, but Thanks to Social Media Photos Have Lost Their Value" (*Forbes*, 24 October 2019) <https://www.forbes.com/sites/petersuciu/2019/10/24/a-photo-used-to-be-worth-a-thousand-words-but-thanks-to-social-media-photos-have-lost-their-value/> accessed 19 October 2024; Olivier Laurent, "How Snapchat, Instagram & Apple Are Reinventing Photography" (*Time*, 24 February 2017) <http://time.com/4659058/snapchat-instagram-apple-photography/> accessed 19 October 2024; Evgeny Tchebotarev, "AI Is Already Changing the Way We Think about Photography" (*Forbes*, 30 May 2018) <https://www.forbes.com/sites/evgenytchebotarev/2018/05/30/ai-is-already-changing-the-way-we-think-about-photography/#78117de7bb6a> accessed 19 October 2024; Jessica Silbey, "Control over Contemporary Photography: A Tangle of Copyright, Right of Publicity, and the First Amendment" (2019) 42 Journal of Law and the Arts 351; Tom de Castella, "Five Ways the Digital Camera Changed Us" *BBC News* (28 February 2012) <http://www.bbc.co.uk/news/magazine-16483509> accessed 11 October 2024.

5 Stephen Heyman, "Photos, Photos Everywhere" *The New York Times* (29 July 2015) <https://www.nytimes.com/2015/07/23/arts/international/photos-photos-everywhere.html> accessed 19 October 2024; Rose Eveleth, "How Many Photographs of You Are Out There in the World?" (*The Atlantic*, 2 November 2015) <https://www.theatlantic.com/technology/archive/2015/11/how-many-photographs-of-you-are-out-there-in-the-world/413389/> accessed 19 October 2024; Mary Meeker, "Internet Trends Report 2018" (*Kleiner Perkins*, 30 May 2018) <https://www.kleinerperkins.com/perspectives/internet-trends-report-2018/> accessed 19 October 2024.

take high-quality technical images without much of an effort.[6] In the past, such images required the technical knowledge, skill, creative choices, and judgement of an experienced professional photographer utilising specific equipment geared towards specific genres of photography to produce high-quality images.

Nowadays, due to the ubiquity of photographs and the prevalence of automation algorithms that fine-tune captured images without requiring much human input, the skill required to take high-quality photographs, along with the intrinsic value attached to photographs, is increasingly diminishing.[7] Apple is one of the companies that is leading the effort to automate photography for the ordinary consumer. Greg Joswiak, Apple's Vice President of product marketing, stated that they want to "make it so it's a single tap and you get the picture you want, even though, in the background, we're doing literally one hundred billion operations to make that photo look as good as it possibly can look."[8]

The ease of creation, coupled with the lack of meaningful depleting resources, virtually removed any limit on the number of photographs one can create. As a result, the production of digital images is believed to be enormous to the point that the images that are uploaded to online platforms such as Facebook,[9] Instagram,[10] X (formerly Twitter),[11] Snapchat,[12] and WhatsApp,[13] among others,[14] are estimated to

6 Hadland, Campbell and Lambert (n 4) 10; Sam Byford, "How AI Is Changing Photography" (*The Verge*, 31 January 2019) <https://www.theverge.com/2019/1/31/18203363/ai-artificial-intelligence-photography-google-photos-apple-huawei> accessed 19 October 2024; Tchebotarev (n 4); Devin Coldewey, "The Future of Photography Is Code" (*TechCrunch*, 22 October 2018) <https://techcrunch.com/2018/10/22/the-future-of-photography-is-code/> accessed 19 October 2024; Terry Sullivan, "Computational Photography Is Ready for Its Close-Up" (*PCMag UK*, 6 August 2018) <https://uk.pcmag.com/features/116743/computational-photography-is-ready-for-its-close-up> accessed 19 October 2024.

7 Laurent (n 4); Eveleth (n 5); Suciu (n 4).

8 Laurent (n 4).

9 "Facebook" (*Facebook*) <https://www.facebook.com/> accessed 19 October 2024.

10 "Instagram" (*Instagram*) <https://instagram.com/> accessed 19 October 2024.

11 "X (Twitter)" (*X*) <https://x.com/> accessed 19 October 2024.

12 "Snapchat!" (*Snapchat*) <https://www.snapchat.com> accessed 19 October 2024.

13 "WhatsApp" (*WhatsApp.com*) <https://www.whatsapp.com/> accessed 19 October 2024.

14 Jim Edwards, "Planet Selfie: We're Now Posting a Staggering 1.8 Billion Photos Every Day" (*Business Insider*, 28 May 2014) <http://www.businessinsider.com/were-now-posting-a-staggering-18-billion-photos-to-social-media-every-day-2014-5> accessed 19 October 2024; Molly Mulshine, "This Mind-Blowing Graphic Shows How Many Snapchat Photos Are Sent per Second" (*Business Insider*) <https://www.businessinsider.com/snapchat-photos-sent-per-second-2015-5> accessed 30 September 2021; "Connecting One Billion Users Every Day" (*WhatsApp.com*, 26 July 2017) <https://blog.whatsapp.com/connecting-one-billion-users-every-day> accessed 19 October 2024; Anita Balakrishnan and Julia Boorstin, "How Many Users Does Instagram Have? Now, 800 Million" (*CNBC*, 25 September 2017) <https://www.cnbc.com/2017/09/25/how-many-users-does-instagram-have-now-800-million.html> accessed 19 October 2024; Milken Institute, "175 Years of Photography: The Impact of Images" (*Youtube*, 30 April 2014) <https://www.youtube.com/watch?v=fRX7xzc7qdI&t=846s> accessed 19 October 2024; Meeker (n 5); Mary Meeker, "Internet Trends 2019" (*Bond*, 11 June 2019) 77 <https://www.bondcap.com/report/itr19/#view/1> accessed 19 October 2024.

exceed more than 1.8 billion images per day without showing any signs of slowing down.[15] Observers expressed that people take pictures not to save a moment but to share and communicate with each other.[16] This different attitude towards photography is popularised by social media platforms such as Snapchat, which is geared towards sharing ephemeral pictures of fleeting moments instead of saving those moments, as is traditionally the case with photography.[17]

The explosive production of photographs in social media is reminiscent of the time when the Kodak Brownie had brought a similar situation, albeit on a much smaller scale, prompting pushback from elitists who felt that the oversaturation of photographs undermined their value.[18] The pursuit of authenticity and intrinsic value led to fighting the aesthetics of digital photography itself. Hipstamatic[19] is a popular digital application that provides digital imaging filters that mimic the imperfections of old photographic processes to elicit the feeling of nostalgia and simulate the seemingly inherent value perceived in vintage photographs. Nathan Jurgenson, a sociologist at Snapchat, argued that vintage photographs' allure of authenticity paved the way for the proliferation of faux-vintage photographs in social media to simulate and invoke feelings of nostalgia.[20] He explained that "Faux-vintage photos placed one's self and one's digitally mediated present into the context of the past and its overtones of the authentic, the important, and the real."[21]

Another manifestation of this relentless pursuit of authenticity and uniqueness is embodied through the rise of non-fungible tokens (NFT). Every single NFT functions as a unique digital certificate that proves that the owner holds the original authentic copy of the digital asset.[22] One could argue that NFT may grant digital images the coveted aura of uniqueness and authenticity, which Walter Benjamin theorised to be the elements that imbued additional cultural value to the original

15 Edwards (n 14); Balakrishnan and Boorstin (n 14); Meeker (n 14).

16 Suciu (n 4); Laurent (n 4).

17 Milken Institute (n 14); Team Snap, "Introducing the New Snapchat" (29 November 2017) <https://newsroom.snap.com/introducing-the-new-snapchat> accessed 19 October 2024; Laurent (n 4); Suciu (n 4).

18 Milken Institute (n 14); Castella (n 4); Gary Sampson, "Histories, Theories, Criticism" in Michael R Peres (ed), *The Focal Encyclopedia of Photography: Digital Imaging, Theory and Applications History and Science* (4 edition, Elsevier 2007) 228.

19 Hipstamatic LLC, "Hipstamatic X Analog Camera" (*Hipstamatic*) <http://hipstamatic.com/x/> accessed 19 October 2024.

20 Nathan Jurgenson, *The Social Photo: On Photography and Social Media* (Kindle edition, Verso 2020) 4–7.

21 ibid 6.

22 "What Are NFTs and Why Are Some Worth Millions?" *BBC News* (23 September 2021) <https://www.bbc.com/news/technology-56371912> accessed 19 October 2024; Jazmin Goodwin, "What Is an NFT? Non-Fungible Tokens Explained" (*CNN*, 17 March 2021) <https://www.cnn.com/2021/03/17/business/what-is-nft-meaning-fe-series/index.html> accessed 19 October 2024; Josie Thaddeus-Johns, "What Are NFTs, Anyway? One Just Sold for $69 Million." *The New York Times* (11 March 2021) <https://www.nytimes.com/2021/03/11/arts/design/what-is-an-nft.html> accessed 19 October 2024.

work, "the aura of the work of art," in a manner that a copy would never be able to reproduce.[23] Alas, it remains to be seen where, in the digital age, the pursuit of authenticity will lead.

Professional photographers lamented the current state of photography following the impact of the internet and digital technology.[24] It seems that photographers are increasingly worried about the broad democratisation of photography and its impact on the value of images. These concerns are exacerbated by the advent of computational photography, which progressively eroded the level of skill needed in the art of photography. This is because the photographer's skill, which is considered one of the main competitive advantages of professional photographers over amateurs, is increasingly becoming less relevant in the face of computational photography paired with AI and machine learning technologies.

### *8.2.1 The Advent of Computational Photography*

The arrival of computational photography accelerated the erosion of skill in the art of photography. Computational photography was defined by Marc Levoy, a researcher and head of a team on computational imaging at Google, as "computational imaging techniques that enhance or extend the capabilities of digital photography [in which the] output is an ordinary photograph, but one that could not have been taken by a traditional camera."[25] In other words, computational photography captures data, and that data is processed to produce stunning images with minimal input from the photographer, effectively shifting the emphasis to the quality of the processing algorithms instead of the photographer's skill.[26]

Observers have contemplated whether computational photography has relegated the position of the photographer to little more than a "glorified button-pusher."[27]

23 Walter Benjamin, "The Work of Art in the Age of Mechanical Reproduction (1935)" in Hannah Arendt (ed), Henry Zohn (tr), *Illuminations: Essays and Reflections* (Houghton Mifflin Harcourt 1968).

24 See: Adrian Hadland and Camilla Barnett, "The State of News Photography 2018" (*World Press Photo*, 2018) 6 <https://www.worldpressphoto.org/getmedia/4f811d9d-ebc7-4b0b-a417-f119f6c49a15/the_state_of_news_photography_2018.pdf> accessed 30 September 2021; Hadland, Campbell and Lambert (n 4) 50; The British Photographic Council, "The British Photographic Council Industry Survey of Photographers 2010" (*British Photographic Council*, 2010) <http://www.british-photographic-council.org/survey/2010> accessed 19 October 2024.

25 Sullivan (n 6); Vince Tabora, "Computational Photography Will Revolutionize Digital Imaging" (*Medium*, 16 October 2018) <https://medium.com/hd-pro/computational-photography-will-revolutionize-digital-imaging-a25d34f37b11> accessed 19 October 2024.

26 Grant Scott, "OK Computer: Computational Photography Is Here to Stay!" (*The United Nations of Photography*, 29 May 2018) <https://unitednationsofphotography.com/2018/05/29/ok-computer-computational-photography-is-here-to-stay/> accessed 19 October 2024.

27 Hans Rosemond, "Has Technology Taken the Fun Out of Photography?" (*Fstoppers*, 9 May 2019) <https://fstoppers.com/originals/has-technology-taken-fun-out-photography-366471> accessed 19 October 2024; Scott (n 26); Katherine Bindley, "AI-Powered Cameras Represent Tech's Biggest Trade-Off" *Wall Street Journal* (7 January 2020) <https://www.wsj.com/articles/ai-powered-cameras-represent-techs-biggest-trade-off-11578414752> accessed 19 October 2024.

One commentator said that computational photography "makes the photographer irrelevant in most cases since the process is intelligent enough to make the image look great even if it wasn't shot by a professional."[28] Indeed, most smartphones come equipped with machine learning and AI technologies that enable the camera to produce high-quality technical images regardless of the skill of the person operating the camera.[29] In fact, AI is capable of deciding when to capture the image without interference from the photographer. In other words, it reached a point where there is no need to press a button since the AI takes control of the camera and decides when to capture the image once the framing meets its parameters.[30]

Computational photography was the subject of controversy, among professional photographers and photojournalists, centred around the authenticity of the images produced. In 2014, this controversy prompted the World Press Photo[31] to publish a research report led by Dr David Campbell titled "The Integrity of the Image."[32] The report examined the impact of the digital revolution on photography and explained that:

> [In the] conventional [analogue] understanding of photography, the camera is understood as a picture-making device… .In the digital era, we still think of the camera of a picture-making device. This, however, is a mistake. In the digital era, we need to understand the camera as a data-collection device, a device which is "gathering as much data as you can about the scene, and then later using advanced computational techniques to process that data into the final image. That creates a much more slippery definition of an original, because what is defined at the time of capture is not necessarily a fully formed picture." With this understanding, we can appreciate that photography has become "computational photography."[33]

The report declared that "We are now in an era of computational photography, where most cameras capture data rather than images. This means that there is no original image, and that all images require processing to exist."[34] Therefore, the quality of an image may progressively be attributed to the processing quality rather than primarily the photographer's skill. Hence, some photographers continue to use

28 Tabora (n 25).

29 ibid; Byford (n 6); Hui Fang, "Using Deep Learning to Create Professional-Level Photographs" (*Google AI Blog*, 13 July 2017) <https://research.google/blog/using-deep-learning-to-create-professional-level-photographs/> accessed 19 October 2024.

30 Navid Shiee and Aseem Agarwala, "Take Your Best Selfie Automatically, with Photobooth on Pixel 3" (*Google AI Blog*, 16 April 2019) <https://research.google/blog/take-your-best-selfie-automatically-with-photobooth-on-pixel-3/> accessed 19 October 2024.

31 World Press Photo, "World Press Photo" (*World Press Photo*) <https://www.worldpressphoto.org/> accessed 19 October 2024.

32 David Campbell, "The Integrity of the Image" (World Press Photo 2014) <https://www.worldpressphoto.org/education/research/integrity-of-the-image-report> accessed 19 October 2024.

33 ibid 7.

34 ibid 2.

film-based cameras and old photographic processes as a creative choice due to their "authentic appeal" that gives the photograph greater intrinsic value, at least compared to digital images.[35] These photographers reject faux-vintage photographs' mimicry of old photographic processes through digital simulation in favour of utilising the old photographic processes themselves to produce their work.[36] Thus, for these photographers, simulated antiquity was simply not enough to capture the value and the nostalgic feelings associated with vintage photographs.

Nowadays, many images are captured for their information and communication capacity, either for sharing and communicating a moment or an experience or serving as data input, especially because limited resources do not hamper digital photography compared to analogue photography. The internet is oversaturated with images uploaded each day in a way that impacts how images are perceived and valued.[37] Many of these images populating social media have little intrinsic value on their own since they are often meant to serve as a tool for visual communication rather than a creative outlet for artistic or documentary aspirations. Nathan Jurgenson labelled these types of images as social photography whose primary objective is to serve social functions to the point that "its existence as a stand-alone media object is subordinate to its existence as a unit of communication."[38]

Nonetheless, the digital era's impact on the position of photographic art with regard to its value as an art form is not the only cause for concern for photographers. The level of technological advancement in the field of digital imaging, such as computational photography, threatens the anchors of creative photographic expressions that were traditionally relied upon to justify copyright protection for photographs.

## 8.3 The Impact of the Digital Era on Photographic Copyright

The impact of the digital era extends beyond changes to the art of photography to reach the very basis for protecting images with copyright. These new technologies threaten the rationale for copyright protection of photographs and the stability of that protection. The previous chapters examined how the anchors that justified the subsistence of copyright in photographs were, traditionally, firmly placed at the creation stage prior to capturing the image, placing the bulk of the weight on the photographer's free choices during the pre-capture stage. The courts justified copyright in photographs on the grounds of the photographer's free creative choices that defined the image rendition and composition. These choices include the choice of

35 Hadland, Campbell and Lambert (n 4) 37, 66; Garage Staff, "The Analog Revival: Why Photographers Are Returning to Film" (*hp: The Garage*, 24 January 2019) <https://garage.hp.com/us/en/modern-life/analog-film-photography-trend-low-tech-photos.html> accessed 19 October 2024.

36 Aline Smithson, "Historic Processes / Contemporary Visions" (*LENSCRATCH*, 16 June 2013) <http://lenscratch.com/2013/06/historic-processescontemporary-visions/> accessed 19 October 2024.

37 Suciu (n 4); Eveleth (n 5); Meeker (n 5); Castella (n 4).

38 Jurgenson (n 20) 8.

angle, depth of field, lighting, colours, focus, shadows, subject matter, etc. The free choices, taken at the pre-capture stage before pressing the button, that impact the image's rendition are what were consistently relied upon to decide whether a photograph is an original creation containing a copyright. This indicates that the courts regard the post-capture stage as of much lesser importance for the purposes of finding copyright in photographs. This is rooted in an analogue view of photography that neglects to consider technological advancements, such as digital imaging and computational photography, that greatly expanded post-capture flexibility to the extent that it alters some of the pre-capture elements of the image.[39]

However, unlike photographic copyright, the art of photography itself was not shackled by its analogue past and went beyond its traditional limitations.[40] One can posit that nowadays, the art of photography contains three important stages: the pre-capture stage, the mid-capture or processing stage, and finally, the post-capture stage. Yet, only the pre-capture stage was traditionally acknowledged in the courts as the stage where originality is to be located for the purposes of copyright protection.[41] The courts routinely do not give weight to the post-capture stage in assessing the originality of photographs despite the fact that the raw photo digital format, which is a format that stores the raw data of an image to be processed and edited with varying results depending on the quality of the processing software used,[42] expands the parameters of adjustments that can be made to an image.

39 See: Fang (n 29); Stephen Mayes, "The Next Revolution in Photography Is Coming" [2015] *Time* <https://time.com/4003527/future-of-photography/> accessed 19 October 2024; Coldewey (n 6); Tchebotarev (n 4); Byford (n 6); Jun-Yan Zhu and others, "Unpaired Image-to-Image Translation Using Cycle-Consistent Adversarial Networks" [2018] arXiv <http://arxiv.org/abs/1703.10593> accessed 19 October 2024; Campbell (n 32); John Aldred, "'Reverse Prisma' AI Turns Paintings into Photos and Turns Winter to Summer" (*DIY Photography*, 4 April 2017) <https://www.diyphotography.net/reverse-prisma-ai-turns-paintings-photos-turns-winter-summer/> accessed 19 October 2024; Stephen Shankland, "With an Eye to the Future, Try Raw Photos Today" (*CNET*, 7 December 2009) <https://www.cnet.com/news/with-an-eye-to-the-future-try-raw-photos-today-10407309/> accessed 19 October 2024; Dane Pestano, "AI in Photography – The Good, The Bad and The Ugly" (*Professional Photo*, 24 January 2024) <https://professionalphoto.online/ai-artificial-intelligence/ai-in-photography-the-good-the-bad-and-the-ugly/> accessed 19 October 2024; Campbell (n 32) 7.

40 Fang (n 29); Mayes (n 39); Coldewey (n 6); Tchebotarev (n 4); Byford (n 6); Zhu and others (n 39); Campbell (n 32) 7; Aldred (n 39); Shankland, "With an Eye to the Future, Try Raw Photos Today" (n 39); Pestano (n 39).

41 See: *Burrow-Giles Lithographic Co v Sarony, 111 US 53 (1884)*; *(C-145/10) Painer v Standard Verlags GmbH [2012] ECDR 6*; see also: Eva E Subotnik, "Originality Proxies: Toward a Theory of Copyright and Creativity" (2010) 76 Brooklyn Law Review 1487; Christine Haight Farley, "The Lingering Effects of Copyright's Response to the Invention of Photography" (2004) 65 University of Pittsburgh Law Review 385; see Chapters 6–7.

42 Shankland, "With an Eye to the Future, Try Raw Photos Today" (n 39); Stephen Shankland, "Digital Photography Begins Its Next Chapter with Radical Changes" (*CNET*, 19 December 2018) <https://www.cnet.com/tech/mobile/digital-photography-gets-radical-changes-smartphone-mirrorless-tech/> accessed 19 October 2024; Stephen Shankland, "Google, Apple, Adobe Make Your Phone Photos Better by Boosting Raw Format" (*CNET*, 14 December 2018) <https://www.cnet.com/news

The mid-capture stage is unknown territory in the realm of copyright in photographs since it combines elements of both the pre-capture (such as angle, depth of field, aperture, staging, lighting, arrangement) and the post-capture stage (such as enhancements, visual manipulation) in one automated process. The mid-capture (or processing) stage is where the collected data is processed to produce the image. It is the stage that saw great developments to the point of extending beyond merely fixing the image; it now processes the captured data, correcting deficiencies to produce the best possible image.[43] Hence, the quality of the photograph depends on the quality of the processing algorithms instead of the photographer's level of skill,[44] a far cry from its analogue past, where it was the stage to bring out and fix the original image captured, something akin to printing it.

The World Press Photo conceded that in the digital era, the camera is no longer "a picture making device," it is instead a "data-collection device" that collects the data of whichever the camera captures, and that data is then processed to produce an image. In other words, the camera not only records light but also captures a bundle of data that requires post-processing in order for an image to exist. The image itself does not exist in its original form.[45] Hence, in the digital era, specifically in computational photography, there is no original image; instead, there is data. What is considered an image is a construct of that data, and its quality depends on the quality of the processing algorithms.[46]

Therefore, what is considered a photograph can be redefined as data given a visual form. The US copyright law does not define photographs since it adopts an open system of copyright subject matters, providing that the subject matter of copyright is "original works of authorship fixed in any tangible medium of expression, now known or later developed, from which they can be perceived, reproduced, or otherwise communicated, either directly or with the aid of a machine or device."[47] Thus, it can be argued that the works produced by computational photography, at least in principle, would not fall outside copyright subject matters under the US copyright law.

However, a question may be raised regarding whether redefining photographs beyond a recording of light presents challenges to the UK copyright law, which is described as a closed system of copyright where it lists the categories of works that are eligible for copyright protection. There is a longstanding presumption in UK courts that copyright subsists in photographs if they were independently created by virtue of being a photograph, one of the works expressly mentioned as a subject matter of copyright. Under Section 4(2) of the UK Copyright, Designs and

/google-apple-adobe-make-your-phone-photos-better-by-boosting-raw-format/> accessed 19 October 2024.

43 Campbell (n 32) 7; Coldewey (n 6); Shankland, "Digital Photography Begins Its Next Chapter with Radical Changes" (n 42).

44 Scott (n 26); Tabora (n 25); Coldewey (n 6).

45 Campbell (n 32).

46 ibid; Scott (n 26); Coldewey (n 6); Tabora (n 25); Hadland, Campbell and Lambert (n 4) 66.

47 Sec. 102 Title 17 of the United States Code (US).

Patents Act 1988 (CDPA 1988), photographic works are placed under the category of artistic works, hence requiring originality, and defined as "a recording of light or other radiation on any medium on which an image is produced or from which an image may by any means be produced, and which is not part of a film."[48] It is not clear whether this definition of photographs is wide enough to cover images produced by computational photography where what is recorded is, fundamentally, data. Nonetheless, the definition appears flexible enough to accommodate computational photography since, ultimately, it is a recording, "data," from which an image can be produced.

Nevertheless, on the subsistence of copyright in photographs, the most pressing issue is the fact that copyright in photographic images was conceived as subsisting due to the author's free creative choices at the pre-capture stage. Whatever these choices may be, what matters is their holistic imprint on the photograph.[49] In spite of this, technological advancements now make it possible to change, in the mid- and post-capture stage, the fundamental elements of an image that are often thought of as firmly placed in the pre-capture stage. These changes may go beyond mere enhancements to reach some of the very anchors for copyright's subsistence in photographs, which represents the photographer's originality as evidenced in his free choices during the capture of the image.

One of these technological advancements is the light-field cameras, which capture the data of individual light rays of a scene in 3D space and store it. Afterwards, that stored data would be possible to manipulate in order to change the image's composition long after it was captured.[50] The user can change the image parameters, such as the focus, depth of field, aperture, angle of the shot, and shadows, during the post-capture stage, going further than mere enhancements to changing the foundational elements of the image itself.[51] Consequently, images captured with light-field cameras are described as "living pictures," since they uproot some of the anchors believed to be the image's firmly fixed elements that were previously incapable of being efficiently adjusted in the post-capture stage.[52]

On the one hand, one can say that despite the changes to photographic technologies, the element of the author's free choice is still firmly present in the art of photography. Since, ultimately, the choice remains with the photographer to choose the camera, whether it is a film-based or digital single-lens reflex or

48 Section 4(2)(b) Copyright, Designs and Patents Act 1988 (UK).

49 See Chapter 7.

50 Harry McCracken, "Lytro: What Really Makes It Revolutionary" (*CNET*, 20 October 2011) <https://www.cnet.com/culture/lytro-what-really-makes-it-revolutionary/> accessed 19 October 2024; Sean O'Kane, "Lytro's 'Living Pictures' Are Now Dead on the Web" (*The Verge*, 6 December 2017) <https://www.theverge.com/2017/12/6/16742314/lytro-focus-photos-support-cameras-illum> accessed 19 October 2024.

51 Michael Zhang, "A Look at the Lytro Illum, The Camera of the Future That Failed" (*PetaPixel*, 1 December 2017) <https://petapixel.com/2017/01/12/look-lytro-illum-camera-future-failed/> accessed 19 October 2024; McCracken (n 50); O'Kane (n 50).

52 O'Kane (n 50); Justin Hughes, "The Photographer's Copyright-Photograph as Art, Photograph as Database" (2011) 25 Harv. JL & Tech. 339, 423, 424.

computational-based camera, along with the perks that come with each. It also could be argued that the choices available to the photographer are greatly expanded and enhanced to allow the photographer considerable room for creative expression.[53] Thus, one could argue that the tools that have become more intelligent and efficient should not be used against the photographer. Indeed, Nathan Jurgenson argues that cameras of all kinds should be regarded as creative partners that "encourage new ways of seeing, new performances of vision."[54] Hence, the camera should be considered subservient to the human agent rather than being perceived as a tyrannical machine that subordinates the human agent.

On the other hand, one can say that technological advancements are, in fact, increasingly diminishing the importance of the photographer's choices beyond the pressing of the button. Photographic images are increasingly becoming more malleable, where the bulk of the work, which is automated, is now happening in the post-capture stage or even during the mid-capture stage itself when the image is being processed.[55] Yet, copyright law predominantly focuses on the pre-capture stage to determine whether a photograph contains a copyright. That is because the law response to photography developed firmly on an analogue view of photography; the law still sees the camera as an authentic "picture-making device."[56]

Professor Justin Hughes shed light on the effects of technological development on the stability of copyright in photographs in his 2011 article.[57] He argued that the originality standard was "stretched and distorted" to accommodate photography.[58] Hughes reasoned that many photographs are, in essence, more akin to a compilation of facts instead of artistic works and this is evidenced by the fact that most of the problems concerning copyright in photographs are similar to the issues encountered by copyright in compilations of facts.[59] Hence, Hughes suggested that photographic copyright should be approached in the same manner we approach copyright in databases.[60] He posits that:

53 Pestano (n 39).

54 Jurgenson (n 20) 21.

55 Michael Zhang, "This AI Can Change Weather, Seasons, and Time of Day in Photos" (*PetaPixel*, 5 December 2017) <https://petapixel.com/2017/12/05/ai-can-change-weather-seasons-time-day-photos/> accessed 19 October 2024; Ming-Yu Liu, Thomas Breuel and Jan Kautz, "Unsupervised Image-to-Image Translation Networks" [2017] NIPS <https://research.nvidia.com/publication/2017-12_Unsupervised-Image-to-Image-Translation> accessed 19 October 2024; James Vincent, "Nvidia Uses AI to Make It Snow on Streets That Are Always Sunny" (*The Verge*, 5 December 2017) <https://www.theverge.com/2017/12/5/16737260/ai-image-translation-nvidia-data-self-driving-cars> accessed 19 October 2024; Byford (n 6); Tchebotarev (n 4).

56 See: Burri (n 2); Hadland and Barnett (n 24) 7; see also: Zachariah Parry, "Digital Manipulation and Photographic Evidence: Defrauding the Courts One Thousand Words at a Time" (2009) 2009 U. Ill. J.L. Tech. & Pol'y 175.

57 Hughes (n 52).

58 ibid 342, 422.

59 ibid 342.

60 ibid.

> Seeing the parallel between photographs and databases has great dividends for those working in copyright law. It is no accident that the strongest, most stable bases for copyright protection of a photograph are selection and arrangement.[61]

However, equating photographs with databases is not an accurate treatment of photography since this neglects their artistic capacity. After all, photography, since its inception, was a curious merge of science, technology, and art. Therefore, instead of equating photography with databases, paintings, or even writings, or as any other work for that matter, it is more suitable to address photographs as their own unique thing, not as paintings, nor as databases, but as photographs.

## 8.4 Photographic Copyright and Its Value in the Era of Photo Ubiquity

### *8.4.1 Photographs, Social Media, and Copyright Infringement*

The internet space is filled with copyrighted works produced by users, amateurs and professionals alike, with an unprecedented and decentralised output of production.[62] The popularity of social media platforms, such as Facebook, X (formerly Twitter), Instagram, Snapchat, TikTok, and Reddit, among other platforms, provided not only unparalleled access to copyrighted works but also cultivated a deeply rooted culture of sharing.[63] Sharing is actively encouraged across social media platforms; this fed into the mistaken belief that whatever is posted in the internet space is free for all to use and share.[64] Social media platforms created an environment where copyrighted works, especially images, were used and "remixed" for a variety of purposes. Chief among them is as a medium for visual

61 ibid 350.

62 See: Meeker (n 14); Jessica Silbey, "Justifying Copyright in the Age of Digital Reproduction: The Case of Photographers" (2019) 9 UC Irvine Law Review 406, 408; Diane Leenheer Zimmerman, "Copyright and Social Media: A Tale of Legislative Abdication" (2014) 35 Pace Law Review 260, 261; Ng (n 1) 867, 883; Elena Cooper, "Reassessing the Challenge of the Digital: An Empirical Perspective on Authorship and Copyright" in Mireille van Eechoud (ed), *The Work of Authorship* (Amsterdam University Press 2014); Daniel Gervais, "Authors, Online" (2014) 38 Columbia Journal of Law & the Arts 385, 390; see also: Ng (n 1) 864.

63 See: Meeker (n 14); see: Lessig, *Remix* (n 1); Lessig, *Free Culture* (n 1); Alison C Storella, "It's Selfie-Evident: Spectrums of Alienability and Copyrighted Content on Social Media Note" [2014] Boston University Law Review 2045; Roxanne A Stokes, "Don't Pin It on Pinterest: Addressing the Conflict between the Culture of Sharing and Secondary Liability for Copyright Infringement" (2014) 14 Journal of High Technology Law 482; Elizabeth J Tao, "A Picture's Worth: The Future of Copyright Protection of User-Generated Images on Social Media" (2017) 24 Indiana Journal of Global Legal Studies 617; Victoria Smith Ekstrand and Derigan Silver, "Remixing, Reposting, and Reblogging: Digital Media, Theories of the Image, and Copyright Law" (2014) 21 Visual Communication Quarterly 96, 96, 97; Ng (n 1) 864, 865.

64 See: Lessig, *Free Culture* (n 1); Lessig, *Remix* (n 1); see: Michael W Carroll, "Pinterest and Copyright's Safe Harbors for Internet Providers Symposium: Social Media and the Law" (2013) 68 University of Miami Law Review 421.

communication, which ranges from mere responses to express a particular emotion to memes without permission from the rightsholders.[65] Social media popularised what Nathan Jurgenson labelled as social photography, in which images are captured and used primarily as "a unit of communication" where communication is the priority rather than the photograph's aesthetic features.[66] This created various issues related to copyright, such as the scope of fair use and fair dealing, the extent of orphaned works, and the problem of copyright infringement and enforcement in the current digital environment.

The practice of sharing copyrighted content is deeply embedded in internet culture to the point that any attempt to limit this is met with strenuous opposition from different stakeholders. This was evidenced via the general response to the controversial attempt by the European Union (EU) to address the issue through the Directive on Copyright in the Digital Single Market,[67] which entered into force despite the campaign against it from diverse stakeholders.[68] Copyrighted images are one of the largest segments of copyrighted works that are being distributed and continuously shared all over the internet, along with short viral clips.[69] Consequently, the scale

65 Taylor Lorenz, "Instagram Wants Memers to Like It Again" (*The Atlantic*, 6 August 2019) <https://www.theatlantic.com/technology/archive/2019/08/instagram-hiring-meme-liaison/595552/> accessed 19 October 2024; Jane C Hu, "Meme and Reposting Accounts Live in a Legal Netherworld" (*Slate Magazine*, 8 August 2019) <https://slate.com/technology/2019/08/copyright-law-meme-accounts-instagram-reposts.html> accessed 19 October 2024.

66 Jurgenson (n 20) 9.

67 Directive 2019/790/EC of 17 April 2019 on copyright and related rights in the Digital Single Market and amending Directives 96/9/EC and 2001/29/EC [2019] OJ L130/92.

68 See: Kent Walker, "Now Is the Time to Fix the EU Copyright Directive" (*Google*, 7 February 2019) <https://blog.google/around-the-globe/google-europe/now-time-fix-eu-copyright-directive/> accessed 19 October 2024; Institute for Information Law, "Academics Against Press Publishers' Right" (*IVIR*, 24 April 2018) <https://www.ivir.nl/academics-against-press-publishers-right/> accessed 19 October 2024; James Vincent, "European Wikipedias Have Been Turned Off for the Day to Protest Dangerous Copyright Laws" (*The Verge*, 21 March 2019) <https://www.theverge.com/2019/3/21/18275462/eu-copyright-directive-protest-wikipedia-twitch-pornhub-final-vote> accessed 19 October 2024; Andrew Griffin, "EU Removes 'Offensive' Blog Post Attacking Internet Campaigners against New Copyright Rules" (*The Independent*, 19 February 2019) <https://www.independent.co.uk/tech/eu-copyright-rules-blog-post-commission-article-11-13-latest-a8786256.html> accessed 19 October 2024; Julia Alexander, "YouTube CEO Calls EU's Proposed Copyright Regulation Financially Impossible" (*The Verge*, 12 November 2018) <https://www.theverge.com/2018/11/12/18087250/youtube-ceo-copyright-directive-article-13-european-union> accessed 19 October 2024; Matt Reynolds, "What Is Article 13? The EU's Divisive New Copyright Plan Explained" [2019] *Wired UK* <https://www.wired.co.uk/article/what-is-article-13-article-11-european-directive-on-copyright-explained-meme-ban> accessed 19 October 2024; Andrew Griffin, "Article 13: What Just Happened to the EU 'Meme Ban' and Why Are People So Angry?" (*The Independent*, 26 March 2019) <https://www.independent.co.uk/life-style/gadgets-and-tech/news/article-13-vote-eu-meme-ban-copyright-law-rule-explained-a8841016.html> accessed 19 October 2024.

69 See: Meeker (n 14) 4, 86.

of infringement is so vast that photographers rarely seek to pursue infringement claims since the costs would far exceed the benefits.[70]

Photographers have long expressed their concerns regarding the scale of infringement that plagued their profession, expressing that, year after year, the issue continues to grow and threaten their industry.[71] The oversaturation of images reduces the value of photographs, which, when met with the prevailing culture on the internet, leads to a wide-scale infringement of images, making it nearly impossible for copyright law to keep up.[72] There are attempts to fill the void left by the law through private actors, a situation referred to as "private ordering."[73] However, private ordering may not be the preferred approach for the purposes of copyright protection,[74] although Daniela Simone argues that, at least in the context of collective authorship, the flexibility and efficiency characterised by private ordering supported by the structure and public interest-oriented approach of public ordering would be the most balanced approach that may lead to greater legal effectiveness.[75]

#### *8.4.1.1 Copyright, Remix Culture, Sharing, and the Author's Control*

The digital age has drastically changed how we interact with knowledge-based content. A striking example is observed on social media platforms where creative works are being used in a manner that blurs the line between authors and users through the proliferation of user-generated content (UGC), based on copyrighted works, beyond the original authors' control.[76] Copyright as a system of protection creates an artificial scarcity of intangible assets by granting a set of limited

70 The British Photographic Council (n 24); Hadland and Barnett (n 24); Hadland, Campbell and Lambert (n 4) 50; Hong Luo and Julie Holland Mortimer, "Copyright Infringement in the Market for Digital Images" (2016) 106 American Economic Review 140, 140, 144.

71 Hadland and Barnett (n 24) 6.

72 Suciu (n 4); Zimmerman (n 62) 261; see: Tao (n 63).

73 See: Jennifer E Rothman, "Copyright's Private Ordering and the Next Great Copyright Act" (2014) 29 Berkeley Technology Law Journal 1595; Severine Dusollier, "Sharing Access to Intellectual Property through Private Ordering" (2007) 82 Chicago-Kent Law Review 1391; Jorge L Contreras, "From Private Ordering to Public Law: The Legal Frameworks Governing Standards-Essential Patents" (2016) 30 Harvard Journal of Law & Technology (Harvard JOLT) 211.

74 See: Zimmerman (n 62).

75 Daniela Simone, *Copyright and Collective Authorship: Locating the Authors of Collaborative Work* (Kindle edition, CUP Cambridge 2019) 216–217, 219–220.

76 Natalia Mielczarek and W Wat Hopkins, "Copyright, Transformativeness, and Protection for Internet Memes" (2021) 98 Journalism & Mass Communication Quarterly 37, 44, 46; Giacomo Bonetto, "Internet Memes as Derivative Works: Copyright Issues under EU Law" (2018) 13 Journal of Intellectual Property Law & Practice 989, 990; see: H Bosher and S Yeşiloğlu, "An Analysis of the Fundamental Tensions between Copyright and Social Media: The Legal Implications of Sharing Images on Instagram" (2019) 33 International Review of Law, Computers & Technology 164; Hayleigh Bosher, "Key Issues around Copyright and Social Media: Ownership, Infringement and Liability" (2020) 15 Journal of Intellectual Property Law & Practice 123.

exclusive rights to the author/copyright owner of the creative work.[77] These exclusionary rights effectively grant the author/copyright owner exclusive control over the work for the duration of the copyright.[78] Hence, copyright is, by design, an instrument of control over intangible works vested in the copyright owner of the work. In contrast, social media fundamentally cultivates a culture of sharing that creates an abundance of cultural works by inviting users to engage with the contents not as passive consumers but as active participants who contribute to the work's value as a communicative instrument.[79] Therefore, it is perhaps more accurate to describe social media users as "Prosumers," a term that refers to individuals who are both consumers and producers who participate in the creation of value in a given ecosystem for themselves and other users.[80] In other words, social media gains value from encouraging their user base to be prosumers and this frequently conflicts with the author/copyright owner's rights to control their work.[81]

Perhaps a clear demonstration of how social media wrestles control out of the author's hand, should he wish to utilise the platform, is located in their terms of service. Instagram, the most popular image-sharing social media platform, notes, in their terms of service, that they "do not claim ownership of [the user's] content, but [the user] grant[s] us a license to use it."[82] However, the particulars of that licence reveal that it effectively divests the user of all control over their content in favour of the platform as long as it remains in their system. Hence, in the instant the user shares, posts, or uploads their content on the platform, they grant Instagram "a non-exclusive, royalty-free, transferable, sub-licensable, worldwide license to host, use, distribute, modify, run, copy, publicly perform or display, translate, and create derivative works of [the user's] content."[83] Several other social media

77 See: Jake Linford, "Copyright and Attention Scarcity" (2020) 42 Cardozo Law Review 143 (Arguing in favour of the artificial scarcity created by copyright, seeing it as driving the creation of new creative works).

78 Lionel Bently and others, *Intellectual Property Law* (5 edition, OUP Oxford 2018) 1, 140; *Dutfield and Suthersanen on Global Intellectual Property Law: Second Edition* (2 revised edition, Edward Elgar Publishing 2020) 14, 98.

79 Mielczarek and Hopkins (n 76) 53–54; Kara Podraza, "When Is a Little Too Much?: The De Minimis Doctrine and Its Implications for Online Communication Tools" (2018) 25 George Mason Law Review 544, 544; Corinne Tan, *Regulating Content on Social Media: Copyright, Terms of Service and Technological Features* (UCL Press 2018) 3–4; Bonetto (n 76) 544; Bosher and Yeşiloğlu (n 76) 164.

80 Myriam Ertz, Xinyuan Cao and José Maria Barragán Maravilla, "The Prosumer" (2024) 4 Encyclopedia 1263.

81 Bosher and Yeşiloğlu (n 76) 181; James Meese and Jennifer Hagedorn, "Mundane Content on Social Media: Creation, Circulation, and the Copyright Problem" (2019) 5 Social Media + Society 44, 46 <https://doi.org/10.1177/2056305119839190> accessed 25 August 2024; Bosher (n 76) 123, 125; Bonetto (n 76) 990.

82 Instagram, "Terms of Use" (*Instagram*) <https://help.instagram.com/581066165581870/?helpref=hc_fnav> accessed 6 October 2024.

83 ibid.

platforms adopt comparable terms of service/user agreement.[84] Palmieri and Reid conducted a systematic analysis of the user agreement of leading social media platforms and revealed that they all required a non-exclusive extensive licence to exploit the user's content if shared on the platform.[85] However, some of these platforms allow users to restrict or limit the scope of certain licensed rights through the user's settings.[86] One notable example of how these licences force the user to virtually relinquish control over their content is found in the social media platform X. X, formerly Twitter, asserts, rather bluntly, that the acquired licence allows for

> additional uses by [X], or other companies, organizations or individuals… with no compensation paid to [the user] with respect to the Content that [they] submit, post, transmit or otherwise make available through the Services as the use of the Services by [them] is hereby agreed as being sufficient compensation for the Content and grant of rights herein.[87]

Across the internet landscape, the user's agreements of social media platforms are designed primarily to serve the platform itself instead of the users who contribute immensely to its value.[88] Inherently, social networks thrive on a sharing culture where participants are eager to share and collaborate in the value creation process and pass the fruits that emerge from it.[89] However, there lies the crux of the conflict, as Bosher noted that "the ethos of sharing on social media platforms contrasts with the nature of copyright as a regime aimed at restricting copying."[90] Consequently, a mismatch is manifested between the prevalent and actively encouraged practices of social media and the rules of copyright law, leading the public to hold inaccurate perceptions of copyright.[91] This mismatch extends not only to ordinary users but also to celebrities, who are generally expected to be more adept with copyright due to the nature of their cultural position.[92] Several celebrities found themselves the

84 See e.g.: "Facebook Terms of Service" (*Facebook*) <https://www.facebook.com/terms.php?_rdr> accessed 7 October 2024; "Pinterest Terms of Service" (*Pinterest Policy*) <https://policy.pinterest.com/en/terms-of-service> accessed 7 October 2024; "Terms of Service | TikTok" (*TikTok*) <https://www.tiktok.com/legal/page/row/terms-of-service/en> accessed 7 October 2024.

85 Isabela M Palmieri and Amanda Reid, "Copyright and Shareability: A Contractual Solution to Embedding via Social Media" (2023) 28 Communication Law and Policy 152, 178–183.

86 ibid 179.

87 X, "X Terms of Service" (*X*) <https://x.com/en/tos> accessed 6 October 2024.

88 Tao (n 63) 619.

89 Brian Leung, "Internet Memes and Copyright: Facilitating the Memetic Remix Discourse by Viewing Joint Authorship Flexibly?" The Journal of World Intellectual Property 1, 3; Lessig, *Remix* (n 1) 146.

90 Bosher (n 76) 124.

91 Bosher and Yeşiloğlu (n 76) 181.

92 See: Emma Perot, "The Conflict between the Copyright of Paparazzi and the Right of Publicity of Celebrities" (2021) 30 Texas Intellectual Property Law Journal 121; Dylan B Reich, "'Gigi, Over Here!': Celebrity Use of Copyrighted Paparazzi Photographs" (2021) 39 Cardozo Arts & Entertainment Law Journal 793.

subject of litigations filed against them for sharing photographs of themselves on Instagram without acquiring a licence from the photographers/the rightsholders.[93]

The "ethos" of social media to share and collaborate in value creation is not aligned with copyright law's function to restrict rather than liberate.[94] This is especially problematic for photographs and images in general since, due to their nature, what ends up being shared is the whole work as intended to be perceived and not just a fragment of it.[95] Perhaps a glaring example of how social media users add value to the works, through remixing and utilising them as communicative tools, is illustrated in internet memes. A "meme" is defined as "a noun that conveys the idea of a unit of cultural transmission, or a unit of imitation."[96] It is a term coined by evolutionary biologist Richard Dawkins in his 1973 book *The Selfish Gene*, which posits that "memes propagate themselves in the meme pool by leaping from brain to brain via a process which, in the broad sense, can be called imitation."[97] One can draw parallels with the process in which internet memes propagate the internet with unprecedented speed due to the powerful communication tools of the internet. Social media platforms amplify and curate these communication tools by encouraging users to collaboratively and organically replicate, remix, and disperse these memes throughout the internet.[98]

Daniel Gervais dubbed the internet as "the Global Meme Factory – it makes possible a great cycle of: (1) access to existing works; (2) copying them; (3) modifying them and (4) disseminating them, which repeats endlessly in various directions."[99] Some commentators even argue that internet memes now serve as an effective "visual language" used for communicative utilitarian purposes that transcend boundaries.[100] One can observe that the raw materials of the most popular internet memes are visual works, such as photographs and images, that were altered in some way, without the prior consent of the copyright owner, to serve as a communicative unit that, in many cases, carries an entirely different message from what the original creator intended.[101] Nevertheless, the original copyright holders of the underlying work sometimes try to assert their control to prevent certain undesirable uses or

93 See e.g.: *Barbera v Grande, No 119-cv-04349 (SDNY May 13, 2019)*; *Xclusive-Lee, Inc v Hadid, 1:19-cv-00520 (EDNY 2019)*; *Xposure Photos UK, Ltd v Kardashian, No 2:17-cv-03088 (CD Cal Apr 25,2017)*; Kelly-Leigh Cooper, "Why Celebrities Are Being Sued over Images of Themselves" (*BBC*, 6 February 2019) <https://www.bbc.com/news/world-us-canada-47128788> accessed 5 October 2024.

94 See: Tim Wu, "Tolerated Use" (2008) 31 Colum. J. L. & Arts 617.

95 Bosher and Yeşiloğlu (n 76) 181; see: Tao (n 63).

96 Richard Dawkins, *The Selfish Gene* (40 anniversary edition, OUP Oxford 2016) 249.

97 ibid 250.

98 Podraza (n 79) 544; Bonetto (n 76) 990; Mielczarek and Hopkins (n 76) 53–54; see also: Leung (n 89).

99 Gervais (n 62) 385.

100 Mielczarek and Hopkins (n 76) 53–64; Podraza (n 79) 544.

101 See e.g.: Matt Furie, "Pepe the Frog's Creator: He Was Never About Hate." (*TIME*, 13 October 2016) <https://time.com/4530128/pepe-the-frog-creator-hate-symbol/> accessed 7 October 2024.

even to exclude certain people from using the meme based on their work.[102] One recent example of this is the US case involving the popular internet meme "Success Kid," which was based on a photograph depicting a toddler clutching sand while looking directly at the camera with a determined expression.[103]

In *Griner v King*,[104] the plaintiff sued the defendant for the unauthorised use of their copyright in the photograph famously adopted as a meme template titled "Success Kid." The defendant, Steve King, is a former congressman and director of the King for Congress campaign committee that owns and manages a website for his political activities. In January 2020, the website posted a "Success Kid" meme with an altered background to promote King's campaign for Congress. The plaintiffs, Larnier Griner and Sammy Griner, sued for copyright infringement and invasion of privacy for using the plaintiff's likeness without authorisation. The district court held for the plaintiff's claim of copyright infringement. On appeal, the defendant raised the fair use defence but to no avail, as the 9th Circuit Court of Appeal affirmed the judgement.[105]

It is beyond the scope of this book to analyse the internet meme phenomenon as it relates to copyright. However, it is a pressing matter for copyright in photographs since they represent one of the categories of works that stand most affected by the proliferation of internet memes. This is because, in the case of photographs, it is most often that the whole image is exploited and not just a fragment of it. Moreover, social media compounded the tension between copyright and UGC since they reassure the users that they remain the owners of their content to then proceed to deprive them of most of their rights through a broad licensing scheme akin to a Trojan horse from which they effectively gain control over the content in lieu of the user, as long as it remains on their platform.

### *8.4.2 Fair Use and Fair Dealing*

The concept of fair use, as it is known in the United States, and fair dealing, as known in the United Kingdom, refers to uses that are permitted by copyright law

102 "Nyan Cat and Keyboard Cat Creators Sue Warner Bros" *BBC News* (3 May 2013) <https://www.bbc.com/news/technology-22397446> accessed 9 September 2024; Katie Van Syckle, "Keyboard Cat and Nyan Cat Come Out Ahead in Lawsuit Against Warner Bros" (26 September 2013) <https://nymag.com/intelligencer/2013/09/keyboard-cat-nyan-cat-win-warner-bros-lawsuit.html> accessed 9 September 2024; "Grumpy Cat Wins $710,000 Payout in Copyright Lawsuit" *BBC* (24 January 2018) <https://www.bbc.com/news/world-us-canada-42808521> accessed 10 September 2024; "InfoWars and Alex Jones Settle 'Pepe The Frog' Copyright Dispute" <https://www.forbes.com/sites/legalentertainment/2019/06/11/infowars-and-alex-jones-settle-pepe-the-frog-copyright-dispute/> accessed 7 October 2024; see: Lee J Matalon, "Modern Problems Require Modern Solutions: Internet Memes and Copyright" (2019) 98 Texas Law Review 405.

103 Laney Griner, "Why I Oughta…" <https://www.flickr.com/photos/sammyjammy/1285612321/> accessed 5 October 2024.

104 *Griner v King* (2021) 568 F Supp 3d 978 (Dist Court); *Griner v King* (2024) 104 F 4th 1 (Court of Appeals, 8th Circuit).

105 *Griner v King* (n 104).

even if they were undertaken without authorisation from the rightsholder.[106] Hence, certain uses of copyrighted works would not be regarded as copyright infringement for the purposes of copyright law. The general aim of these permitted acts was to balance the rights of copyright holders with users, advancing the public interests through allowing the exercise of certain acts in relation to the copyrighted work without hindrance.[107] The nature and extent of the permitted acts differ between the two jurisdictions since each adopts a different approach.

On the one hand, the approach adopted by the UK copyright law sets out specific categories of permitted acts that fall under the scope of fair dealing if done for specific purposes, such as being for non-commercial research, education, private study, criticism, review, quotation, parody, pastiche, among other uses listed in Chapter 3 of the CDPA 1988.[108] In order for the specific use to be considered fair dealing, it must first fall under one of the listed categories and then be considered fair.[109] Whether the use is fair or not under that category is an assessment that takes into account several factors and is determined on an ad hoc basis subject to each individual case as a matter of degree and impression.[110] The United Kingdom adopts a restrictive approach concerning the permitted acts since it requires that the use satisfies two requirements. The first requirement is that the use should fall under one of the specific categories of permitted acts. The second requirement is that that particular use is regarded as fair.[111] Hence, the use must satisfy both requirements in order to be considered fair dealing. In such a manner, it is immaterial whether the use is fair for purposes not specified in the copyright law or if the use is generally considered to be fair without falling under one of the listed uses.[112]

On the other hand, the US copyright law conception of fair use differs in the sense that it adopts a flexible approach that follows a set of guidelines in order to determine whether a particular use is fair on a fact-based ad hoc basis.[113] Section 107 of the US Copyright Code confirms the statutory recognition of fair use and provides illustrative examples as well as non-exclusive factors that can be

106 Chapter 3 and 3A Copyright, Designs and Patents Act 1988 (UK); Section 107 Title 17 of the United States Code (US).

107 Nicholas Caddick, Gwilym Harbottle and Uma Suthersanen, *Copinger and Skone James on Copyright* (18 edition, Sweet & Maxwell Ltd 2020) paras 9–01; William Patry, *Patry on Copyright* (March 2019, Thomson West 2012) s 10:1.50.

108 Chapter 3 Copyright, Designs and Patents Act 1988 (UK).

109 Bently and others (n 78) 229; Caddick, Harbottle and Suthersanen (n 107) paras 9–19, 9–39; Michael Tappin and others, *Laddie, Prescott and Vitoria: The Modern Law of Copyright* (5 edition, LexisNexis Butterworths 2018) s 21.34.

110 *Hubbard v Vosper, [1972] 2 QB 84*; Caddick, Harbottle and Suthersanen (n 107) paras 9–19, 9–39; Bently and others (n 78) 229, 230; Tappin and others (n 109) s 21.34.

111 Bently and others (n 78) 229; Caddick, Harbottle and Suthersanen (n 107) paras 9–39.

112 Caddick, Harbottle and Suthersanen (n 107) paras 9–19, 9–39; Bently and others (n 78) 229; *Contemporary Intellectual Property: Law and Policy* (5 edition, OUP Oxford 2019) 160.

113 Patry (n 107) s [10:1.60]; see: *Campbell v Acuff-Rose Music, Inc, 510 US 569 (1994)*; *Harper & Row Publishers, Inc v Nation Enterprises, 471 US 539 (1985)*.

considered to determine whether a particular use constitutes fair use of the copyrighted work.[114] These four factors are:

> (1) the purpose and character of the use, including whether such use is of a commercial nature or is for non-profit educational purposes; (2) the nature of the copyrighted work; (3) the amount and substantiality of the portion used in relation to the copyrighted work as a whole; and (4) the effect of the use upon the potential market for or value of the copyrighted work.[115]

The US Supreme Court stated that fair use was both a question of fact and law and stated that additional factors could be considered, such as whether the use was transformative.[116] Transformative use refers to a new work that supersedes the original work or

> adds something new, with a further purpose or different character, altering the first with new expression, meaning, or message…the more transformative the new work, the less will be the significance of other factors, like commercialism, that may weigh against a finding of fair use.[117]

Transformative use focuses on the use itself rather than the user. Hence, it is immaterial whether the user is a professional or amateur photographer, or whether the use is commercial or non-commercial.[118] The US copyright law approach to permitted uses is often hailed as being flexible and broad enough to encompass new activities, especially those brought about by the advent of the digital age.[119]

The application of fair use and fair dealing on visual works such as photographs presents a complex issue.[120] One of the reasons is that, ultimately, what is used is often the entire work in the form of the copyrighted image itself. In fact, it was stated by US courts that for the purposes of fair use in the context of

114 Patry (n 107) s [10:1.60], [10:8].

115 Section 107 Title 17 of the United States Code (US).

116 See: *Google LLC v Oracle America, Inc, 141 SCt 1183 (2021).*

117 *Campbell v Acuff-Rose Music, Inc, 510 U.S. 569 (1994)* (n 113) 579.

118 Patry (n 107) s [10:13]; *Otto v Hearst Communications, Inc WL 6510801 (2018)* 25, 8 (Rejecting fair use defence by a media company who argued that the copyright owner captured the photograph for personal purposes while they used it for a news article).

119 Caddick, Harbottle and Suthersanen (n 107) paras 9–39; Patry (n 107) s 10:1.60, 10:21; *Contemporary Intellectual Property: Law and Policy* (n 112) 166; see: *Authors Guild v Google, Inc, 804 F3d 202 (2d Cir 2015).*

120 See: Molly Torsen Stech, "Detangling Copyright, Transformation and Ideas (in Photographs)" (2016) 11 Journal of Intellectual Property Law & Practice 339; Teresa M Bruce, "In the Language of Pictures: How Copyright Law Fails to Adequately Account for Photography" (2012) 115 West Virginia Law Review 93; Mary Wong, "Tranformative User-Generated Content in Copyright Law: Infringing Derivative Works or Fair Use" (2008) 11 Vanderbilt Journal of Entertainment and Technology Law 1075; see also: Bryce Clayton Newell, "Freedom of Panorama: A Comparative Look at International Restrictions on Public Photography Intellectual Property Law" (2010) 44 Creighton Law Review 405.

photographs, the amount taken is given less weight as a factor towards evaluating fair use.[121] Furthermore, the factual nature of a photograph, in the sense that it was not staged, may be considered favourably to the finding of fair use.[122] The breadth of fair use, especially as it applies to photographs, has been criticised as risking depriving the photographer of his exclusive right to authorise derivative works or make adaptations.[123] The cases that have dealt with fair use and fair dealing in the context of photographs showcased the difficulties of balancing copyright protection with the extent of permitted acts, especially with the advent of digital technology and the internet.[124] Nonetheless, it is worth noting that the UK copyright law expressly exempted photographs from coming under fair dealing for reporting current events.[125] Hence, the United Kingdom provides a higher level of control over photographic copyright, with their restrictive approach to fair dealing, if compared to the United States' copyright law, which subjugates it to the general assessment of fair use based on the specific facts of the case.

For professional photographers, fair use represents an encroachment on their property. Photographers are strenuously opposed to any unauthorised use of their work, fair use or not, as a matter of principle. Qualitative research conducted by Silbey, Subotnik, and DiCola found that, through interviewing several established professional photographers, they tend to be copyright maximalists.[126] The photographers interviewed expressed that copyright ought to give them full control over their own creations, justifying this by arguing that their work is an extension of their own personality. Hence, photographers perceive copyright as an integral part of their identity and consider unauthorised use of their work as compelled speech; they invoke personhood theory for copyright as a justification for asserting a high level of control over their work and the way it ought to

121 See: *North Jersey Media Group Inc v Pirro, 74 FSupp3d 605 (2015)*; *Fitzgerald v CBS Broadcasting, Inc, 491 FSupp2d 177 (2007)* 188.

122 See: *North Jersey Media Group Inc v Pirro, 74 FSupp3d 605 (2015)* (n 121); *Fitzgerald v CBS Broadcasting, Inc, 491 FSupp2d 177 (2007)* (n 121) 188; *Katz v Google Inc, 802 F3d 1178 (2015) (11th Circuit)*.

123 Stech (n 120) 340, 354.

124 See e.g.: *Hyde Park Residence Ltd v Yelland [2000] EMLR 363* (UK); *Football Association Premier League Ltd v Panini UK Ltd [2003] EWCA Civ 995* (UK); *Fraser-Woodward Ltd v BBC [2005] EWHC 472 (Ch)* (UK); see also: *Andy Warhol Foundation Visual Arts v Goldsmith* (2022) 598 US 508 (Supreme Court) (US); *Otto v Hearst Communications, Inc WL 6510801 (2018)* (n 118) (US); *Kienitz v Sconnie Nation LLC, 766 F3d 756 (2014)* 4; *Blanch v Koons, 467 F3d 244 (2006)* (US); *Cariou v Prince, 714 F3d 694 (2013)*; *Brammer v Violent Hues Productions, LLC, 922 F3d 255 (2019) (4th Circuit)* 13; *Graham v Prince, 265 FSupp3d 366 (2017)*; *Leibovitz v Paramount Pictures Corp, 137 F3d 109 (1998)* (US); *Monge v Maya Magazines, Inc, 688 F3d 1164 (2012) (9th Circuit)*; *North Jersey Media Group Inc v Pirro, 74 FSupp3d 605 (2015)* (n 121); *Philpot v Media Research Center Inc, 279 FSupp3d 708 (2018)*; *Ferdman v CBS Interactive Inc, 2018 WL 4572241(2018)* 29.

125 Section 30(2) Copyright, Designs and Patents Act 1988 (UK); Tappin and others (n 109) s 4.72.

126 See: Jessica Silbey, Eva E Subotnik and Peter DiCola, "Existential Copyright and Professional Photography" (2019) 95 Notre Dame Law Review 263.

be communicated.[127] Perceiving copyright as speech is not something uniquely exhibited by professional photographers; legal scholars also examined copyright from a similar theoretical basis.[128] Perhaps the fact that photographers are so protective of their copyright, regarding unauthorised use as compelled speech that encroaches on their personhood, is one of the reasons that photographers exhibited rigorous opposition to any legislation that addresses the issue of orphaned works in relation to photographs.[129]

### *8.4.3 Orphan Works and Photographic Copyright*

The issue of orphan works, which refers to works where the rightsholders could not be identified or located,[130] was amplified following the digital revolution and the advent of the internet.[131] Photographs, in particular, could be regarded as the

127 Silbey (n 62) 426; Silbey (n 4) 353–354, 361; Silbey, Subotnik and DiCola (n 126) 311, 312.

128 See e.g.: Anne Barron, "Kant, Copyright and Communicative Freedom" (2012) 31 Law and Philosophy 1; Maurizio Borghi, "Copyright and Truth Copyright Culture, Copyright History" (2011) 12 Theoretical Inquiries in Law 1; Kim Treiger-Bar-Am, "Kant on Copyright: Rights on Transformative Authorship" (2007) 25 Cardozo Arts & Entertainment Law Journal 1059; Lionel Bently, "Drassinower's Vision of Copyright" (2016) 29 Intellectual Property Journal; Scarborough 19, 20,21; Christopher S Yoo, "Rethinking Copyright and Personhood" (2019) 2019 University of Illinois Law Review 41; see also Abraham Drassinower, *What's Wrong with Copying?* (Harvard University Press 2015) (Where the author presents a vision to reconceptualize copyright as speech, re-envisioning copyright on a model based on communication).

129 See: The British Photographic Council (n 24) 36; Dave Lee, "Photographers' Anger at Law Change" *BBC News* (29 April 2013) <https://www.bbc.com/news/technology-22337406> accessed 19 October 2024; Andrew Orlowski, "UK's Planned Copyright Landgrab Will Spark US Litigation 'Firestorm'" (*The Register*, 12 November 2012) <https://www.theregister.co.uk/2012/11/12/uk_theft_firestorm_photographers_artists/> accessed 19 October 2024; Andrew Orlowski, "UK.Gov Passes Instagram Act: All Your Pics Belong to Everyone Now" (*The Register*, 19 April 2013) <https://www.theregister.co.uk/2013/04/29/err_act_landgrab/> accessed 19 October 2024; Stop43, "Stop Confiscation of Your Property and Human Rights in the UK Enterprise and Regulatory Reform Bill" (*Stop43.org.uk*) <http://www.stop43.org.uk/> accessed 30 September 2021; Michael Zhang, "Orphan Works Copyright Law Being Considered Again in the US" (*PetaPixel*, 21 July 2015) <https://petapixel.com/2015/07/21/orphan-works-copyright-law-being-considered-again-in-the-us/> accessed 19 October 2024; Neil Turner, "The Copyright Fight – David Bailey Weighs In…" (*The BPPA*, 16 April 2013) <https://thebppa.wordpress.com/2013/04/16/the-copyright-fight-david-bailey-weighs-in/> accessed 19 October 2024.

130 US Copyright Office, "Report on Orphan Works" (The Register of Copyrights 2006) 15 <https://www.copyright.gov/orphan/orphan-report-full.pdf> accessed 19 October 2024; Reg 3(4) The Copyright and Rights in Performances (Licensing of Orphan Works) Regulations 2014; US Copyright Office, "Orphan Works and Mass Digitization: A Report of the Register of Copyrights" (2015) 9 <https://www.copyright.gov/orphan/> accessed 19 October 2024.

131 See: Ian Hargreaves, "Digital Opportunity: A Review of Intellectual Property and Growth" (2011) <https://www.gov.uk/government/publications/digital-opportunity-review-of-intellectual-property-and-growth> accessed 19 October 2024; US Copyright Office, "Orphan Works and Mass Digitization: A Report of the Register of Copyrights" (n 130) 2, 36.

most prevalent type of orphaned works on the internet.[132] No wonder, then, that photographers were specifically worried about the adverse effect of orphan works legislation on their industry and the value of photographs in the internet space.[133] This is because photographs are susceptible to having their metadata removed, which is data embedded in digital images that provides descriptive information about the image, and the images can circulate quickly over social media in a manner that makes it difficult to identify and locate the rightsholders.[134] Photographers feared that an orphan works regime would, in practice, strip them of their rights to control the use of their photographs since the majority of images circulating the internet may potentially be considered orphaned works.

Photographers feared the perceived negative impact that could befall their rights if legislation on orphan works were to pass along the aforementioned lines. Several scholars also suggested reintroducing some form of copyright formalities, such as copyright registration, to curb the spread of orphaned works and better address the prevalence of copyright in the digital age.[135] This was because one of the main factors that exacerbated the issue of orphaned works is the fact that copyright is

132 US Copyright Office, "Orphan Works and Mass Digitization: A Report of the Register of Copyrights" (n 130) 2,7, 9, 25, 75, 78; Intellectual Property Office, "Copyright: Orphan Works" (*GOV. UK*, 12 May 2015) <https://www.gov.uk/guidance/copyright-orphan-works> accessed 19 October 2024; Andrew Gowers, "Gowers Review of Intellectual Property" (2006) para 4.93 <https://www.gov.uk/government/publications/gowers-review-of-intellectual-property> accessed 19 October 2024.

133 See: The British Photographic Council (n 24) 36; Lee (n 129); Orlowski, "UK's Planned Copyright Landgrab Will Spark US Litigation 'Firestorm'" (n 129); Orlowski, "UK.Gov Passes Instagram Act" (n 129); Stop43 (n 129); Zhang, "Orphan Works Copyright Law Being Considered Again in the US" (n 129); Turner (n 129); Bently and others (n 78) 346–347.

134 Hargreaves (n 131) para 4.59; see: US Copyright Office, "Orphan Works and Mass Digitization: A Report of the Register of Copyrights" (n 130); Turner (n 129).

135 See: Bingbin Lu, "The Orphan Works Copyright Issue: Suggestions for International Response" (2012) 60 Journal of the Copyright Society of the USA 255; Daniel Gervais and Dashiell Renaud, "The Future of United States Copyright Formalities: Why We Should Prioritize Recordation, and How to Do It Symposium: Reform(aliz)ing Copyright for the Internet Age" (2013) 28 Berkeley Technology Law Journal 1459; Molly Shaffer Van Houweling, "Land Recording and Copyright Reform Symposium: Reform(aliz)ing Copyright for the Internet Age" (2013) 28 Berkeley Technology Law Journal 1497; Niva Elkin-Koren, "Can Formalities Save the Public Domain; Reconsidering Formalities for the 2010s Symposium: Reform(aliz)ing Copyright for the Internet Age" (2013) 28 Berkeley Technology Law Journal 1537; Jane C Ginsburg, "With Untired Spirits and Formal Constancy: Berne Compatibility of Formal Declaratory Measures to Enhance Copyright Title-Searching Symposium: Reform(aliz)ing Copyright for the Internet Age" (2013) 28 Berkeley Technology Law Journal 1583; Michael W Carroll, "A Realist Approach to Copyright Law's Formalities Symposium: Reform(aliz)ing Copyright for the Internet Age" (2013) 28 Berkeley Technology Law Journal 1511; Stef Van Gompel, "Unlocking the Potential of Pre-Existing Content: How to Address the Issue of Orphan Works in Europe?" 1; Lu; Ginsburg; Peter S Menell, "Economic Analysis of Copyright Notice: Tracing and Scope in the Digital Age Symposium: Notice and Notice Failure in Intellectual Property Law: Panel V" (2016) 96 Boston University Law Review 967.

automatic, requiring no formalities in order to be granted.[136] The Gowers report of 2006 even recommended establishing a simplified voluntary registration system in the United Kingdom as a way to address the issue of orphaned works.[137] In spite of the fact that images are one of the works most vulnerable to being orphaned, photographers rarely register their copyrights.[138]

At the EU level, the Orphan Works Directive[139] was passed in 2012 with a limited scope to the extent it aims to allow public bodies such as libraries, museums, and public archives to digitise their collections.[140] The directive excluded stand-alone photographs from its scope, perhaps due to the extensive opposition from photographers and visual artists.[141] The EU directive was implemented in the United Kingdom in 2014 alongside the United Kingdom's own orphan works scheme, which enables the licensing of orphaned works.[142]

The UK orphan works regime has a much greater reach than the EU directive since it applies to all types of works, including photographs, and covers non-commercial and commercial uses.[143] The UK regulation allows the Intellectual Property Office (IPO) to grant non-exclusive licences to use the registered orphaned works for a limited duration if the rightsholders cannot be located following a diligent search.[144] Despite the fact that the United Kingdom has a relatively extensive orphan works scheme, its utilisation was minimal and did not reflect the extent of the orphaned works populating the UK museums and galleries, let alone the internet landscape.[145] Moreover, still images represent the largest segment of orphaned works registered in the UK IPO by a large margin.[146] This indicates the extent

136 US Copyright Office, "Report on Orphan Works" (n 130) 43–44; Gowers (n 132) para 4.92; US Copyright Office, "Orphan Works and Mass Digitization: A Report of the Register of Copyrights" (n 130) 10.

137 Gowers (n 132) para 4.101.

138 The British Photographic Council (n 24) 54–55; Silbey, Subotnik and DiCola (n 126) 283.

139 Directive 2012/28/EU of 25 October 2012 on certain permitted uses of orphan works [2012] OJ L299/5 2012.

140 Article 1 ibid.

141 See: The British Photographic Council (n 24) 36; Lee (n 129); Orlowski, "UK's Planned Copyright Landgrab Will Spark US Litigation 'Firestorm'" (n 129); Orlowski, "UK.Gov Passes Instagram Act" (n 129); Stop43 (n 129); Zhang, "Orphan Works Copyright Law Being Considered Again in the US" (n 129); Turner (n 129).

142 Section 116A, Sch. ZA1 Copyright, Designs and Patents Act 1988 (UK); The Copyright and Rights in Performances (Licensing of Orphan Works) Regulations 2014.

143 Bently and others (n 78) 347–348.

144 Reg. 4, Reg. 6 The Copyright and Rights in Performances (Licensing of Orphan Works) Regulations 2014; Section 116A Copyright, Designs and Patents Act 1988 (UK).

145 A conservative estimate in 2009 reveals that 25 million orphan works existed in public sector organizations. See Naomi Korn and Collections Trust, "In from the Cold: An Assessment of the Scope of 'Orphan Works' and Its Impact on the Delivery of Services to the Public" (2009) 5, 6 <https://naomikorn.com/wp-content/uploads/2020/09/SCA_CollTrust_Orphan_Works_v1-final.pdf> accessed 19 October 2024; Hargreaves (n 131) 38–40; US Copyright Office, "Orphan Works and Mass Digitization: A Report of the Register of Copyrights" (n 130) 36–39.

146 "View the Orphan Works Register" (*GOV.UK*) <https://www.orphanworkslicensing.service.gov.uk/view-register> accessed 19 October 2024; Bently and others (n 78) 348.

of the issue, especially in the context of photographic works, yet photographers remain fearful of any orphaned works scheme that takes control away from the creators regardless of whether the rightsholders could be located or not. David Bailey, a renowned British photographer, expressed his fears in a letter to the then Chancellor of the Exchequer by lamenting that:

> everyone will be able to get their hands on our so-called "orphans" so libraries and museums can publish old photographs whose authors have long been forgotten. But never mind what's lying around on dusty old shelves, what about the millions of "orphans" that are being created now every day!...our government refuses to give us the right to our names by our pictures (Moral rights). So now commercial organisations will be allowed to make money from our "orphans," but not us, the creators.[147]

In comparison, the United States does not have specific statutory provisions that address orphaned works. However, following the case of *Authors Guild v Google, Inc (2015)*,[148] it seems that fair use is seen as flexible enough to cover situations that involve the use of orphaned works.[149] Furthermore, the US Copyright Office issued a report on orphan works and mass digitisation, acknowledging that fair use might be an avenue to protect users of orphaned works.[150] However, the Copyright Office recommended that for the purposes of certainty and consistency, as well as to encourage users to diligently search for rightsholders before using the orphaned work, a specific legislative framework that addresses the issue of orphaned works would be the more appropriate avenue.[151] Furthermore, the US Copyright Office recommended a limited liability model instead of a government-licence model for any future orphaned works legislation.[152] This is because evidence showed that the UK scheme was rarely utilised. This is in spite of the fact that the United Kingdom has a relatively narrow fair dealing scope compared to the US fair use, which may have prompted the expectations of a higher rate of utilisation of the UK orphaned works scheme to avoid infringement due to the limitation of the fair dealing exceptions. Nonetheless, many professional photographers expressed their fears of any type of scheme that may potentially impact the industry's value.

147 David Bailey's letter as reported in Turner (n 129).

148 *Authors Guild v Google, Inc, 804 F3d 202 (2d Cir. 2015)* (n 119).

149 US Copyright Office, "Orphan Works and Mass Digitization: A Report of the Register of Copyrights" (n 130) 3; US Copyright Office, "Report on Orphan Works" (n 130) 4; Graham Dutfield and Uma Suthersanen, *Dutfield and Suthersanen on Global Intellectual Property Law* (2 edition, Edward Elgar Publishing 2020) 370.

150 US Copyright Office, "Orphan Works and Mass Digitization: A Report of the Register of Copyrights" (n 130) 3, 106.

151 ibid.

152 ibid 3.

### *8.4.4 The Value of Photographic Copyright and Its Enforcement*

Professional photographers' attachment to their work and what copyright means to their profession goes beyond its economic dimension. Photographers place great value on copyright, so much to the point that they are hostile to any suggestions that they perceive to lessen the status of photographs as an art form. The characteristic importance of copyright for the status of photography as an art is demonstrated throughout the history of photography.[153] To this day, professional photographers tend to retain their copyright in spite of acknowledging that retaining copyright holds little economic value after they grant the initial expanded licence to their clients.[154] In fact, professional photographers have stated that the use of copyright in their business is, quite often, for the purpose of economic benefits, regarded as nothing more than a leveraging tool during the stage of negotiation.[155] Hence, the economic value of retaining copyright after licensing their work was considered to be very minimal.[156]

Yet, professional photographers justified retaining copyright by expressing that copyright was valuable as a symbol of their own identity as artists and professionals, a class of photographers distinguished from amateurs, and as a sign of having an elevated status as creators compared to their amateur brethren.[157] In essence, photographers value their copyright as a "status" symbol and as a reassurance of control over their own creations, which they perceive as an extension of their own personhood, even if that control was, in practice, difficult to assert.[158]

In spite of photographers generally feeling empowered in their efforts to stop legislation that they perceive to be harmful to the value of their copyright, they exhibit hopelessness over protecting their copyright. Interviews and surveys with professional photographers indicated that, quite often, it is hardly worth it to enforce their copyright in the face of the colossal scale of infringement taking place on the internet.[159] Moreover, photographers often complained about the disproportionate costs associated with pursuing infringement claims, describing it as both time-consuming and costly to the point that it becomes economically unfeasible in a lot of cases to pursue infringement claims.[160] Therefore, photographers rarely pursue claims in courts solely for economic reasons and are only persuaded if the infringing use affects their moral rights or their photographed subject.[161] Hence, this indicates that photographers place greater value on the moral rights side of

153 See Chapters 2–4.
154 Silbey, Subotnik and DiCola (n 126) 270, 278, 281; The British Photographic Council (n 24) 1, 27.
155 Silbey, Subotnik and DiCola (n 126) 278, 301.
156 ibid 268, 278; The British Photographic Council (n 24).
157 Silbey, Subotnik and DiCola (n 126) 269, 306, 308, 310, 312; Silbey (n 4) 354.
158 Silbey, Subotnik and DiCola (n 126) 269, 306, 308, 310, 312; Silbey (n 4) 354.
159 The British Photographic Council (n 24) 50; Silbey, Subotnik and DiCola (n 126) 267, 324; Silbey (n 4) 364; Hadland and Barnett (n 24) 6; see also: Luo and Mortimer (n 70).
160 US Copyright Office, "Copyright Small Claims: A Report of the Register of Copyrights" 201, 1; Silbey (n 4) 364; Silbey, Subotnik and DiCola (n 126) 269.
161 Silbey, Subotnik and DiCola (n 126) 306, 312, 319, 324; Silbey (n 4) 358–359, 364.

copyright than its economic side as a determinative factor in pursuing infringement claims.

Perhaps due to the time-consuming and costly process of enforcing copyright in photographs, especially considering the level of infringement that plagued their profession, photographers often pursue a simple money claim for unpaid fees against infringing users instead of a copyright infringement claim.[162] Hence, due to the fact that photographers feel powerless to stop unauthorised use, they do not seek to stop the use itself; rather, for the majority of the time, they seek to remedy the issue through post-licensing. Their strategy was to turn infringers into customers instead of stopping the unauthorised use to bring infringers to the negotiation table.[163] Even though money claims were seen as the simpler and economically feasible option for photographers, it was still not ideal since they would not be able to claim damages in relation to the infringement.

Therefore, in the United Kingdom, if rightsholders pursue an infringement claim to seek damages and not just unpaid fees, their most preferred route is through the Intellectual Property Enterprise Court Small Claims Track (IPEC SCT).[164] The IPEC court is a specialist listing of the High Court that deals with copyright-related claims with a value that does not exceed £500,000.[165] The IPEC was established in 2013 to provide a simpler and cheaper route to bring copyright-related claims.[166] The IPEC provides two sets of tracks depending on the case's value and level of complexity. These two tracks are the IPEC multi-track and the IPEC SCT. The IPEC SCT deals with straightforward cases with a value of less than £10,000, while the IPEC multi-track deals with relatively more complex cases with a higher value.[167] The IPEC SCT represents the forum most favoured by photographers as most cases involving copyright in photographs in the United Kingdom are brought under the IPEC SCT since it provides the most appropriate route for these types of cases.[168]

Elena Cooper and Sheona Burrow examined the claims that involved photographic copyrights that were decided under the IPEC SCT between 2013 and 2015, and found that the vast majority of cases were regarding unauthorised use on the internet.[169] Moreover, the overwhelming majority of these claims, which are mostly brought by freelance photographers, sought financial remedies without seeking an

162 Elena Cooper and Sheona Burrow, "Photographic Copyright and the Intellectual Property Enterprise Court in Historical Perspective" (2019) 39 Legal Studies 143, 16.

163 ibid 15, 21, 27; Silbey, Subotnik and DiCola (n 126) 301–302.

164 Cooper and Burrow (n 162) 4, 17.

165 Part 63 The Civil Procedure Rules 1998 (UK); see: HM Courts & Tribunals Service, "The Intellectual Property Enterprise Court Guide," *The Intellectual Property Enterprise Court: Practice and Procedure* (2 edition, Sweet & Maxwell 2016) paras 2–002.

166 Bently and others (n 78) 1306; HM Courts & Tribunals Service, "Guide to the Intellectual Property Enterprise Court Small Claims Track" 3.

167 See: HM Courts & Tribunals Service (n 166); HM Courts & Tribunals Service (n 165).

168 Cooper and Burrow (n 162) 4, 11.

169 ibid 27–28.

injunction.[170] This indicates that the main issue is not necessarily the unauthorised use itself; rather, it was the fact that the use was not remunerated.[171] Cooper and Burrow indicate that the most frequent defence in these claims reiterates the argument that the infringing party thought the image was free to use since it was posted on the internet without a copyright notice, an argument that the court firmly and continuously rejected.[172]

In relation to the amount of damages awarded by the IPEC, Cooper and Burrow reveal that, when it comes to photographic copyright, the IPEC SCT tends to adopt the rates followed by collecting societies and stock image providers, such as Getty Images[173]and Flicker,[174] rather than calculating the compensatory damages based on the rates reached if there was a bilateral agreement between the parties.[175] Cooper and Burrow interpreted this as evidence that, under the IPEC SCT, copyright in the context of photographs moved towards a liability-oriented model. They posited that:

> the legal rulings of the IPEC, in utilising picture library standards, provide aspects of the bureaucratic "simulation" of property with legal force; bureaucratic standards – rather than mere "representations" – become part of copyright's legal reality through their judicial application in court decisions…in this particular context: copyright law as applied by the IPEC SCT to the practices of freelance professional photographers, takes on features of a liability rule.[176]

In the United States, for some time now, stakeholders, especially creators of visual works such as photographs, have campaigned for a forum suitable for small copyright claims, especially given the impact of the digital age and the internet.[177] The US Copyright Office published an extensive report in 2013 expressing the urgent

170 ibid 27.
171 ibid 15, 27.
172 ibid 27.
173 "Getty Images" (*Getty Images*) <https://www.gettyimages.co.uk/> accessed 19 October 2024.
174 "Flickr" (*Flickr*) <https://www.flickr.com/> accessed 19 October 2024.
175 Cooper and Burrow (n 162) 4, 45–46.
176 ibid 46.
177 See: Trisha Barber, "ASMP Perspective and Action on Copyright Reform" (*ASMP*, 4 January 2017) <https://www.asmp.org/advocacy/asmp-perspective-action-copyright-reform/> accessed 19 October 2024; Professional Photographers of America, "Advocacy & Copyright Protection" (*PPA*) <https://www.ppa.com/benefits/advocacy-copyright-protection> accessed 19 October 2024; Michael Zhang, "Why Photographers Need a Copyright Small Claims System" (*PetaPixel*, 11 June 2016) <https://petapixel.com/2016/06/11/photographers-need-copyright-small-claims-system/> accessed 19 October 2024; Professional Photographers of America, "Copyright Fight for Artists' Rights" (*PPA*) <https://www.ppa.com/benefits/advocacy-copyright-protection/fight-for-artists-rights> accessed 19 October 2024.

need for an alternative forum that makes it simpler and cheaper for rightsholders to pursue small copyright claims.[178]

The US Copyright Office recommendation was heeded in the form of the Copyright Alternative in Small-Claims Enforcement Act of 2019 (the CASE Act), signed into law in December 2020.[179] The CASE Act will establish a Copyright Claims Board tribunal as a voluntary path for small copyright claims where the damages may not exceed $30,000.[180] The CASE Act also provides statutory damages for registered copyright. The relatively easier access to copyright enforcement may, in return, increase the rate of copyright registration for photographs. Currently, photographers rarely register their works[181] but this may change since now it is beneficial to register the work in terms both of combating the issue of orphaned works and of potentially increasing the amount of damages awarded.

## 8.5 Conclusion

The ubiquity of images on the internet has changed the way we interact and value images as well as the reason we create them. The prevailing sharing culture of the internet presented complex issues related to copyright, such as the scope of fair use and fair dealing. The widespread orphaned works and the enormous scale of copyright infringement taking place on the internet sphere presented near insurmountable challenges to the effectiveness of copyright enforcement. Photographers feel powerless to enforce their copyright protection in the face of the massive scale of infringement to the point that some photographers stated that they are only persuaded to enforce their copyright to assert their moral rights instead of pursuing infringement claims for economic incentives.

On the nature of photographic copyright, the impact of the digital age on the art of photography was substantial to the point that it touched on all aspects of photographs, from their creation to their exploitation. Social media platforms have changed how photographs are perceived and utilised, and they are increasingly used as a communicative unit instead of a medium of artistic expression. The terms of service of social media platforms assure the users that they own their content's copyright to then draw a broad licence that effectively divests the user's control over their copyright.

178 See: US Copyright Office, "Copyright Small Claims: A Report of the Register of Copyrights" (n 160) 111.

179 "H.R.2426 – 116th Congress (2019–2020): Copyright Alternative in Small-Claims Enforcement (CASE) Act of 2019" (23 October 2019) <https://www.congress.gov/bill/116th-congress/house-bill/2426> accessed 19 October 2024; "H.R.133 – 116th Congress (2019–2020): Consolidated Appropriations Act, 2021" (27 December 2020) <https://www.congress.gov/bill/116th-congress/house-bill/133/text> accessed 19 October 2024.

180 Section 1504, CASE Act 2019 "H.R.2426 – 116th Congress (2019–2020): Copyright Alternative in Small-Claims Enforcement (CASE) Act of 2019" (n 179).

181 The British Photographic Council (n 24) 55; Silbey (n 4) 353; Silbey, Subotnik and DiCola (n 126) 283.

Photographic technologies are increasingly minimising the impact of the photographer and his level of skill on the quality of the image by automating many aspects of the art of photography. The camera is no longer considered a "picture-making device"; instead, it is more accurately referred to as a "data-collecting device." Hence, the quality of the images is increasingly moving away from relying on the photographer's skill to the quality of the processing algorithms. This threatens to unearth the roots that traditionally justified the copyright protection of photographs.

The changes to photographic technologies threaten to destabilise the already fragile grounds for the subsistence of copyright in photographs. Traditionally, the author's conception of a photograph in a manner that indicates his own intellectual creation was deemed to be only evident in the pre-capture stage, neglecting the mid-capture and post-capture stages. Whatever comes after the pre-capture stage was traditionally thought to be the translation of the mindless machine, the camera. But with the advent of computational photography, the "mindless machine" developed to acquire a mind of its own. It is no longer helpful to analogise photography with other copyrighted works to find authorship and originality. It is high time to acknowledge that photographs are justified copyright protection as their own thing, not as writings or paintings, nor as databases, but as photographs.

# 9 The Way Forward for Photographic Copyright? A Focus on Copyright Authorship

## 9.1 Introduction

Since the beginning, photographs have struggled to maintain a stable position within copyright law's tendency to adopt a one-size-fits-all approach, often requiring the distortion of the tried and tested copyright concepts to accommodate different types of photographic works. This has shaken the consistency of copyright law and the coherency of its concepts. In fact, many of the issues that plagued copyright in photographic works can be described as legacy issues that owed their persistence to the way copyright protection was first extended and rationalised for photographic works. This emanated from the fact that photographic works were protected not by virtue of their unique characteristics as photographs but by virtue of their similarity, whether apparent, perceived, or otherwise, to other works in terms of their fundamental elements of expression. Indeed, photographs were compared to the model of literary works and paintings, at different points of abstraction, in order to justify their protection.[1]

This chapter aims to provide the groundwork to remedy the legacy issues of copyright in photographic works at its core via advocating for a tailored approach to copyright key concepts that actively considers the unique characteristics of the category of works in question. This chapter is divided into two main parts and presents its arguments by utilising photographic works as the main model for analysis. The first part argues that originality is not sufficiently suitable for determining the level of protection afforded to photographic works. It argues that authorship, instead, should determine the level of copyright protection in photographic works through a two-tier system of copyright protection based on Professor Ginsburg's framework of high and low authorship.[2] It posits that utilising the concept of authorship as the engine behind a two-tier system would bring more stability and coherence to the copyright protection of photographic works. The second part lays the groundwork for a tailored conception of authorship to serve as the engine that operates the proposed two-tier system of copyright protection for photographic works. It examines the concept of authorship through selected theories in order to construct

1 See Chapters 5–6.

2 Jane C Ginsburg, "Creation and Commercial Value: Copyright Protection of Works of Information" (1990) 90 Columbia Law Review 1865.

DOI: 10.4324/9781003586555-9

an original theory of authorship tailored for photographic works. Henceforth, this chapter serves as a building block from which the proposed theory and system are presented and illustrated in Chapter 10.

## 9.2 Part 1: The Suitable Device for Categorising Photographic Works' Copyright Protection

### *9.2.1 Why Originality Is Not Suitable as a Test for Copyright in Photographic Works*

Historically, the level of copyright protection has been linked to the work's originality.[3] As a starting point, there are two undisputed tenets of originality. The first one is origination and independent creation, in that originality requires that the work was not copied from another.[4] The second tenet is associated with free creative choices, selections, and arrangements, in other words, the elements of expression that evidence an "intellectual creation."[5] It is through the notion of "intellectual creation" that originality may be explored beyond its basic tenets. Intellectual creation is also integral to authorship; the difference in the role it plays in authorship and originality is linked to its position within the creation process. For illustration, it may be beneficial to visualise authorship as a road that leads to a place; the "place" symbolises the work, while originality is located in the elements that make up that place (the work of authorship). Hence, originality should be evaluated within the confines of the work itself and should not be confused with authorship.

An intellectual creation is evidenced when the author exercises intellectual or creative choices to produce a work. The essence of an intellectual creation, which is the essence of originality in copyright law, is intimately linked to the notion of

3 See: Elizabeth F Judge and Daniel Gervais, "Of Silos and Constellations: Comparing Notions of Originality in Copyright Law" (2009) 27 Cardozo Arts & Entertainment Law Journal 375; see also Chapter 6.

4 Lionel Bently and others, *Intellectual Property Law* (5 edition, OUP Oxford 2018) 93, 94; Paul Goldstein, *International Copyright: Principles, Law, and Practice* (OUP Oxford 2001) 161; Graham Dutfield and Uma Suthersanen, *Dutfield and Suthersanen on Global Intellectual Property Law* (2 edition, Edward Elgar Publishing 2020) 105; Nicholas Caddick, Gwilym Harbottle and Uma Suthersanen, *Copinger and Skone James on Copyright* (18 edition, Sweet & Maxwell Ltd 2020) paras 2–10; William W Fisher III, "Recalibrating Originality" (2016) 54 Houston Law Review 437, 438; *University of London Press Ltd v University Tutorial Press Ltd [1916] 2 Ch 601*; *Burrow-Giles Lithographic Co v Sarony, 111 US 53 (1884)*.

5 Bently and others (n 4) 93, 95, 100–101; Goldstein (n 4) 162, 176; Dutfield and Suthersanen (n 4) 105, 106; Michael Tappin and others, *Laddie, Prescott and Vitoria: The Modern Law of Copyright* (5 edition, LexisNexis Butterworths 2018) s 3.40; Judge and Gervais (n 3) 404; Fisher III (n 4) 438; Daniel J Gervais, "Feist Goes Global: A Comparative Analysis of the Notion of Originality in Copyright Law Part I" (2001) 49 Journal of the Copyright Society of the USA 949, 974; Article 10 (2) Agreement on Trade-Related Aspects of Intellectual Property Rights (TRIPS) (as amended on 23 January 2017); Article 2(5) Berne Convention for the Protection of Literary and Artistic Works 1886; Article 3 (1) Directive 96/9/EC of 11 March 1996 on the legal protection of databases [1996] OJ L77/20; *(C-5/08) Infopaq International A/S v Danske Dagblades Forening [2009] ECR I-6569* [45].

"creative choice."[6] Professor Daniel Gervais posits that through defining what a "creative choice" is, a definition of originality for the purposes of copyright law can emerge. Gervais proceeded to present his definition of the notion of "creative choice" for the purposes of copyright law as "[one] made by the author that is not dictated by the function of the work, the method or technique used, or by applicable standards or relevant 'good practice.'"[7] He indicated that "purely arbitrary" selection not supported by "a conscious, human choice" may not be sufficient to regard a choice as creative as to evidence originality.[8]

Accordingly, Gervais argues that an intellectual creation involves three types of choices, and only one of these types is relevant to originality in copyright law.[9] His analysis provides that a work's creation involves the following choices: first, technical choices, which are choices dictated by the choice of the medium;[10] second, functional choices, which are choices taken purely for functional considerations;[11] third, creative choices, which are the ones relevant to copyright law, and they are free choices made by the author that are not dictated by merely an application of principles or good practices associated with the type of work.[12] The creative choices, and by extension originality, are examined through a qualitative assessment that avoids aesthetic evaluation[13] and is only concerned with the choices that reflect the work's expression and not the ideas themselves that are behind the work.[14] On this notion, placing a creative choice on either side of the idea/expression or fact/expression dichotomies may prove to be a deeply complicated matter, especially since they are ill-suited for visual works such as photographs.[15]

Nonetheless, Gervais proceeded to test his definition of originality in photographic works. He indicated that the art of photography involves many choices,

6 Gervais (n 5) 974, 975; Judge and Gervais (n 3) 402.
7 Gervais (n 5) 976–977.
8 ibid 977.
9 ibid 978–979, 980; Judge and Gervais (n 3) 377.
10 Gervais (n 5) 978; Judge and Gervais (n 3) 377.
11 Gervais (n 5) 978; Judge and Gervais (n 3) 377.
12 Gervais (n 5) 978; Judge and Gervais (n 3) 377.
13 Bently and others (n 4) 94, 101–103; Eleonora Rosati, *Originality in EU Copyright: Full Harmonization through Case Law* (Edward Elgar Publishing 2013) 78, 113; *Feist Publications, Inc v Rural Telephone Service Co, Inc, 499 US 340 (1991)* 362, 363; *Newspaper Licensing Agency Ltd v Meltwater Holding BV [2011] RPC 7* [74, 75]; *(C-5/08) Infopaq International A/S v Danske Dagblades Forening [2009] ECR I-6569* (n 5) para 45.
14 Bently and others (n 4) 94, 101–102; Judge and Gervais (n 3) 404; Article 9(2) Agreement on Trade-Related Aspects of Intellectual Property Rights (TRIPS) (as amended on 23 January 2017).
15 See: Teresa M Bruce, "In the Language of Pictures: How Copyright Law Fails to Adequately Account for Photography" (2012) 115 West Virginia Law Review 93; Carl Mazurek, "Through the Looking Glass: Photography and the Idea/Expression Dichotomy" (2017) 6 Journal of Intellectual Property and Entertainment Law 32; *Baigent v Random House Group Ltd [2008] EMLR 7*; *Temple Island Collections Ltd v New English Teas Ltd [2012] EWPCC 1*; *Mannion v Coors Brewing Co, 377 FSupp2d 444 (2005)*; *Harney v Sony Pictures Television, Inc, 704 F3d 173 (2013)*; William Patry, *Patry on Copyright* (March 2019, Thomson West 2012) s 3.118.

from the type of camera to aperture, choice of filter, shutter speed, focus, etc.[16] These choices are dictated by the art of photography and are, themselves, not enough for a photograph to be original unless they were manipulated and combined with the free choices dictated by the author, such as the choice of angle, lighting, and selection, among other arrangements that form the depiction illustrated in the photograph.[17] The latter half of these choices are given the bulk of the weight when assessing the originality of a photograph. However, Professor Farley pointed out that, in fact, the courts may acknowledge technical considerations as creative choices that justify a photograph's originality, as illustrated in the US case of *Time Inc v Bernard Geis Associates*.[18] In this case, Farley explained that:

> the court could not list pre-shutter choices, but had to engage with the technology much more so than had previously been done. The court recognized that the selection of the camera, film and lens were creative choices. However, as if that were not enough, the court went on to assert that Zapruder had selected the location from which to film and the time to film. Thus, the court felt it necessary to describe happenstance as creative direction in order to come within Burrow-Giles.[19]

Hence, it may not be obvious to demarcate the choices that formulate an intellectual creation. This is because creative choices may encompass the choice of the medium and other technical aspects that were chosen purely to stress the author's creative liberty and not just because of their functional or technical aspects. An arbitrary delineated classification of the choices may not be ideal because these choices converge and combine to produce works of authorship. An example of this is the choice of an analogue camera, such as a Polaroid instead of a digital single-lens reflex camera, to capture photographs in a manner that expresses the author's artistic choice. It could not be denied that this choice did impact the photographs' creative expression.[20] Moreover, the notion of creativity in the term "creative choice," as suggested by Gervais, may lead to attempts to specify, for the purposes of copyright law, what it means to classify a choice as being "creative" as opposed to another choice, which is a matter that is heavily contested.[21]

16 Gervais (n 5) 979, 980.

17 ibid.

18 *Time Inc v Bernard Geis Associates, 293 FSupp 130 (1968)* 143.

19 Christine Haight Farley, "The Lingering Effects of Copyright's Response to the Invention of Photography" (2004) 65 University of Pittsburgh Law Review 385, 447.

20 For more about the resurgence of film photography, see Cody Rooney, "The Analogue Revival: Memory, Nostalgia and Error in Contemporary Film Photography" (*Glossi Mag*, 31 May 2017) <https://glossimag.com/analogue-revival-memory-nostalgia-error-contemporary-film-photography/> accessed 19 October 2024.

21 "Creativity" for the purposes of copyright is a widely contested concept. See: Olufunmilayo B Arewa, "The Freedom to Copy: Copyright, Creation, and Context" (2007) 41 UC Davis Law Review 477; Bently and others (n 4) 101–102; Erlend Lavik and Stef van Gompel, "On the Prospects of Raising the Originality Requirement in Copyright Law: Perspectives from the Humanities" (2012) 60 Journal of the Copyright Society of the USA 387, 411; Mitzi S Phalen, "How Much Is

The courts have a tendency to look at the choices outside the confines of photographs in order to establish their originality.[22] Professor Justin Hughes criticised how the courts tend to measure originality through what existed before a photograph's creation and argued that we should measure originality by considering what the photograph allowed to exist after its creation.[23] Furthermore, he posited that most photographs circulating today "do not qualify for copyright protection under a reasonably administered originality standard."[24] In response, Professor Terry Kogan heavily contested Hughes's views and asserted that the courts are correct in assuming that most photographs would be able to satisfy the Anglo-American's originality standards and consequently qualify for copyright protection.[25] Kogan argued that one of the main problems with copyright assessment of photographic works lies in the courts' tendency to look through the photograph, as a window, instead of at it, as a canvas.[26] It seems the diverging views on originality render the concept close to being a mirage when it comes to locating it in photographic works.

This is unsurprising since the concept of originality is bound to create inconsistencies due to its elusive nature.[27] Originality, for the purposes of copyright, is highly challenging to utilise, beyond its basic tenets, with consistency as a determining factor of a work's level of copyright protection.[28] In fact, Professor Jessica Litman levelled a strong criticism of the concept of originality, describing it as a "conceit" and a mere "apparition; [that] does not, and cannot, provide a basis for

Enough – The Search for a Standard of Creativity in Works of Authorship under Section 102(a) of the Copyright Act of 1976 Comment" (1989) 68 Nebraska Law Review 835, 850. See also: Gideon Parchomovsky and Alex Stein, "Originality" (2009) 95 Virginia Law Review 1505; Shyamkrishna Balganesh, "Tiered Originality and the Dualism of Copyright Incentives" (2009) 95 Virginia Law Review 67; Christopher Buccafusco and others, "Experimental Tests of Intellectual Property Laws' Creativity Thresholds" (2014) 92 Texas Law Review 1921; Ryan Littrell, "Toward a Stricter Originality Standard for Copyright Law Note" (2001) 43 Boston College Law Review 193; Dutfield and Suthersanen (n 4) 108–109.

22 See Chapters 6–7.

23 Justin Hughes, "The Photographer's Copyright-Photograph as Art, Photograph as Database" (2011) 25 Harv. JL & Tech. 339, 416–417.

24 ibid 342, 381, 425 (Hughes proposed that the copyright rules associated with databases should be applied to photographs).

25 Terry S Kogan, "The Enigma of Photography, Depiction, and Copyright Originality" (2014) 25 Fordham Intellectual Property, Media & Entertainment Law Journal 869, 878 (Proposed using the concept of depiction in art theory to inform how photograph's originality is to be evaluated within the confines of the photograph).

26 See: ibid 910, 923, 931.

27 See Chapter 6.

28 Regarding the formless nature of originality, see Eva E Subotnik, "Originality Proxies: Toward a Theory of Copyright and Creativity" (2010) 76 Brooklyn Law Review 1487; Balganesh, "Tiered Originality and the Dualism of Copyright Incentives" (n 21); Farley (n 19); Fisher III (n 4); Paul J Heald, "The Vices of Originality" (1991) 199 The Supreme Court Review 143; Eleonora Rosati, "Why Originality in Copyright Is Not and Should Not Be a Meaningless Requirement" (2018) 13 Journal of Intellectual Property Law & Practice 597; Russ VerSteeg, "Rethinking Originality" (1992) 34 William and Mary Law Review 801; Diane Leenheer Zimmerman, "It's an Original! (?): In Pursuit of Copyright's Elusive Essence" (2004) 28 Columbia Journal of Law & the Arts 187; Bently and others (n 4) 96.

deciding copyright cases."[29] Moreover, in the Court of Justice of the European Union case of *Football Dataco Ltd*,[30] Advocate General Mengozzi expressed that "clearly, it is not possible to define, once and for all and in general terms, what constitutes an 'intellectual creation.'"[31] Yet, Article 6 of Directive 2006/116/EC states that no criteria other than originality should be applied to determine whether a photograph is eligible for copyright protection and proceeds to state that "Member States may provide for the protection of other photographs."[32] This allowed several European Union (EU) member states to continue to utilise a two-tier system of protection for photographic works, as if originality could be quantified and measured objectively, in order to provide a lesser scope of protection for photographs that do not meet the originality standard.[33] Furthermore, despite the EU's effort to harmonise the laws related to copyright protection in relation to original photographic works, the sui generis protection for "other" photographs that do not meet the originality requirement, if they exist, was left without any move towards harmonisation. This has created wide diverging standards of protection between EU member states for photographs that do not meet the originality standards.[34]

Germany,[35] Spain,[36] Italy,[37] and a few other countries employ variations of a two-tier system of protection for photographs that categorise works of photography into two main categories depending on whether or not a specific photograph passes the originality threshold.[38] In general, the higher tier addresses photographic works deemed to satisfy the originality requirement of the respective jurisdiction

29 Jessica Litman, "The Public Domain" (1990) 39 Emory Law Journal 965, 1019, 1023.

30 *(C-604/10) Football Dataco Ltd v Yahoo! UK Ltd [2013] FSR 1.*

31 ibid AG38.

32 Directive 2006/116/EC of 12 December 2006 on the term of protection of copyright and certain related rights [2006] OJ L372/12.

33 These countries are Germany, Spain, Italy, Austria, Denmark, Finland, Sweden.

34 For a general overview, see: Ysolde Gendreau, Axel Nordemann and Rainer Oesch (eds), *Copyright and Photographs, An International Survey* (Kluwer Law International 1999); see also: Daniele Fabris, "A European 'Copyright Polynesia'? Copyright on Photographs and a Case of European Non-Harmonisation"; Thomas Margoni, "The Digitisation of Cultural Heritage: Originality, Derivative Works and (Non) Original Photographs" [2015] Institute for Information Law (IViR) 12–13, 52–53 <https://papers.ssrn.com/sol3/papers.cfm?abstract_id=2573104> accessed 19 October 2024.

35 Germany's Section 72 provides that the term of protection for photographs that do not satisfy the originality standard extends to 50 years. Gesetz über Urheberrecht und verwandte Schutzrechte (Urheberrechtsgesetz, geändert durch das Gesetz vom 01. September 2017) (Germany).

36 Article 128 of the Spanish Copyright law states that protection for mere photographs extends to 25 years from making of the photographs. Texto refundido de la Ley de Propiedad Intelectual, regularizando, aclarando y armonizando las disposiciones legales vigentes (aprobado por el Real Decreto Legislativo N° 1/1996 de 12 de abril de 1996, y modificado hasta el Real Decreto-Ley N° 26/2020 de 7 de julio de 2020) (Spain).

37 Italy's Chapter 5, Art 92 provides that the term of protection for photographs that do not meet the originality standard extends to only 20 years from the making of the photographs. Legge 22 aprile 1941, n. 633 sulla protezione del diritto d'autore e di altri diritti connessi al suo esercizio (aggiornata con le modifiche introdotte dal decreto-legge 30 aprile 2010, n. 64 (Italy).

38 For an international overview on copyright protection for photographs, see: Gendreau, Nordemann and Oesch (n 34).

and consequently grants full copyright protection on the same level as other copyright- protected works. The lower tier is often referred to as simple photographs, non-original photographs, or "other" photographs that do not meet the originality requirement of the respective jurisdictions and consequently are granted a lesser form of copyright protection, as neighbouring/related rights, with a lesser term of protection. The lesser level of protection can even be subject to specific formalities, as is the case in Italian copyright law.[39] In fact, Italian copyright law goes even further to the point of specifying the category of photographs covered by related-right protection as well as specifying the types of photographs that are excluded from copyright protection altogether, such as photographs made for mere documentary purposes.[40]

Across jurisdictions, legacy issues still endured due to the persistence of the one-size-fits-all approach, modelled on traditional works, to copyright concepts instead of a tailored contextual approach geared towards the categories of works in question. This strains and distorts key concepts such as originality to accommodate untraditional works such as photographic works on the paradigm fashioned for other works. These concepts are often contorted to fit the desired result in a way that makes it a convenient mirage that does not lead to a consistent and coherent framework in which to judge a photograph's copyright protection. These issues persisted despite the fact that the originality standards, across different jurisdictions, are still fundamentally regarded as a low threshold that is detached from the work's artistic merits.

The need for a different approach regarding copyright in photographic works in the Anglo-American copyright law was pointed out by legal scholars in an effort to suggest a more stable framework that fits the current technological realities of photography.[41] LJ Richard Arnold explained in a journal article that copyright law addresses two main categories of copyrights, content copyrights and signal copyrights.[42] He explained that content copyrights require originality and are attached to the immaterial property that represents the work's expression regardless of the medium used to convey that protectable authorial expression. Content copyrights subsist in "original literary, dramatic, musical or artistic"

39 Article 90(1), Legge 22 aprile 1941, n. 633 sulla protezione del diritto d'autore e di altri diritti connessi al suo esercizio (aggiornata con le modifiche introdotte dal decreto-legge 30 aprile 2010, n. 64 (Italy).

40 Article 2, Article 87(1),(2) ibid (Italy); for more on Italian copyright law, see: Luigi Carlo Ubertazzi, "Italy" in Ysolde Gendreau, Axel Nordemann and Rainer Oesch (eds), *Copyright and Photographs, An International Survey* (Kluwer Law International 1999) 161–178; see also: Margoni (n 34) 40–41; Fabris (n 34) 607, 608.

41 For example, see: Hughes (n 23); Kogan (n 25); Terry S Kogan, "How Photographs Infringe" (2017) 19 Vanderbilt Journal of Entertainment and Technology Law 354; Bruce (n 15); Richard Arnold, "Copyright in Photographs a Case for Reform" (2005) 27 European Intellectual Property Review 303.

42 Richard Arnold, "Content Copyrights and Signal Copyrights: The Case for a Rational Scheme of Protection" (2011) 1 Queen Mary Journal of Intellectual Property 272, 272–273.

expressions.[43] In contrast, signal copyrights do not require originality, and they attach to the medium used to record and convey that expression in order to reward the producer's investment and prevent free-riding. The subject matter of signal copyrights is entrepreneurial works such as films, sound recordings, broadcasts, and typographical arrangements.[44] LJ Arnold suggested that photographic works should be protected under the paradigm of signal copyrights that parallel the rights conferred to entrepreneurial works.[45] However, LJ Arnold's suggestion neglects the historical struggle of photographers to be recognised as artists in their own capacity as photographers who utilise the tools of photography as an art form, in and of itself, and not as merely a recording device.

There is an enduring persistence to the refusal to accept photographic works on their own unique capacity as photographs. The unique characteristics of photography are often dismissed as merely mechanical despite the fact that photography, since its inception, has been a curious mix of technology, science, and art that has created a uniquely accessible creative medium. There is a tendency to pierce the veil of the photograph to look through and beyond it, instead of at it, to determine originality.[46]

In summary, adopting a system that involves two tiers of copyright protection may prove useful in protecting investments in works such as photographs without continuously distorting the originality standards to accommodate different categories and types of works. However, the core of the issue is using originality itself as a test for the two-tier system, since relying on originality as a classification device as well as positioning it as the primary gear determining the tier of copyright protection awarded to photographic works is bound to create inconsistencies due to the amorphous nature of originality, which is even more pronounced for visual works such as photographs. Furthermore, any system that refuses to acknowledge and accept photographic works in their own capacity as photographs with all the unique characteristics of photography is bound to face issues. Henceforth, the idea behind the two-tier system for copyright protection is sound, but the tools are not efficient for such a purpose. Therefore, a contextual approach that utilises the concept of authorship should serve as the more suitable tool, at least comparably to originality, to determine the tiers of protection afforded to photographic works under a two-tier system of copyright protection.

### *9.2.2 Authorship as the Suitable Test for Photographic Works' Copyright Protection*

The concept of authorship represents the most significant pillar of copyright law that could be utilised more effectively as a device that determines the tier of

43 ibid 272–273, 276–277; Section 1(1)(a) Copyright, Designs and Patents Act 1988 (UK).
44 Arnold (n 42) 272–273, 276–277; Bently and others (n 4) 118; Section 1(1)(b)(c) Copyright, Designs and Patents Act 1988 (UK).
45 Arnold (n 42) 277; Arnold (n 41) 304–305.
46 Kogan (n 25) 875, 910, 937.

copyright protection for photographic works. The position of authorship across the development of modern copyright law has always been placed at the centre of the system since the creation of the Berne Convention.[47] Moreover, utilising authorship as the primary gear in a two-tier system for photographic works would not introduce drastic changes to the existing copyright system. In fact, it would merely recalibrate it through reusing the tools already in operation. This approach of working within the system of copyright law to reconfigure ideas to promote a more coherent and stable system is advocated by Professor Balganesh since it may lead to less resistance and more refinement of copyright law.[48]

Henceforth, how would authorship function as an engine of the proposed two-tier system of protection for photographic works? Professor Jane Ginsburg's proposal for copyright protection for low authorship informational works serves as an important guide from which to derive an approach for a two-tier system for photographic works.[49] Ginsburg divided informational works into two classes, high and low authorship, to determine the rules associated with each. She proceeded to explain that, in the context of informational works, high authorship refers to works with "authorial presence" such as historical narratives, theories, and novels. On the other hand, low authorship informational works are works such as compilations of facts where the value of the work is in the facts themselves and the labour that went into compiling them.[50] Ginsburg proposed that low authorship works should be protected by copyright, but that protection should be subject to a compulsory licence scheme that ensures that the work is available to maximise the public benefit from utilising such works. Hence, Ginsburg explained that "The point at which low and high authorship works diverge would not be the securing of copyright status, but the organization of the scope of protection."[51]

Ginsburg's framework may prove beneficial for photographic works. However, a compulsory licence scheme, although reasonable for low authorship informational works like compilations of facts, may not be as reasonable for photographic works. This is because, in compilations of facts, there is intrinsic value in the facts themselves. Consequently, the copyright system may wish to encourage their production to advance the public benefits but wish to do so without protecting the facts themselves since limiting the use of these facts risks public harm.[52] So, for Ginsburg, a compulsory licence scheme may be the most efficient way to remedy the conflict in this context.[53] However, photographs are depictions of a scene; the copyright in photographs protects the photograph's depiction and rarely the scene

47 Article 1 Berne Convention for the Protection of Literary and Artistic Works; Section 9, 11 Copyright, Designs and Patents Act 1988 (UK); Section 102 Title 17 of the United States Code (US); Article 1, Section 8 United States Constitution.

48 Balganesh, "Tiered Originality and the Dualism of Copyright Incentives" (n 21) 77.

49 Ginsburg (n 2).

50 ibid 1870.

51 ibid 1937.

52 ibid 1916, 1922.

53 ibid 1927, 1938.

itself. They are not compilations of facts, as Justin Hughes suggested;[54] rather, they can be depictions of facts but never the facts themselves.[55] Susan Sontag, a philosopher and essayist, touched on this notion and expressed that:

> The photographer was thought to be an acute but non-interfering observer – a scribe, not a poet. But as people quickly discovered that nobody takes the same picture of the same thing, the supposition that cameras furnish an impersonal, objective image yielded to the fact that photographs are evidence not only of what's there but of what an individual sees, not just a record but an evaluation of the world. It became clear that there was not just a simple, unitary activity called seeing (recorded by, aided by cameras) but "photographic seeing," which was both a new way for people to see and a new activity for them to perform.[56]

In other words, photographs are depictions; they add an interpretation rather than provide purely objective records of facts. Hence, a compulsory licence scheme is not ideal for low authorship photographs because it may risk creating fixed licence fees, regardless of the type of photographs, and cause what Robert Merges referred to as "legislative lock-in" in terms of the value of the licence and royalties in a way that distorts the market.[57] A situation such as this transpired in the United States with musical works' "mechanical license" where the legislative compulsory licence value remained stagnant from 1909 until the 1970s, whereupon the 1976 Copyright Act implemented a flexible rate-setting framework under Section 801, which was recently amended by the Music Moderation Act 2018.[58] Therefore, a general liability rule model, other than a compulsory licence, for low authorship photographs may be the more efficient option that still leaves room for a flexible valuation of compensations.

Professors Calabresi and Melamed provided a useful framework for illustrating the dynamics of the protection rules attached to legal entitlements and how they differ in three different categories, which are property rules, liability rules, and inalienability rules.[59] Property rules dictate that an entitlement, in normal circumstances, can only be subject to the holder's voluntary transaction.[60] Accordingly, under the proposed two-tier system of protection, photographic works that are deemed to be of high authorship will be protected by property rules. On the other

54 Hughes (n 23).

55 See: Kogan (n 25).

56 Susan Sontag, *On Photography* (RosettaBooks 2005) 68.

57 Robert P Merges, "Contracting into Liability Rules: Intellectual Property Rights and Collective Rights Organizations" (1996) 84 California Law Review 1293, 1299, 1309–1310.

58 Title 17 of the United States Code (US); see: Merges (n 57) 1310; Jacob Victor, "Reconceptualizing Compulsory Copyright Licenses" (2020) 72 Stanford Law Review 915, 921–922; Orrin G. Hatch-Bob Goodlatte Music Modernization Act, Pub. L. No. 115-264 2018 (MMA).

59 Guido Calabresi and A Douglas Melamed, "Property Rules, Liability Rules, and Inalienability: One View of the Cathedral" (1971) 85 Harvard Law Review 1089.

60 ibid 1092.

hand, liability rules dictate that an entitlement is protected on "the basis of a value determined by some organ of the state rather than the parties themselves," and upon payment of that "objectively determined value," the exploitation of that entitlement is allowed.[61] It is along these lines that low authorship photographs should be granted protection. This would allow mundane photographs, such as Chinese food dishes,[62] dental photographs,[63] and surveillance cameras,[64] to be protected as low authorship works without distorting the originality standard or discouraging their production with no protection.

On the one hand, one may certainly argue that low authorship works should not be protected by copyright in the first place. However, it was often the revenue generated from these types of works, which may be regarded as low authorship works, that allows authors to support themselves to pursue highly creative and ambitious projects.[65] Thus, protecting low authorship works is not without merits. The rate-setting standard for low authorship photographs should be based on the fair and appropriate market value standard and be decided on a case-by-case basis. Lemley and Wiser advocated for case-specific liability rules, instead of universal ones such as compulsory licences, as the more fitting model for copyright since it promotes the economic efficiency and flexibility of the system.[66]

The liability rule entitlements for low authorship photographs should only, in normal circumstances, take the form of case-specific monetary remedies based on the objective fair market value of the photograph's licence. The value of the photograph's licence could be determined by the courts based on appraisals from experts, collecting societies, and/or the standard licence fees for similar photographs from commercial picture libraries. Hence, the infringer will only be strictly liable for compensations, without injunctions, for his particular use of the low authorship photographs. Strict liability will be imposed if wholesale use of the low authorship photographs is found.[67] Thus, there is still room to find fair use in situations that may not involve wholesale copying or for uses that fall under the narrower fair dealing exceptions. This may require an amendment to the UK Copyright, Designs and Patents Act 1988 Section 30(2)[68] to allow newspapers to use low authorship photographs for reporting current events and be liable only for compensations,

61 ibid.

62 *Oriental Art Printing, Inc v Goldstar Printing Corp, 175 FSupp2d 542 (2001)* (US).

63 *Pohl v MH SUB I, LLC, 314 FSupp3d 1225 (2018)* (US).

64 *Hyde Park Residence Ltd v Yelland [2000] EMLR 363* (UK).

65 Subotnik (n 28) 1495; Bently and others (n 4) 95; Dutfield and Suthersanen (n 4) 105–106; Brittany Hillen, "Report: 'Photographer' among 2018's Worst Jobs Due to Rise of Freelancing, Smartphones" (*DPReview*, 22 April 2019) <https://www.dpreview.com/news/7564938322/photographer-among-2018-worst-jobs-due-to-rise-of-freelancing-and-smartphones> accessed 19 October 2024.

66 Mark A Lemley and Philip J Weiser, "Should Property or Liability Rules Govern Information?" (2006) 85 Texas Law Review 783, 794–796, 820, 827–829, 833, 841.

67 For a discussion about whether copyright infringement is a strict liability tort, see: Patrick R Goold, "Is Copyright Infringement a Strict Liability Tort?" (2015) 30 Berkeley Technology Law Journal 306.

68 Copyright, Designs and Patents Act 1988 (UK).

instead of injunctions that may lead to high removal costs. This may balance the high search costs often associated with copyright and overall reduce the stress on the copyright system when it comes to photographic works.[69]

The crux of such a proposal is not too foreign, given how copyright holders in photographs organically came to protect their photographs through money claims for unpaid licence fees.[70] This is due to the fact that it was often economically not feasible for photographers to pursue copyright infringement claims.[71] But with the proposed liability rule protection for low authorship photographs, photographers would be guaranteed monetary remedies against infringers without the fear that their work may not meet the originality standard and consequently not be entitled to protection. Cooper and Burrow examined the UK's Intellectual Property Enterprise Court Small Claims Track (IPEC SCT) cases from 2012 to 2015 that involved disputes regarding photographic works and observed that IPEC SCT tend to rely on the rates found on commercial picture libraries, such as Getty Images, to determine the collective value of the compensation.[72] Consequentially, they concluded that the IPEC SCT exhibits liability rule features for photographic works.[73] This substantiates Robert Merges's argument that "the property rule entitlements granted at the outset actually lead to a liability rule-like regime, though one based on a collective valuation by firms, rather than by an arm of government."[74]

All in all, a liability rule protection, requiring compensation based on the objective fair market value standard of similar photographs without the right to injunctions, other than a pre-set compulsory licence scheme, may be suitable for low authorship photographic works. On that account, repurposing Ginsburg's proposal to fit photographic works may prove beneficial to the stability of the copyright system, since the originality standards would not be strained under a two-tier system of copyright protection to deal with different types of photographs and authorial traditions. Through the aforementioned liability rule protection, low authorship photographs would gain some form of protection instead of no protection without distorting the concept of originality or implementing a different duration of protection. However, in order to allow such a system to function with a reasonable level of stability and coherence, the concept of authorship itself must be first identified and recalibrated to function for the purposes of the two-tier system. In other words,

69 Stewart E Sterk, "Property Rules, Liability Rules, and Uncertainty about Property Rights" (2007) 106 Michigan Law Review 1285, 1227–1228, 1327–1329, 1331.

70 Elena Cooper and Sheona Burrow, "Photographic Copyright and the Intellectual Property Enterprise Court in Historical Perspective" (2019) 39 Legal Studies 143, 15–16, 21, 27; Jessica Silbey, Eva E Subotnik and Peter DiCola, "Existential Copyright and Professional Photography" (2019) 95 Notre Dame Law Review 263, 301–302.

71 US Copyright Office, "Copyright Small Claims: A Report of the Register of Copyrights" 201, 1; Jessica Silbey, "Control over Contemporary Photography: A Tangle of Copyright, Right of Publicity, and the First Amendment" (2019) 42 Journal of Law and the Arts 351, 364; Silbey, Subotnik and DiCola (n 70) 269.

72 Cooper and Burrow (n 70) 4, 8, 28, 46.

73 ibid 12, 28–29, 46–47.

74 Merges (n 57) 1303.

what constitutes high authorship and low authorship works in the context of photographic works could be satisfactorily identified if the system is accompanied by a theory of authorship tailored for photographic works and takes into account their unique characteristics.

## 9.3 Part 2: Recalibrating Authorship

This part advocates a more tailored and nuanced approach to the concept of authorship based on the category of work in question to avoid creating legacy issues. This is to prevent the distortion of the authorship concept based on the literary model as a one-size-fits-all approach to works of authorship.

This part begins by providing a definition of authorship based on the scholarship of Professor Jane Ginsburg. Afterwards, it will examine selected theories of copyright authorship to construct an original conception of authorship tailored to photographic works.

### *9.3.1 A Definition of Authorship through Comparative Law*

Professor Jane Ginsburg examined the concept of authorship across different common law and civil law jurisdictions, showcasing the disparity surrounding it in spite of being one of the central pillars of copyright law.[75] Ginsburg identified six principles related to the concept of authorship that reared their heads across the different jurisdictions she examined.[76]

The first principle provides that the one who conceptualised the work and controlled its development tends to have a stronger claim of authorship than the one who merely followed instructions and executed the work. The second principle expresses that the involvement of a machine, such as a camera, does not invalidate authorship, provided that the author showcased a greater role in the work's conception and depiction than the role of that machine.[77] Hence, the purely mechanical application of photography, such as surveillance cameras, does not, in itself, create works of authorship. Therefore, during the creation process, the camera must remain subservient to the human operator and not the other way around. The third principle found by Ginsburg reveals that the jurisdictions examined tend to address authorship and originality interchangeably.[78] This was not surprising since the concept of originality is even more elusive to define than authorship.[79] However, originality and authorship are not the same. Originality for the purposes of copyright primarily requires that the work exhibits minimum creativity and not be the result

75 See Jane C Ginsburg, "The Concept of Authorship in Comparative Copyright Law" (2003) 52 DePaul Law Review 1063.

76 ibid 1072.

77 ibid 1074.

78 ibid 1078.

79 ibid 1081, 1082.

of copying.[80] On this point, Professor Balganesh explained that "even if originality is otherwise a notional stand-in for authorship in the modern context, it does so through the 'work of authorship' construct and not as authorship qua act of authoring."[81]

Proceeding from there, Ginsburg presents the fourth principle as "the author need not be creative, so long as she perspires."[82] Nevertheless, the courts in different jurisdictions are reluctant to award authorship to works that faithfully reproduce other public domain works, even if that reproduction requires considerable skill and labour to create.[83] The fifth principle is the "Intent to be an author," which was a standard proposed by Professor David Nimmer in his article regarding copyright in the Dead Sea Scrolls.[84] Ginsburg criticised this principle and stated that it has the potential to encroach on the public domain and may even present problems with the authorship of photographs, derivative works and works that exhibit elements of chance or unintended features.[85] Nonetheless, she explained that intent might prove helpful in determining authorship in situations involving multiple contributors to the same work of authorship.[86] The sixth and final principle provides that the employer of the commissioned party will be assigned authorship and/or ownership of the commissioned work. Ginsburg points out that this was primarily a pragmatic principle designed for legal efficiency.[87] This is because it was often the standard, in normal circumstances, that the first copyright owner in a work is the author of that work.

Upon examining the concept of authorship through comparative law, Ginsburg critically analysed these six principles to fashion the following definition of authorship for the purposes of copyright law:

> in copyright law, an author is (or should be) a human creator who, notwithstanding the constraints of her task, succeeds in exercising minimal personal autonomy in her fashioning of the work. Because, and to the extent that, she moulds the work to her vision (be it even a myopic one), she is entitled not only to recognition and payment, but to exert some artistic control over it.[88]

This definition of authorship, or perhaps one should say a definition of who is an author of a copyrighted work, seems to encompass various acts and works of authorship. An average photographer's work, such as snapshot photographs, would

80 ibid 1078, 1080.
81 Shyamkrishna Balganesh, "Causing Copyright" (2017) 117 Columbia Law Review 1, 39.
82 Ginsburg (n 75) 1082.
83 ibid 1082, 1083.
84 ibid 1085; see: David Nimmer, "Authorship and Originality: Copyright in the Dead Sea Scrolls" (2001) 38 Houston Law Review 1.
85 Ginsburg (n 75) 1085, 1086.
86 ibid 1087.
87 ibid 1088, 1089.
88 ibid 1092.

certainly be the work of an author under this definition without the need to stretch the traditional views regarding authorship. Furthermore, this definition may have reduced the confusion surrounding the famous *monkey selfie case*.[89] On the one hand, the photographer, David Slater, in the aforementioned case, would not have faced uncertainty regarding his authorship of the monkey selfie photographs since he demonstrated "minimal personal autonomy in fashioning the work" by adjusting the camera's parameters to make it possible for the photographs to be produced.[90] The fact that the monkey executed the work by pressing the shutter should not raise questions about the principal photographer's authorship status.

On the other hand, there is a concern regarding this definition's mention of a human creator in the sense that it may be interpreted rigidly in a way that may sustain the uncertainty surrounding the authorship of the monkey selfie photographs. This is because the photograph could be deemed as created by the animal without giving credit to the unorthodox creation process exhibited by the human creator, which allowed the photographs to be captured by the animal. However, an argument could be made that, within the confines of Ginsburg's definition of authorship, the principal photographer exhibited "minimal personal autonomy" that should not be denied regardless of the unorthodox method in which he chose to express his creativity in the photograph.

Moreover, Ginsburg's definition of authorship may raise legitimate grounds for the existence of the element of authorship in untraditional works. One example that may illustrate the potential of this definition is related to works that utilise Google Street View images if we consider these works as depictions rather than copies. Google Street View captures panoramic photographs around the world utilising artificial intelligence (AI) and automated cameras.[91] Since non-human actors created these works without a human's minimal personal autonomy, it is very likely that a copyright's authorship could not be located. Nevertheless, there is a growing practice by artists whereby they utilise Google Street View images, by screenshotting or rephotographing the images, to present them in a different frame as artistic images.[92] One could reasonably argue that these appropriation artists, such as Jon

89 David J Slater, "Sulawesi Monkey – Photographs by David J Slater" (*DJS Photography*) <http://www.djsphotography.co.uk/original_story.html> accessed 18 October 2024; *Naruto v Slater No 15-cv-04324-WHO, 2016 WL 362231 unreported (2016)* 4; Andres Guadamuz, "Can the Monkey Selfie Case Teach Us Anything about Copyright Law?" (*WIPO Magazine*, February 2018) <http://www.wipo.int/wipo_magazine/en/2018/01/article_0007.html> accessed 18 October 2024.

90 Slater (n 89).

91 Google, "Street View" (*Google Maps*) <https://www.google.com/streetview/> accessed 18 October 2024.

92 Geoff Dyer, "How Google Street View Is Inspiring New Photography" *The Observer* (14 July 2012) <https://www.theguardian.com/artanddesign/2012/jul/14/google-street-view-new-photography> accessed 18 October 2024.

Raffman[93] and Michael Wolf,[94] despite the constraints of their task, have exercised minimal personal autonomy and succeeded in "moulding" the work to their vision even though their contribution, as appropriation artists, may be regarded as minimal.[95]

Ginsburg's definition is helpful in addressing what an author is for the purposes of copyright law, but how a work of copyrightable authorship manifests itself depending on the category of work for the purposes of copyright law remains yet to be clarified. In more precise words, Ginsburg defines authorship through conceptualising the author but falls short of providing a theory of authorship that addresses how a work manifests that authorship, in a full circle, to be regarded as a work of authorship for the purposes of copyright law. This flaw was observed by Justine Pila, who pointed out that Ginsburg's conception is "problematic" since it "proceeds from the existence of a 'work', which is part of the object it is seeking to establish."[96] In other words, Ginsburg's conception of authorship focuses on how an author would be attached to the work of authorship, but it does not explain how a work of authorship manifests itself.

We explored in Chapter 5 that the concept of work in copyright law remains underdeveloped, at times used as synonyms with authorship and originality. While the concept of work is indeed strongly connected with originality and authorship, it remains a separate concept altogether. Professor J.A.L. Sterling provided a simple yet elegant attempt to define what constitutes a work in copyright law by conceptualising a work as "the ordered expression of thoughts."[97] The "ordered" element may refer to the general authorial traditions and rules that attach the work to a particular category of works or to the general selection and arrangement that gave birth to the work. In the context of photographs, the expression is ordered through the medium of photography, with all its rules and authorial traditions. Hence, the concept of work might be inseparably connected to the concept of authorship. Therefore, a conception of authorship that is tailored and centred around the work of authorship may serve as the appropriate way forward in addressing copyright authorship for the two-tier system of protection for photographic works.

93 Jon Rafman, "IMG MGMT: The Nine Eyes of Google Street View" (*ArtFCity*, 12 August 2009) <http://artfcity.com/2009/08/12/img-mgmt-the-nine-eyes-of-google-street-view/> accessed 18 October 2024.

94 Jim Casper, "A Series of Unfortunate Events – Photographs by Michael Wolf" (*LensCulture*) <https://www.lensculture.com/articles/michael-wolf-a-series-of-unfortunate-events> accessed 18 October 2024.

95 Dyer (n 92).

96 Justine Pila, "Copyright and Its Categories of Original Works" (2010) 30 Oxford Journal of Legal Studies 229, 242.

97 JAL Sterling, "Philosophical and Legal Challenges in the Context of Copyright and Digital Technology" (2000) 31 International Review of Intellectual Property and Competition Law 508, 513.

### *9.3.2 Reconceptualising Copyright Authorship in Photographic Works*

Many legal scholars endeavoured to develop new understandings of the element of authorship in copyright law. These scholars endeavoured to illuminate the concept of authorship for the purposes of copyright law in a manner that is consistent across different types of works.[98] However, it is there where the crux of the issue lies. Confirming copyright law's tendency for a one-size-fits-all approach would inevitably create legacy issues as soon as new forms of works emerge, as was the case with photographic works. Hence, a tailored approach that takes into account the categories of the works in question may provide a better and more stable way forward. This is because instead of a universal model that would be inevitably stretched and distorted to accommodate different categories of works, a tailored approach could be adjusted without affecting the approach to other categories of works. Daniela Simone, in her work regarding the treatment of collective authorship in Anglo-American copyright law, argues that the law needs to adopt a contextual approach to authorship that is sensitive to the changing creative practices of the type of work in question.[99] She advocated for contextuality that takes into

98 See: Shyamkrishna Balganesh, "The Folklore and Symbolism of Authorship in American Copyright Law" (2016) 54 Houston Law Review 403; Laura Biron and Elena Cooper, "Authorship, Aesthetics and the Artworld: Reforming Copyright's Joint Authorship Doctrine" (2016) 35 Law and Philosophy 55; Alina Ng Boyte, "The Conceits of Our Legal Imagination: Legal Fictions and the Concept of Deemed Authorship" (2013) 17 New York University Journal of Legislation and Public Policy 707; Oren Bracha, "The Ideology of Authorship Revisited: Authors, Markets, and Liberal Values in Early American Copyright" (2008) 118 The Yale Law Journal 186; Christopher Buccafusco, "A Theory of Copyright Authorship" (2016) 102 Virginia Law Review 1229; Margaret Chon, "The Romantic Collective Author Copyright and Creativity: Perspectives on Originality, Authorship, and Expression January 27, 2012" (2011) 14 Vanderbilt Journal of Entertainment and Technology Law 829; Alan L Durham, "Copyright and Information Theory: Toward an Alternative Model of 'Authorship'" [2004] Brigham Young University Law Review 61; Alan L Durham, "The Random Muse: Authorship and Indeterminacy" (2002) 44 William and Mary Law Review 569; Ginsburg (n 75); Darren Hudson Hick, "Authorship, Co-Authorship, and Multiple Authorship" (2014) 72 The Journal of Aesthetics and Art Criticism 147; Molly Van Houweling, "Authors Versus Owners" Houston Law Review 33; Anne Jamison, "Collaboration v. Imitation: Authorship and the Law" (2006) 18 Law and Literature 199; Peter Jaszi, "Toward a Theory of Copyright: The Metamorphoses of 'Authorship'" (1991) 1991 Duke Law Journal 455; Alina Ng, "When Users Are Authors: Authorship in the Age of Digital Media" (2009) 12 Vanderbilt Journal of Entertainment and Technology Law 853; Mark Rose, *Authors and Owners: The Invention of Copyright* (Harvard University Press 1993); Balganesh, "Causing Copyright" (n 81); Jack Stillinger, *Multiple Authorship and the Myth of Solitary Genius* (OUP Oxford 1991); Kim Treiger-Bar-Am, "Kant on Copyright: Rights on Transformative Authorship" (2007) 25 Cardozo Arts & Entertainment Law Journal 1059; Russ VerSteeg, "Defining 'Author' for Purposes of Copyright" (1996) 45 The American University Law Review 1323; Martha Woodmansee, "The Genius and the Copyright: Economic and Legal Conditions of the Emergence of the 'Author'" (1984) 17 Eighteenth-Century Studies 425; Lionel Bently and Laura Biron, "Discontinuities between Legal Conceptions of Authorship and Social Practices. What, If Anything, Is to Be Done?" in Mireille van Eechoud (ed), *The Work of Authorship* (Amsterdam University Press 2014) 260.

99 Daniela Simone, *Copyright and Collective Authorship: Locating the Authors of Collaborative Work* (Kindle edition, CUP Cambridge 2019) 270.

account the good social norms of a work's authorial community and the changing nature of creative practices. She argues that this would be the best approach for a one-size-fits-all copyright regime to operate flexibly and efficiently.[100] Simone did not provide a theory of authorship but stressed that authorship, at least collective authorship, should be approached contextually.

In order to construct a theory of copyright authorship that is tailored for photographic works to serve as the engine behind the two-tier system of protection for photographic works, the following section explores selected theories of copyright authorship curated for that purpose.

#### *9.3.2.1 Authorship Based on Categorical Intention to Create Mental Effects*

Professor Christopher Buccafusco presented an attractive theory of authorship for copyright law that centres around the author's intention to produce mental effects rather than an intent to be an author.[101] The theory provides that a human being's "categori[c]al intention" to conceptualise a work to produce mental effects, through any medium of expression capable of producing the mental effects, in a manner that was "original, minimally creative and fixed" in a permanent form, would be deemed as the author of the copyrighted work.[102] The mental effects themselves are regarded as similar to ideas. Their particular nature and whether the author managed to communicate the intended effects are not relevant to finding authorship; they are immaterial to copyright law.[103]

Buccafusco explains, drawing from the philosopher Jerrold Levinson, that "categori[c]al intention" does not concern itself with what the author intended to mean with his work, in other words, his semantic intentions. Instead, categorical intention refers to the author's intentions to classify the work in which such intended classification or categorisation will inevitably determine how the work is "conceptualised and approached on a fundamental level"[104] to be created in the form it was presented.[105] For example, utilising the United Kingdom's categories of works system, suppose an author wrote a text with the intention to present it as a poem or wrote the same text on a canvas and intended to present his work as a painting. The author's first categorical intention made the first work fall under "literary works" as a poem. The author's second categorical intention made the work fall under "artistic works" as a painting. His categorical intention fundamentally

100 ibid 234, 251–252, 270.

101 Buccafusco (n 98) 1232.

102 ibid.

103 Buccafusco explained that he opted out of using the term "mental image" to prevent the impression that his theory was only addressing visual works. ibid 1262, 1263, 1266, 1274.

104 Levinson, "Intention and Interpretation: A Last Look," 232–233 (italics in original) (as cited and quoted in Stephen Davies, "Authors' Intentions, Literary Interpretation, and Literary Value" [2006] 46 The British Journal of Aesthetics 223, 234).

105 Davies (n 104); Buccafusco (n 98) 1261, 1262.

affected how the work is conceived and generally perceived by the audience.[106] Buccafusco further clarified that for the purposes of copyright,

> a putative author's intentions should be assessed at the time of creation. A creator should not be able to assert different intentions or adopt different readings of her work after she has created it, at least not for purposes of subsequently establishing a copyright.[107]

Applying his theory on photographs' authorship, Buccafusco reasoned that:

> For works like photographs, where the creation of a mental effect was obviously intended, we need only consider the manner by which that effect was created...copyright attaches to the manner or form by which the photographer attempted to achieve the production of a mental effect.[108]

He further elaborates that the scope of the photographer's authorship is concentrated on the relationship "created between the objects in the image...and how they were depicted" in the photograph.[109] Thus, his proposal "considers the relationship between creators' categori[c]al intentions to create mental effects and the choices they made to do so."[110]

Buccafusco referenced the famous *monkey selfie case*[111] and reasoned, based on his theory, that because the photograph was captured by an animal who was incapable of categorical intention, it contains no copyright protection.[112] However, Buccafusco neglected the case intricacies in that the photographer, David Slater, made arrangements and enabled the conditions for such photographs to be created by setting up the camera and its parameters.[113] Should the fact that a non-human actor pressed the shutter be considered sufficient enough to diminish the human influence and creative thought, exercised by the principal photographer, that went into setting the conditions that allowed the photograph to be created in this manner? While it was true that the timing, and perhaps the angle, was chosen by the monkey, but since an animal cannot be an author for the purposes of copyright, it could be argued that the animal could not have taken the photographs without the arrangement, setup, and creativity of the principal photographer. Hence, the author was the one who directed the capture in a manner that rendered him the principal photographer.[114] Buccafusco's take on the *monkey selfie case* neglects this important element. It would not be far-fetched

106 Buccafusco (n 98) 1261, 1263.
107 ibid 1264.
108 ibid 1269, 1270.
109 ibid 1286, 1287.
110 ibid 1287.
111 *Naruto v Slater No. 15-cv-04324-WHO, 2016 WL 362231 unreported (2016)* (n 89).
112 Buccafusco (n 98) 1263, 1276.
113 See here David Slater's account on the monkey selfie photograph: Slater (n 89).
114 *Burrow-Giles Lithographic Co v Sarony, 111 US 53 (1884)* (n 4) (US); *Melville v Mirror of Life Co [1895] 2 Ch 531* (UK); *Nottage v Jackson (1883) 11 QBD 627* (UK).

to regard Slater's enabling activities as directorial and thus amount to a categorical intention that evidences his authorship.

As per Buccafusco's theory, in order to find authorship in photographs, the categorical intention that influenced the choices and the relationship created between what is depicted and how it was depicted, at the time of the photograph's creation, to generate mental effects are key to finding authorship in photographs. However, in many photographs, the selection comes after the photographs were captured. Therefore, it may prove difficult to reconcile Buccafusco's theory of authorship on various applications of photography, such as the ones that adopt untraditional creation processes, for instance, and works based on AI-captured photographs or works that heavily utilise computational photography. Nevertheless, Buccafusco's theory of authorship provides an important piece towards constructing a tailored theory of copyright authorship. This piece is the categorical intention and prior mental conception that dictates the work's category and the authorial tradition followed.

#### *9.3.2.2 A Selection-Based Theory of Copyright Authorship*

Professor Alan Durham's model of copyright authorship, which he described as "unromantic selection-oriented model"[115] of authorship, provides another important piece for constructing our theory of copyrightable authorship. Durham's model of authorship draws from the field of information theory and invites us to picture the author as a "channel," a medium of conveying information, that merely adds "noise" to the source; hence, the author is not principally the source as posited by the romantic model of authorship.[116] The elements "channelled," described by Durham as the "noise," along with the source, are what comes from within the author; hence, they are the protectable elements of expression that evidence a work of authorship. These elements are influenced by the author's freedom of selection and amount to being his "channelled" expression.[117] The "noise" (expression) is what the "channel" (the author) adds to the transmitted source in a way that influences how it was transmitted and eventually depicted to materialise a work of authorship.[118] The source, which did not originate from within the author, is regarded as similar to ideas or facts and, therefore, unauthored.[119]

Under this model, one's selection and expression that added information to the source in a way that sufficiently evidences authorship in the resulting work render him the author of that work.[120] Durham explains that:

115 Durham (n 98) 156.
116 ibid 146, 148, 150.
117 ibid 150.
118 ibid 148, 150.
119 ibid 146, 148, 153.
120 ibid 150.

> An author is in some respects a source, a channel, and an encoder. In each role, an author exercises choice. An author chooses the ideas to be included in the work and chooses how they will be expressed.[121]

Durham stresses that this "selection-based model of authorship would have to operate in conjunction with the traditional dichotomies of copyright law" in order to be compatible with the purposes of copyright law.[122] This model of authorship as a product of a channel symbolising the author, and not necessarily a source, lends itself well to different types of photographic works since whatever was depicted in a photograph, more often than not, does not originate from the photographer, nor does it need to be in order to evidence authorship. The angle, lighting, arrangements, and shadows, along with other means of expression within the confines of the art of photography, need not be under the complete control of the photographer so long as the act of "selection has occurred."[123]

Nonetheless, it is not clear how Durham's model applies when the bulk of the "noise" channelled does not necessarily owe its presence to the photographer but to AI and complex algorithms instead, as is the case with computational photography. Would the "noise" added to the source being "channelled" be that of the photographer or of the machine? All in all, Durham's model provides us with another important piece towards constructing a tailored theory of authorship for photographic works. That piece is channelled selection. Channelled selection entails that an author, by being a channel rather than a source that conveys selection-based expression, is capable of producing a work of authorship for the purposes of copyright law.

#### *9.3.2.3 Causation and Copyrightable Authorship*

Professor Shyamkrishna Balganesh's article "Causing Copyright" invoked an insightful discussion about causation in copyright law and showcased that, from the onset, authorial causation was an element hidden within copyright doctrines.[124] In order to locate authorship, Balganesh draws from causation in tort law to explain that authorial causation refers to a human agent's causal responsibility, as a matter of fact, for the creation of a work.[125] Balganesh elaborates that "In assigning authorship, copyright law (much like tort law) is therefore about allocating responsibility for an outcome, except that the allocation is of a positive one rather than a negative one."[126] It is positive in the sense that it "allocates an exclusive entitlement over the expression to the causally responsible individual."[127] Balganesh argues that an express acknowledgement of authorial causation in copyright jurisprudence

121 ibid 151.
122 ibid 157.
123 ibid 153.
124 Balganesh, "Causing Copyright" (n 81) 6–7, 14, 17, 18, 33–34.
125 ibid 54, 55.
126 ibid 55.
127 ibid 54.

would be a natural fit that will bring great benefits to copyright law, in terms of coherence and consistency, when it comes to the element of authorship on the doctrinal level.[128] He further elaborated that authorial causation should be implemented in a "copyrightable causation" requirement within the copyright system to determine copyright's authorship following a two-step inquiry inspired by tort law.[129] The first step examines causal authorship as a matter of fact; satisfying this test leads to the second step, which looks at authorship as a matter of copyright law to determine copyrightable causation.[130]

The first step of the copyrightable causation inquiry is concerned with authorial causation as a matter of fact.[131] It applies a modified version of tort law's causation tests, such as the "But-for" or the "Necessary Element of a Sufficient Set (NESS)" test, for the purposes of copyright law to assign the work's authorship.[132] The "But-for" test set out to determine whether or not for "that individual's actions, the particular work of expression in question would not have come into existence."[133] If the work involves multiple contributors, such as works of joint authorship, in a way that renders their actions as multiple causes for a single work, then the NESS test would be more suitable to determine creation in fact.[134] The NESS test evaluates the multiple causes to determine whether each cause is considered an essential element of "a set of antecedent actual conditions that was – as a whole – sufficient" to be considered an essential cause for creating the work.[135]

Once authorship, as a matter of fact, was established, the second inquiry was concerned with authorship as a matter of copyright law.[136] Balganesh illustrates that this inquiry was to be conducted on copyright authorship claims through three principal tests that evaluate authorship for the purposes of copyright law.[137] These tests are of control, whether the putative author demonstrated insufficient control in the work's creation process;[138] of disproportionality, whether the author's contribution was disproportionate to the claim of authorship;[139] and personality conflation test, which evaluates whether the original work author's causality to a derivative work by another author conflates the original work's authorship, to the point of being regarded as a co-author.[140] These three evaluative tests represent the exclusionary nature of authorship in law as they were designed to evaluate authorship claims strictly for the purposes of copyright law. Hence, if an authorship claim

128 ibid 7–9, 11.
129 ibid 53.
130 ibid 53, 61.
131 ibid 53, 54.
132 ibid 55–56, 57.
133 ibid 55–56.
134 ibid 57, 59–60.
135 ibid 59–60.
136 ibid 61.
137 ibid 64, 71.
138 ibid 64.
139 ibid 67.
140 ibid 68–70.

failed to pass any of the aforementioned tests, then copyrightable causation would not be established even if authorship, as a matter of fact, was established.[141]

Equipped with the aforementioned analysis framework, Balganesh examined the *monkey selfie case*,[142] with reference to causation, and reasoned that even though the monkey was the nearest to be the immediate cause of the photograph due to being the one who had chosen the angle and pressed the shutter, copyright law focuses primarily on human agency.[143] Therefore, an animal or a machine cannot be regarded as the causal creator of a work for the purposes of copyright law.[144] The photographer, instead, should be regarded as the causal element that created the photograph since if not for him fulfilling the necessary conditions for the photographs to be produced, the photograph would not have existed in the form it did.

While Balganesh's proposal may provide a more consistent framework of analysis, authorial causation in photographs was not as simple as it may seem. Despite the fact that the immediate cause could be argued to be embodied through the act of capture or pressing the shutter, as without it, the image would not exist in a fixed form, that act was still the most automated act in the medium of photography. It may represent a considerable argument for causation but not necessarily for copyright authorship. This is precisely where the conundrum lies. Is a photograph's causation primarily linked to the circumstances surrounding the act of fixation? The one who pressed the shutter certainly caused the permanent fixation of the photograph, but could it be equally argued that he was also the authorial cause for its creation in the traditional sense?

For example, Bob Martin, a famous sports photographer, was asked about his involvement in his work and how he regards photographs as "his" when he uses assistants. He answered that:

> if you determine the parameters it's your picture; if you ask someone else to do it for you, it's his or her picture. Since I set up the camera, determined all the parameters, and selected the best frame, the horse jumping picture is totally mine, and it would still be mine if had I told an assistant when to press the shutter release.[145]

One could deduce that Martin views his authorship claim as proportionate to his level of control over the creative process. His authorial causation may be evidenced in a NESS test in that his contribution was an essential element "in a set

141 ibid 61, 63–64, 71.

142 *Naruto v Slater No. 15-cv-04324-WHO, 2016 WL 362231 unreported (2016)* (n 89).

143 Balganesh, "Causing Copyright" (n 81) 55, 56.

144 ibid.

145 Frank Walker, "Meet a Pro: Elite Sports Photographer Bob Martin" (*Adorama Learning Center*, 5 August 2016) <https://www.adorama.com/alc/meet-a-pro-elite-sports-photographer-bob-martin> accessed 18 October 2024.

of antecedent actual conditions that was – as a whole – sufficient"[146] to cause the creation of the photograph in the manner it did.

Henceforth, the level of the photographer's control over the creative process would have to be evaluated to determine whether the level of control was sufficient to evidence authorial causation. Snapshots may prove to be challenging types of photographs due to the fact that, more often than not, a photographer may have control only over the timing and angle but little to no control over how the subjects and objects are depicted in a photograph. In fact, in many instances, the photographer may only be aware of how they were depicted after the capture of the photograph.[147] Moreover, it may prove challenging to locate authorial causation for the purposes of copyright law, with consistency, over different applications of photography, especially the ones that heavily employ computational photography. This is because the choices that influenced how the images are depicted were often largely due to AI and countless complex algorithms, all geared towards minimising the photographer's impact on the quality of the image.[148] This may raise questions regarding whether the camera is subservient to the human agent or vice versa.

All in all, Balganesh's proposal for a copyrightable causation requirement is promising. It offers a framework anchored on causation to tackle the issues of copyright authorship through multiple stages of analysis designed to examine causation through the lens of copyright law. However, applying the framework may prove to be complicated when faced with works involving unorthodox creation processes since it may end up placing considerable weight on the most automated aspects of certain categories of works, such as the pressing of the shutter in photographic works. In tricky examples, there is a risk that the cause of fixation may be mixed with the cause of copyright in the work. Nevertheless, the element of copyright causation provides the final important piece for our endeavour to construct a tailored theory of authorship for photographic works. This tailored theory of authorship is presented in Chapter 10.

## 9.4 Conclusion

The unstable position of copyright in photographic works is due to copyright law's tendency to adopt a one-size-fits-all approach regarding copyright concepts and apply it to different categories of works. This has created legacy issues where the

146 Balganesh, "Causing Copyright" (n 81) 58, 59.

147 See: William W Fisher III and others, "Reflections on the Hope Poster Case" (2012) 25 Harvard Journal of Law & Technology 96, 255; "Mannie Garcia: The Photo That Sparked 'Hope'" (*NPR.org*, 26 February 2009) <https://www.npr.org/2009/02/26/101184444/mannie-garcia-the-photo-that-sparked-hope> accessed 19 October 2024.

148 Vince Tabora, "Computational Photography Will Revolutionize Digital Imaging" (*Medium*, 16 October 2018) <https://medium.com/hd-pro/computational-photography-will-revolutionize-digital-imaging-a25d34f37b11> accessed 19 October 2024; Olivier Laurent, "How Snapchat, Instagram & Apple Are Reinventing Photography" (*Time*, 24 February 2017) <http://time.com/4659058/snapchat-instagram-apple-photography/> accessed 19 October 2024; see Chapter 8.

models of these concepts were stretched and distorted to accommodate different types of works. In the hope of remedying this issue, it is recommended that a tailored approach to copyrightable authorship that takes into account the categories of works in question be applied. This recommendation proposes recalibrating copyright key concepts to better fit photographs as photographs with all their unique characteristics. Hence, it suggests abandoning the one-size-fits-all approach, considering it a liability rather than an advantage, in favour of a tailored approach. It argues that this would lead to a stable development of copyright law that acknowledges the differences in the categories of works and addresses photographs in their own capacity instead of using the perspective of another category, such as literary works, paintings, or even databases, to justify copyright protection for photographs.

It is advanced that a repurposed model built on Ginsburg's model of high/low authorship for informational work paired with Ginsburg's definition of authorship would serve as the groundwork for constructing a system suitable for photographic works, for the purposes of copyright law, that is flexible enough to accommodate different types of works, and especially photographic works. Within the proposed two-tier system, photographic works would be protected either as high or low authorship photographs. The difference between the two tiers is manifested in the level of protection granted. On the one hand, high authorship photographs would be protected by property rule protection just as other copyrighted works. On the other hand, low authorship photographs would be protected by a case-specific liability rule copyright protection in the form of compensation without the right to injunctive relief. It is forwarded that an original theory of copyright authorship, which will be presented in the next chapter, paired with Ginsburg's definition of authorship, would provide a stable conception of authorship for the purposes of copyright law that is flexible enough to accommodate different types of works, and especially photographic works. On this, it is recommended that authorship should be the engine that operates a two-tier system of protection for photographic works that classifies photographs as either of high or low authorship.

Ginsburg's definition of authorship will serve as a starting point; it provides that "an author is (or should be) a human creator who, notwithstanding the constraints of her task, succeeds in exercising minimal personal autonomy in her fashioning of the work."[149] However, this definition may be accurately described as a definition of the figure of the author in copyright law instead of a definition of the concept of authorship. Hence, the selected theories of authorship that were examined sought to provide a nuanced approach to the element of authorship, not the figure of the author itself, to attain a relatively clear and more consistent framework for copyright authorship. The selected theories endeavoured to reconceptualise authorship specifically for the purposes of copyright law, advocating for a definite separation of what authorship means in the semantic and philosophical sense from its legal meaning for the purposes of copyright law. These theories provided important pieces towards constructing a theory of authorship that takes into account the

149 Ginsburg (n 75) 1092.

unique nature of photographic works. These important pieces are: 1) categorical intention, 2) channelled selection, 3) copyright causation. It is argued here that by adopting a tailored approach to copyright authorship based on the category of the work in question, the stability of copyright concepts would be enhanced due to reducing the risk of creating legacy issues emerging from the tendency to examine one art not through the confines of its own overarching rules and authorial traditions but through that of another. This phenomenon persists in the traditional approach followed by the Anglo-American courts regarding copyright authorship in photographic works. The next chapter presents the proposed two-tier system of protection for photographic works based on an original theory of authorship tailored for photographic works.

# 10 An Original Two-Tier System for Copyright in Photographic Works

## 10.1 Introduction

The previous chapter examined the futility of applying copyright concepts designed on the paradigm of traditional works, in a one-size-fits-all approach, to untraditional works such as photographs. It explored how originality is too elusive of a concept to utilise as the anchor that operates a two-tier system of copyright protection for photographic works. Henceforth, it argued that in order to design a forward-thinking system that is able to adapt to different types of works, it must adopt a contextual and tailored approach to authorship, instead of originality, as well as other copyright concepts based on the category of work in question. It suggested that this will lead to a stable and flexible system that could accommodate the unique characteristics of photographic works in their own capacity as photographs, unhindered by the rigid one-size-fits-all approach to copyright concepts.

This chapter consolidates the discussion in the previous chapters by presenting and exploring the proposed two-tier system of copyright protection for photographic works anchored on an original theory of copyrightable authorship. Firstly, this chapter presents an original theory of copyrightable authorship constructed from select theories of authorship. This original theory of copyrightable authorship is described as a tailored work-based approach to copyright authorship. Secondly, this chapter presents the model of the proposed two-tier system of copyright protection of photographic works. Thirdly, it provides a framework that illustrates how the proposed system is envisioned to operate. Finally, this chapter showcases the merits of the proposed system by revisiting select cases, previously examined in Chapter 7, and demonstrating how it would approach these cases.

## 10.2 A Tailored Work-Based Approach to Copyright Authorship

The previous chapter repurposed Professor Ginsburg's high-low authorship model for informational works to fit photographic works in a two-tier system. The difference between the two tiers is reflected in the type of protection granted. On the one hand, high authorship photographs would be protected by property rule type of protection. On the other hand, low authorship photographs would be protected by a liability rule type of protection, without injunctions, based on case-specific monetary remedies centred on the objective fair market value of the photograph's

DOI: 10.4324/9781003586555-10

licence. The copyright author is defined according to Professor Ginsburg's definition of authorship in that the author is "a human creator who, notwithstanding the constraints of her task, succeeds in exercising minimal personal autonomy in her fashioning of the work."[1] The strength of the authorial presence reflected in the photograph will determine the photograph's tier of protection. The manner in which the authorial presence is measured would be based on an original theory of copyright authorship tailored to the category of works in question.

This section constructs a tailored approach to copyright authorship, instead of the one-size-fits-all approach, by piecing together elements inspired by the selected theories previously examined in Chapter 9. This section seeks to provide a theory of copyrightable authorship that considers the category of the works in question, tailored for photographic works in order to serve in conjunction with the proposed two-tier system of copyright protection. It builds on the theories examined in Chapter 9 to construct an original theory of copyrightable authorship crafted with photographic works in mind. This theory serves as the core of the proposed two-tier copyright protection of photographic works.

### *10.2.1 A Tailored Theory for Copyright Authorship in Photographic Works*

To reiterate, the three important components of the forthcoming tailored theory of copyright authorship are categorical intention, channelled selection, and copyrightable causation. Categorical intention, Buccafusco's theory of authorship,[2] symbolises the first act of authorship that embodies selection. This is because by choosing the category of the work, one will inevitably draw the boundaries on the form of that work and be constrained by the extent of its overarching rules and authorial traditions, regardless of how much these rules can be stretched. That categorical intention is fuelled and materialised based on a prior mental conception, or image, of the work. A writer is bound by the overarching rules and traditions of the language, a painter is bound by the overarching rules and traditions of painting, and the same could be said for the other categories of works such as sculptures, collages, etc. Equally, a photographer is bound by the overarching rules, authorial traditions, and constraints of photography. These overarching rules and authorial traditions governing each category of work may extend beyond their traditional boundaries, but their categorical boundaries would still resonate regardless, placing the work within the confines of its categorical limit.[3] A categorical intention denotes a prior mental conception of the work. This represents the first important element of the act of authorship in copyright law, albeit yet to materialise into full

1 Jane C Ginsburg, "The Concept of Authorship in Comparative Copyright Law" (2003) 52 DePaul Law Review 1063, 1092.

2 See: Christopher Buccafusco, "A Theory of Copyright Authorship" (2016) 102 Virginia Law Review 1229.

3 See: William P Seeley, "Concepts and Categories of Art: A Very Brief Primer" in William P Seeley (ed), *Attentional Engines: A Perceptual Theory of the Arts* (OUP Oxford 2020) <https://doi.org/10.1093/oso/9780190662158.003.0004> accessed 19 October 2024.

authorship. That prior mental conception, despite how faint it was during the onset of the process of authorship, would still cast a residual shadow upon the work.

The impact of categorical intention is not only limited to the aesthetic form of the work, but it also dictates the authorial tradition that was followed to create it. This was a point stressed by Justine Pila's criticism of the influence of formalism theory,[4] in that an object exists and is perceived according to its form, on the categories of works in the UK copyright system.[5] She reasoned, deriving from Kendal Walton's scholarship,[6] that in order to categorise a work for the purposes of copyright law, it is essential that the work is first correctly perceived.[7] She argues that in order to perceive a work correctly, one must take into account the evolving authorial traditions associated with its category.[8] Hence, she argues that a category of work not only indicates the form of the work but, equally, the category of the authorial tradition associated with it.[9] Indeed, a photograph's form is influenced by the authorial tradition that shaped it. Cartier-Bresson's "decisive moment" style would demand different considerations compared to prearranged fine art photographs. Both authorial traditions associated with these types of works would have an immense impact on the work's form as well as its elements of expression.[10]

Accordingly, the first piece and element of the act of authorship, for our purposes, is the categorical intention and prior mental conception that would inevitably dictate the authorial tradition followed as well as influence the form of the work on a fundamental level. This represents the first element of authorship in copyright law that, if fully materialising and satisfying the two forthcoming additional elements, would produce a work of authorship. However, the puzzle of authorship remains yet incomplete, which takes us to the second piece, channelled selection.

Channelled selection, an idea derived from Alan Durham's selection-based theory of authorship,[11] is the act of channelling a source where the author, seen as a channel, contributes the elements of expression along with the channelled source to process the prior mental conception and categorical intention towards the creation of the work. A channelled selection denotes the idea that the author is not necessarily the sole originator of the source, which should be considered akin to ideas and facts.[12] Instead, the author is the channel through which the source

4 For a discussion on formalism theory and how it relates to art, see: ibid 94–114; Kendall L Walton, "Categories of Art" (1970) 79 The Philosophical Review 334; Richard Wollheim, "On Formalism and Pictorial Organization" (2001) 59 The Journal of Aesthetics and Art Criticism 127.

5 Justine Pila, "Copyright and Its Categories of Original Works" (2010) 30 Oxford Journal of Legal Studies 229, 231, 241, 251.

6 Walton (n 4).

7 Pila (n 5) 244–245.

8 ibid 251.

9 ibid 245, 251.

10 ibid 245.

11 Alan L Durham, "Copyright and Information Theory: Toward an Alternative Model of 'Authorship'" [2004] Brigham Young University Law Review 61.

12 ibid 146, 148, 153.

is then streamed and mixed with his own "noise," the author's expression, influenced by his categorical intention and prior mental conception.[13] One may inquire about the benefit of referring to selection as being channelled. This is rationalised through the fact that the word "channelled" indicates that the selection reflected in the work does not necessarily denote origins but an act of communication[14] that materialises the author's expression into a work of authorship. An example of this is when an author chooses a genre of literary works, such as horror, or a genre of musical composition, such as classical music, or a genre of photography, such as street photography, whereby the categorical design and authorial traditions of that category inform his channelled selection through them.

Channelled selection represents the next necessary step for copyright authorship to materialise the categorical intention and prior mental conception of the work to full fruition into a work of authorship. However, the two elements of authorship, categorical intention and channelled selection, must have a causal relationship with the work and this is where Balganesh's nuanced approach to copyright causation comes to complete the process of copyright authorship.

The final piece, derived from Balganesh's scholarship, is the concept of "Copyrightable Causation."[15] Causation completes the authorship of copyright and materialises it into being. It attaches the work of authorship to the putative author who was deemed to be the cause of the channelled selection that was influenced by the categorical intention and prior mental conception. This is because categorical intention alone, although it may evidence a causal link to the channelled selection, cannot be regarded as sufficient to evidence authorship for the purposes of copyright law. This is owed to the fact that a categorical intention may be dictated by someone other than the author, such as commissioned works, but ultimately, the channelled selection is what contains the author's expression. Hence, categorical intention and prior mental image are the very first step to copyright authorship that must be followed by channelled selection linked to the putative author in such a way as to position him as the principal cause of the copyright in the materialised work of authorship for the purposes of copyright law. To determine whether the putative author is the cause of the copyright, an inquiry into the level of control over the channelled selection and the proportionality of the claimed authorship may serve as guiding posts.

All these three elements accumulate to serve as building blocks for constructing a tailored theory of copyright authorship. This proposed original theory of copyright authorship is as follows:

13 Durham (n 11).

14 See: Abraham Drassinower, *What's Wrong with Copying?* (Harvard University Press 2015) (Proposing to reconceptualise copyright to a dialogue model and the work of authorship as a communicative act); compare: Lionel Bently, "Drassinower's Vision of Copyright" (2016) 29 Intellectual Property Journal; Scarborough 19.

15 Shyamkrishna Balganesh, "Causing Copyright" (2017) 117 Columbia Law Review 1.

> A copyrightable authorship is a product of a human agent's *categorical intention* and *prior mental conception* that influenced his *channelled selection*, expression, to *cause* a work of authorship to materialise for the purposes of copyright law.

This theory of copyrightable authorship is referred to as tailored authorship. It is tailored because, based on the categorical intention and prior mental conception of the work, the authorship is tailored to the confines of that work. Hence, it is not a universal one-size-fits-all approach to copyrightable authorship. As a consequence, this theory would ease legacy issues emerging from the traditional one-size-fits-all approach based on a model of one type of works, such as literary works, and distorting it to be a universal model in which to judge the authorship of other types of works such as photographs.[16]

This tailored approach to authorship would be well suited for untraditional works and authorial processes that are closely connected to technology, such as photographic works. Under this theory of copyright authorship, common photographic practices, such as snapshots and prearranged photographs, would mostly lead to copyrightable authorship without major issues. That is because a categorical intention and prior mental conception, or image, can be easily located by virtue of the photographs being photographs and not by virtue of being photographs that exhibit similar expressive elements with other types of works.[17] Furthermore, these photographs, regardless of their type, have a source, an independent reality, or a created scene that was "channelled" with a selection of elements of expression (such as framing, angle, depth of field) to materialise the photographs and cause them to exists in their form by the putative author/s in a manner that evidences copyrightable authorship.

With this understanding of copyright authorship for photographic works, the authorship of the monkey selfie photographs[18] would not have created nearly as much confusion. This is because David Slater, the photographer, had the categorical intention and prior mental conception of the photographs and set up the parameters and the method of capture, his channelled selection, to cause a work of authorship

16 An issue that is well documented. See for example: Kevin Garnett and Alistair Abbott, "Who Is the 'Author' of a Photograph?" (1998) 20 European Intellectual Property Review 204; Rebecca Tushnet, "Worth a Thousand Words: The Images of Copyright" (2012) 125 Harvard Law Review 683; Teresa M Bruce, "In the Language of Pictures: How Copyright Law Fails to Adequately Account for Photography" (2012) 115 West Virginia Law Review 93; Christine Haight Farley, "The Lingering Effects of Copyright's Response to the Invention of Photography" (2004) 65 University of Pittsburgh Law Review 385; Eva E Subotnik, "The Author Was Not an Author: The Copyright Interests of Photographic Subjects from Wilde to Garcia" (2015) 39 Columbia Journal of Law & the Arts 449; *Sarony v Burrow-Giles Lithographic Co, 17 F 591 (1883)*; *Nottage v Jackson (1883) 11 QBD 627*; Carl Mazurek, "Through the Looking Glass: Photography and the Idea/Expression Dichotomy" (2017) 6 Journal of Intellectual Property and Entertainment Law 32.

17 Which was the case with landmark cases such as: *Burrow-Giles Lithographic Co v Sarony, 111 US 53 (1884)*; see also: *Nottage v Jackson (1883) 11 QBD 627* (n 16); see Chapters 3–4, 5.

18 *Naruto v Slater, 888 F3d 418 (2018).*

to materialise in this form.[19] The unorthodox creation process and authorial tradition that was followed did not remove Slater's causal link, as the principal photographer, to the work. In addition, the element of chance is well documented as an element of creative choice with an established authorial tradition behind it.[20]

On the one hand, a similar argument could be raised to support finding copyright in photographs that follow the authorial tradition of accurate depiction. On the other hand, photographs that accurately depict public domain works, such as works held by museums, represent a tricky situation that generated a discussion regarding the appropriate balance of copyright law.[21] Indeed, that situation is tricky due to the fact that it is locked into a binary paradigm represented by either property rule copyright protection or no protection. However, it is suggested that this situation could be remedied if we applied the forthcoming proposed two-tier system of protection to regard accurate depiction of public domain works as low authorship works that can only be protected against verbatim copying through a case-specific liability rule protection instead of property rule protection. It is argued that this would remedy both the fears that the lack of protection may discourage investment in producing these types of photographs as well as the fears that granting full copyright protection may prevent the free dissemination of public domain works since museums control access to these public domain works.

Moreover, the proposed theory of authorship would provide a basis for evidence of copyrightable authorship in unorthodox creative creation methods in the context of photographs and accommodate drastic changes in photographic technologies, such as computational photography. In fact, during the 2020 COVID-19 pandemic, professional photographers found ways to continue to work virtually through taking screenshots or photographs of the screen during virtual photo-shoot sessions or capturing images while taking a virtual tour in Google Street View.[22] One could

19 David J Slater, "Sulawesi Monkey – Photographs by David J Slater" (*DJS Photography*) <http://www.djsphotography.co.uk/original_story.html> accessed 18 October 2024.

20 See: Nadya Bair, "The Decisive Network: Producing Henri Cartier-Bresson at Mid-Century" (2016) 40 History of Photography 146; see also: Alan L Durham, "The Random Muse: Authorship and Indeterminacy" (2002) 44 William and Mary Law Review 569; see also: *Alfred Bell & Co v Catalda Fine Arts, 191 F2d 99 (1951)* 105.

21 For discussion about this, see: Robin J Allan, "After 'Bridgeman': Copyright, Museums, and Public Domain Works of Art" (2007) 155 University of Pennsylvania Law Review 961; Terry S Kogan, "Photographic Reproductions, Copyright and the Slavish Copy" (2011) 35 Columbia Journal of Law & the Arts 445; Mitch Tuchman, "Inauthentic Works of Art: Why Bridgeman May Ultimately Be Irrelevant to Art Museums" (2000) 24 Columbia-VLA Journal of Law & the Arts 287; Ronan Deazley, "Photography, Copyright and the South Kensington Experiment" in Estelle Derclaye, *Copyright and Cultural Heritage* (Edward Elgar Publishing 2010); see also: *Bridgeman Art Library, Ltd v Corel Corp, 25 FSupp2d 421 (1998).*

22 See: Vince Tabora, "Virtual Photography in the Time of Social Distancing" (*Medium*, 13 April 2020) <https://medium.com/hd-pro/virtual-photography-in-the-time-of-social-distancing-cabf79bfc893> accessed 19 October 2024; David Williams, "Photographer Uses FaceTime to Shoot Portraits of His Friends under Lockdown" (*CNN*, 7 May 2020) <https://www.cnn.com/style/article/virtual-photographer-coronavirus-trnd/index.html> accessed 19 October 2024; Tim Medlideo, "I Took a Virtual Photography Road Trip Using Google Street View" (*PetaPixel*, 16 April 2020) <https://petapixel

argue that the categorical intention and prior mental conception to transform the work would be evidenced by the artist's intention to select the authorial tradition of appropriation art to take the screenshot or the desired position to rephotograph the screen. Consequently, this may evidence low authorship of that photograph, notwithstanding the unorthodox creative process that went into capturing it. The photographers could be regarded as the authorial cause of these works by virtue of their channelled selection of a source that was not itself subject to copyright to cause the work to exist in the form it took. However, if these practices amounted to copying rather than a form of depiction, then they would not be deemed as independently created and, therefore, would not be subject to copyright protection.

Other untraditional works of photography that have seen a surge in recent times are attributed to the practice of "virtual photography," which refers to images captured virtually to simulate traditional photographs.[23] More predominantly, virtual photography is associated with images taken within virtual in-game worlds either through screenshotting or photographing the screen or using the game's tools to produce virtual photographs.[24] It represents a growing subculture within the video game community due to the advent of sharing and remixing culture on the internet,[25] and it is actively encouraged by the gaming industry to the point that a dedicated photo mode has become nearly a stable feature of high-production video games.[26] These photo modes come equipped with standard virtual photography

---

.com/2020/04/16/i-took-a-virtual-photography-road-trip-using-google-street-view/> accessed 19 October 2024.

23 Eron Rauch, "Hybrid Light: A Few Thoughts on the Future of Virtual Photography" (*videogametourism.at*, 15 July 2015) <https://videogametourism.at/content/hybrid-light-few-thoughts-future-virtual-photography> accessed 19 October 2024; Adobe, "Virtual Photography: Picture-Perfect Photos, No Studio Required" (*PRINT Magazine*, 9 November 2020) <https://www.printmag.com/3d-visualization/virtual-photography-picture-perfect-photos-no-studio-required/> accessed 19 October 2024; Alistair Campbell, "Landscape Photographer Explores the Rise of In-Game Photography" (*DigitalCameraWorld*, 9 September 2020) <https://www.digitalcameraworld.com/news/landscape-photographer-explores-the-rise-of-in-game-photography> accessed 19 October 2024.

24 See: David Gilmour, "The Art of Video Game Photography" (*Vice*, 18 July 2015) <https://www.vice.com/en_us/article/8qxpp4/the-art-of-video-game-photography> accessed 19 October 2024; Rainer Sigl, "The Art of In-Game Photography" (*Videogametourism.at*, 25 July 2012) <https://videogametourism.at/content/art-game-photography> accessed 19 October 2024; Rauch (n 23); Eron Rauch, "Virtual Light: Exploring In-Game Photography and Photo History" (*videogametourism.at*, 28 August 2012) <https://videogametourism.at/content/virtual-light-exploring-game-photography-and-photo-history> accessed 19 October 2024.

25 Lawrence Lessig, *Remix: Making Art and Commerce Thrive in the Hybrid Economy* (Penguin Books 2009).

26 Teddy Amenabar, "Video Games Are Now So Beautiful Players Are Spending Hours Framing Stunning Works of Internet Art" *Washington Post* (20 November 2018) <https://www.washingtonpost.com/technology/2018/11/20/video-game-photography-is-rise-producing-stunning-works-internet-art/> accessed 19 October 2024; Adam Vjestica and Rhys Wood, "Best Video Game Photo Modes: Capture the Perfect In-Game Picture" (*TechRadar*, 2 April 2021) <https://www.techradar.com/best/best-video-game-photo-modes-capture-the-perfect-in-game-picture> accessed 19 October 2024; Christopher Isak, "What Is Video Game Photography? [Interview]" (*TechAcute*, 9 October 2020) <https://techacute.com/what-is-video-game-photography-interview/> accessed 19 October 2024;

features and offer considerable freedom to capture images within virtual worlds and share them on social media platforms.[27] In fact, Nvidia, a tech company specialising in producing high-end graphics cards, developed Ansel, named after the famous nature photographer Ansel Adams, an advanced virtual photography tool for use in supported video games.[28]

With the proposed theory of authorship, even these types of photographic practices may evidence copyrightable authorship, either low or high authorship, for the purposes of copyright law. This is because the categorical intention and mental conception are evidenced by virtue of the work as a virtual photograph that follows the authorial traditions of photographic works, even though it was not technically capturing light or its data. The channelled selection could be evidenced in the fact that the source, being a video game, was channelled with the artist's own expression, such as framing and angle, to cause a work of authorship to materialise. The elements of expression in these examples, no matter how faint they may seem,[29] could be regarded as evidence of copyrightable authorship. The fact that it adopted an unorthodox creation process and did not exhibit elements associated with other categories of works should not be summoned to deny them protection under this tailored theory of copyright authorship.

Nonetheless, a question could be raised regarding the element of causation in that the direct cause of virtual photographs is video game developers and not the photographers. After all, a video game's world is crafted by the game developers. However, this argument could be countered by the fact that just as a photographer does not need to create the subject he depicts in order to produce works of authorship, the same could be raised for virtual photography in that a photographer need not create the virtual gaming worlds himself in order to depict them and produce a work of authorship.[30] Virtual photographs, just as traditional photographs, could be

---

*Cyberpunk 2077 – Photo Mode Trailer* (Directed by Cyberpunk 2077, 2020) <https://www.youtube.com/watch?v=IHfs98k86EA&feature=emb_title> accessed 19 October 2024.

27 See: Isak (n 26).

28 Andrew Burnes, "NVIDIA Ansel: Revolutionizing Screenshot Capture for GeForce GTX Gamers" (*NVIDIA*, 6 May 2016) <https://www.nvidia.com/en-us/geforce/news/ansel-revolutionizing-game-screenshots/> accessed 19 October 2024.

29 "The copy is the personal reaction of an individual upon nature. Personality always contains something unique. It expresses its singularity even in handwriting, and a very modest grade of art has in it something irreducible, which is one man's alone," in *Bleistein v Donaldson Lithographing Co, 188 US 239 (1903)* 4, 250 (per Judge Holmes).

30 For more discussion on the position of works based on virtual worlds, see: Thomas Jr Pichta, "The Virtual Photography Paradox: How Courts Could Analyze Copyright of Virtual Photography of User Generated Content Using Software, Real World, or Toy Copyright Analyses" (2008) 12 SMU Science and Technology Law Review 275; Matthew Brett Freedman, "Machinima and Copyright Law Note" (2005) 13 Journal of Intellectual Property Law 235; Tyler T Ochoa, "Who Owns an Avatar – Copyright, Creativity, and Virtual Worlds Copyright and Creativity: Perspectives on Originality, Authorship, and Expression January 27, 2012" (2011) 14 Vanderbilt Journal of Entertainment and Technology Law 959; Cindy Poremba, "Point and Shoot: Remediating Photography in Gamespace" (2007) 2 Games and Culture 49.

seen to focus on depiction and not recreation.[31] Hence, by channelling the source, an artist may be able to fulfil his mental conception of the work through his categorical intention to depict that source in the desired manner. A similar notion is advocated by Eron Rauch,[32] one of the leading proponents of virtual photography as a new sub-art of photography, where he invoked author Seth Godin's view of "a 'node' based system of culture" in that

> it's not about how much attention you call to yourself, but how much value you add to things that pass [through] your node, that now determines how interesting an artist is. As a node, virtual photography seems to embrace that role.[33]

## 10.3 The Shape of the Authorship-Based Two-Tier System of Protection for Photographic Works

The discussion in the book consolidates to shape the following proposed system of copyright protection for photographic works (Figure 10.1).

As illustrated in Figure 10.1, the nature of copyright protection for photographic works would centre around the level of authorship exhibited by the photograph, whereupon, accordingly, it may be classified into one of two tiers. This classification stage is only reached if the work of authorship was independently created in the sense that it was not the result of copying.[34] Therefore, originality still occupies a pivotal role in the granting of copyright protection. In such a manner, even though

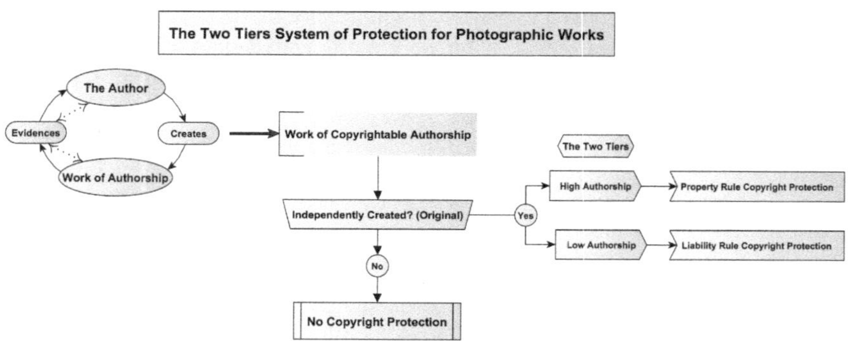


*Figure 10.1* The proposed two-tier system of copyright protection.

31 Pichta (n 30) 284, 304.

32 "Eron Rauch" (*Eron Rauch*) <https://www.eronrauch.com> accessed 19 October 2024.

33 Rauch (n 23).

34 Independent creation should be understood along the lines advanced by the following cases: *Bleistein v Donaldson Lithographing Co, 188 US 239 (1903)*; *University of London Press Ltd v University Tutorial Press Ltd [1916] 2 Ch 601*; *Walter v Lane [1900] AC 539*; *(C-5/08) Infopaq International A/S v Danske Dagblades Forening [2009] ECR I-6569*; *(C-145/10) Painer v Standard Verlags GmbH [2012] ECDR 6.*

the proposed system centres the level of protection on authorship, it does not seek to remove the originality requirement altogether. Instead, it aims to simplify the concept of originality for photographic works and prevent it from being utilised as a qualitative classification device. Hence, the importance of originality is not diminished; on the contrary, it remains the "sine qua non of copyright,"[35] since without it, a photograph could not acquire copyright protection.

Therefore, as long as the photographs were created independently and were not directly copied, they would be deemed independently created for copyright protection purposes. Accordingly, it could be argued that most, if not all, photographs that were captured independently would satisfy this requirement and advance to the classification stage of the proposed system. At this point, the level of authorship exhibited would determine the tier of protection afforded to the photographs in question. Moreover, originality will still play a critical role in assessing copyright infringement in the proposed two-tier system of protection. The substantial similarity test, which determines whether there is a copying of a substantial part of the works' original expression in a manner that constitutes an infringement,[36] can benefit from the proposed system in the context of photographic works. This is because the test would be simplified depending on whether the photograph is of high or low authorship. This will reduce the overreliance on one-size-fits-all tests that might not be compatible with visual works such as photographs. After all, the substantiality assessment is an area that has seen intense discourse surrounding its suitability to determine copyright infringement.[37] In fact, at least one scholar even argued that the substantiality test is "meaningless" and "inadequate" to determine copyright infringement.[38]

Moreover, adding to the notion that substantiality is an unstable anchor to determine copyright infringement, a 2014 study revealed that fact-finders, in their substantiality assessment, are very sensitive to additional information even if such information goes beyond the confines of the works in question.[39] The study posits

35 *Feist Publications, Inc v Rural Telephone Service Co, Inc, 499 US 340 (1991)* 1287.

36 ibid 361 (US); Howard B Abrams and Tyler T Ochoa, *Law of Copyright* (Clark Boardman Callaghan 2020) s 14:2; *Designers Guild Ltd v Russell Williams (Textiles) Ltd (t/a Washington DC) [2001] FSR 11* [38–41] (UK); *(C-5/08) Infopaq International A/S v Danske Dagblades Forening [2009] ECR I-6569* (n 34) para 51 (EU); Nicholas Caddick, Gwilym Harbottle and Uma Suthersanen, *Copinger and Skone James on Copyright* (18 edition, Sweet & Maxwell Ltd 2020) ss 7–15, 7–28, 7–58.

37 See for example: Rachael Wallace, "Framing the Issue: Avoiding a Substantial Similarity Finding in Reproduced Visual Art" (2014) 10 Washington Journal of Law, Technology & Arts 89; Mark A Lemley, "Our Bizarre System for Proving Copyright Infringement" (2010) 57 Journal of the Copyright Society of the USA 719; Daryl Lim, "Saving Substantial Similarity" (2021) 73 Florida Law Review; Moon Hee Lee, "Seeing's Insight: Toward a Visual Substantial Similarity Test for Copyright Infringement of Pictorial, Graphic, and Sculptural Works" (2017) 111 Northwestern University Law Review 833.

38 See: Amy B Cohen, "Masking Copyright Decisionmaking: The Meaninglessness of Substantial Similarity" (1987) 20 UC Davis Law Review 719.

39 Shyamkrishna Balganesh, Irina D Manta and Tess Wilkinson-Ryan, "Judging Similarity Essays" (2014) 100 Iowa Law Review 267, 270–271, 289–290.

that the mere knowledge of copying coupled with the work's creation narrative, which highlights the creator's effort into producing the original work, plays a key role in finding similarity even if the works were not substantially similar.[40] Hence, one can see the persistent influence of the narrative surrounding the work's creation, which plays a vital role beyond the confines of the work in determining copyright infringement through the substantiality assessment.

Indeed, an empirical study with an extensive scale provided the first in-depth analysis of the substantial similarity assessment in American courts across a randomised sample of over one thousand cases between 1978 and 2020.[41] The study, led by Professor Clark Asay and his team, revealed the degree of inconsistency related to the substantiality assessment and made manifestly clear that the test exhibits significant heterogeneity.[42] In fact, due to the absence of guidance from the US Supreme Court regarding the substantiality assessment, American courts use multiple subtests along with copyright limitations in order to determine the substantiality inquiry.[43] Furthermore, the study revealed that one of the critical elements that tilt the court's decision to either party of the case was the extent to which the court engages, in their substantiality assessment, with any relevant copyright limitations. The study claimed that "whether or not a court engages with copyright limitations…literally flips the script as to a party's chances of success: defendants overwhelmingly win when courts discuss copyright limitations, whereas plaintiffs win at about the same rate when courts do not."[44]

Although a similar study was not conducted to examine UK cases involving the substantiality assessment, it is long established that substantiality was difficult to apply with consistency in general, particularly so to visual works such as photographs.[45] In essence, the substantiality assessment aims to determine whether a substantial part of the copyrighted work has been copied. The elements that constitute a substantial part of the copyrighted work are those that represent the expression of the author's own intellectual creation.[46] However, beyond these general principles, the substantiality assessment is "essentially a matter of impression"[47] that is influenced by several factors, such as the type of work, the work's creation

40 ibid 289.

41 Clark D Asay, "An Empirical Study of Copyright's Substantial Similarity Test" (19 January 2022) <https://papers.ssrn.com/abstract=4013095> accessed 19 October 2024.

42 ibid 1, 12–13, 16, 56.

43 ibid 4–5, 12–13, 16, 58, 63.

44 ibid 5–6.

45 See: *Designers Guild Ltd v Russell Williams (Textiles) Ltd (t/a Washington DC) [2001] FSR 11* (n 36); *Temple Island Collections Ltd v New English Teas Ltd [2012] EWPCC 1*; see also: Fiona Macmillan, "Is Copyright Blind to the Visual?" (2008) 7 Visual Communication 97; Caddick, Harbottle and Suthersanen (n 36) ss 7–56, 7–57, 7–111, 7–112.

46 See: *(C-5/08) Infopaq International A/S v Danske Dagblades Forening [2009] ECR I-6569* (n 34); *SAS Institute Inc v World Programming Ltd [2013] EWCA Civ 1482*; *Duchess of Sussex v Associated Newspapers Ltd [2021] ECDR 25*.

47 *Designers Guild Ltd v Russell Williams (Textiles) Ltd (t/a Washington DC) [2001] FSR 11* (n 36) paras 35, 41.

narrative, as well as other surrounding circumstances that may be important in establishing whether there was a copying of a substantial part of the expression that contains the author's own intellectual creation.[48]

In dealing with copyright in photographs, the proposed two-tier system would lessen the stress on the substantiality assessment by simplifying the process of examination when it comes to visual works such as photographs. On the one hand, if a photograph was deemed as a high authorship photograph, then the more rigorous test of substantially would normally apply to determine the extent of that protection against alleged infringements. However, if the photograph was deemed to be a low authorship photograph, then the test to be applied would examine whether there is verbatim copying of the photograph without the need to distort originality with arbitrary abstractions to reach a desired result. This would reduce the stress on the concept of originality in the context of photographic works since the substantiality assessment, with all of its iterations,[49] is known to be subjective and notoriously challenging to apply to visual works such as photographs.[50]

In this manner, the proposed two-tier system would still work within the paradigms of the current Anglo-American copyright system, but it recalibrates, simplifies, and repositions the concepts and tests to promote a more coherent system for photographic works copyright protection that takes into account their unique characteristics.

## 10.4 Determining Whether a Photograph Is High or Low Authorship Work

Whether a photograph is regarded as being of high authorship and subsequently protected by property rule, or of low authorship and subsequently protected by the proposed liability rule protection, should be determined by the courts on an ad hoc basis regardless of the genre/type of photographs in question. The courts should not determine whether a photograph is of high or low authorship purely based on preconceptions associated with the particular genre/type of photographs under which

48 Caddick, Harbottle and Suthersanen (n 36) ss 7–56, 7–57, 7–111, 7–112; Michael Tappin and others, *Laddie, Prescott and Vitoria: The Modern Law of Copyright* (5 edition, LexisNexis Butterworths 2018) s 3.125, 3.132, 4.47, 4.48; Lionel Bently and others, *Intellectual Property Law* (5 edition, OUP Oxford 2018) 203–205, 207.

49 US Circuits applies different tests and terminologies and formulas for the test to examine whether there is a copying of a substantial part that constitutes a copyright infringement. See: Abrams and Ochoa (n 36) s 14:2, 14:3, 14:5, 14:6.

50 See Chapter 7 Terry S Kogan, "How Photographs Infringe" (2017) 19 Vanderbilt Journal of Entertainment and Technology Law 354; see also: Tushnet (n 16); for a critical analysis of the US general substantial similarity test, see: Lemley (n 37); Michael D Murray, "Copyright, Originality, and the End of the Scenes a Faire and Merger Doctrines for Visual Works" (2006) 58 Baylor Law Review 779; Wallace (n 37); On the idea/expression dichotomy and substantial similarity in the context of photographs, see: Bruce (n 16); Morgan M Stoddard, "Mother Nature as Muse: Copyright Protection for Works of Art and Photographs Inspired by, Based on, or Depicting Nature" (2007) 86 North Carolina Law Review 572; Lee (n 37).

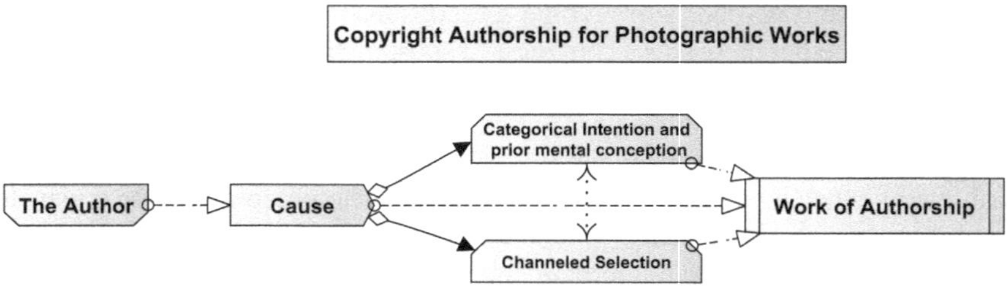


*Figure 10.2* Copyright authorship for photographic works.

the photograph in question happens to fall. Hence, under the proposed two-tier system, the courts should not substitute a nuanced examination of the photographs in question with presumptions, as a generalised rule, regarding the tier of protection usually awarded to particular types of photographs. This is a critical risk to avoid in order to prevent the courts from influencing photographic practices.

The classification of the tier of protection awarded to photographs is built upon a conception of authorship tailored for photographic works. The conception of authorship that would operate the proposed two-tier system for photographic works' copyright protection is illustrated in Figure 10.2.

The author, for the purposes of the proposed system, is to be defined along the lines drawn by Ginsburg's definition of authorship, which provides that the author is "a human creator who, notwithstanding the constraints of her task, succeeds in exercising minimal personal autonomy in her fashioning of the work."[51] The work of authorship that manifests and evidences that authorship, in a full circle, is to be defined as the product of a human agent's *categorical intention* and *prior mental conception* that influenced his *channelled selection*, expression, to *cause* a work of authorship to materialise for the purposes of copyright law.

Thus, Figure 10.2 illustrates that the putative author's categorical intention and prior mental conception of the work influence his channelled selection, which influences the categorical intention and the mental conception of the work as if they are constantly bouncing off each other. Both the categorical intention and channelled selection must be caused by the author in order to materialise a work of copyrightable authorship. This conception of copyright authorship and its dynamics would serve as the engine behind the proposed two-tier system of protection for photographic works. The courts would carefully scale the balance of these elements to determine whether the photographic work in question tilts towards one tier more than the other.

51 Ginsburg (n 1) 1092.

## 10.5 Showcasing the Proposed Two-Tier System for Photographic Work Copyright

Under the proposed system, even the contentious *monkey selfie case*[52] would not be as perplexing to deal with since the photograph, whether it was deemed to be of high or low authorship, would still gain some form of copyright protection awarded to the photographer. The only difference would be whether that copyright protection was subject to property rule or liability rule protection. In the *monkey selfie case*, a monkey took a photograph of himself that proved to be popular. Subsequently, questions were raised about the authorship of the photographs and whether the photographs were a work of authorship subject to copyright protection.[53] The photographer, David Slater, claimed authorship of the photographs by virtue of being the principal photographer who set up the camera parameters and laid the groundwork for the photographs to be taken by the monkeys.

With the proposed system, the court would not be pressured between copyright protection or no protection and forced to bend or twist copyright concepts to reach a desired result. Through utilising the proposed conception of authorship tailored for photographic works, the court would evaluate whether Slater's authorial presence evidences high or low authorship. The court would look at the first stage of authorship, represented by categorical intention and channelled selection, to determine whether the photographs are the work of copyrightable authorship. It is apparent that Slater's categorical intentions were strongly present in the photographs in question. Slater is a nature photographer and follows the authorial tradition associated with this genre of photography. He set out to take photographs of Sulawesi crested macaques and observed them for days to that end.[54]

Slater's channelled selection was evident in configuring and setting the camera's expressive elements, such as the angle, type of lens, and focus, in order for the photographs to be captured. He employed untraditional creative practices by soliciting the monkeys to fiddle with the prepared camera in order to capture these unique photographs. Despite that, his categorical intentions and channelled selection remain pervasive in the photographs, positioning himself as the principal photographer. Hence, it could be argued that the photographs carry Slater's authorial presence. Copyright causation can also be traced to David Slater since he was the one whose categorical intention and channelled selection were manifested in the photographs' expression to cause it to exist for the purposes of copyright law. He is the author of the photographs since, despite the constraints of his task, he succeeded "in exercising minimal personal autonomy" in creating the photographs. Hence, it could be argued that the monkey selfie photographs contain high authorial presence and consequently would be protected as high authorship work with property rule type of protection.

52 *Naruto v Slater No 15-cv-04324-WHO, 2016 WL 362231 unreported (2016)* 4.

53 See Chapter 5.

54 David Slater, "Sulawesi Monkey – Photographs by David J Slater" <https://www.djsphotography.co.uk/original_story.html> accessed 19 October 2024.

On the other hand, if the court regarded Slater's authorial presence as merely residual upon the categorical intention and channelled selection for the monkey selfie photographs, then his work may be deemed to be of low authorship and subsequently protected by liability rule protection, ascertaining his right only to compensation according to the proposed liability rule protection without the right to injunctions. In both situations, Slater's work that resulted from a creative, albeit untraditional, creation process would be awarded some form of copyright protection instead of no protection. As a result, copyright protection is awarded regardless; the only difference is the form and extent of the protection.

Another case that may illustrate the advantages of the proposed system is the UK case of *Creation Records Ltd v News Group Newspapers Ltd [1997]*.[55] In this case, the photographer arranged the scene and designed the set to be photographed in order to produce a photograph for an album cover for the musical band Oasis. The scene was creative, constructed to the minute detail, and included many objects arranged in a certain way to achieve the desired scene. The dispute arose concerning a claim over another photograph of the scene that was taken without permission by a photojournalist working for a newspaper.[56] The court dismissed the plaintiff's motion for copyright infringement on the grounds that one cannot prevent another from making a photograph of the same subject matter if the subject matter itself was not copyrighted.[57]

While the underlying reasoning for the decision was sound, one can see that this created an unfair situation where the original author of the scene and the photojournalist who took a photograph of the scene were equally regarded as authors of the photographs that emerged of the scene and subsequently awarded with the same level of protection. In spite of that, it was clear that the authorial presence of these two photographers was not on equal footing as one could strongly argue that the photographer who constructed the scene that was depicted in the photographs had shown a stronger authorial presence that evidences his imprint of personality. The same could not be said about the photojournalist whose photograph did not exhibit a strong authorial presence, at least given the facts of the case.

Hence, under the proposed two-tier system, an arguably more fair and balanced result would be achieved if the original photograph from the principal photographer who created and arranged the scene would be regarded as high authorship work and subsequently gained property rule copyright protection. Through applying the proposed theory of copyrightable authorship, the creator of the scene exhibited categorical intention and prior mental conception of the photograph by conceptualising the work as photographs and creating and arranging the scene. Furthermore, the principal photographer channelled elements of expression, such as the angle, focus, and arrangement of the objects, to cause the work of authorship to manifest. Thus, the original principal photographer exhibited high authorial presence in his

55 *Creation Records Ltd v News Group Newspapers Ltd [1997] EMLR 444* (UK).

56 See Chapter 7.

57 *Creation Records Ltd v News Group Newspapers Ltd [1997] EMLR 444* (n 55) 450.

photograph, and consequently, the work would be classified as a high authorship photograph subject to property rule copyright protection.

On the other hand, the photojournalist's photograph did not exhibit a high authorial presence due to the fact that his photograph displayed low categorical intention and prior mental conception since he took the photograph for its documentary nature and did not conceptualise the work to cement his authorial presence. The photojournalist channelled his expression through the medium of photography by choosing the angle, focus, depth, and other expressive elements of photography and caused the photograph to manifest. Notwithstanding the fact that the photojournalist's photograph exhibited low authorial presence, the photograph remains a work of authorship because, despite the constraints of his tasks, he managed to express minimal personal autonomy in making the photograph. However, due to the facts of the case that evidence his low authorial presence in the photograph, it would be classified as a low authorship work subject to liability rule copyright protection.

In that fashion, the unauthorised photograph taken by the photojournalist would be considered as low authorship work due to exhibiting low authorial presence and subsequently be protected by liability rule protection. In contrast, the original photograph from the one who created the scene would be protected by property rule copyright protection for exhibiting high authorial presence. Therefore, the court would be able to acknowledge the high authorial presence of the original principal photographer and award the appropriate tier of protection to his photograph. At the same time, the court grants protection to the photojournalist's photograph without equating their protection to the original photograph due to the fact that the photojournalist's photograph exhibited low authorial presence.

The US case of *Harney v Sony Pictures Television, Inc*[58] may further demonstrate the advantages of the proposed two-tier system. In this case, the plaintiff, Harney, is a photographer who claimed copyright infringement against Sony Pictures for recreating a photograph he took of a daughter riding on her father's shoulders. The photograph turned out to be of significant importance since the man photographed abducted his daughter and was a criminal with multiple identities. Sony Pictures made a documentary on the man and recreated the photograph. Harney's claim was unsuccessful as the appeals court confirmed the lower court's judgement and held that Sony did not copy the photograph's expression but only recreated and adapted the photograph to the extent necessary to produce the impression of the original photograph's factual contents.[59]

One can see the issue with this decision and its implications on the adaptation rights attached to photographic works. This is because even though Sony Pictures admitted that they sought to recreate the photograph, and despite the similarities, the court found that the two photographs were not substantially similar as a matter of

58 *Harney v Sony Pictures Television, Inc, 704 F3d 173 (2013)*; for more dicsussion of this case, see Chapter 7.

59 ibid 188.

law. Using the proposed two-tier system for copyright protection for photographs, an arguably more balanced treatment could be achieved without necessarily altering the decision since these types of cases are facts specific and determined on an ad hoc basis. Through applying the proposed theory of authorship, Harney's authorial presence was evident in the original photograph since it carries his categorical intention and prior mental conception following the authorial traditions of street portrait photography. These types of photographs have a long and distinguished history; in fact, some of the most famous and widely regarded photographs fall under the category of candid street photography. Alfred Eisenstaedt's 1945 photograph "V-J Day in Times Square," which depicted a navy sailor kissing a stranger in New York's Times Square, is hailed as one of the most iconic American photographs. Eisenstaedt happened upon the scene and captured it, and the photograph resulting from it became a cultural icon and proved to be popular, which allowed Eisenstaedt to benefit from its copyright.[60] In Harney's original photograph, his categorical intentions influenced his channelled selection that was reflected in the photograph's elements of expressions and how the subjects were depicted. Harney took a direct photograph of the subjects looking at the camera, demanding their attention, in the style of street portrait photography and did not merely capture the scene without influencing it. Consequently, he caused the photograph to exist as it did due to his categorical intention and channelled expression. Thus, it could be argued that Harney's photograph exhibits high authorial presence to be a high authorship photograph protected by property rule copyright protection.

On the other hand, Sony's recreation of the photograph could be argued to exhibit low authorial presence despite being prearranged and staged since it was created solely to recreate Harney's photograph. It could be argued that the categorical intention, prior mental conception, and the channelled selection exhibited in Sony's photograph were low since it sought, with their own admission, to copy the impression of Harney's photograph. Hence, due to the low authorial presence, Sony's recreated photograph could be regarded as low authorship work that is only protected by liability rule copyright protection. In this manner, the court could reach the same result while acknowledging the difference between Harney's original photograph and Sony's recreation with regard to the tier of protection awarded to each photograph. Furthermore, the court could employ the idea/expression dichotomy to reach the same judgement while acknowledging that Harney's photograph exhibits high authorial presence.[61] With this conceptualisation, the "frustration of photographers" regarding the treatment of copyright in photographic works may gain some form of relief. After all, a sizable faction of professional photographers

60 Eliza Berman, "V-J Day Kiss in Times Square: Go Behind the Lens of That Famous Photo" (*LIFE*, 14 August 2015) <https://www.life.com/history/v-j-day-kiss-times-square/> accessed 19 October 2024.

61 For cases that share some similarity with the Harney case, see: *Rentmeester v Nike, Inc, 883 F3d 1111 (2018)* 19 (US); *Temple Island Collections Ltd v New English Teas Ltd [2012] EWPCC 1* (n 45) (UK); for an examination of these two cases, see Chapter 7.

value copyright in order to assert their status as artists and differentiate themselves from amateur photographers.[62]

Furthermore, the proposed two-tier system may clear the uncertainty surrounding the copyrightability of photographs created for the sole purpose of accurately depicting subject matters, such as reproductions of public domain works of art produced by museums. These types of photographs that often reproduce public domain works held by museums are valued for their high fidelity and accuracy in depicting subject matters, such as paintings and other valuable public domain works of art, of historical and cultural importance. In the US case of *Bridgeman Art Library, Ltd v Corel Corp*,[63] the court dismissed a copyright infringement claim brought by a UK-based company that marketed reproductions of public domain works of art on the grounds of lack of originality. The court regarded the reproductions as slavish copies that did not meet the standard of originality for copyright in both the United Kingdom and the United States and, consequently, were not eligible for copyright protection.

The court was pressured to reach this result in order to maintain the balance between copyright and the public domain. This was because the court was locked into a binary paradigm of property rule copyright protection or no protection. Hence, in fear of harming the public domain, the court held that the works in question were not subject to copyright because they were slavish copies that did not meet the originality standard.[64] However, if we applied the proposed two-tier system, a third option that may lead to a fairer and more balanced result could be achieved. Within the proposed two-tier system, these accurate reproductions of public domain works of art could be classified as low authorship photographs and be awarded liability rule copyright protection that enables the museums to receive remuneration without the right to injunctive relief. Therefore, museums would be motivated to allocate resources to produce these types of expensive photographs that benefit the public since they would still gain some form of copyright protection instead of no protection. Henceforth, these photographs would be protected as low authorship photographs subject to liability rule copyright protection, giving museums a way to recuperate their investments but denying them the level of control associated with property rule copyright protection. Furthermore, an additional advantage of the proposed two-tier system is that it avoids intrusion in the public domain since the protection for low authorship photographs extends only to direct verbatim copying. Hence, in the words of Justice Holmes, "Others are free to copy the original, but are not free to copy the copy."[65]

62 See: Jessica Silbey, Eva E Subotnik and Peter DiCola, "Existential Copyright and Professional Photography" (2019) 95 Notre Dame Law Review 263; see also Chapter 8.

63 *Bridgeman Art Library, Ltd v Corel Corp, 25 FSupp.2d 421 (1998)* (n 21).

64 For more on museums and reproduction, sSee: Allan (n 21); Burton Ong, "Originality from Copying: Fitting Recreative Works into the Copyright Universe" (2010) 2 Intellectual Property Quarterly 165; Deazley (n 21).

65 *Bleistein v Donaldson Lithographing Co, 188 US 239 (1903)* (n 34) 249.

This, however, does not deny the possibility for certain types of reproductions to exhibit high authorial presence to the extent eligible for protection as high authorship work. After all, the authorial tradition of accurate depiction in the art of photography requires a considerable amount of technical knowledge, experience, skill, and command of the expressive elements of photography.[66]

Indeed, the UK case of *Sawkins v Hyperion Records [2005]*[67] involved the question of copyright in performing editions of public domain musical works where the court held that the performing editions are subject to copyright since they meet the originality standard. Furthermore, Article 14 of the European Union directive on the Digital Single Market explicitly addressed the reproduction of public domain works of art and stated that

> when the term of protection of a work of visual art has expired, any material resulting from an act of reproduction of that work is not subject to copyright or related rights, unless the material resulting from that act of reproduction is original in the sense that it is the author's own intellectual creation.[68]

Photographic depictions involve many elements of expression that influence how the subject is depicted, even if accuracy was the primary objective. The photographer's categorical intention and prior mental conception could be evidenced through the authorial tradition associated with accurate depictions that shaped the photographer's creative choices. These choices are the products of the photographer's channelled selection – such as focus, tonal balance, lights, colours, glare, shadows, and other expressive elements of photography – to cause a work of authorship to manifest. However, the authorial presence in the resulting photographs could be classified as low if the predominant feature of these types of photographs was solely the level of accuracy in reproducing the subject matter. Despite the arguably low authorial presence in these types of photographs, they are still works of authorship that were produced by authors who, despite the constraints of their tasks, exercised "minimal personal autonomy" in creating the works.[69] The same line of reasoning utilising the proposed two-tier system could also be used to justify copyright protection for mundane photographs, such as photographs of generic food dishes.[70]

66 For examples regarding the range of creative choices that typically involve photographing artworks, see: *Artwork Photography at Klein Imaging* (Directed by Klein Imaging, 2021) <https://www.youtube.com/watch?v=7W2WVcH1K-A> accessed 18 October 2024; *Ask The Expert: Artwork Photography* (Directed by Klein Imaging, 2018) <https://www.youtube.com/watch?v=yNRbwxkHalE> accessed 18 October 2024.

67 *Sawkins v Hyperion Records Ltd [2005] EWCA Civ 565.*

68 Directive 2019/790/EC of 17 April 2019 on copyright and related rights in the Digital Single Market and amending Directives 96/9/EC and 2001/29/EC [2019] OJ L130/92.

69 Ginsburg (n 1) 1092.

70 See: *Oriental Art Printing, Inc v Goldstar Printing Corp, 175 FSupp2d 542 (2001)* (Held that pictures of generic Chinese dishes were not copyrightable for lack of originality).

Another area that may benefit from the advantages of the proposed two-tier system is virtual photographs and artificial intelligence images. The authorial presence in these images would be examined to determine the tier of protection, if any, to be awarded to these types of works. If no authorial presence exists according to the theory presented, then no protection is awarded due to the absence of copyrightable authorship. On the one hand, if the courts regarded virtual photographs as depictions, then subsequently protecting them would not be absurd, especially if they were protected as low authorship works. Hence, a work of authorship might be evidenced if the categorical intention and channelled selection reflected in the virtual photographs, such as the ones based on video games' virtual worlds, exhibited enough authorial presence to cause the work of authorship to manifest in the depicted image. On the other hand, if virtual photographs were considered mere copies for copyright law purposes, then there would be no protection since they were not deemed as independently created works for the purposes of copyright and contain no copyrightable authorship.[71]

All in all, the examples provided sought to illuminate the possible advantages of the proposed system. It is beyond the scope of this part to provide a detailed guide of under which tier a type of photograph would potentially fall. Instead, this part sought to argue that the proposed system and theory of copyrightable authorship provide the courts with the tools necessary to better deal with cases involving copyright in photographs without resorting to distorting copyright concepts to reach a desired result. The proposed system places authorship as the central concept for the level of copyright protection for photographic works.

## 10.6 Conclusion

This chapter presented an original theory of authorship to serve as the engine that operates the proposed system of two-tier copyright protection for photographic works. The theory of tailored authorship, which was crafted and tailored to photographic works, provides that copyrightable authorship is "a product of a human agent's categorical intention and prior mental conception that influenced a channelled source with channelled selection, expression, to cause a work of authorship to materialise for the purposes of copyright law." In this system, the author of a work of copyrightable authorship is defined according to Ginsburg's definition of authorship, which provides that an author is "a human creator who, notwithstanding the constraints of her task, succeeds in exercising minimal personal autonomy in her fashioning of the work."[72] This conception of copyrightable authorship and the figure of author represents the gears that operate the proposed two-tier system of protection for photographic works. It examines the level of authorial presence, whether high or low, exhibited in the photographs in question based on the level of

71 Pichta (n 30) 284, 304.
72 Ginsburg (n 1) 1092.

categorical intention and channelled selection caused by the author and whether it manifested a work of authorship in the photographs.

The proposed system provides an efficient framework and tools for the courts to organically and flexibly deal with copyright in photographic works on a case-by-case basis without the burden of being pressured to fit photographic works into moulds made for other categories of works or being locked into a binary choice of property rule copyright protection or no protection. Furthermore, instead of introducing new concepts that might face resistance within copyright law, this proposed system recalibrates and repurposes certain copyright concepts to better fit photographic works. Henceforth, the merits of the proposed two-tier system lie in the fact that it is based on authorship and specifically tailored for photographic works. Since it addresses photographic works in their own capacity and not through the lens of other categories of works, this would prevent the distortion of copyright concepts, foster an appropriate balance of photographic works' copyright protection with the public interest, as well as strengthen the stability of copyright law. This is because, under the proposed system, most photographs would be protected, but that protection is balanced and tailored in a way that takes into account the unique nature of photographic works and the facts of each case. Hence, based on the level of authorial presence exhibited in the photograph in question, it could be either a high or low authorship photograph.

The difference between the tiers of protection is manifested in the type of protection granted. Thus, under the proposed two-tier system, low authorship photographic works would be protected through a case-specific liability rule copyright protection in the form of compensation, based on the objective fair market value standard, without the right to injunctive relief. In contrast, property rule protection would only be reserved for high authorship photographic works. This would promote copyright law's objectives of inciting the production of high authorship works without prejudicing low authorship photographs, since photographers often rely on the revenue generated from such works to fund their high authorship creations. It is argued that a two-tier system of protection for photographic works is more efficient and better equipped for the future than technology-specific legislation that may be rendered obsolete on arrival.

# 11 Conclusion

The development of photographic works' copyright protection did not follow a straight trajectory in Anglo-American copyright law. Photographic works had a unique and challenging journey towards being protected by copyright. This journey owes its turbulence to the unique dual nature of photographs that exhibited both industrial and mechanical characteristics while simultaneously being capable of creative artistic expressions. This dual nature of photographic works made it a prime place for the conflicts of ideas concerning art, industry, and copyright and also the meaning of the concept of work under copyright law. The residue of the debates that surrounded photographs' copyright protection since their inclusion still resonates today, leaving a legacy that increasingly stands as the culprit behind the incompatibility issues plaguing photographic works' copyright.

Across the different copyright traditions, copyright laws struggled with the dual nature of photographic works that acted as a pendulum that swung back and forth between the mechanical and creative paradigms. Anglo-American copyright law was the first to embrace photographic works, granting them copyright protection even before France, the birthplace of photography. Despite embracing photographic works, the debates surrounding their capacity for creative expression that expresses the author's personality and authorship were never quelled. Those in opposition viewed photographs as nothing more than the work of a soulless machine devoid of the author's own intellectual creation on a level that did not amount to authorship since the pressing of a button was all that was required to create a photograph. With their long-ingrained traditions, the traditional art establishments objected to considering photographers as authors and artists, opting instead to regard them as mere operators of a mechanical apparatus that fixes and prints images. Hence, photographers were deemed to be subservient to the camera.

Those favouring photography as an art form rejected the notion above by stating that photographers imbue their personality and intellectual expression into the photographs without any industrial uniformity, in contrast to mechanical processes that are characterised by uniformity. They further argued that the elements that define art are the author's creative judgement, free selection, and choice, which allows his expression to flow into any medium capable of translating these creative elements into fruition. They affirmed that photography is certainly, without a doubt, a medium capable of conveying the author's intellectual expression. Hence, it was

DOI: 10.4324/9781003586555-11

not that the photographer was subservient to the camera; in fact, it was the other way around. It was the camera that was subservient to the photographer.

The arguments favouring photographic works' copyright prevailed eventually, but not without vestiges of the opposition's ideas being ingrained into the DNA of photographic works' copyright, serving as a legacy that resonated ever so often within the corpus of photographs' copyright protection. A key factor that exacerbated this issue lies in the fact that the approach to photographic works was anchored in an analogue view of photography that emphasised prior arrangement through the proxy of analogy to painting and writing and not in photographs' own capacity as photographs. This created a legacy that led to increasing incompatibility issues between photographic works and copyright's key concepts, such as authorship and originality.

The concept of authorship took centre stage during the debates surrounding photographic works, sparking contentions regarding the essence of authorship in copyright law. The concept of authorship itself escaped a universal definition even within the context of copyright law. Furthermore, the dual nature of photographs made them ill-fitted for the traditional notion of authorship, which was built on the textual model and influenced by a romantic view of authorship based on a deeply rooted analogue approach to creative works. The courts were pressured to approach authorship in photographs through the proxy of analogy to the model of writing and painting. As a result, the person nearest to the position of the author from the lens of writing or painting was deemed to be the author of photographs without needing to engage directly with photography by considering its unique characteristics. In other words, to locate authorship in photographs and originality by extension, the courts felt the need to emphasise the prior arrangements and selection that led to a photograph's creation instead of directly engaging with the photograph's features. Hence, the courts often neglected what Professor Kogan referred to as the design markings on the photograph's surface in favour of looking through the photograph to locate the design elements themselves instead of their effects as reflected by the photograph.[1]

Even though authorship is considered a central foundational concept in the copyright system, it remains challenging to apply uniformly across different categories of works. In fact, authorship was often conflated with originality despite being different, albeit closely connected, concepts. To illustrate the inherent difference between the two concepts, one could picture authorship as the road that leads to a place; that place is originality, as reflected in the work of authorship. Originality itself is a notoriously elusive concept to pin down, even in the context of traditional works of authorship. Originality remained an amorphous mirage that was approached and utilised through different proxies to achieve different policy objectives without defining it directly beyond affirming that it is a low threshold.

1 Terry S Kogan, "The Enigma of Photography, Depiction, and Copyright Originality" (2014) 25 Fordham Intellectual Property, Media & Entertainment Law Journal 869.

The elusiveness of originality made it increasingly difficult to assess photographic works' originality for the purposes of copyright protection.

The courts often located photographic works' originality in three main aspects: the photograph's rendition and composition, the creation of subject matter, and timing. The elements that comprise these three main aspects are not taken in isolation since what evidences originality is the combined holistic effects of these elements reflected in the photograph's expression in a manner that constitutes the author's intellectual creation. Despite the existence of a pattern regarding a photograph's originality, it remained highly inconsistent to utilise for the purposes of copyright protection, especially in the context of visual works such as photographs since originality is often examined through a reliance on the proxy of narrative. This book posits that due to the elusive nature of originality, it is ill-suited to determine the level of copyright protection afforded to photographic works. This is particularly so with the digital advancement of photo technology that has made the process of photography increasingly more automated.

The advent of computational photography fundamentally changed photography from being an art that utilises picture-making devices to an art that utilises data-collecting devices. Increasingly, many aspects that once required the skill and judgement of a professional photographer are being handled by complex algorithms that gradually make the photographer's influence hardly relevant. The ubiquity of images in cyberspace with the popularity of social media revealed the need for more clarity regarding the level of protection afforded to photographs. This exposed the weakness of copyright's one-size-fits-all approach to photographic works anchored in an analogue view based predominantly on the model of writing or painting. This chiefly emphasised the need for a tailored contextual approach to copyright works that take into account the category of work in question and its unique characteristics. The one-size-fits-all approach is argued to be the culprit behind the stretching and distortion of copyright's traditional notions regarding the concepts of originality and authorship. A tailored approach based on the relatively more stable concept of authorship, as opposed to the elusive concept of originality, may prove the more suitable tool for stabilising copyright law's approach to photographic works.

This book recommends abandoning the one-size-fits-all approach, considering it a liability, in favour of a contextual and tailored approach that considers the unique characteristics of the categories of work under a two-tier system of copyright protection anchored on the concept of authorship. Under the proposed two-tier system of protection, photographic works' copyright protection would be classified into two tiers, either high or low authorship, depending on the level of authorship exhibited by the work in question. The difference between the two tiers is manifested in the type of protection attached to each tier fashioned through utilising Calabresi and Melamed's model of legal entitlements.[2] On the higher tier,

2 Guido Calabresi and A Douglas Melamed, "Property Rules, Liability Rules, and Inalienability: One View of the Cathedral" (1971) 85 Harvard Law Review 1089.

photographs classified as high authorship works would be protected by property rule copyright protection. On the lower tier, photographs classified as low authorship works would be protected by liability rule copyright protection that awards only compensations, without injunctions, that are based on the objective fair market value standard. The book posits that this will stabilise the copyright law approach to photographic works without distorting copyright's traditional concepts of authorship and originality.

The book argues that in order for this proposed two-tier system to function with a reasonable degree of consistency and stability, authorship should be tailored to the specific category of work in question, taking into consideration the work's unique characteristics. Therefore, the book presents its own theory of authorship tailored and calibrated for photographic works. The book conceptualises copyrightable authorship as a product of a human agent's *categorical intention* and *prior mental conception* that influenced his *channelled selection* (expression) to *cause* a work of authorship to materialise for the purposes of copyright law. The author's categorical intention and prior mental conception fundamentally shape the work and the authorial tradition adopted, which in return influence the author's channelled selection, imbuing it with his intellectual expression, creating a causal connection that causes the work of authorship to be manifested for the purposes of copyright law. For the purposes of this system, the author that is attached to that work is defined according to Ginsburg's definition of authorship, which provides that the author is "a human creator who, notwithstanding the constraints of her task, succeeds in exercising minimal personal autonomy in her fashioning of the work."[3]

A tailored approach to authorship to serve as the mechanism behind the two-tier system of protection for photographic works will lead to a more stable and efficient development of copyright law that is geared to the future compared to technology-specific legislation that may be rendered obsolete on arrival. The proposed system would benefit from a stable development since it approaches photographic works in their own capacity as photographs instead of invoking the proxy of analogy with other categories of work on a one-size-fits-all approach. This would remedy the legacy issues that have plagued photographic works since the time of its inclusion to the list of works protected by copyright law.

3 Jane C Ginsburg, "The Concept of Authorship in Comparative Copyright Law" (2003) 52 DePaul Law Review 1063, 1092.

# Index

Note: Page references in *italics* indicate figures; Page references with "n" represent note number.

FSC
www.fsc.org
MIX
Papier | Fördert gute Waldnutzung
FSC® C083411

Kolibri 360 GmbH
Ferdinand-Jühlke-Straße 7
99095 Erfurt, Deutschland
produktsicherheit@kolibri360.de